Sharon
D0403393

From Conflict
to Resolution

A NORTON PROFESSIONAL BOOK

From Conflict to Resolution

*Strategies for diagnosis
and treatment of distressed
individuals, couples, and families*

SUSAN HEITLER, *Ph.D.*

W • W • Norton & Company • NEW YORK • LONDON

Copyright © 1990 by Susan Heitler

All rights reserved.

Printed in the United States of America.

First Edition

Library of Congress Cataloging-in-Publication Data

Heitler, Susan M. (Susan McCrensky), 1945–
    From conflict to resolution : strategies for diagnosis and
treatment of distressed individuals, couples, and families / Susan
Heitler.
        p.   cm.
    Includes bibliographical references (p. 331)
    1. Psychology, Pathological.   2. Conflict (Psychology)   3. Problem
solving.   4. Psychotherapy.   I. Title.
    RC454.H424   1990   616.89–dc20   89-23234

ISBN 0-393-70081-X

W. W. Norton & Company, Inc., 500 Fifth Avenue, New York, N. Y. 10110
W. W. Norton & Company Ltd., 37 Great Russell Street, London WC1B 3NU

1 2 3 4 5 6 7 8 9 0

To my parents, Harold and Mary McCrensky,
and my brother and sisters,
Jay McCrensky, Paula Singer, and Andrea Kremer,
with love

Contents

List of Tables

Acknowledgments

LONG FASCINATED BY THE QUESTION of how conflicts move to resolution, I first had the opportunity to begin library research on this topic during a half year sabbatical spent with my family in Israel. The year was 1982, and while the children were in school I devoted my time to two passions, tennis and conflict resolution research. Then, in June, war broke out. One day I had been taking tennis lessons at the Jerusalem Israel Tennis Center in the mornings and reading about conflict resolution in the afternoons. The next day my lessons had been canceled. My tennis instructor, Yossi Zaytuni, had been called to fight in Lebanon. The following day, Yossi was dead, shot and killed. War had always seemed senseless to me. Now it also had personally touched me, devastated me. Yossi had been a fine tennis coach and a generous human being. Many of the ideas about coaching developed in this book have come from him. His death intensified my determination to do what I could to replace fighting with cooperative problem-solving.

This interest had been long gestating. As an undergraduate at Harvard in the 1960s, I learned much in a course innocuously entitled Social Relations 120. "Soc Rel 120" offered students the opportunity to study the psychology of groups by reflecting on the development of their own classroom group. In his end-of-the-year feedback to us the instructor, Dean Whitlock, observed to me, "Your particular interest seems to be conflict. Whenever the group begins to get blocked, divided, or distressed over a conflict, you emerge as the negotiator who guides the passage." I feel indebted to Dean Whitlock for crystallizing for me an interest that has since become the focus of my professional work.

Inspiration and assistance in writing this book have come from my colleagues in the Society for the Exploration of Psychotherapy Integration

(SEPI). I greatly appreciate Paul Wachtel who invited me to SEPI's first annual meeting, launching the integration movement, in June of 1985. I thank Bernie Beitman for discussing with me whether to write a book and how to contact publishers, and then for reading through one of my first manuscript drafts, giving me invaluable direction. Stan Messer coached me in the stages of book development, encouraging me to start with articles, two of which subsequently became parts of this book. Jim Prochaska offered me the opportunity to write my first article, and Nolan Saltzman the second article, requesting them for the *Journal of Integrative and Eclectic Psychotherapy*. John Norcross sent the request for integrative book proposals that launched the writing of this book. Don Freedheim and Bob Sollod gave me vital encouragement and joined me on SEPI panels where the ideas of the book could be discussed with colleagues. Ellen Wachtel, Barry Wolfe, David Ricks, Leslie Greenberg, Drew Westen, Arnold Lazarus, Ellen Tobey Klass, and many others within the organization have contributed books, talks, papers and mealtime conversations that have enriched the thinking in this book.

My psychologist colleagues in private practice, Ruth Solomons, Pegi Touff, and Betsy House, have supported me by listening and offering constructive refinements of my treatment ideas throughout the years of their development. Physician-writer Richard Abrams contributed practical advice about the book-writing process. Nancy Simon, the resourceful Rose Medical Center librarian, provided essential library services. Sandy Pierson helped with multiple sessions of chart-typing and laser printing.

My heartfelt appreciation goes also to psychologist Itamar Barnea, with whom many of the understandings in this book were jointly developed; to the several clinicians who gave me feedback that guided early drafts of the book — Lynn Heitler, Laurie Honor, Stanley Lifschitz, Eric Aronson, and Aart Lovenstein; to the friends and relatives who generously donated editing time and lay perspectives on the book — Amy Kremer, Ralphine Gross, Ronna Blaser, Joan Baronberg, Janet Schoeberlein, Michael Touff, and my parents, Harold and Mary McCrensky; to Dorothy Bales, the violin teacher who modeled principles of effective teaching; and to Barbara Geller and Ronen Moralli who spurred me on with steady encouragement.

On the other end of the telephone wires and the mailbag, my editor Susan Barrows has been critical to the team. At every stage of the writing process I have relied on her sensible guidance. My secretaries, Janet Olson and Becky Boomsma, have supported me throughtout the writing years with consistently good-humored and capable assistance.

Without my patients, there would have been no book. Their growth and their willingness to share insights about their lives have enabled this project to proceed.

Psychologist Howard Lambert has devoted many hours to careful reading and detailed discussion of every chapter. I greatly esteem his judgment and perceptivity, and thank him profoundly for his major contribution as the book's primary clinical consultant.

Finally, my deepest appreciation goes to my family. I leave home each morning refreshed by them. Our phone conversations provide invigorating breathers during the day. And I return home in the late afternoons happy to put aside my clinical work and the manuscript and to indulge again in the warm blessing of their companionship. To Abigail, Sara, Jesse, and Jacob, and especially to my husband Bruce, thank you.

Preface

> And nation shall not lift up sword against nation, neither shall they
> study war any more. — Isaiah.

In this time of nuclear threat, when our capacity to destroy ourselves and
our entire planet is unparalleled in the history of the world, the need to
understand how people can live together cooperatively takes on new
urgency. As a therapist I am asked daily to help people find cooperative
solutions to troubling personal and family conflicts.

A fundamental assumption underlying this book is that conflict resolution principles apply on all levels, from the international conflicts that
threaten the world to the personal inner conflicts that are evident only in the
privacy of our thoughts. *From Conflict to Resolution* focuses primarily on
personal and family upsets, but the same resolution strategies govern the
settlement of global conflict, business disputes, domestic tensions, and
inner personal struggles.

In the realms of government, law, and business, when a third party
assists in the resolution of a difficult conflict, the process is termed
mediation or negotiation; in the realms of personal and family distress the
similar process is termed counseling or therapy. *From Conflict to Resolution* integrates the negotiation literature that has emerged from schools of
law, business, and international relations with the psychological literature,
which has delineated communication skills, types of emotional disturbances, and many forms of treatment. Negotiators and therapists have
much to learn from one another. By sharpening our skills in conflict
negotiation, mankind has the potential to put aside much violence and
emotional suffering. We can learn to live in peace, nation next to nation,
with our neighbors, in our families, and within ourselves.

From Conflict to Resolution is arranged in three parts. The first section orients readers by clarifying the elements of healthy movement from conflict to resolution. The first chapter draws from multiple disciplines, while the second adds the psychological and communication elements that facilitate the process of resolution.

Section II focuses on psychopathology. Chapters 3 and 4 provide an overview, suggesting the patterns of conflict resolution characteristic of common emotional and behavioral problems. Chapters 5 through 8 explore more fully each of these patterns, focusing particularly on depression, anxiety, anger, and escape maneuvers such as addictions and obsessive-compulsive disorders. Chapter 9 concludes this section with a systems perspective, exploring dysfunctional family conflict resolution patterns.

In Section III the focus shifts from diagnosis to treatment, from analysis of what has gone wrong to strategies for setting things right. Chapters 10 and 11 delineate the elements of conflict-based treatment by describing the assessment and treatment of a distressed couple. A conflict resolution framework maps assessment and treatment with the same basic format whether patients are individuals, couples, or families. With this mapping, multiple intervention routes become options. Criteria are suggested for determining which strategies are most appropriate at which points in treatment. Determination of who should be in treatment or whether treatment should focus on individuals, couples, and/or families is a particularly critical issue that is explored with a review of research.

Chapter 12 suggests guidelines for assessing when symptom relief needs to be a primary treatment focus and offers a number of symptom reduction techniques suggested by the conflict resolution model. Chapters 13, 14, 15, and 16 delineate methods for guiding patients from conflict to resolution on specific troubling issues. Chapters 17, 18, and 19 explore the coaching aspects of therapy. Therapists can teach patients new skills so that they can handle subsequent personal, family, or work conflicts more effectively. Chapter 20 looks briefly through the lens of conflict resolution theory at resistance, a critical element which must be managed adeptly in any treatment. To conclude, Chapter 21 explores ethical aspects of our strategies for handling conflict in therapy, in business and politics, and in our personal lives.

One of my personal interests within the field of psychotherapy, an interest shared by my colleagues in the Society for Exploration of Psychotherapy Integration, has been finding ways to integrate the many profuse schools of thought in psychology, psychiatry, and the other helping professions. *From Conflict to Resolution* suggests a framework that offers intriguing potential as an integrating perspective.

For instance, each diagnostic entity, such as depression, anxiety, or addiction, is currently described in the psychological literature with a different set of theoretical constructs. No one system ties these syndromes together and shows how they interrelate. A conflict resolution perspective can reconceptualize the various types of psychopathology within one integrative framework.

Similarly, diagnosis and treatment are often viewed from different conceptual schemas, making diagnosis relatively unrelated to treatment. Yet the point of diagnosis is to guide treatment. This objective is more easily attained when the language of diagnosis describes the problem in ways that clarify how the problem can be corrected. Because a conflict resolution perspective can integrate diagnosis and treatment under one set of conceptualizations, the assessment then creates a map for treatment.

A vast array of treatment options is available now to therapists and to patients seeking therapy. Conflict resolution theory offers a flexible framework within which these many puzzle pieces of individual, couple and family treatments emerge into one comprehensible picture. With this fuller picture, decisions about which interventions to utilize when and toward precisely what objectives become easier.

The same framework can be similarly useful for guiding business and governmental negotiations. Many of the interventions customarily used by therapists could become powerful tools for negotiators. A conflict resolution overview makes the therapist's repertoire potentially more accessible to negotiators at the same time as it allows the experience of negotiators to benefit therapists.

To the extent that therapists, negotiators, and all of us in our personal and work lives clearly comprehend the pathways from upsetting conflict to satisfaction, we can resolve conflicts more efficiently and effectively. This book maps the territory in the journey from distress to relief, from conflict to resolution.

SECTION I

Healthy Functioning

CHAPTER 1

Overview and Underpinnings

FROM CONFLICT TO RESOLUTION is based on the premise that poorly handled conflicts lie at the core of emotional distress. With more effective conflict resolution patterns, individuals, couples, and families in distress can move toward resolution of their underlying difficulties and resume emotionally healthy living.

When people in distress turn to psychotherapists for help, they are seeking guidance through the confusing terrain of their upsetting personal and family conflicts. Therapists are expected to be experts in this terrain, to know well the pathways from conflict to resolution. Individual therapy relies on the therapist's ability to guide patients to resolution of intrapsychic, and sometimes interpersonal, conflicts. Marital and family therapies focus on the conflicts among family members, and also assist in bringing family members' inner conflicts to more satisfying resolutions.

Business people, lawyers, political leaders, parents and children—in fact, all of us—deal with conflicts daily. Few of us want altercations to disrupt the smooth flow of our lives. We want what we want, but without loss of a cooperative atmosphere in our homes and at our workplaces.

OVERVIEW

All of us, simply because we are human, repeatedly face conflictual dilemmas. Within ourselves, for instance, our many personal needs, wants, feelings and values require ongoing mediation. We want affection from loved ones, and we also want to maintain self-sufficiency and independence. We want to relax and play, and we also want to accomplish work goals. We value time with our families and yet we feel an urge to take time

3

alone, away from everyone. Every individual must learn to mediate these conflicting impulses.

In addition, humans are by nature social. We live with others and consequently repeatedly face decisions in which both our preferences and those of others must be heeded. Moreover, we exist simultaneously as individuals and as members of groups. Whether the group consists of a couple, family, extended family, work group, community, or country, our participation requires that we somehow negotiate our personal preferences with the context of the group's demands. As Andreas Angyal (1965) pointed out, we live in paradox, functioning simultaneously as *we* and as *I*. Neither alone is sufficient. Either without the other can jeopardize our emotional well-being. Somehow we need to negotiate competing interests in a manner that gets us what we want without sacrificing our membership in significant groups. Healthy functioning enables a person to resolve these conflicts in a manner that enables both differentiation and belonging to flourish.

Since groups coexist and overlap, they must negotiate with one another. If, for instance, a person lives in a nuclear family and in an extended family, these two systems may sometimes have contrary needs. For example, an extended family member may be planning a large wedding during the week the nuclear family has saved for much-needed vacation time alone together. Larger systems, such as communities, corporations, and nations, also need to negotiate with one another, particularly when they are in competition for a common resource. The city of Denver and its neighbor, the city of Aurora, both want the land of a proposed regional shopping mall, because sales taxes from shopping centers constitute the base of their governmental income. Opposing interests are as inevitable between groups as they are within groups, within and between individuals, and between groups and their individual members.

History, unfortunately, is replete with episodes in which whole communities have been the victims of poor conflict resolution. Dark periods have occurred in which the rights of one group of people have been trampled upon by a more powerful group whose members listened only to their own concerns, oblivious to the needs and suffering of the less powerful.

In far too many parts of the world today, domination of some groups over others is still seen as normal rather than unethical. Economic exploitation, oppression of political dissidents, terrorism, violence, and war signal the continued existence of pathological national and international approaches to conflict resolution.

In addition to intrapsychic, interpersonal, and intergroup conflict, life challenges us regularly with conflicts between what we want and the realities that face us. Economic downturns, physical illnesses, deaths of loved ones, the ticking of our biological clocks as we age—these are just some of the many reality factors that confront us all, often in opposition to what we want. To these givens we can respond with denial, helplessness, or rage, or with constructive problem-solving and creative adaptivity.

The principles of conflict resolution apply to conflict in any sphere, from the private worlds of our inner conflicts to global conflicts between nations. The broader perspective suggested here underscores the importance of understanding constructive movement and its aberrations. Therapists, however, focus primarily on the conflicts faced by people in their personal lives. It is on these intrapsychic and family conflicts that the remainder of this book will be focused.

What constitutes conflict?

The term conflict is used here with a particular and specific meaning: *a situation in which seemingly incompatible elements exert force in opposing or divergent directions.* These divergent forces evoke tension, but not necessarily hostility or fighting. As used in this book, the word conflict does not necessarily connote argument or battle. Conflicts may be silent and unexpressed. Individuals who avoid speaking to one another, or who refrain from discussion of sensitive issues, may be manifesting signs of conflict. The term conflict denotes only that elements appear to be in opposition.

The term conflict has been defined similarly by several other theorists. The influential social psychologist Kurt Lewin (1951) defined conflict as "the overlapping of two force fields." In his concept of force fields, Lewin included forces with both positive and negative valences, that is, impulses to do something and impulses to *not* do something. While Lewin stressed the push and pull of feelings, Pruitt and Rubin (1986), social scientists who have focused on conflict resolution, define conflict in terms of perceptions and beliefs. For them, "conflict" means "perceived divergence of interest, or a belief that the parties' current aspirations cannot be achieved simultaneously" (p. 4). This definition of conflict in terms of belief is helpful, since many instances of perceived conflict turn out, after exploration, to involve forces that are in *apparent* but not *actual* opposition. Conflict exists if people think it exists, even if the situation does not in fact include inherently contradictory factors.

What constitutes resolution?

Resolution refers to the attainment of a solution that satisfies the requirements of all of the seemingly conflicting forces and thereby produces a feeling of closure for all participants.

In mathematics, resolution is the act or process of reducing a complex notion or formula to a simpler form. In music, resolution is the passing from dissonance to consonance. In literature, resolution refers to the point at which the chief dramatic complication has been worked out and appears settled. In law, "resolved" means "decided."

Resolution of conflicts within or between people involves all of the above elements. Psychological resolution exists when two or more apparently contradictory elements have been transformed into one element that exists without opposition. As in mathematical resolution, what looked complex has been transformed to apparent simplicity. As in music, the feeling tones switch from dissonance to consonance. As in literature, at the point of resolution oppositions give way to solution and a feeling that all has been settled. The drama seems over. All has been decided.

How can conflicts best be resolved?

No single best way exists for handling all conflict. Within the value system of this book, however, "effectively" resolved conflicts have certain common characteristics:

- The process is based on talking, not on verbal or physical violence.
- The process is predominantly cooperative, not avoidant, competitive, antagonistic or coercive.
- The outcome is a settlement that all participants find acceptable and that addresses the concerns of all participants.

Not all individuals, societies and cultures share this aversion to violence or prefer outcomes that leave all sides feeling satisfied. For many, saving face and winning, or at least not losing, are high priorities that pit husband against wife, brother against brother, nation against nation. For others, maintenance of at least an appearance of harmony is valued to the extreme and, paradoxically, sometimes brutally enforced. Totalitarian regimes such as Stalin's in the Soviet Union and the rule of the Red Guard in China, for instance, used violent means to establish unanimity.

In response to a party that uses violence, values winning over cooperating, or seeks self-gain irrespective of the harm this gain may do to others, the cooperative strategies described below are not necessarily optimal or appropriate. To the contrary, cooperative conflict resolution strategies work only when both sides share a willingness to pursue mutually optimal solutions. When an opponent in a conflict is looking only to win and/or to destroy, it may be preferable to meet selfishness with selfishness, to meet force with counterforce, to somehow avoid dealing directly with the conflict at all, perhaps even to surrender. This issue will be addressed again later in this chapter and from time to time throughout the book.

CONFLICT IN PSYCHOTHERAPY THEORIES

Theoreticians from almost every school of therapy have described therapy as an opportunity for people to deal with their conflicts. The major treatment orientations — psychoanalytic, behavioral, and family systems — all include conflict as a significant component of their ideas about pathology and treatment. Yet the *process* of conflict resolution has been virtually ignored in the psychotherapy literature.

In a review article, Marmor (1971) points out the psychodynamic assumption that conflict is at the root of the vast majority of neurotic disorders. Wachtel (1984) similarly emphasizes that the psychodynamic point of view focuses on intrapsychic conflict as a central element. Indeed, Freud's battling id and superego provided the first model of psychopathology emerging from intrapsychic conflict. Jung continued the conflict model, looking at conflicting archetypes and polarities rather than impulses and values. Fritz Perls' gestalt therapy added a host of new techniques for accessing unconscious conflicts. However, most of the focus within psychodynamic writings has been on the *content* of conflicts. Competing needs for dependence, independence, control, nurturance, sexual and aggressive release and restraint, and conformity with the shoulds and oughts of our society have been identified. How competing needs and values interact has been less clearly delineated.

A number of behavioral theorists have also conceptualized conflicting feelings as sources of dysfunction. Mahoney (1984), reflecting on similarities between behaviorism and psychoanalysis, writes that both approaches draw heavily upon a conflict-based model of psychological movement. Dollard and Miller (1950) utilized a conflict model of neurosis, focusing on the role of fear and elucidating the way conflict could be learned in the course of early feeding situations, cleanliness training, etc. Skinner (1969), within operant theory, described conflict between responses competing for selective retention. More recently, Linehan (1988) has modified the linear behavioral thinking of stimulus and response with a conflict-based interactional model. Expanding traditional behaviorism into what she calls "dialectical behaviorism," Linehan defines psychological growth as "the synthesis of bipolar tensions."

With the emergence of systemic perspectives, many therapists have expanded their focus from the individual's inner turmoil to turmoil within the family. From its beginnings, family therapy has emphasized clarification of conflicts as part of the family diagnostic process. Ackerman (1958) pointed out that delineation of specific family conflicts and clarification of the nature and effectiveness of the family's methods of coping with conflict should be part of the initial family assessment. Minuchin (1965), whose family treatment approach grew out of a psychodynamic perspective, even called his initial systemic work "conflict-resolution family therapy."

The content of family battles has been explored by many family therapists. In some of his earlier writings Haley (1976) suggested that marital conflict often centers on "(a) disagreements about the rules for living together, (b) disagreements about who is to set those rules, and (c) attempts to enforce rules which are incompatible with each other"(p.188). Family therapists (Carter & McGoldrick, 1988; Pittman, 1987) later focused on events in the family life cycle, hypothesizing that family conflict generally erupts at transitions between life cycle stages, as well as with entrances and exits from the family system.

Recent research has corroborated the strong relationship between conflict (in the vernacular sense of fighting) and psychopathology. For example, the role played by family conflict is evident in the emotional adjustment of children after divorce (Dancy & Handal, 1984; Enos & Handal, 1986; Slater & Haber, 1984).

Although the content and impact of typical conflicts have been quite thoroughly delineated, the actual *process* of conflict resolution has received surprisingly little attention in the psychotherapy literature. In her landmark description of various "mechanisms" of defense, Anna Freud (1936) revealed a variety of patterns of unsuccessful intrapsychic conflict resolution; yet, the process of healthy intrapsychic conflict resolution has been virtually ignored.

Greenberg and colleagues (Johnson & Greenberg, 1987; Rice & Greenberg, 1984), who have pioneered task analyses of conflict resolution, offer a notable exception. Based on gestalt theory and technique, their work details many of the behaviors involved in the achievement of resolution. Their concept of "softening" is particularly useful and is discussed in Section III on treatment (in Chapter 15) as an indicator of cooperative interactions. Linehan (1988) also details an aspect of the conflict resolution *process*, focusing on cognitive patterns. In her work with severely suicidal borderline patients, Linehan emphasizes the need for these patients to learn to shift from rigid dichotomous thinking to dialectical, synthesizing thought.

As a result of the general dearth of information about the conflict resolution process, some fairly naive and even damaging notions have prevailed. For instance, as Wachtel (1977) has pointed out, the idea of renunciation as a means of resolving neurotic conflict is implicit in much psychoanalytic treatment. Renunciation assumes that once patients become fully aware of what they have been seeking, they will be in a position to give up their strivings and turn elsewhere. This idea is based on the premise that patients must be satisfied with either-or solutions rather than seek solutions that gratify multiple needs. Renunciation thus runs contrary to one of the essential principles of effective conflict resolution, namely, that solutions must be responsive to all the significant underlying concerns.

Although explicit focus on the resolution process has been sparse in the psychological literature, communication patterns in interpersonal conflict situations have received considerable attention. Research efforts by Gottman (1979), Markman and Floyd (1980), Stuart (1980), Jacobson and Holtzworth-Munroe (1986), and others have clarified that certain communication habits disrupt dialogue and others are essential to constructive problem-solving. The skills involved in assertiveness and empathic listening, for instance, are critical to the flow of healthy discussion of problems. These skills have not, however, been integrated into a larger model of conflict resolution or into a general theory of psychotherapy.

In sum, the *content* of conflicts has been the subject of much important research and thought in the psychological literature. The *process* of conflict resolution has been studied only in piecemeal fashion, and primarily with respect to addressing interpersonal, not intrapsychic, issues.

UNDERPINNINGS FROM OTHER AREAS

Two lines of thinking from fields other than psychology have given particular impetus to the ideas in this book. One has been game theory in mathematics, which has developed the study of cooperative versus competitive strategies for resolving conflicts. A problem known as the "Prisoner's Dilemma" has provided a particularly thought-provoking research format. "Tit for Tat" a widely studied solution to the Prisoner's Dilemma game, not only suggests strong advantages of cooperative over antagonistic conflict resolution, but also defines when cooperation is inappropriate (Axelrod, 1984).

A second line of thinking has emerged from the practical study of negotiation for use by lawyers, businessmen, and mediators in governmental and international disputes. Business and political theorists such as Nierenberg (1968), Fisher and Ury (1981), Pruitt and Rubin (1986), Raiffa (1982), and Moore (1986) have taken the lead in clarifying paradigms for resolution of conflictual positions. The work of these theorists is referred to in upcoming chapters. Although developed to meet the needs of people working in the economic and political world, these ideas have direct relevance to the work of psychotherapy.

Game theory

Any interaction between two elements, i.e., between two competing desires within one person, between two individuals, between groups or between groups and individuals, can be analyzed in terms of game theory. A *game* is defined as a situation in which each participant has, at specified times, a range of choices of action (Fisher & Ury, 1981). Like children's games, each interactive situation has a set of spoken or unspoken *rules* for interaction, to which participants are expected to conform. Within these rules, many options exist. The totality of the choices made by all participants determines the outcome or *payoffs*. In most games, maximization of payoffs is a desired outcome. In mathematical games, as in many of the games that children and adults play "for fun," the payoffs are points. Some of the payoffs that people seek in real world everyday interactions are love, appreciation, maintenance of relationships, money, power, prestige, fun, laughter, health—all the good things in life.

ZERO, POSITIVE, AND NEGATIVE SUM GAMES

Games can be categorized on the basis of the type of payoff. In a *zero sum game* the sum of the payoffs to the players is zero. The more player A wins, the more player B loses; one's gain is the other's loss. Competitive sports are generally structured this way, with winners and losers.

By contrast, in a *positive sum game* there is no loser, only winners. Both sides obtain something of value. Each player's outcome can be enhanced by the other's outcome; the more one wins, the more the other wins. At any given moment players may need to forego a move with higher potential payoff in order to maintain the condition of mutual benefit, but in the long run their gains are maximized by cooperating. Business partnerships and marriages, for instance, generally aim to be positive sum games. Both partners hope to gain by their mutual association.

A *negative sum game* is an interaction in which both sides suffer net losses. War is probably the ultimate negative sum game. People sometimes believe that a war has winners and losers, but in most instances the toll in human suffering on both sides dwarfs any positive outcomes that the war was initiated to accomplish. Wars, at best, end with a dominant and a surrendering side; for this ending, both sides pay high costs.

Many interactions can be played as either zero, negative, or positive sum games. An individual psychotherapy interaction, for instance, can be analyzed as a game in which two sides, patients and a therapist, interact in order to reduce the patients' emotional distress. Patients are expected to offer information, participation, and monetary payment, and in return to obtain payoffs in emotional relief and personal growth. The therapist is expected to contribute expertise and empathy, and in return to receive payoffs in financial remuneration, self-esteem, and altruistic satisfaction. Like most games in life, therapy can be undertaken selfishly (as a zero sum game), or self-defeatingly (as a negative sum game in which no one gets desired outcomes), but works best when regarded as a cooperative (positive sum) endeavor. That is, a therapist who is focused primarily on his/her financial gain from treatment or a patient who is looking to receive help without contributing actively in the treatment is operating from a self-only zero sum game orientation. Occasionally, therapy becomes oriented as a negative sum game, with the therapist locked into proving that a patient is hopeless, or a patient determined to prove that s/he, the therapist, or therapy in general is bad in some way. This kind of negative sum interaction gives gains to neither patient nor therapist. Both sides lose. By contrast, the payoffs, financial and emotional for both patient and therapist, are optimized when both parties contribute cooperatively to the therapy process, with positive sum interactions.

Variable sum games depend upon the extent to which the interests of the players are seen to be coincident or opposed. In a variable sum game players will experience some impulses to cooperate for common interests and some impulses to compete in order to maximize their own gain. The final payoffs are not fixed; rather, they vary depending on how the game is played. In real life most games or situations are variable sum games. They include some inducements toward cooperation and some seduction toward personal gain to the detriment of the other participant(s).

This book focuses on individuals who debate internally and interact with others as if they were involved in zero sum or negative sum games. Whether the desired payoff is affection, power, prestige, money, sexual gratification, joy or any of life's gratifications, interactions based on zero or negative sum assumptions often lead to negative outcomes and emotional distress. Therapy is a process of helping people transform the interactions in their lives from frustrating zero and negative sum patterns to more satisfying positive sum interactions. The road from conflict to resolution can best be traveled with this cooperative orientation.

COOPERATION VERSUS COMPETITION

Game theory has provided a thought-provoking format for investigating the behaviors we label competition and cooperation. Competition is the evaluation of the rightness of one's actions by a comparison with the actions of an opponent. People with a competitive orientation feel that they have won in an interaction if they have done better than someone else, rather than by whether or not they have gained what they personally sought.

Competition is inherently selfish. Viewed in the framework of conflict resolution and game theory, selfishness is behavior that takes into account only maximization of personal gain. Data about others' interests are ignored, deemed irrelevant, or blocked in some other fashion. Cooperation, by contrast, is behavior that looks at the gain both for oneself and for the other players in the game, with the objective of optimizing everyone's gain, even at the expense of some gain for oneself. With a cooperative perspective one player feels successful to the extent that both players feel successful, i.e., feel that they have obtained their desired objectives. Cooperation, thus, inherently involves an altruistic as well as a self-gain perspective. The goal is not for one player to do better than the other, but for both to do their best and to facilitate the other's best attempts.

Thus, two strategies for handling conflict can be conceptualized. The purely competitive strategy seeks to maximize the individual's gain relative to the gain of the other. The competitor operates from a zero sum game conviction that the more one person wins, the more the other inevitably must lose. The greater the discrepancy between the winner and the loser, the more successful this player feels. The competitive strategy is also individualistic, i.e., concerned with maximizing self-gain and devoid of altruistic concern for the other.

The second strategy relies on cooperation, focusing on mutually beneficial, "win-win" solutions. The underlying belief in this strategy is that both players will do better if they work together, helping each other while simultaneously watching out for their own benefit. Satisfying marriages operate on these positive sum game principles. Both marital partners gain when they make sure that each decision is responsive to their spouse's concerns as well as their own.

Many interactions have elements of both competition and cooperation. For instance, tennis players who are playing for fun rather than for tournament prizes may play their best in order to beat opponents, while also encouraging opponents on good points and enjoying their companionship.

What determines whether players will cooperate, compete, or do some of both? The specific contingencies, i.e., the payoffs, for a competitive versus a cooperative move may make one or the other of these strategies more attractive. If the rewards for cooperation are adequate and fairly risk-free, they will be appealing. If the risks are low and the payoff for self-interested moves is high, an atmosphere of competition may prevail. For example, once big prize money is involved in a tennis match, cooperation among competitors is likely to give way to strict competition.

The strategy chosen by either player may also affect the strategy chosen by the other. If one player is willing or able to play only from the individualistic, zero sum game position, the option of playing successfully from a cooperative position is ruled out for the other. A person who is married to a persistently egocentric spouse is likely to learn to be self-centered. An individual whose altruism is repeatedly met with taking and no return giving generally experiences resentment and eventually reciprocates with selfishness.

The nature of the players' relationship — long or short term, trusting or distrustful, etc. — is another factor influencing response style in any given game interaction. A person can get away with selfish exploitation of others in single interactions. If the interactions are to continue over time, however, self-only moves may cause the other to harden in response, making subsequent self-only moves unproductive. Thus, the highest yield strategy for one-time business interactions and the best strategy for ongoing interactions may be quite different. A used car salesman can sell the customer an overpriced car, provided he does not want that customer's repeat business. By contrast, since marital partners deal with each other day after day, both lose if one is seen as having taken advantage of the other. Furthermore, in order to cooperate, an attitude of *trust* that the other will continue to cooperate is essential. Cooperation breeds trust, which in turn breeds more cooperation.

A comment in defense of competition is in order. Competition may be beneficial, exhilarating and productive; in fact, interactions that are always cooperative may lack adequate stimulation and interest. A race can be more exciting than a practice run.

Rapaport and Chammah (1970) point out that the most psychologically interesting games occur when the interests of players are partly coincident and partly opposed. Each participant then is continually challenged by the impulse to cooperate for common interest and the simultaneous impulse to compete to maximize individual gain. Many real life situations seem to include some inducements in both directions.

THE PRISONER'S DILEMMA AND TIT FOR TAT

The Prisoner's Dilemma refers to a game theory paradigm that has proven to be useful for experimental research on cooperation and competition (Luce & Raiffa, 1957). The game gets its name from a hypothetical problem. Two prisoners have been arrested for a crime. Each faces a potential long jail term. Either alone can confess against the other. This defection (abandonment of concern for the other in favor of considering only what seems to be in one's own self-interest) will enable the confessor to be released and result in the other prisoner's serving the full jail term. If, however, both prisoners defect by confessing against the other, both will serve the full sentence. On the other hand, if the two prisoners cooperate by refusing to confess, both will be convicted on minor charges and both will serve short jail terms.

Many variations of the Prisoner's Dilemma have been developed to test experimentally how people react when offered the opportunity to either cooperate or compete. In different versions, different variables have been altered; for instance, the payoffs may be set higher or lower. In general, however, participants are informed that the goal of the game is to maximize the number of points earned over a series of interactions.

The game usually involves two players who interact in a set number of rounds of play. In each round each player has two options, cooperation or defection. If both players choose cooperation, both earn a moderate number of points. If one player chooses to defect, the defector earns a large number of points and the person who cooperated gets nothing. On the other hand, if both players attempt to defect in any given round, both earn zero points for that round. Thus, defection maximizes gain as long as the other player doesn't also choose that option. Players are not allowed to communicate between rounds, so they cannot tell each other if they are going to cooperate or compete.

Axelrod (1984) explored when it is most advantageous for a person to cooperate and when to act solely with regard to self-interest. In a series of computer tournaments with his version of Prisoner's Dilemma, he sought to determine what strategies would yield the highest scores over multiple encounters with various kinds of players. Axelrod arranged the consequences for choosing to cooperate for moderate gain versus choosing to try for a larger gain at the other player's expense in the manner set forth in Table 1.1. If two players, A and B, both choose a cooperative move in any given round, they each receive three points. If both defect, neither receives any points. If one defects and the other cooperates, the defector receives five points and the cooperator zero.

Axelrod invited game theorists from the diverse fields of economics, psychology, sociology, political science, physics, biology and mathematics to submit computer programs for playing this game. The winning program would be the one that earned the highest total number of points over multiple rounds of play against each of the other programs submitted. A variety of programs were entered into the competition. Some operated on

TABLE 1.1
Payoffs for the Prisoner's Dilemma
With two players, Player A and Player B

	Player B Cooperates	Player B Defects
Player A: Cooperates	A gets 3 B gets 3	A gets 0 B gets 5
Player A Defects	A gets 5 B gets 0	A gets 0 B gets 0

random selection of cooperative and competitive moves. Others included consistent cooperation, consistent defection, or more complex strategies such as a pattern of cooperation interspersed with occasional attempts to gain extra points with brief defections.

Tit for Tat, a program conceived by Professor Anatol Rapoport of the University of Toronto, won Axelrod's competition. A simple and predominantly cooperative method of handling conflict, Tit for Tat offered the most effective strategy for earning points. Although it did not necessarily amass more points than any given opponent program in any given round of play, Tit for Tat amassed by far the highest overall score in multiple rounds of play with multiple alternative programs.

Tit for Tat begins with a cooperative move and then proceeds by returning cooperative for cooperative moves and selfishness for selfishness. Thus, when operating by the rules of Tit for Tat, a player begins by being "nice," that is, by moving cooperatively. S/he continues with only cooperative moves unless the opponent moves selfishly. Should that occur, the player's immediate response is "tit for tat," that is, a selfish move. His/her play will continue to be selfish, responding in kind to selfish moves even if both sides become locked in consistent lose-lose patterns. If the opponent begins again to act cooperatively, however, the Tit for Tat player immediately responds with a cooperative move. In this way the opponent's self-interest moves are rebuked with self-interest and cooperation is rewarded with cooperation.

As he tested the utility of Tit for Tat against the various other computerized Prisoner Dilemma strategies, Axelrod discovered several principles, each quite suggestive for the handling of conflicts in real life:

First, Tit for Tat was remarkable in its *robustness*. That is, starting "nice" and then returning kindness with kindness and meanness with meanness proved to be the most successful long-term strategy with a host of different other players. While there is no absolutely best rule or strategy independent of the environment (the kinds of other players and strategies), Tit for Tat does very well over a wide range of environments. A method of dealing with conflict that is effective with a broad range of others' game plans is most applicable to real life. Most people interact with a number of others who vary broadly in the extent to which they can be counted on to be empathic, altruistic, or selfish.

Second, acting on pure self-interest may maximize gain in brief encounters. For *ongoing relationships*, however, solutions that optimize what both players receive, rather than those that attempt to maximize one player's gains at the other's expense, yield the higher gains. By cooperating and apparently seeking less in any one move, over time each individual as well as both players together actually obtain higher scores that they would if they followed self-interest-only strategies. In real life, most interactions, such as those among family members or between business associates, occur within ongoing relationships rather than as one-shot encounters. In these relationships, cooperative rather than antagonistic attitudes should have the best long-term payoff.

Third, *niceness* pays. Niceness refers to launching the relationship with cooperative moves and then never being the first to defect. Most people intuit that an initial positive impression, an impression of good will, pays off in generating good will in return. A more difficult situation occurs when there has been a series of self-optimizing defections from cooperation. For instance, in marital therapy the question of which spouse should initiate the first positive moves frequently arises, particularly if spouses have had a long period of hostile interacting. Some patients need extensive reassurance, and even scientific explanations from game theory, before being convinced that initiating niceness indeed does have potential for better payoffs than continued hostile encounters.

Selfishness costs. In Axelrod's study frequent unprovoked selfish moves were characteristic of many of the strategies that ended with the lowest long-run scores. Marriages in which one partner insists on being "right" quickly become ungratifying for both partners. Likewise, marriages in which one partner insists on having his/her way to the detriment of the other's preferences tend to become ungratifying for both partners over time.

Excessive pessimism can be similarly expensive. Pessimism, defined as the expectation that the other will make selfish moves, can cause needless losses. When patients first come to therapy they tend to be viewing themselves and their significant relatives in persistently negative ways, saying, for example, "He doesn't care what I want," or "She just wants to hurt my feelings." An essential ingredient of effective therapy is modification of these bleak views so that pessimistic expectations no longer rule out cooperative behavior. By contrast, *optimism*, i.e., the expectation that others will cooperate, enhances the effectiveness of Tit for Tat. Such optimism may be the essential ingredient of what Erikson (1950) termed basic trust.

Tit for Tat is highly *responsive*. The strategy operates on a principle of optimism until shown cause for pessimism, and then distrust until the next cooperative indicator. Only one defection is necessary to reverse the pattern of cooperation, and only one cooperative move from the other can in turn reverse the pessimism.

Such quick shifts between pessimism and optimism, between stingy and generous, contrast with the way less emotionally resilient people operate. People who are consistently preoccupied with their own self-interest or who have become fixedly pessimistic about others tend to ignore, misread, or mistrust instances of cooperative action, making the switch from mutual defection to cooperation increasingly less likely. This pattern frequently occurs in troubled marriages, as each partner comes to believe that the other is hopelessly hurtful and unloving and ignores evidence to the contrary.

On the other hand, individuals who are naively forgiving of others' defections, even disregarding indications of others' selfishness, can invite repeated victimization. By responding too slowly, ineffectively, or not at all to others' hurtful actions, they may fail to set appropriate limits on others, inadvertently encouraging continued abuse. Nonetheless, *forgiveness,* defined as the propensity to cooperate at least once more even after the other player has defected, to give, as it were, a "second chance," enhances the effectiveness of Tit for Tat. That is, defecting only if the other player has defected on two previous moves (rather than just one) actually improves the long-term outcome for Tit for Tat players. Married couples, business partners, athletic teammates, and others who work together over time need to accept their own and their partner's occasional mistakes without overreacting with immediate retribution.

Increasing the degree of *retaliation* seems to decrease Tit for Tat's effectiveness. Excessive reaction to others' selfish moves is not generally in a player's, or anyone's, best interest. At the same time, predictable retaliatory moves (consistent defections in response to defections) are essential and preferable to excessive forgiveness. How much forgiveness and/or retaliation is enough or even too much seems to depend on the characteristics of the other player. In general, slightly overdoing the forgiveness seems to enhance effectiveness while overdoing retaliation seems counterproductive. Patients who manifest high levels of guilt, rage, blame, shame, or other harshly punitive responses to their own or others' mistakes are showing indications of excessive retaliation.

Lastly, *clarity* appears to be a major benefit. The player who utilizes an incomprehensible strategy is at a disadvantage. Strategies that employed random defections, or that utilized decision rules too complex for opponents to decipher and use to predict future moves, scored less well than Tit for Tat. The marital partner or parent who reacts unpredictably, e.g., with angry outbursts or depressive bouts, demoralizes other family members and decreases his own and family members' net payoffs of affection and sense of well-being. Clarity of response rules elicits trust and long-term cooperation.

Negotiation theory

Negotiation is a form of dispute settlement that has evolved with ever-increasing rapidity in the business/legal/political world over the last decade. It is ironic that therapists, whose objective is to help their patients resolve conflicts, have in general been unfamiliar with this extensive literature on conflict resolution.

Because use of the court system can be a lengthy and costly way to settle intractable disputes, legal professionals often look to negotiation and mediation to streamline the process. Cooperative problem-solving is more effective than traditional bargaining in providing lasting and mutually beneficial solutions to business problems. Such groups as Harvard University's Project for Negotiation have sought to define ways that businessmen, lawyers and politicians can create amicable settlements that yield optimal solutions for all parties, precluding the necessity for court involvement.

Some of the groundwork for theorizing on negotiation strategies was actually laid in studies by social psychologists in the '60s and earlier. As early as 1957, Festinger listed a number of key aspects of successful negotiations, all of which are components of effective conflict resolution in the context of psychotherapy. These factors included:

1. Clarification of issues.
2. Improvement in each party's understanding of the other's position, and consequent rapprochement in the two sides' diverse perceptions.
3. Reduction of hostile attitudes.
4. Assistance of a third party as mediator.

5. Separation of broad issues into more manageable and clearly defined units.
6. Identification of common superordinate goals important to both sides.
7. Establishment of mechanisms for resolving conflicts as they arise rather than waiting for crises.
8. Awareness of the framework of the entire organization (we might now use the word "system") in order to see major organizational features that might be problematic.

Literature parallel to the social psychology literature on negotiation began emerging from the business world in the 1960s. Nierenberg (1968) explored the do's and don'ts of effective negotiation from an atheoretical anecdotal standpoint. Interestingly, although his goal was to explain how to maximize gain in business negotiations, Nierenberg's central premise turned out to be similar to the idea of cooperation implied in Tit for Tat. His premise was that in a successful negotiation everybody wins. Furthermore, the negotiator who pushes for too much risks losing all. An apparent total victory is likely to sow the seeds for a subsequent loss. Nierenberg concluded that full understanding of yourself and of your opponent is the key to optimizing your gain. This principle is a cornerstone of the conflict resolution ideas we have developed in the context of psychotherapy.

Roger Fisher and William Ury carried these ideas further in their book *Getting to Yes* (1981), a product of the Harvard Negotiation Project. This bestseller popularized the notion that conflicts can be handled through a process that anyone can learn. They call the process "win-win negotiating," a colorful term for what in mathematical game theory is referred to as a positive sum game. As the term "win-win" suggests, this approach posits that negotiation works best if handled so that all parties emerge feeling like winners.

POSITIONAL BARGAINING

Fisher and Ury coined the term "positional bargaining" for win-lose zero sum negotiation. Positional bargaining occurs when one side says x and the other y, and the opponents then fight over who is right, whose way should be chosen, or how much of each person's way will be accepted. The outcome of positional bargaining is determined by the relative forcefulness of the parties. Winners in positional bargaining are the ones who are in some way stronger or able to persist until they dominate; losers are the ones who are more willing to give up or who lack the strength to attain domination. Person A may say, "I think you should buy my product," and person B answer, "I'm not interested in buying your product at the price you are charging. You'll have to lower your price." If the two individuals then lock horns by each continuing to insist on their initial requests, then A and B are involved in positional bargaining. Each is trying to get the other to do something specific that is unacceptable to the other. They may end up with a winner and a loser, or with two losers, but it is unlikely that they will find a solution that leaves both sides satisfied.

A *compromise* is a subcategory of positional bargaining. In a compromise, both sides lose some and gain some in order to meet in the middle. Person A says, "I'll sell it to you for $25." B says, "I'll give you $15." A and B agree to split the difference. "OK, we'll make it a sale at $20." Each gives up some in order to reach agreement.

Fisher and Ury point out that within positional bargaining, which creates a zero sum game of winners and losers or a compromise in which each side wins some and loses some, participants may be characterized as either soft or hard bargainers. A hard bargainer sees him/herself as an adversary whose goal is victory. A soft bargainer, by contrast, strives to maintain the relationship at the same time as s/he pursues a solution. Whereas hard bargainers focus primarily on the explicit negotiation, soft bargainers are equally or more concerned with the relationship between the two parties. As a consequence, soft bargainers tend to insist less forcefully on an outcome based on their original position, provided the relationship between the participants remains intact. That is, in order to "win" with regard to maintenance of the relationship, soft bargainers are willing to suffer losses on the substantive issues at hand.

INTEREST-BASED BARGAINING

Fisher and Ury propose that the alternative to positional bargaining is a process of mutual problem-solving which they term interest-based bargaining. In order for this positive sum process to occur, participants must work cooperatively for their common interest. In addition, they must switch their focus from interests to positions. Instead of locking horns in attempts to convince each other to satisfy one another's initial position statements of what they want (positional bargaining), they must look instead at "the desires and concerns that lie behind positions" (p.42).

> Your position is something you have decided upon. Your interests are what caused you to so decide. . . . Reconciling interests rather than positions works for two reasons. First, for every interest there usually exists several possible positions that could satisfy it. All too often people simply adopt the most obvious position. . . . When you do look behind opposed positions for the motivating interests, you can often find an alternative position which meets not only your interests but theirs as well.

Reconciling interests rather than compromising between positions also works because behind opposed positions lie many more interests than conflicting ones. Behind opposed positions lie shared and compatible interests, as well as conflicting ones. We tend to assume that because the other side's positions are opposed to ours, their interests must also be opposed. In many negotiations, however, a close examination of the underlying interests will reveal the existence of many more interests that are shared or compatible than ones that are opposed. (p. 43)

In contrast with compromise and positional bargaining, interest-based negotiation would explore why each participant is making the offer suggested. Perhaps our seller wants a long-term payoff of $25, but is in no hurry for the money. The buyer may be interested primarily in cash flow, being low on money at the present time but anticipating having more in the future. An optimal solution then may be for the buyer to pay an initial $5 for the purchase and to take a loan from the seller for the remaining $20. By the time the loan is repaid, the gross amount paid by the buyer to the seller will be $25, but the buyer will have obtained the goods in spite of his cash flow problem, having put down only a minimum of cash. By exploring the underlying interests — or concerns as they will referred to in this book — a solution can be found that meets the parameters of importance to both participants.

Interest-based bargaining involves three main phases, each of which includes a number of essential mini-steps. Delineation of these main phases and mini-steps is the goal of the next chapter.

CHAPTER 2

The Cooperative Pathway from Conflict to Resolution

RECENTLY I HAD OCCASION TO map a route for a foreign friend who wanted to travel from Denver across this large country to Mobile, Alabama. As I looked closely at a map, I sensed his anxiety. "No problem," I said, having found that highways 70, then 55, then 10, would bring him there. "Just three streets and you'll be in Mobile." My friend and I chuckled, knowing that "just three streets" would encompass an arduous and also extremely interesting journey. The route from conflict to resolution can feel similarly long, frightening, and tempting. But like the trip from Denver to Mobile, it can be regarded as proceeding along a sequence of three stages, each offering challenge and gratification.

Maps simplify and clarify; reality offers far more complexity. Like a map, the schematization of the conflict resolution pathway presented in this chapter is a simplification for heuristic purposes, not a replication of full reality. In keeping with this objective, the case examples are quite straightforward. In subsequent chapters dealing with actual clinical cases, more complexity will be included.

MAPPING THE ROUTE

A cooperative process of conflict resolution generally involves three phases:

- Expression of *initial positions*
- Exploration of *underlying concerns*
- Selection of mutually satisfying *solutions*

Positions are initial statements of what one wants. A conflict generally begins when two or more wishes are perceived to oppose one another. The wish may be phrased as a concern, e.g., "I need to finish my homework," or proposed as a specific plan of action, e.g., "I'm going to do my homework now."

The negotiation literature uses the term "positions" to denote opening wishes and from this term derives the phrase "positional bargaining" (Fisher & Ury, 1981). Positional bargaining evolves when participants fight about whose initial position will prevail instead of proceeding to the next two steps of exploring underlying concerns and choosing mutually acceptable solutions. If teenager Sara says, "I'm going to do my homework now," and her mother, Mrs. Smith, says, "I want you to wash the dinner dishes now," they may become involved in a positional tug of war.

Initial positions may suggest incompatible plans of action when in fact the participants' underlying concerns are quite consonant. In these cases needless conflict can result. Many arguments take this form. In the above instance, for example, Sara and Mrs. Smith both agree that Sara's homework is important and that the dishes need washing, but the format leads to a power struggle.

A *concern* is a thought stemming from a value, feeling, desire, preference, fear, or other factor. Concerns are usually statements about oneself. They therefore often have "I" as the subject. Because they are subjective and descriptive, not objective or prescriptive, concerns need to be heard nonjudgmentally and accepted at face value.

Concerns define the parameters of a problem and therefore serve, consciously or unconsciously, as the criteria for successful resolution. For instance, Sara's concern may be that she wants to do well on her next day's chemistry test. Mrs. Smith's concerns may center on the fact that visitors will soon be arriving, that she likes to have a clean kitchen when she has guests, and that she needs to prepare the next evening's supper.

In proposing a conceptual model it is helpful to be aware of the metaphorical connotations of the terminology. In place of the negotiation term *interests* (Fisher & Ury, 1981), I use the term *concerns*. Whereas the term interests suffices for business and political negotiation, therapists assist patients with conflicts in their personal as well as their work worlds. For dealing with issues in these multiple spheres, the broader connotations of the word "concerns" seem more appropriate. Moreover, asking patients to explore their underlying "concerns" facilitates expression of emotional dimensions, while the word "interests" draws forth more limited financial, political, or other rational considerations. For many people, also, "interests" sound selfish, whereas "concerns" sound more legitimate, and therefore more likely to be received with empathy.

Fisher and Ury (1981) view interests as *lying behind* positions, a horizontal conceptualization that connotes negotiators with secret agendas that need to be brought out in the open and laid on the table. In the context of personal explorations, however, a vertical conceptualization of concerns as *underlying* solutions seems more fitting. Therapists' working metaphors for psychological phenomena generally involve ideas of conscious and subconscious thoughts and feelings. The vertical model also fosters conceptualization of levels and depth of understanding, another metaphor that is standard in psychological thinking. Note that the question in choosing terms and metaphors is not which conceptualization is more *right*, but rather which is more *functional*, more useful in clinical work (Auerswald, 1987).

Solutions are potential courses of action. Solutions are specific action options for accomplishing the objectives delineated as concerns. A solution to the dishes vs. homework disagreement, for instance, might be to ask another family member to trade dishwashing nights with Sara. Sara could then focus on her homework, Mrs. Smith would be relieved to see the kitchen cleaned up, and their conflict would be resolved.

Solution-building is often surprisingly easy. After two initially antagonistic parties have cooperatively explored their underlying concerns, they most often discover that their apparent conflict actually involves concerns that are complementary. One creative solution can make everyone happy. Occasionally, however, instances do arise in which there is in fact only one small pie to be divided, a limited resource and no alternative options to draw from. In these instances it can be helpful to find objective criteria for determining how this limited pie is to be divided.

Fortunately, most problems (and particularly parent-child and money-related problems) generally have occurred before in the lives of other people; consequently, societal conventions develop with respect to what is "fair" in most areas. If both parties can turn to socially agreed upon external standards for settlement, both can leave the negotiation feeling that they have reached an acceptable settlement. For example, teenagers and parents who are in disagreement about curfew hours can gather information about the curfews agreed upon by other families in their community. Divorcing spouses can look to the standards set by their state's courts for defining what is "fair" in terms of child support payments. Fisher and Ury (1981), emphasizing the importance in solution-building of objective criteria that all parties can agree upon, suggest the following sources of standards (p. 89):

market value	what a court would decide
precedent	moral standards
scientific judgment	equal treatment
professional standards	tradition
efficiency	reciprocity
costs	etc.

Like the term "solution," the term "position" generally connotes a plan of action. "Position," however, carries the implication that the speaker has an attachment to this option. Excessive attachment to a specific solution at any point in the negotiation process can detour cooperative problem-solving into positional bargaining. The ability to remain flexible in the consideration of multiple options, as opposed to becoming rigidly attached to a specific solution, is one of the hallmarks of effective, cooperative problem-solvers.

Clear differentiation between *solutions* and *concerns* is critical in the journey from conflict to mutually satisfactory resolution. Whereas concerns are underlying parameters of a problem, solutions are action plans. Preoccupation with solutions in the early stages of discussion leads to positional bargaining and power struggles. The movement from initial positions to exploration of underlying concerns enables a cooperative process of information-gathering to evolve, eventuating in the creation of mutually acceptable solutions.

CASE EXAMPLES

The following examples illustrate the flow of a conflict from initial expression of positions, through exploration of underlying concerns, to selection of mutual solutions. The first example involves an intrapsychic conflict. The resolution process actually occurred over a series of three sessions. The material that was covered is presented in condensed form, and with the data rearranged for didactic purposes. Therapy is seldom this orderly. The second conflict example demonstrates a hypothetical couple conflict. The point again is to clarify the elements of effective conflict resolution rather than to present an actual case.

In real-life conflicts, discussion in each of the three phases may be sometimes shorter, sometimes longer. Sometimes discussion will move forward and then retreat, with some discussion of concerns, some proposing of solutions, and then a return to further exploration of concerns

before a mutually satisfactory resolution is obtained. A key hypothesis of
this book, however, is that, whatever the particular path, a successful
journey from conflict to resolution will pass through these three critical
areas.

Intrapsychic conflict resolution

Raymond, an athletic young man, sought help because he was upset by
anxious and depressed emotions in the face of his first major career
decision. Raymond's dilemma emerged as a conflict between what he
wanted and what he felt he *should* be doing.

EXPRESSION OF INITIAL POSITIONS

Shoulds voice: I guess I have to take this job coaching soccer.

Wants voice: I don't want to be coaching. I want to work on my own
game and then see if I can make it on a professional team.

EXPLORATION OF UNDERLYING CONCERNS

Shoulds voice: I really should earn some money. I'm 21 now and I should
begin to be self-supporting.

Wants voice: I agree. I want to be considered a responsible adult, which
is what earning money stands for at this point for me. And I want to have
money to do things without feeling always penniless and without options. Is
that the only reason that taking the coaching job feels imperative?

Shoulds voice: I also feel a debt to the organization that gave me all the
coaching and chances to play competitively that I had as a kid. I feel like I
should give back what my coaches and supporters gave to me.

Wants voice: Yes, that's important. I received everything I know about
soccer from them, and financial support to travel around the world playing
on our national junior team too.

Shoulds voice: I have some other concerns. I feel like I have to be
realistic. Realistically, in the small town where I'm living I can't find anyone
to coach me, or people to work out with, at the skill level I need to prepare
for professional competition. Worst of all I'm afraid that I may not be
realistic about my potential to make it as a world class player. I shouldn't
devote my days to practicing instead of earning a living if pro soccer is all
just an unrealistic dream. All my friends have jobs now. When they ask me
what I'm doing I don't want to say, "Oh, I'm still playing soccer" if it's not
likely to lead to any real success.

Wants voice: Those fears scare me too. I have no desire to devote my
hours and energy to a lost cause. Still something inside of me isn't ready yet

to relinquish the hope. That urge to at least try to play as a pro is so strong. I really want to test out how far I can go as an athlete.

Shoulds voice: Why is that so important to you?

Wants voice: Partly I want to clarify who I am, what I am capable of accomplishing, who I can be—and soccer is my thing, the activity I love and the arena where I shine. Also, that's the arena where, if I really succeeded, big money could come out of it. How else would I ever have the hope of some day earning in the six digits? Or of representing my country around the world?

CHOOSING SOLUTIONS

Both voices: I do need to earn money. If I take a job outside of my public soccer training center, coaching privately, I could earn just as much with way fewer hours. To do that I would have to move to another city, but that also would open up opportunities to find a place with more pro-level players and coaches to work with.

If I find a new coach for myself that I really trust, I could ask him to be honest and to tell me straight how far he thinks I could go professionally so I don't waste my time working hard and long at a goal that's just not realistic. If I don't have the talent and the skills for the big time, just knowing that would make me feel better about returning home and taking the coaching job.

I still should, and want to, help out my soccer center, to return what they gave to me. If I succeed on the pro level though, that would mean even more to them than my coaching now. Also, then I could contribute money to them as well as coaching time. And though I don't want to coach with them now, I can return once I've gotten this professional team urge out of my system.

Phew! Now I don't feel guilty about saying no to the coaching job. And I don't feel trapped and depressed anymore like I did when I thought I was going to have to take the job. I'm just excited to get going.

Prior to therapy, Raymond's decision-making pattern had been a positional bargaining based on a tug-of-war battle between two seemingly incompatible options. When Raymond had resigned himself to following his should voice, he had experienced depression. When he listened instead to his wants, he felt guilty. The longer he procrastinated in making a decision, the more anxious he was becoming. Either/or solutions, however, were all he had been considering as options.

The movement from initial positions to exploration of underlying concerns required a brief delay in reaching a decision so that Raymond could develop a more detailed understanding of the underlying parameters of the problem. Raymond was encouraged to accept all the concerns of both sides as valid. This self-acceptance contrasted with his prior style of amassing new information as ammunition or reinforcements for one side or the other of the battle.

The resolution then bridged all of Raymond's multiple concerns. More complex than the initial either/or positions (to take or not to take the job), the eventual plan was designed to take into account all of Raymond's values and wishes. With his inner conflict resolved, Raymond experienced a sense of closure and feelings of enthusiasm. (Note: Raymond did find excellent coaches, whose evaluation was that he had the potential to rank among the world's top players. He now is playing professionally with considerable success.)

Interpersonal conflict resolution

The movement from conflict to resolution flows through the same three stages when the conflict occurs between people as when it occurs within an individual's conflicting values and impulses. Table 2.1 outlines this flow with a simple dilemma, deciding what to do for dinner.

This particular mini-dilemma poses a simple conflict situation that virtually everyone can relate to and yet that seldom raises strong feelings for people. As a result, the "dinner dilemma" is useful as a problem to pose to couples and families (and also, in slightly different form, to individuals) to assess their baseline conflict resolution patterns. As patients try resolving this conflict, they will replicate key aspects of their usual conflict pattern. Clinical use of this hypothetical conflict for assessment purposes is described in more detail in Chapter 18.

In the dinner dilemma, Barbara's initial position frames the problem. "Let's go out for dinner." When Charles expresses an opposing wish, "I'd rather fix dinner at home," the two proposals seem wholly incompatible. At that point the conflict seems to be heading toward a power struggle, positional bargaining. The outcome then would be a winner and a loser, that is, a zero sum game, or at best a compromise in which each side wins some and loses some.

Instead of proceeding with a contest of wills, Charles and Barbara follow an alternative route, a cooperative route. Their transition is accomplished by shifting the discussion to the level of concerns. Both Charles and Barbara strongly want their concerns to be met; their initial positions were suggested as means to that end. But instead of becoming overattached to their specific

TABLE 2.1
The Three Stages of Conflict Resolution

I. INITIAL POSITIONS	II. UNDERLYING CONCERNS	III. MUTUAL SOLUTIONS
Barbara I'm hungry. I want to go to the restaurant around the corner for dinner.	I'm in a hurry; I'd like to get something fast, no waiting. I want something light, not a full or heavy meal. I'd like to eat somewhere bright and cheery. I'd rather not have to cook or do dishes.	Charles could make quick sandwiches, or heat up soup, that they could eat at home. Barbara could pick up a barbecued chicken and salad from the grocery store.
Charles I'm hungry too, but I want to stay home.	I don't want to get dressed up, and I feel too grubby to go out looking like this. I want to be home to see the evening news on TV. I don't mind preparing dinner or cleaning up.	They could eat by the window in their bright kitchen, with the TV news on. Charles would clean up afterwards.

initially suggested solutions, they overcome this temptation and switch the discussion to a clarification of their underlying concerns. Barbara wants food that is fast, light, in a cheerful place, and without work. Charles wants to eat at home, and to see the TV news. Solutions may be incompatible; concerns seldom are.

If concerns seem to be incompatible, then the concepts of *depth* and *breadth* come into play. Underlying any given concern is usually a deeper concern. Participants in a conflict sometimes need to explore their concerns at deeper levels in order to find mutually compatible solutions. Furthermore, most people experience a diversity of concerns with respect to a given conflict. Weighing these concerns makes it possible for both sides to feel satisfied that at least they have won on their primary concerns and have let go only of minor interests. These concepts of depth and intensity of concerns will be expanded later in this chapter and in the chapters on treatment. Charles and Barbara need little depth or breadth; solutions easily become apparent. They enjoy an easy meal at home; Charles handles the preparation and clean-up; Barbara enjoys the kitchen brightness; both are pleased.

Thus the movement from (1) initial proposals to (2) concerns and then to (3) new solutions that meet the concerns on both sides provides the basic outline of movement from conflict to resolution.

COMMUNICATION SKILLS

The above description of the resolution process focused upon the *nouns*, the *names* of the three stages. Wishes, concerns and solutions are one aspect of effective resolution, but they need to be evoked and expressed; that is, the verbs in each stage also are critical.

Effective resolution depends initially on the requirement that the conflicting positions be *expressed*. This implies that the conflict must be verbalized, not suppressed or acted out. The verbalization needs to be explicit, rather than subtly hinted. Expression also implies a nonthreatening tone and a grammatical construction that conveys the data without assaulting or insulting the other person with it.

Once the conflicting positions have been expressed, they must be *explored*. If attack, debate, or judgmental analysis ensues, the process can sidetrack into argument or end without mutually satisfactory resolution. Both expression and exploration imply empathy on the part of the listener and require that both sides speak and listen symmetrically.

Lastly, solutions need to be carefully and explicitly *selected*. Selection implies the creative generation of alternatives followed by an active process of choice. Passively waiting for solutions to appear does not constitute selection. Likewise, selection implies the exercise of judgment. All potential solutions do not bring about equally satisfactory resolutions. Thus, the activities that predominate in the last phase of conflict resolution are creative thinking, active choice, and utilization of evaluative judgment.

The activities of expression, exploration and selection require a particular kind of emotional climate if they are not only to occur but also to flourish. If the emotional tone surrounding a negotiation is of lurking distrust or animosity, participants will be reluctant to risk expressing feelings that might increase their vulnerability. Exploration of underlying issues is also risky in an atmosphere thick with criticism or anger. Without a climate of kindly respect, participants are unlikely to want to generate or select mutually beneficial solutions. A safe emotional climate is created in part by communciation habits that invite openness and in part by the participants' attitudes.

The following schematic example illlustrates in further detail the communication habits and emotional climate essential for accomplishment of each step in the resolution process.

Expression of initial positions

DON: Let's take a trip to Alaska for our vacation.
BETH: I'd rather not travel. I'd like to stay home and relax around the house.
DON: You want to stay here the whole week?
BETH: That's truthfully what sounds best to me. You really want to travel to Alaska?
DON: I sure do. I guess we've got a problem, if I want us to take off and you want us to stay home.

This dialogue illustrates in simple form the essential components of the first stage of effective conflict resolution. Several key ingredients characteristically emerge: expression of wishes (saying), expression of having heard the other's wishes (hearing), and symmetry (evident in equal air time).

SAYING

The first step in launching problem-solving is to bring the issue out into the open. Someone needs to say out loud what s/he wants. This point seems obvious. In fact, however, many people have difficulty articulating what they want. Expression of wishes is blocked when people fear that their feelings and wishes are not legitimate or acceptable. For instance, a person who lacks self-acceptance or expects disparagement from others may feel uncomfortable speaking out. Other individuals expect people to meet their needs without their having to ask, an assumption that may be based on immature ideas about relationships, including the belief that loved ones are supposed to be able to intuit one another's wishes without verbal communications. Close relationships hopefully foster extra sensitivity, but mind-reading, which is appropriate for parent-infant interactions, needs to give way to more explicit communications with the development of language skills.

Difficulty in expressing preferences directly may result in passive or aggressive communications. Passive methods include saying nothing, hinting, saying what one *doesn't* want, and asking a question instead of making a statement. For instance, Beth may have said nothing, thinking, "He should know that I want to stay home this year." She might have hinted, "Maybe something around here would be nicer." If Beth had expressed what she didn't want without stating her preferences in the positive, this negative, like a negative of a photo, might have been, "I sure don't want an always-on-the-move vacation." Asking "Wouldn't you like to ...?" also would have avoided a self-statement.

Aggressive phrasing can take the form of complaints, blame, or criticism. Aggressive expressions of wishes often begin with the pronoun "you" instead of "I." For example, Don might have expressed his wish with an attacking criticism, "You always put a damper on my plans for adventure." The subject of discussion then would have switched from vacation planning to Beth's personality. Fisher and Ury (1981) make this point about what psychologists refer to as "I-statements" and "you-statements" with their aphorisms: "Focus on the problem, not the people," and "Speak about yourself, not about the other." Similarly, the words "always" and "never" clue listeners that they are being criticized. Because these words make global complaints out of specific problem incidents or behaviors, "always" and "never" tend to antagonize more than they inform.

Both passive and aggressive expressions of wants disrupt the flow of communications instead of keeping the discussion on a productive track. They hide more than they communicate, muddying the problem instead of adding clarification. Instead of increasing understanding, they typically evoke defensiveness in the listener, engendering confusion or counterattack. It is important, nonetheless, for a therapist to realize that these forms of statement are intended to communicate wishes. Paradoxically, these disguised communications tend to be utilized because people think that giving hints or criticisms is safer than explicitly stating what they want. Although excessively self-protective forms of expression tend to be self-defeating, it can be important to assume that they are intended to be constructive.

LISTENING

Along with the ability to express thoughts and feelings in a direct and nonthreatening fashion, effective listening skills are critical in the introduction of problematic topics. Effective listening has three aspects. First, the listener has to be focused on what the other person is saying. If a listener is focused on rebuttal or distracted by other thoughts, data from the speaker will not penetrate his/her consciousness.

Second, the listener needs to focus on what is right, what makes sense about what the speaker is saying, rather than on what is wrong with it. Careful scrutiny for what is wrong is appropriate when a lawyer reads a legal document, when an editor reads a manuscript, or when a child examines a "What's Wrong With This Picture?" game in a puzzle book. However, in cooperative relationships a judgmental listening stance is distinctly counterproductive. Listening for what is wrong rather than for what makes sense leads to argument rather than understanding.

Third, the listener needs to give the speaker some evidence that the speaker's words have been received. This feedback can be given in a multitude of forms. A smile and head nod are nonverbal "I hear you" clues. "Yes" or "um hmm" conveys that the listener is processing the speaker's information. Better yet, some form of restatement of the speaker's comments, a paraphrasing or even exact echo, confirms that what has been spoken has been heard. This verbal confirmation engenders forward progress in the discussion, leaving no uncertainty as to whether or not the speaker's points have been understood and accepted.

In the example above, Don and Beth each reiterate what they have heard expressed by the other. Some people fear that repetition will get tedious. In fact, slower movement from speaker to speaker actually speeds up the dialogue, since it increases the likelihood that the points made in each comment will enter the cumulative pool of understanding.

A response from a listener that begins with the words "yes, but..." indicates the antithesis of constructive listening. These two words almost guarantee that the subsequent discussion will yield polarization instead of cooperation. "Yes, but . . . " invalidates what has just been said, rejecting instead of incorporating it into the mutual database. By contrast, a listener who responds "yes, and . . ." conveys acceptance of what has been said, fostering cooperative problem-solving.

Some people, particularly those with paranoid tendencies, listen with an interpretive ear. Rather than take at face value what others say, they listen for what they think the person is *really* saying. This hyper-alert listening, which may involve considerable projection of the listener's own feelings, can be provocative to a speaker and detrimental to the resolution process. A related but positive habit, empathic listening, involves a similar close attunement, but yields accurate understandings of the speaker and fosters cooperative trust.

In the communication skills literature effective listening is sometimes labeled "active listening." This term implies, correctly, that although listening may not be visible or audible to others, it requires clear mental activity from the listener. The term also implies the need to give feedback, an active response that indicates to the speaker that the data have been received. In addition, listening needs to be "receptive," offering empathic understanding rather than projective interpretation or judgmental critique.

SYMMETRY

In the illustrative dialogue, *both* Don and Beth verbalize what they want. They *both* confirm their active listening by verbalizing what they have heard the other saying. And these communications are accomplished with more or less equal air time. Their dialogue has full symmetry.

If a lack of symmetry occurs because only one participant is saying and/or listening, dialogue may continue at length but with decreasing odds of reaching a mutual resolution. With a lack of symmetry, as monologues continue, frustration mounts on one or both sides. When one partner is "a talker" and the other more taciturn, the unequal air time can evoke negative feelings that contaminate the content of their discussion. Another unfortunate form of asymmetry occurs when discussants, especially spouses, have widely discrepant voice volume or speech rates. When one voice is louder or one person speaks more slowly, both parties' irritation can pollute the atmosphere of cooperation.

SUMMARIZING

With both speakers expressing some form of initial statement of wants, both giving evidence that they take the other's wishes seriously, and both proceeding with symmetrical air time and speech patterns, successful completion of the first conflict resolution stage has been almost accomplished.

To insure that a transition point has been reached, one of the participants can state a full review of the points made. Summarizing insures that what has been understood by one is understood by all, freeing the participants to move on to the next stage of discussion. Don accomplishes this mini-closure by reiterating, "I want us to take off and you want us to stay home."

It should be clear at this point that certain modes of communicating lead to progress in cooperative conflict resolution. Others lead to a high probability that the communications will be disrupted and that the discussion will detour into emotional escalations, tension, abandonment of attempts to build a bilateral consensus, or one side giving up and giving in. Any of the communication behaviors summarized in Table 2.2 can indicate that these detours are imminent.

TABLE 2.2
Red Flags Indicating Disruptive Communication Habits

INSTEAD IF SAYING WHAT IS WANTED

- Saying nothing
- Hinting
- Expressing dislikes, the negative of what one wants: "I don't want to . . ."
- Asking questions instead of stating feelings: "What do *you* want to do?" or, "Don't you think that . . .?"
- Launching statements with the pronoun you as the subject: "You shouldn't . . ."
- Criticisms: "Why did you have to . . .?!"
- Blame: "If you hadn't . . ."
- Complaints: "I don't like you to . . ." or "I never get to . . ."
- Critical innuendo
- Irritated or accusatory tone of voice

INSTEAD OF RECEPTIVE LISTENING

- Continuing with own train of though, ignoring instead of incorporating what the other person has just said
- Focus on what is wrong instead of what is right in what the other is saying
- Interpretive response, especially if it includes projections of own feelings attributed to the speaker: "You just want . . ."
- Contradicting response: "Yes, but . . ."
- No response, verbal or nonverbal

INSTEAD OF SYMMETRY

- Unequal air time (length that each person talks)
- Different voice volumes
- Different rates of speech
- Unequal speaking and listening roles

INSTEAD OF A SUMMARIZING STATEMENT

- No summarizing statements
- Summarizing statements that omit what one person said

A START, NOT A SETTLEMENT

Despite a good start, if the spouses in this example had attempted to decide their vacation plan at this point, the outcome would probably have been less than optimal. If Don had insisted on his initial recommendation or Beth on hers, the ensuing positional bargaining probably would have yielded a win-lose, a lose-lose, or at best, a compromise solution.

Some couples with win-lose decision-making amicably short-circuit discussion at this point. They may routinely take turns getting what they want. Alternatively, they may decide on the basis of who seems to feel more strongly on the issue. These patterns of settlement may be less than optimal but do prevent argument. Other spouses vie for the winning position, in which case they may fight, overtly or covertly, until one dominates and the other gives up.

Couples who seek compromise solutions may look for a hybrid plan such as spending half of the vacation at home and half in Alaska. Splitting the difference might also be arranged geographically; i.e., instead staying home or going to Alaska, Beth and Don would vacation in Portland.

Sometimes, when the fighting gets too intense, or to avoid fighting, a couple agrees that neither person will get what s/he wants. Attempts at settlement may be abandoned or they may agree explicitly on a third solution that is different from what either wanted. A lose-lose solution has the appeal of fairness. Proceeding with the second and third stages of the resolution process, however, opens up the potential for more fully satisfying outcomes.

Exploration of underlying concerns

BETH: I guess we have a problem with finding a vacation plan we'll both like. Why do you want to go to Alaska?

DON: I was thinking of an exploring vacation because I want to be physically active. At work I sit at my desk all day. I'm yearning to move around, walk long distances, meet new people, see new sights.

BETH: I'm also reacting to work, and I have the opposite situation. I'm constantly on the move there, and I guess that's why doing nothing sounds so appealing. I just want to relax, to slow down and recuperate from all this busy-ness business. I also want time to read; it feels like years since I've read a novel.

TEAMWORK

The second stage typically begins with several shifts. First, opposition needs to give way to cooperation. The participants need to shift from viewing themselves as antagonists to assuming that they are two members of one team. As one spouse said, "We need to go from feeling like we are sitting on opposite sides of the table to both sitting on the same side with the problem on the table in front of us." A change of pronouns from "I" to "we" expresses and enhances this shift from opposition to teamwork.

Second, it is helpful to reframe the problem at a level of abstraction that includes both members' initial expressions of wishes. Beth broadens the framing of the problem from "what I want" or "what you want" to "finding a vacation plan we'll both like." She moves from each individual's statement of positions to an overview of the problem they are trying to solve. Now Don and Beth are working as allies facing a common challenge, the vacation plans.

Having set a cooperative tone and a broader definition of the problem, Beth launches the exploration process per se by asking Don to verbalize the concerns underlying his suggestion of the Alaska trip. She begins her question with the word "why."

Individuals and couples who have built up a reservoir of good will and trust can generally respond constructively to "why" questions, hearing the "why" as "in response to what?" or, better yet, "toward what goal?" or "for what?" Spoken in a less genuinely interested tone of voice or received in a less benign emotional climate, a similar "why ... ?" question can imply criticism, belittlement, or demand for justification of what has been said. Either a critical why or a misinterpretation of the intent of the question can derail effective communication at this point.

Don hears Beth's question as coming from genuine interest. He proceeds to introspect and to verbalize his introspections. The habit of introspection seems to develop with both talent and practice. Fortunately, the ability to introspect, though more highly developed in some people than in others, seems to be present in at least rudimentary form in most people who have developed basic language skills. Severely limited intelligence may hinder ability to look beneath the simple concrete and surface level concerns, but even clarification of superficial concerns can add helpful information to the decision-making process. For instance, a young child who tugs on his parent's arm and insists, "I want to go home," can generally, if asked, tell the parent why, e.g., "I'm hungry," or "I have to go to the bathroom."

SELF-ACCEPTANCE AND ACCEPTANCE OF THE OTHER

Capacity for insight seems related to an internalized attitude of self-acceptance. If previous encounters with people in general, and within the current relationship in particular, have been safely accepting, insight is more likely. The rule for free association in traditional psychoanalytic therapy is "Say whatever comes into awareness." This rule, softened perhaps by a bit of tact, characterizes healthy exploration of underlying concerns. Whatever concerns emerge into awareness need to be experienced as legitimate enough to be verbalized, without expectation of criticism, belittlement or disregard.

Probably there are reciprocal relationships between self-acceptance, acceptance of others, and others' acceptance of one's own thoughts, wishes and concerns. If prior experience has established to someone that listeners will generally respond with accepting, nonjudgmental interest, that person is likely to feel a sense of legitimacy about his/her thoughts and comfort in expressing them. At the same time, when a person speaks his mind with a feeling of self-acceptance, others are likely to listen with attentive respect. Similarly, someone who listens attentively to others may set a tone of considerate listening in return.

SPECIFIC DETAILS

Don and Beth express their concerns in considerable detail. Specifics are essential in laying the groundwork for consensual solutions. If Don had said he wanted to go to Alaska because it "sounds like fun," the vagueness of his reply would have obfuscated the exploration process. Many people overestimate the extent to which other people can read their minds. They expect that others' associations to words will resemble their own more than they in fact do. Thus the word "fun" may mean climbing mountains to Don while it connotes romantic dancing to Beth. Don uses the term "physically active," and then specifies the activities he is picturing in his own mind when he uses those words, i.e., long walks, meeting new people, seeing new sights.

A classic exercise used in negotiation workshops teaches the importance of details in exploration of underlying concerns. In this "Ugli Orange" exercise, Company A and Company B are competing to buy the same shipload of oranges. They remain at an impasse, each company's representative seeking unsuccessfully to convince the other that his company deserves the oranges. Only workshop participants who seek specific details of each company's concerns can successfully solve the dilemma with a win-win solution. By inquiring of each other what precisely, in full detail, each side wants the oranges for, participants discover that Company A needs just the peels whereas Company B wants only the juice. That is, specific details uncovered in the explorations of concerns lay the foundations for optimal resolution.

DEPTH

Don and Beth begin their explorations of underlying concerns at a surface level, with their immediate and most pressing interests. Don wants physical activity to compensate for limits to movement in his workday world. Beth wants a restful vacation as a change from her high activity level at work. Often these first concerns that come to mind provide enough information to yield resolution possibilities. Sometimes, however, exploration of deeper levels of concerns is necessary in order to find complementarity and common ground.

Exploring "underlying" concerns implies depth, but what precisely do we mean by "depth" in this context? Norcross (1986) clarifies the way in which this word has come to be used in psychological conceptualizing. Depth refers to variation on two dimensions, an awareness (consciousness) continuum and a historical continuum. On the awareness continuum, a concern that is easily accessible to immediate awareness would fall toward one end. A concern that is deeply buried and is extremely difficult to bring to awareness would lie on the opposite extreme. On a historical continuum, concerns that arise from current here-and-now realities would fall on one extreme and concerns derived from earliest family of origin experiences on the other. "Deeper" underlying concerns then would mean that the concerns are less accessible to conscious awareness and/or originate from childhood rather than contemporary events.

Behavioral therapists have a reputation for focusing primarily on the more conscious and contemporary ends of these continua, and therapists trained in psychodynamic treatments are thought to focus mainly on the more unconscious and historically remote ends. In reality, effective therapists of both types seem to develop ways to gather the full range of data. Effective resolution of difficult conflicts makes that kind of flexibility essential.

In the conflict illustration above, the initial concerns that are expressed do not yield enough information to indicate likely common solutions, so exploration continues at a deeper level.

DON: When I was a kid we never had enough money, so travel was out of the question. Now you and I at least have some extra money in the bank. The sign for me that we're really secure is to splurge on a big trip.

BETH: I never thought of that, but it makes sense. Knowing how little money there was in your family for the necessitites of life, I guess travel must have been unthinkable.

Looking back on my childhood, I see why the ultimate luxury for me is a vacation with freedom to do nothing. My parents were well-meaning, but they were so intent on giving us "quality time" as a family that they used to supersaturate our vacations. By the end of a week of running here and there all over the globe I used to be exhausted, and mad at them for taking my vacation away from me. When you suggest traveling to Alaska I can feel the old resentment building in me. It's that old feeling of having to follow someone else's agenda. What I wanted never seemed to count.

DON: So you're worried we'll run around instead of relaxing, and we'll do only what I want?

BETH: Those probably are the most important factors for me.

Rice and Greenberg (1984) use the term "softening" to describe the listening
stance of compassionate understanding that seems to emerge as individuals
listen to one another's deeper level concerns. They suggest that softening is
an indication that resolution is near. One more major step remains. A
summary of concerns on both sides can facilitate the transition to this last
step.

Selecting mutually satisfying solutions

DON: I want to be able to move around a lot, to meet new people and see
new places, and to splurge financially. You want to be able to sit still,
read and relax, and to feel certain that I am heeding what you want.
How about if we fly to a foreign seacoast? You could sit and relax on
the beach; I could swim, hike and explore.

BETH: That sounds great. Once I get there I could have a stay-put vacation,
and I like the romance of being in a new place. Are you sure you
wouldn't mind going off adventuring on your own?

DON: It sounds a little scary to me, but that's part of the sense of adventure.
Let's just be sure we spend our evenings together. And, for some of
the time, sunning on the beach with you appeals to me too.

BETH: Actually, as long as I don't *have* to go with you on your jaunts, I
might in fact decide to join some of your exploring. The vacation
sounds great!

SUMMARIZING STATEMENTS

Transitions between stages in the resolution process seem to flow more
smoothly if eased with summarizing statements. A summary of the points
of agreement, of the concerns on both sides that are to be considered in
solution-building, propels Don and Beth's negotiation into the final phase.
Don's summary gave equal weight to his and Beth's concerns. The importance of symmetry at all levels of the resolution process cannot be
overemphasized.

GENERATING OPTIONS

People anticipate that the last stage of the resolution process will be the
most difficult because with faulty process it never occurs. In fact, generation of mutually agreeable options often turns out to be relatively simple,
provided someone launches this last phase by asking, "So what shall we do
to solve this?"

People who have never ventured this far in mutual problem-solving sometimes prematurely settle on the first suggestion, too relieved to realize they can generate more options. In fact, some degree of brainstorming to create multiple options can be helpful. Some people seem to have more facility at coming up with creative alternatives than others. Individuals also differ in their characteristic levels of productivity, the trait referred to on Rorschach tests as R (which reflects the total number of responses generated by the cards). The result is that some individuals and couples are able to create multiple options for themselves, and others feel thankful to determine at least one that is mutually acceptable. In the example above, one proposal suffices.

SELECTION OF A SOLUTION

A sense of relief often accompanies agreement on a specific solution. Beth says, "sounds great," hearing a solution that satisfies her agenda perhaps even more successfully than her original suggestion of staying home for the vacation. Going to a foreign seacoast is different from Don's initial idea, an Alaska trip, but he too ends up feeling he has "won." The solution incorporates the concerns of both people.

CHECKING FOR UNFINISHED BUSINESS

The couple has chosen a solution, but one more question often holds the key that determines whether the agreed upon plan will succeed.

BETH: Are there any pieces of the plan that don't feel quite right to you? Anything that still feels unfinished?

DON: The only question left on my mind is where we go. I'd love to go to Mexico, since I've never been there and I hear the coastline is beautiful.

BETH: Mexico sounds good to me. I like the idea of reviewing a Spanish book while I sit on the beach. And Mexico is easy to get to, with a minimum of travel hassles.

DON: How about you—anything still feel unfinished?

BETH: Booking hotel and flight arrangements! I feel too overwhelmed with other responsibilities to add planning a vacation. Would you be willing to handle all the arrangements, and just touch base with me on when we leave?

DON: That's fine with me. What you see as a "chore," I regard as part of the adventure. I'm glad to take on the planning details.

Checking for remaining unfinished pieces of the problem prevents later dissatisfactions or confusions that might undermine what is generally an excellent plan. Like every other step through the resolution process, checking for unfinished business needs to be symmetrical. Both sides need to stand back and rethink what the new solution leaves unclear or unsatisfactory. After these final loose ends have been addressed, the final package is ready to be wrapped and ribboned.

FINAL CLOSURE

Summarizing marked the transitions between stages and now marks the end of the last stage. Clear final verbalization of the agreement decreases the likelihood of later misunderstandings.

BETH: It's off to the Mexican coast, with a lovely beach for relaxing and
      plenty of exploring potential. I think we've solved it.
DON: Mission accomplished. Hasta luego!

The conflict has been resolved. Smiles, nods of approval, hugs, and comments indicating satisfaction give an "amen" of closing punctuation.

WHEN DO CONFLICTS OCCUR?

Some individuals and families seem to flow through their days with relatively little argument or tension. These individuals and families handle conflict smoothly, automatically engaging in the process detailed in this chapter, calling it "talking things over" or "discussing decisions together." Neither an individual's internal network of values and desires, nor differing viewpoints among family members, nor even the twists and turns of life seem to evoke oppositional stances. These people seem to expect that, as Schwartz (1989) says, "the data are always friendly." They experience their and others' feelings with self-acceptance (Wile, 1989). They assume that reality problems such as maintaining health and financial security can be solved. Because they expect other people and new situations to be reasonable, they launch into interactions with a cooperative stance, with what the tit for tat paradigm refers to as "niceness." In most instances, niceness begets niceness. Consequently, in the lives of these individuals and families, relatively few situations develop the tension level necessary to experience a dilemma as a conflict.

On the opposite extreme, some individuals' and families' existences seem replete with continual tension, turbulence, and strife. Whatever happens in their lives, good and bad, these people are more likely to react with criticism, self-criticism, blame, and self-blame. The more they react with negativity, defensiveness, irritability or selfishness toward challenges that confront them in daily living, the more their lives become conflictual. These attitudes invite negativity from others, "bad luck," and more upsetting interactions.

McLuhan (1964) said the medium is the message. In psychological functioning, the process can become the problem. In psychotherapy, new processes can be learned and become part of the solutions.

Diagnosis

CHAPTER 3

Understanding and Describing Distressed People

A CONFLICT RESOLUTION FRAMEWORK for understanding emotional distress rests on the following postulates, which will be explored in this chapter and the next:

- The health of any given system, be it an individual, couple, or group, can be seen as a function of its ability to negotiate conflicts.
- Emotional and behavioral problems result from deficiencies in the handling of inner conflict, conflict with other people, and/or conflict with life circumstances. Emotional problems are produced not by needs per se but rather by inadequacies in how people go about getting those needs met.
- A full diagnostic evaluation includes description of symptoms, listing of the problems about which the patients feels conflicted, and delineation of the patterns characteristically used in conflictual situations.
- Specific symptoms, such as depression, anxiety, anger, or addiction, are associated with specific patterns of conflict management. A system that delineates these less adaptive conflict patterns can integrate our conceptualizations of a wide range of pathologies.
- The same conflict patterns pertain to both intrapsychic and interpersonal conflict management. People seem to rely on similar conflict patterns for handling both their inner conflicts and their conflicts with others.
- Certain conflict patterns, such as perpetual fighting, are inherently

47

dysfunctional. Other patterns can be useful from time to time in various contexts.

• Conflict resolution patterns, like language, are learned initially in the family of origin. Difficulties may erupt when the patterns are insufficient for coping with particularly challenging circumstances. A child's language skills would be inadequate for coping with college studies; likewise, simpler patterns of conflict resolution may be inadequte for an individual, couple, or family facing difficult life challenges. Also, difficulties can emerge if the conflict patterns that were suitable for survival in the family of origin are inappropriate for a different environment.

ORGANIZING THE DATA IN A CONFLICT-BASED ASSESSMENT

A comprehensive clinical assessment includes data-gathering about the individual, the marital dyad, and the family unit. Most clinicians explore realms that could be seen as behavioral (observable behaviors and reported symptoms), dynamic (underlying motivations, conscious and unconscious, and their family of origin roots), and systemic (structural and other issues of the family unit). A system for arranging this vast array of data into meaningful patterns is critical.

The following system manages this broad database by arranging the data within a conflict resolution framework. Clinicians have long looked at symptoms, process and content. These three traditional categories, enhanced by the central organizing construct of conflict, offer an excellent sorting system for analyzing the flood of raw data presented to clinicians:

• *symptoms,* which lead to a DSM diagnosis.
• *processes*, or patterns, for resolving conflicts, and
• *content* of conflicts, i.e., a problem list of individual, couple, and systemic issues.

Symptoms

Symptoms are signs. They signal that a problem exists, that something is wrong in the emotional or psychic life of an individual or family. They are behaviors, feelings, or thoughts that bother people or that therapists view as pathological, abnormal or dysfunctional.

Symptoms often are solutions—attempts by an individual or family to cope with problems. Alcohol addiction, for instance, may emerge as an attempt to ease the pain felt after the death of a loved family member.

Sometimes symptoms are by-products of solutions. For instance, a family may face difficult decisions about whether to move to a new city in order to find better financial opportunities. If this decision is resolved in a detrimental fashion, resentment, guilt, depression, anxiety, or alcoholism could be by-products.

Symptoms are feelings or behaviors that suggest disturbance of normal functioning. Excessive crying, appetite loss, anxiety, hallucinations, outbursts of rage, arguments, job failure, unsatisfactory sexual relationship, violence, cognitive distortions, collapsed hierarchy in a family, sibling rivalry, and so on indicate that people are experiencing significant distress and/or inability to function effectively.

Assessment of symptoms includes listing of specific troubling behaviors and feelings, the history of these symptoms, and diagnosis in terms of DSM categories. When treatment includes multiple family members, assessment of each individual's symptomatology, along with evaluation of couple and family issues, is essential for a full understanding of the problems to be treated.

> Tammy presented for treatment in response to her sister's urging. She had been considering divorce. She felt unhappy in her marriage, guilty about having succumbed to several extramarital sexual relationships, and demoralized by continuous arguments with her husband. She felt guilty that her children were witnessing loud angry interchanges during which she and her husband disparaged one another with name-calling and cursing. Several episodes had become violent, with Tammy striking out at her husband.
>
> The marriage, of five years' duration, initially had been satisfactory. About the time that Tammy had begun working outside the home, arguments and affairs had commenced. Subsequent to the arrival of a second child, the intensity and frequency of the arguments had again increased.

The above case description portrays Tammy by delineating her symptoms, including the history of their development. *DSM* diagnostic decisions are primarily based on this kind of data. Tammy's symptoms cluster around anger and sexual acting-out, suggesting a possible individual diagnosis of histrionic personality disorder, narcissistic personality disorder, borderline disorder, or adjustment disorder of adult life with mixed emotional features. Because of Tammy's generally healthy functioning in other areas of family, work, and social life, and because of the therapist's subjective intuitions, the diagnosis was determined to be adjustment disorder. Tammy and her family were adapting poorly to her return to work outside the home and to the birth of their second child.

Tammy's anger and sexual acting-out can be seen as symptoms that indicate conflicts. Her symptoms can also be regarded as solutions to these underlying dilemmas. Tammy felt torn between wanting to stay in her marriage and wanting to leave. Her solution involved staying, but at the same time pushing her husband away with anger and enhancing her social world with extramarital relationships. These solutions may not have been optimal choices, but they were the solutions she was utilizing when she presented for consultation. This notion of symptoms as solutions is critical to an understanding of psychopathology based on conflict and how conflict is handled.

Process

Process refers to *how* conflicts are dealt with. A process is a sequence of behaviors occurring over time. Process descriptions focus on the *patterns* of responses to conflictual situations.

> In response to the question, "How do you and your husband try to settle your disagreements?" Tammy said that their biggest problem seemed to be an inability to communicate. She said that she often raised issues, but discussion quickly turned into mutual exchange of insults. She blamed this pattern primarily on her husband, saying that even with the children he tended to be short-tempered, angering quickly rather than exploring what the problem might be when the children were not behaving as he felt they should. It was not clear to what extent Tammy's way of raising issues for discussion invited a defensive attacking response.

Tammy presented an argumentative pattern for dealing with conflicts. Her communications with her husband had deteriorated into bickering and name-calling. In her descriptions of their marriage, Tammy focused on her husband's faults rather than her own wants. Her attempts to deal with her personal and marital conflicts seemed to be characterized by a similar pattern of blame more than by information-gathering or insight. The negative style with which she approached conflicts was also evident later when she was asked to explore her feelings with regard to staying in the marriage or leaving. She could articulate what she feared and didn't want, but not what she did want.

This skill deficit suggested that when she was grappling with either intrapsychic or interpersonal dilemmas Tammy would experience difficulties in the first stage of conflict resolution, expression of wishes. Focusing on the negative, she expressed herself in complaints rather than requests. This pattern may have ignited some of the couple's fights. It also probably compounded Tammy's inner distress. Repeatedly telling herself what she didn't want could not lead her toward positive objectives such as making the marriage better or striking out on her own.

Strengths in patients' conflict patterns are also vital to note. Tammy addressed each question that the therapist asked with thoughtful intelligence. She expressed feelings appropriately, crying briefly when sensitive issues were uncovered. She showed courage as she plowed on with good-humored determination to clear a path of understanding through the complexities of her situation. While she seemed psychologically naive, she caught on quickly and appreciatively as the therapist helped her to refocus from blaming her husband to recognizing her personal needs and the needs of the couple and family.

In sum, Tammy seemed to have become locked in an attack-attack response to conflict with her husband and within her inner conflicts. At the same time, her ability to discuss her difficulties in an open, insightful, and constructive manner with the therapist suggested the potential for more effective patterns.

Content

Content refers to *what* the conflict is about, to the unresolved problems that make people uncomfortable. Content includes problematic situations, and also the competing concerns evoked by these troubling situations. Concerns can take the form of desires, such as longings for affection, for validation, for control, for independence, for nurturance from others, for rest and health, for financial security, and for meaning and purpose. Concerns also can take the form of fears, such as fears of failure, rejection, abandonment, illness, or death. Exploration of underlying concerns, longings, and fears has traditionally been a central focus of psychodynamic psychotherapies.

Values, referred to as superego concerns in psychoanalytic nomenclature, likewise can be an element in the content of conflicts. Values generally get expressed as "should" statements. Perry London (1986) suggests that, in part out of a concern for therapist neutrality, that is, reluctance to impose their value system on their clients, many therapists insufficiently explore values with their clients. In fact, however, much intrapsychic conflict occurs when values and wishes seem to be at odds.

Conflict can also arise out of structural concerns, concerns about the design of a life space and of a family system. Allotment of time and energy to work, family, and recreational activities, for instance, is a structural as well as a values issue. Concerns about the closeness/distance of family members, division of labor, hierarchy and control, and boundary clarity, rigidity, and/or permeability fall under the rubric of structural concerns. Exits and entrances of family members, developmental changes (such as from infancy to school years and to adolescence), or reality changes (such as financial shifts or the advent of chronic illness) require families to restructure themselves to adapt to new conditions. These problems about which people feel conflicted and conflict with one another constitute the *content* of conflicts.

Tammy disliked feeling locked into a dependent relationship, excessively taken care of by a paternalistic spouse. Although her husband had indicated willingness to do his part in changing the parent-child aspects of their relationship, Tammy had not cooperated in negotiating the changes. She wanted a better relationship, but she also wanted it to remain bad so that she could leave.

The couple had begun arguing when Tammy first returned to work. At her work she had become involved socially and eventually sexually with other men. She enjoyed their companionship. They offered a sharp contrast to her husband, with whom she shared virtually no common interests and had little compatibility in terms of intellectual style.

Tammy valued her husband's fathering qualities, but she had become increasingly ambivalent about being treated by him as a dependent and did not find him appropriate as a life companion. Her choice of a spouse had been made on the basis of availability when she was 18 and wanted to leave home, rather than on the basis of compatibility. While her husband was satisfied working as a manual laborer, Tammy was intellectually and financially more ambitious. Whereas she was an ardent conversationalist and an intellectual explorer, he was content watching sports on TV and disliked discussions on the topics that intrigued her.

Tammy worked evenings so that she could take care of her children during the days. This schedule created additional structural problems in the marriage. She and her husband no longer shared common leisure time. The dearth of time together as a couple seemed to be both a cause and an outgrowth of increased distance between the spouses. The arrangement of separate and shared times was not satisfactory to either of them. On the other hand, it did give Tammy more sense of being separate without having to obtain an actual divorce.

Countering Tammy's impulses to leave the marriage was a genuine fondness for her husband, whom she saw as trying to be a good husband and father. Her Catholic religious background also condemned divorce. On a deeper (less conscious) level, the primary fear blocking Tammy from ending the marriage was of "falling on her face." This metaphor translated into fear of being shamed by her mother if she were to have difficulties living alone. The youngest of seven children, Tammy had been babied by her parents and older siblings and had internalized the message that she could not take care of herself. The financial pressures that would be inevitable as a single parent with two young children and meager economic resources further blocked her from terminating the marriage. Realistically, Tammy would have great difficulties sustaining herself and her children alone.

Tammy's case illustrates multiple levels and arenas in which the content of psychological distress can be explored. Both current realities and recurring themes in a patient's life are important. Tammy was distressed about her marriage and wanted to escape from an unfortunate mismatch. She felt locked into a dependent relationship that replicated the dependent relationships she still had with her parents and her many siblings. Although she longed for self-reliance, she feared failure. In the realm of values, Tammy's Catholicism ruled against divorce. Her values also left her feeling guilty about the affairs in which she had engaged out of disaffection with the marital relationship. Neither of these solutions to her affectional and autonomy needs—divorce or affairs—was consonant with her values. A systemic/structural problem further exacerbated the marital dissatisfaction. With her husband working days and Tammy working evenings and weekends, the couple shared so little time together that the relationship was undernourished.

In sum, content can be explored in multiple dimensions. Developmental needs, current desires, neurotic and realistic fears, personal values, and systemic/structural issues may all be relevant in any given case.

THE CHICKEN AND THE EGG

Which of the three aspects of conflicts are causes and which effects? Which must be changed for all three factors—symptoms, process and content—to be changed? These causality questions can be important in choosing treatment interventions.

Whenever conflict processing is poor, symptoms are likely to emerge. For instance, depressive or anxious symptoms can emerge when vital concerns are barred from awareness. On the other hand, they can create dysfunctional conflict patterns and exacerbate problems. For example, individuals suffering from major depression may be too de-energized to express what they want. Schizophrenics' inner voices may render them deaf to reality demands from the world outside the mind. People who are biologically prone to anxiety can be immobilized with fear that inhibits them from accomplishing what they want.

Poor process also can create problems, adding to the content areas that are distressing. When spouses develop a pattern of fighting, for instance, they may begin to argue over issues about which there is no genuine disagreement, creating new topics of dissension in each interchange. A host of issues can become problems simply because the couple has developed antagonistic instead of cooperative communication habits.

Likewise, troubling life dilemmas, i.e., content, can affect communication patterns (processes) and symptoms. Even people whose skills at resolving conflicts are generally adequate may find their ability to cope excessively strained by a particularly difficult life problem. A previously well-functioning individual, couple, or family may then become overwhelmed, resort to ineffective responses to conflict, and even manifest clinical symptomatology. For instance, a couple with a fine relationship may develop patterns of angry bickering in response to differences in how to handle money problems. Likewise, a family member's severe illness can overwhelm a family's ability to resolve the new conflicts about who is now responsible for what, who gets how much attention, and when. In these instances the content of difficult circumstances precipitates a degeneration in conflict processing and the onset of stress symptoms.

To complicate even further the relationship among these three dimensions of conflict, the reality is that sometimes the categories overlap. Poor process can be a symptom, as when violence is the process used for solving conflicts and is also the presenting symptom. Likewise, the content can be the process. A couple may seek therapy explicitly to resolve conflicts about the appropriateness of violence as a means of settling disputes. Symptom, process and/or content may be overlapping categories.

Although the relationship among the symptoms, process, and content of conflicts can be linear (one causes another) or identical (they are one and the same), complex three-dimensional reciprocal causality offers an alternative, perhaps more useful model. That is, each problem may be caused initially by any of the others, and in turn may exacerbate the others. Depressive symptomatology, for instance, can be a by-product of a dominant-submissive conflict resolution pattern and a particularly intransigent problem. On the other hand, that pattern will be reinforced when one partner is depressed, because a depressed person has no energy for negotiating and just submits when differences occur. Likewise, underlying issues may become aggravated by poor conflict negotiating. Poor process and symptoms make the content of the conflicts loom larger and larger.

Fortunately, the reciprocal impact can also work in the opposite direction. As process improves, the same content shrinks in toxicity. As the content seems less threatening, effective processing is easier to maintain. As one couple blithely noticed toward the end of treatment, "Oh, it's just that old issue again. We used to get so alarmed whenever that came up. Now it's no big deal. We just have to talk for a few minutes about how to readjust our solution. It's just a mini-glitch now, no longer a mountain." Symptoms, poor conflict processing, and the fears, desires and other content of conflicts all can interact to perpetuate, exacerbate, or attenuate one another.

ASSESSING THE ASSESSMENT

As suggested above, *symptoms*, *process* and *content* of conflict are terms that are familiar to most therapists, including practitioners from the full spectrum of treatment modalities. While a language that most clinicians already speak with ease, these ways of describing people are also accessible to lay people.

One advantage of the three-part conflict-based system is its focus on how people are functioning, how they are behaving and feeling and living their lives, rather than on what they "have." The metaphorical implications when we say someone "has" a problem such as a borderline disorder or depression or agoraphobia is that the problem needs to be removed. The implication for therapy is that some form of emotional catharsis, medication or surgery is necessary to rout out the problem. By contrast, if symptoms are viewed as suboptimal solutions to problems, the therapeutic implication is that better solutions need to be found. This implication fosters problem–solving and psychoeducation rather than a treatment that focuses on extirpation. Similarly, processes are patterns of behavior. Patterns of behavior can be understood. Their origins and intents can be clarified. They can be modified, discarded, and improved upon. Likewise, the content of conflicts comprises the very real issues that need to be satisfactorily resolved for life to proceed in more gratifying ways.

Unlike descriptions of patients' problems that utilize traditional diagnostic terminology such as "neuroses" and "personality disorders," regarding patients in terms of their conflicts, processes for handling these conflicts, and related symptoms does not inherently make patients sound "sick." All of us have problems in our lives, deal with these problems with various strategies, and from time to time manifest emotional symptoms of distress. Because this terminology can be used to describe healthy as well as pathological functioning, it keeps all of us simply human, instead of dichotomizing people into normal and mentally ill.

At the same time, the symptoms category does assume that clinicians must assess psychopathology along traditional criteria. This aspect of understanding and describing patients is an essential component of responsible diagnosis and treatment that must never be overlooked. As a practical matter, an official diagnosis is necessary for insurance reimbursement of treatment expenses. More fundamentally, correct naming (or ruling out) is a crucial first step in treatment planning, as disorders with elements that interfere with ability to function (such as schizophrenia, mood disorders, addictions, explosive epsiodes, etc.) may require immediate symptom reduction (see chapters 11 and 12). Diagnosis in terms of labeling psychopathology (symptoms) is, however, only one step in the assessment process.

Perhaps the most important aspect of organizing data in terms of symptoms of conflict, processes for handling conflict, and content of conflicts, however, is the breadth of data which these categories span. A limitation of conventional nomenclature for describing patients is that the terms refer to individuals or to family systems, but not to both. A conflict-based view can be used to describe individuals, their intrapsychic functioning, their interpersonal interactions, and also their families with the same three basic concepts. Likewise, conceptualization of psychological dysfunction in terms of symptoms, content and processes allows for psychoanalytic, behavioral, existential, and systemic data, as well as for raw data that do not clearly fit any of our traditional conceptualizations. The effectiveness of this way of describing distressed people is in large part dependent on the breadth of a clinician's psychological knowledge base. What has been added is an integrative framework that enables the various kinds of psychological data to be viewed all together on one cognitive map.

CHAPTER 4

From Conflict to Distress

WHEN PEOPLE ARE TROUBLED BY upsetting feelings like depression, anxiety, or anger, they are responding to conflicts in their lives with specific predictable patterns. That is, certain patterns of conflict handling consistently emerge in conjunction with specific symptoms. This coupling of conflict patterns (processes) and symptoms occurs whether the upsetting conflicts are intrapsychic, interpersonal, or both. Awareness of these patterns helps a therapist to intervene efficiently, redirecting patients from distress to relief.

OPTIONS IN CONFLICT SITUATIONS

The multitude of colors we see in the world comes from blends of only three primary colors. Similarly, there seem to be four primitive responses to conflict. A young child who wants to keep playing with a toy that his friend is trying to take from him can fight to hold on to it, give up and surrender to the other's wishes, run away from the battle, or stay still, frozen and immobilized. Animals show the same four basic nonverbal responses to conflict situations. They can fight, give up, take flight, or become immobilized and freeze. For instance, a cat threatened by another cat can raise its fur, growl, bare its teeth, and, if need be, escalate into a full-scale clawing and biting attack. Surrender may be indicated by the cat's rolling onto its back. If the other cat is showing a determined fight response or is far enough away so that escape looks feasible, the cat may choose flight, dashing away to safety. Distraction with an irrelevant activity, such as preening, can be a more subtle form of flight, since acting as if there is no conflict sometimes seems to make the conflict go away. Or the cat can become immobilized and freeze.

57

Fortunately, the unique human medium of language offers a fifth option, problem-solving. If Mr. and Mrs. Smith both want the last piece of apple pie, rather than fighting over it, giving up on the tempting morsel, experiencing rising tensions while neither adversary takes definitive action, or running away from the confrontation, the Smiths can discuss their situation. Talking through the dilemma can broaden the range of potential solutions, raising possibilities that would satisfy both spouses. Discussion could lead to a decision to divide the pie. The Smiths might look about the kitchen and find an additional dessert. Or they might remind themselves of their desires to lose weight and give the pie to one of their children. Language gives people the option of working out cooperative solutions.

Animals do cooperate. They hunt in packs, bring food to their young, and spend idle time in pairs and prides. However, once an animal perceives itself in conflict with another, it can settle the dispute only via dominance, submission, retreat, or freezing until the conflict disappears. The option of exploring concerns and finding mutually agreeable solutions does not exist in a nonverbal world (see Table 4.1). In a verbal world all five options become available and can be enacted via words as well as by physical actions. In the literature of political negotiation these five responses to controversy are defined by Pruitt and Rubin (1986) as contending, yielding, withdrawing, inaction, and joint problem-solving.

INTRAPSYCHIC CONFLICT REACTIONS

When inner conflicts create emotional discomfort, the most sanguine resolution strategy is generally to listen with a self-accepting ear to conflicting feelings, and then to determine optimal plans of action. Freud's classic summation of the process of therapy, "Where id was, let ego be," can be seen as the recommendation to acknowledge, think about, discuss, and make decisions about conflicting thoughts and feelings rather than fight, squelch, ignore or flee from them. Open-minded acceptance of competing feelings and concerns, followed by problem-solving thought and action, raises the odds that a satisfactory resolution will be found.

Realistically, alas, no one functions optimally all the time. Most people sometimes slip, at least from time to time, into defensive, blocked, self-critical, or self-protective postures instead of openly addressing thoughts and feelings with cooperative inner dialogue and problem-solving. To the extent that defensive responses to uncomfortable thoughts and feelings hinder family or work functioning or cause distressed feelings, these "defenses" can be seen as counterproductive. Table 4.2 lists some of

TABLE 4.1
Strategies Available to Parties in Conflict

ANIMALS CAN:	PEOPLE CAN:*	BY:
Fight	Contend: Try to impose one's preferred solution on the other party.	Insisting Blaming Criticizing Accusing Shouting Using force
Submit	Yield: Lower aspirations and settle for less than one would have liked.	Giving in Giving up Agreeing, just to end the conflict Surrendering to what the other wants
Flee	Withdraw: Choose to leave the scene of the conflict.	Ceasing to talk Leaving physically cognitively and/or emotionally Changing the topic
Freeze	Inaction: Choose to wait for the other's next move.	Waiting Doing nothing
(not applicable)	Problem-solve: Pursue alternatives that satisfy both sides.	Talking Listening Gathering information Thinking Generating options Resolving

*The terms and definitions in this column are from Pruitt and Rubin (1986), pp. 2–3.

the classic intrapsychic defenses (A. Freud, 1936) and suggests their relationship to the four basic categories of self-protective maneuvers.

INTERPERSONAL CONFLICT REACTIONS

Fight, submission, flight, and immobilization can also be utilized as interpersonal strategies. Whether their use should be considered normal or dysfunctional depends on the extent to which the strategies enhance or

TABLE 4.2
Responses to Inner Conflicts

STRATEGY	CLINICAL LABEL	DESCRIPTION
Fight	Projection	Blame and criticism of another in lieu of seeing these qualities in oneself
	Self-criticism	Attacking one's own feelings or thoughts
Submit	Depression	Giving in to one side in order to end inner conflicts
Flee	Suppression Repression	Blocking out from awareness, especially of angry or sexual impulses
	Denial	An extreme blocking from awareness of uncomfortable thoughts, feelings, or realities
	Compulsive behaviors	Behaviors such as rituals, eating disorders and addictions that distract from uncomfortable thoughts or feelings
	Obsessional thinking	Preoccupation with compelling but safe thoughts that block out frightening thoughts
Freeze	Anxiety Passivity	Doing nothing in hopes that the situation will spontaneously improve
Problem-solve	Healthy ego functioning i.e., thought, leading to constructive action	Listening to the conflicting thoughts and feelings, and finding solutions that take all of these into account

impair problem-solving, enhance or impair the relationship, and involve a loss in reality-testing. For instance, most people from time to time try to get their way by some form of fight strategy. They insist, demand, or raise their voices to convince others to give them what they want. This fight strategy becomes clinically significant or pathological to the extent that it fails to obtain good solutions, involves misreadings of people's thoughts and feelings, disrupts relationships, or injures others. If a mother's voice gets louder when she reiterates to her son that he must clean his room now, that may be within the realm of helpful insistence. If she adds negative epithets—"You lazy boy!"—she is stepping into the realm of hurting him. And if she then physically attacks the boy, the fight strategy could be escalating into the pathological realm.

Table 4.3 categorizes commonly diagnosed psychological disturbances in terms of their manifestations in interpersonal conflict situations. For purposes of brevity, only the most salient aspects of each syndrome are included in the descriptions.

RECIPROCAL INTERACTION PATTERNS

Conflict inherently involves two sides. The viewpoint presented thus far in this chapter, by focusing primarily on one side's options, tells only part of the story. An interactional view, one that looks at patterns of reciprocal interactions, is helpful. Interactional patterns are reciprocal when each triggers the other, with either or both launching the pattern. One side's expectation that the other is going to take the standard move can be enough to initiate the interaction. Then after each action by one side, the other returns the reciprocal action and vice versa. For instance, a criticism ("You should have. . . .") can engender a countering criticism a("Well, that was because you should have . . ."), evoking yet another critical remark from the first speaker, the second speaker's defensively critical next response, and so on. Table 4.4 delineates common interactional patterns and some of their associated symptomatology.

Sometimes the intensity level escalates in each round of the conflict. This kind of tornado-like escalation of the cyclic pattern is particularly common in fight-fight interactions. An argument can start with a critical innuendo, which receives a hostile retort, evoking in turn angry blame, and ending in shouting or even physical violence. Volume and intent to hurt increase with each round. Conflict–avoidant flee-flee interactions also tend to escalate, with escalations seen in increasing frequency of addictive behavior or in stepwise disengagement within a family system.

When one strategy is clearly not working, participants may switch to another. Escalating argumentative interactions, for instance, typically reach a point of intensity at which one or both participants choose to discontinue the interaction. At that point participants may experience a stalemate,

TABLE 4.3
Clinical Syndromes Categorized by Interpersonal Conflict Strategy

STRATEGY	DIAGNOSIS	DESCRIPTION
Fight	Paranoia	Projection of own feelings onto others, and angry response to other on the basis of this projected reading
	Hysteria	Escalation of feelings in order to be heard, dominate or gain control in a frustrating situation
Submission	Depression	Giving up on obtaining what one wants, accompanied by feelings of resignation and negativity toward self, others and the future
Flight	Addictive behavior	Overeating; binge-purge syndromes; abuse of alcohol or other drugs; overinvolvement in work, TV viewing, sexuality or other activity
	Schizoid isolation	Avoidance of social situations that are seen as threatening
Immobilization	Anxiety	Experience of fear without movement toward negotiating, escaping, conquering or submitting to the feared phenomenon
	Catatonia	Inability to move or talk in response to perceived threats.

establishing a cold war (freeze-freeze mutual immobilization). They may change to dominant-submission, with one participant giving up. They may disengage (flee-flee), and then avoid the topic for a period of time. They may even switch to cooperative problem-solving, the transformation that therapists hope to effect in the process of treatment.

Sometimes the same dysfunctional pattern or series of patterns (e.g.,

TABLE 4.4
Interactional Conflict Patterns

INTERACTION	INDIVIDUAL'S SYMPTOMS	COUPLE/FAMILY MANIFESTATIONS
Fight-fight	Inner turmoil Self-accusation	Arguments Can escalate into verbal or physical violence
Fight-freeze	Procrastination	Nagging and passive-aggressive response
Fight-submit	Low self-esteem Guilt	One partner dominating and the other denying own preferences to keep dominating partner from being critical Submissive partner may feel virtuous, martyred, resentful, or depressed
Freeze-freeze	Anxiety, apprehension chronic tension	Stalemated negotiations Marital tension
Flee-flee	Addictive, obsessive-compulsive, and schizoid patterns	Addict and co-dependent Disengaged families

immobilized anxiety, exploding in fighting, and then followed by a dominant-submissive conclusion) is repeated for a lifetime. In other cases, one pattern characterizes a period in a person's or couple's life, and then is exchanged for another for a subsequent lengthy period. A couple, for instance, may have of months or years of mounting tensions, followed by an era of continuous bickering, and then an episode of disengaged avoidance of one another.

Common to all noncooperative strategies is one assumption: that conflict is inevitably a zero or negative sum game. If A wins, B loses; if B wins, then A must lose; both can lose, but both cannot emerge as winners. Cooperation, a strategy that seeks win-win solutions, does not seem possible. In what ways then are these patterns dysfunctional?

- They cause undue emotional pain.
- They yield suboptimal or no solutions to the conflictual issues.
- They satisfy one party at the expense of the other, or satisfy neither.
- They yield secondary symptomatology such as depression, anxiety, addictions, etc.

THE RELATIONSHIP BETWEEN INTRAPSYCHIC AND INTERPERSONAL CONFLICT PATTERNS

One of the central hypotheses of this book is that a given individual's patterns for handling conflicts tend to be similar in both the intrapsychic and interpersonal spheres. Depressed people seem to show a dominant-submissive pattern both in inner dialogue between conflicting shoulds and wants and in negotiations with other people. Angry people tend to be critical toward themselves as well as toward others. Individuals functioning in a borderline mode experience inner chaos analogous to the chaos they find, and tend to develop, around them. In the following case example, a young married woman utilizes the same pattern of conflict responses in her intrapsychic decision-making and in her interactions with her father, her husband, and her daughter.

> Deanna sought help with several problems. She was particularly concerned about her inability to make decisions and her difficulties in getting her daughter to mind her. When Deanna wanted to make a decision, she would hear what she envisioned as "a chorus of experts" in the back of her mind admonishing her about what she should do, which was always contrary to what she wanted to do. In general she would dutifully but unhappily comply with the "experts'" advice.
>
> Observing Deanna interact with her husband, Justin, the therapist noticed a pattern of deferring also with him. Justin had been raised by a mother "who was always right." When he spoke, his self-assured style quietly conveyed that he always knew what was best, for himself and for his wife. In this regard, Deanna and Justin's family of origin patterns dovetailed, with his having learned the dominant role and her the submissive role. Because Justin's style was gentle and kindly, Deanna did not complain about their relationship. The pattern nonetheless was strongly dominant-submissive.
>
> At one therapy session involving Deanna and her three-year-old daughter Lacey, the little girl decided at the outset that she did not want to enter the therapy room. Looking angrily at her mother, she launched into a tantrum of loud crying. Although in this instance Deanna artfully soothed her, in general such episodes left Lacey in control. The collapsed mother-daughter hierarchy, with little Lacey dominating with her tantrums, followed the same dominant-submissive decision-making pattern as Deanna's intrapsychic and husband-wife interactions.
>
> Where was this pattern learned? Deanna's father had been authoritarian in his parenting style, placing a high value on obedience. Even as an adult Deanna found it difficult to have an opinion different from his. Though her father had mellowed in his senior years, he still voiced strong opinions in a manner that implied the foolishness of contrary opinions. Oak furniture, for instance, which Deanna and Justin loved and collected, was unattractive to her father, who clearly let them know the folly of their taste.
>
> Treatment, consisting of individual, couple, and family sessions, helped

Deanna see the pattern common to all of these situations. To deal with the intrapsychic pattern Deanna visualized the should voices, the "chorus of experts," and then made them shrink into the background. Her preferred technique for shrinking them was to raise the volume in her expression of her own concerns. The more she listened to herself, the more the chorus shriveled into powerlessness.

Expansion of her parenting skills enabled Deanna to take control with her daughter, softening the control with prevention and distraction techniques so that Deanna would not have the same impact on Lacey as her authoritarian parents had had on her. Marital sessions added exploration of Justin's family of origin, encouraging him to let go of his overly authoritative stance and to listen more attentively to Deanna's perspectives. Lastly, Deanna experimented with visualization and practiced in vivo until she could hear her own opinions and felt more comfortable making decisions.

Individuals who are open with regard to hearing their own inner competing feelings and values tend to be similarly open about expressing their preferences in discussions with others. Likewise, those who are reluctant to admit their own feelings to themselves may tend to be less than open in conflicts with others. Those who deal harshly with themselves, who on the sports fields shout "Damn it, you idiot!" when they miss a ball, may be inclined to deal harshly with others. Those who heed their shoulds ("I should invite those people for dinner") over what they want ("I'd rather not spend time with them") are similarly inclined to give up on obtaining what they want in the face of competing requests from others.

Thus, families that settle arguments by deeming one person right and the other(s) wrong may produce individuals whose inner debates take a dominant-submissive form and who develop depressive symptomatology when stressful inner conflicts arise. The argumentative family may produce an adult who feels the continuous shock waves of inner turmoil. The family that avoids discussions of sensitive subjects may produce children who grow into adults who escape inner conflicts via drugs, schizoid withdrawal, or obsessive-compulsive distractions, and who develop disengaged marital systems.

CATEGORIES OF EMOTIONAL DISTURBANCE

Psychosis, neurosis, and personality disorder are terms which are broadly used by clinicians to clarify different kinds of emotional disorders. How do these terms become clarified with a focus on conflict as the central organizing element in psychodiagnosis?

Psychosis implies a disorder with an organic basis that affects the intensity of emotions or the functioning of cognitions. The term thus focuses on symptoms as opposed to the content of conflicts or the process of handling conflict (although the various kinds of psychotic reactions, like lesser emotional disorders, involve aggressive fight, depressive yielding, avoidant flight, and immobilizing anxiety). The precipitant for a psychotic disorder may be a stressful life event, but the treatment generally needs to focus initially on symptom reduction. In general, a diagnosis of psychosis suggests that psychotropic medications are likely to be an important part of treatment and that consideration must be given to the need for hospitalization or other measures to provide safety for the patient from harm to him/herself or others. Once symptomatic thinking and emotions are back within a normal range of functioning, treatment can address the content of, and processes of dealing with, the precipitating conflicts.

Neurosis refers to a recurring conflict. The term has been gradually dropped from the official diagnostic nomenclature (the *DSM* system), and yet it does have a certain clinical utility. Although its connotations are perhaps excessively negative, and also excessively suggestive of a psychoanalytic frame of reference, the term does make sense within a conflict-focused conceptualization of emotional distress and treatment (see below).

The third term discussed below, personality disorder, refers to relatively stable patterns of thinking, feeling, behaving, or relating that are demonstrated over a wide range of situations. The avoidant (flight) patterns include schizoid, schizotypal, compulsive, passive-aggressive, addictive and dependent personality disorders. The patterns with a major component of anger expression include histrionic, borderline, narcissistic, antisocial, and paranoid. A pattern of worrying and immobilization would characterize a chronically anxious individual, and the tendency to give up can yield a depressive personality style.

The three terms, psychosis, neurosis, and personality disorder, are by no means mutually exclusive. One individual can show signs of one, two, or all three types of disturbances. This coincidence makes sense when the terms are viewed as referring to disturbances in different realms, the first in the realm of symptoms, the second in the realm of upsetting content of conflicts, and the third in patterns of handling conflict.

Neurosis from a conflict resolution vantage point

Neurosis can be defined within the conflict resolution framework as a conflict that persists, repeatedly recurring in varying forms throughout a person's life because it has not been satisfactorily resolved. One side or another of the conflict may "win" each time the issue comes up, or the issue may be avoided, but it is not satisfactorily brought to closure. Each recurrence of the conflict may on the surface be about a different issue. The underlying concerns, however, will be the same "neurotic" (meaning unresolved, unmet, unsettled) conflicting needs or fears.

> Felicia began experiencing anxiety attacks in the weeks just prior to getting married. Felicia wanted to marry her fiance, Ryan. Early in the course of treatment she expressed the fear that if she were to allow herself to become too attached, Ryan might someday abandon her. Her concern was that she would become dependent on him, and then he would get sick and die.
>
> In a later session, Felicia's fears focused on an upcoming bicycle trip. Although initially her feelings about the trip seemed to have little to do with her fears of the marriage, probing yielded similar underlying concerns that attachment would be followed by loss. Felicia feared that her fiance might want to take a different route than she wanted on the trip, get angry at her, and decide to abandon her.

Neurotic conflicts tend to emerge around reality situations that have some point in common with the situation around which the conflict originally arose. Although the past and present conflicts may share at least one aspect in common, the remainder of the situations may be quite different. In this regard a "neurotic" reaction will seem inappropriate to observers who are unaware of the original situation in which the conflict became emotionally powerful.

> Felicia had experienced multiple abandonments in her childhood, as her mother was sickly and required frequent and lengthy hospitalizations. In Felicia's adult life, any situation that involved a loved one's being close and/or leaving evoked anxiety, as if the total situation were the same as her unfortunate and terrifying childhood.

Luborsky, Crits-Christoph, & Mellon (1986) refer to conflicts that emerge repeatedly throughout someone's life as "core conflicts." Their research suggests that upsetting incidents in a given person's life tend to activate a same few repeated fears or concerns. They posit that these repeated themes become the issues involved in what psychoanalytic therapists describe as transference. Transference refers to patients' tendencies in therapy to develop conflicts with the therapist that reenact early conflictual issues. Core conflicts and transference will be discussed in further detail in the context of treatment in Chapter 15.

Wachtel (1987) offers a useful explanation for why people perpetually replay old conflicts. He notes that in these instances people are reacting to new situations as if these were the same as earlier ones in their lives. Utilizing the Piagetian concept of schema, Wachtel (1981) suggests that neurotic stuckness occurs because of a failure of the adaptational process of assimilation/accommodation. Because new data, i.e., data that show how this situation is different, have not been accommodated (digested in a manner that has changed the earlier schemas), the earlier schemas, or views of how things are, persist. When someone behaves as if the new situation is the same as the old (i.e., on the basis of the unchanged schema), that behavior evokes responses from others similar to those in the earlier playing out of the same conflicts.

A reciprocal causation emerges. A person acts as if the new situation were the same as the original; others respond in the same old way, calling forth a continuation of the neurotic interaction patterns in a vicious cycle (Wachtel & Wachtel, 1986). What these individuals need are new solutions, "re-solutions" to the familiar conflictual situations. A key to obtaining new solutions is therefore incorporation of new data that causes modifications in the old schemas and ways of behaving.

> Felicia's fears regarding the bicycle trip were not unfounded. In fact, Felicia and Ryan had poor strategies for making joint decisions such as which route to take. They typically engaged in positional bargaining. Each stubbornly insisted on doing things his/her way, a style of argument both had learned in their respective families of origin. Felicia was the more insistent of the two. Her dominance would irritate Ryan, who then would have thoughts of leaving her.
>
> As the couple learned in therapy to negotiate their mututal decisions more cooperatively, Felicia rightly sensed that their relationship became less tenuous. As Ryan felt equal power in their discussions, he expressed clearer commitment to the marriage. Felicia's anxiety also eased as she realized that she could exert considerable control over Ryan's commitment to the relationship by doing her part in discussing decisions cooperatively and productively.

Couples and families exhibit a phenomenon analogous to individual neurosis. Couples tend to fight repeatedly about the same few conflicts, which are emotionally upsetting each time they are brought up for discussion. Often these themes can be traced back to issues that have recurred over the years as unresolved, and in this sense "neurotic," conflicts in one or both spouses' families of origins. The themes may have developed initially in parent-child interactions, in interactions between siblings, or in childhood observation of parents' frustrations in their relationship with each other. Often these issues can be traced back through several generations within each family of origin. The core conflicts that continue to trouble a couple usually involve dovetailing themes from each family of origin.

> Felicia feared abandonment because of the frequent separations from her mother caused by her mother's illness, and Ryan brought fears of dealing with

others' anger. When his mother used to become upset, his father had always deferred. Ryan similarly tended to back down in the face of irritated insistence from Felicia. He feared marrying Felicia because he dreaded a life of intermittent exposure to her ire. Each time he responded to her piqued insistence by pulling back from his commitment to her, Felicia reciprocated with abandonment fears. The fears were expressed as outbursts of anger – and the cycle would recur.

Personality disorders

Whereas the term neurosis usually focuses on specific repeated conflictual fears and longings, personality disorders can be seen as a function of the skill level and range of options with which people deal with conflict. When an individual's conflict-handling repertoire is deficient, rigidified in one counterproductive mode, the person may be diagnosed as having a particular character style or personality disorder.

Emotional health involves adaptability, including the ability to react with different strategies to different conflict situations. Emotionally resilient people generally handle information about their own and other's preferences in a cooperative manner, looking to synthesize and integrate rather than balking in an antagonistic mode. When conflicts do emerge, they seek to handle them with cooperative negotiation. Yet they can draw the line and fight against someone who is exploitative, can defer when continued insistence on a point will only engender antagonism, or can gracefully withdraw when a discussion is becoming unproductive.

By contrast, less flexible individuals are likely to have a narrower repertoire and to utilize predominantly defensive strategies (fight, flight, freeze and submit) rather than cooperative ones. Individuals who show a hysteric conflict style habitually react to conflict by dramatizing their needs in order to be heard (and to hear themselves). Those with a paranoid style deal with conflict by attacking and blaming. Obsessive individuals escape from dealing directly with conflict by obfuscating the issues in excessive extraneous detail within which they can hide their true concerns, a conflict avoidant (flight) strategy. Anxious worriers chronically hover over problems, unable either to deal with or to let go of situations. Narcissistic individuals typically have difficulty hearing others' needs. Sometimes they err on the other extreme. They become finely attuned to what others want, ignoring their own needs until they feel starved, at which point they flip and appear extremely self-centered.

Where do we learn our conflict patterns? As usual, both nature and nurture play a role; in fact, there may be a reciprocal interaction between them. With respect to nature, receptivity to utilizing each strategy may have biological bases in temperament. Children who are physically small or who have quiet voices, for instance, may be less likely than large and loud children to rely on domination and fighting to get what they want. High-strung, physiologically highly reactive children may be more likely to become oriented toward anxiety/immobilization. Frail children may be more likely to become submissive or to utilize withdrawal in conflict situations.

With respect to the nurture aspect of learning, communication patterns in a person's family of origin may provide the template for intrapsychic self-talk in adult life. Knobloch and Knobloch (1979) posit that internal dialogue replicates the voices from parents and other key figures in a person's development. I would expand that idea to include both intrapsychic and interpersonal conflict-handling patterns. Children learn from their child-parent interactions, their interactions with their siblings, and from their parents' interactions with each other. Patients sometimes report, "I'm making myself do things I don't want to do just the way my father used to force me to ignore what I wanted and just pay attention to what he wanted," or, "I sound like my mother when she was mad at my father." Children who grow up in households where French is spoken learn to speak French. The languages of violence, avoidance, submissiveness, tension and problem-solving are similarly developed in the home environment.

Interestingly, when a family conflict pattern is fight-submit or fight-withdraw, with two complementary strategies, children seem to learn both sides. They may predominantly demonstrate the role of the parent with whom they most strongly identify. The conflict strategy that individuals utilize may also be affected by the person with whom they are interacting. With older and stronger family members, for instance, children may adopt a submissive or escape strategy, while they attack and dominate younger siblings.

The Martin family included Mom and Dad and four teenagers—a college-aged son, Jim, and three sisters, Lila, Monica, and Mandy. A near-fatal suicide attempt by Lila had prompted the family to seek therapeutic help. Suicide is a complex behavior that can involve elements of submissive giving up, of anger expression, and of escape from frustrating circumstances. All the Martin family members demonstrated a diversity of non-problem-solving responses to conflict. Jim, like his father, handled most conflict situations with attempts to dominate by verbally attacking opponents. He might start with simple insistence, could progress by raising his voice and adding subtle barbs or innuendos, and was generally willing to fight to the finish. The three daughters, by contrast, would briefly duel and then submit when challenged by their parents or brother. Submission was their mother's characteristic response in disagreements with her husband. When the daughters fought each other, however, no one sister consistently dominated, and none of them easily relented from their positions. Because virtually none of the family's conflict patterns involved cooperative problem–solving, tensions, frustrations, misunderstandings and arguments often drowned out the genuine caring they felt for one another.

In sum, individuals can be seen as psychologically healthy to the extent that they are able to express, hear and integrate their own and others' wishes, needs and concerns. Similarly, a couple or family system is functioning in a healthy manner to the extent that it is able to respond to the concerns of each of its members, as well as the needs of the couple or family as a group. By contrast, psychological dysfunction occurs to the extent that conflict resolution processes take into consideration only one or neither participants' concerns. These principles pertain to intrapsychic conflict, to conflicts between individuals, to conflicts within families, or within and between other groups.

CHAPTER 5

Depression:
The Submissive Route

DEPRESSION SEEMS TO OCCUR in conjunction with a dominant-submissive pattern of conflict resolution. The pattern may cause the depression; depression may cause a submissive posture; and/or the interaction may be reciprocal. Whatever the cause, the coincidence is striking. Furthermore, return of a determined, as opposed to submissive, spirit coincides with the lifting of depressed feelings and thoughts.

The *symptoms* of depression typically include loss of pleasure or interest in usual activities; feelings of worthlessness, self-reproach or guilt; diminished ability to think or concentrate; energy, appetite, sexuality and sleep changes (marked increases or decreases); tearfulness or crying; brooding about past events and pessimism about the future; and, in more extreme cases, thoughts of death or suicide. Depressions are subtyped with respect to the apparent triggering factor (reactive or endogenous), the length and intensity of the depression (dysphoria versus major depressive episode), the type of thinking (nonpsychotic or psychotic, and with mood-congruent or mood-incongruent features), and the life phase of the depressed individual (postpartum, involutional, etc).

Various researchers and clinicians have focused on different aspects of this diagnostic picture. Beck (1967) considers the sine qua non of depression to be cognitive negativity, i.e., the tendency of depressed individuals to see themselves, their future, and their world as if they were looking through dark glasses. Negative thoughts about self, others, and the future constitute Beck's "negative cognitive triad." Seligman (1975), looking at the behaviors of depressed individuals, has identified a pattern of cessation of attempts to

72

find solutions to problems, a state of resignation that he terms "learned helplessness." Bibring (1953), looking more at patients' experience of being-in-the-world, described an attitudinal state of pervasive "hopelessness and helplessness." Freud (1917) likened depression to the state of lowered energy and sadness that accompanies mourning and commented on the self-reproach characteristic in depressive functioning. He and Abraham (1948) emphasized the extent to which depressed individuals appear to be angry at themselves, with more severely depressed individuals typically tormented by guilt and self-hatred. Systemic therapists such as Madanes focus on the family interactions, noting the power disparities between depressed and nondepressed family members.

While depressive *symptoms* show a certain amount of consistency, the *content* of depressive problems varies widely. Although losses such as relationship endings, job terminations, decreases in physical functioning from accident or illness, or death of loved ones are common precipitants, many seemingly positive life events—the arrival of a baby, a job promotion, a move to a larger house, etc.—can also trigger depression. In these instances some aspect of the event is experienced as undesirable but inevitable, thereby triggering the dominant-submissive paradigm. The same outcome could occur without precipitating depression if the resolution process had been experienced as cooperative and concensual. A sense of loss is experienced in a conflict that is resolved in dominant-submissive fashion because conflicts resolved in this manner result in a winner and a loser. "Losers" experience a sensation of loss.

From a conflict-based perspective the sine qua non of depression is the dominant-submissive conflict resolution *process*. The remainder of this chapter explores the ingredients of dominant-submissive interactions. A selection of cases illustrates various aspects of the pattern as they appear in a variety of different kinds of depressions. The chapter concludes with a review of multiple depression theories that can be integrated under the umbrella conceptualization of depression as a concomitant of dominant-submissive resolution to dilemmas.

THE DOMINANT-SUBMISSIVE RESOLUTION PATTERN

A dominant-submissive pattern involves opposing wishes interacting in a pattern in which one side is insistent and the other gives up. The pattern is best regarded as interactive. Evidence of giving up induces one side to dominate; simultaneously, domination induces the other side to submit. For instance, although one would not expect a dominant-submissive relationship to occur with a tiny infant as the dominant figure and an adult mother as the submissive individual, in the first postpartum weeks a mother's physical vitality may be so minimal that the cry of an infant is enough to overwhelm her. Sleep loss is a powerful predictor of postpartum depression; lengthy labor and medical problems in the delivery can further increase probabilities of significant depression in the postpartum weeks (Heitler, 1975). A mother's lack of physical stamina may inadvertently thrust the tiny newborn into a dominating role.

When a conflict is intrapsychic, the content of the dominant side seems most often to be what people feel they *should* do or *have to* do—in psychoanalytic terminology, a superego message. Often this message involves what the individual believes, rightly or wrongly, that others want him/her to do. Such is not always the case however. Wishes and feelings can take a dominant role as well.

> Patrick became depressed over a conflict in which his passions were dominating his values. Cravings for continued intimate contact with a woman with whom he had shared a brief and intense extramarital relationship were dominating his traditional values about marital fidelity. He felt powerless to control his sexual urgings and depressed by his sense of having to follow his passions irrespective of the havoc they were causing in his life and the pain they were causing his wife.

When a problem is interpersonal, the conflict pits one person's values, beliefs, desires, and/or proposal for action against another's. The disagreement can be about any decision that needs to be made mutually between two people or that affects both of them.

> Patrick felt locked into his extramarital relationship. His wife Janice was able to forgive his initial episodes with the other woman, but felt that continuation of this involvement was totally unacceptable to her. Patricks's infidelity continued nonetheless. Janice felt overcome by helplessness and negativity about herself and her future.

When a conflict erupts between an individual and an external reality, the dominant side may be a difficult situation such as bankruptcy, physical illness, a job loss, or an impossible work assignment. These external realities often seem most intransigent. A successful conflict resolution process, however, can often reverse the emotional impact of such circumstances. Exploration in detail of various aspects of both the dominant and the submissive sides of the conflict can yield solutions that, as the saying goes, change lemons into lemonade.

> Danny failed his real estate broker's exam for the third time in succession. Initially he felt helpless and discouraged about this reality disappointment,

blow to his ego, and blockage to his career plan. Gradually he began to think through the situation by clarifying the concerns underlying his wishes to pass the exam and his failures to do so. As this exploration continued, Danny began to realize that although he wanted the earning potential of a broker, he found the subject matter difficult to master. Perhaps other career paths might offer a better match with his talents and job objectives. Instead of continuing to pursue a real estate broker's license, Danny applied for and obtained work in sales of high-end retail goods. Because he was personable and a natural salesperson, he discovered that this work suited him well, paid well, and offered him a more steadily secure salary than real estate sales in his city's depressed economy would have provided.

The above examples should help to clarify why the term "dominant" (suggested by the work of Arieti and Bemporad, 1978) is apt for describing the more powerful side in the depressive negotiation pattern. A dominant-submissive interaction connotes a pattern in which one side comes to the fore and the other gives up. Unlike terms such as "fight" or "contending," which connote the hostile aggression which sometimes, but by no means always, characterizes the behavior of the stronger side, "dominance" implies only a position of superior power or influence, a position which can be enacted passively or aggressively. The term "dominant" implies that the concerns of that side are heeded unilaterally in the solution to the conflict. Dominating can be accomplished via a wide range of styles, from a firm manner to aggressive attack.

Similarly, the term "submissive" is not meant to imply any particular tone or style of yielding or surrender, but simply that the concerns of that side do not become incorporated into the solution-building database. In depressogenic interactions, responsivity to the concerns of the submissive side is minimal, with those concerns relegated to second-class status. If the concerns on this side are of only minimal importance, they may be given up in a willingly compliant manner without engendering depressed feelings. When the issue is more critical, giving up may incur more sense of loss, suppressed anger, hopelessness, and helplessness. Still, the style and tone of submission can vary widely, engendering reactions varying from a brief sigh to prolonged despair. The consistent element is that the submissive individual or side engages in adversarial circumstances as what Fisher and Ury (1981) term a "soft bargainer." Soft bargainers are willing to yield on obtaining their interests in order to keep peace, prevent escalation, be liked, and/or maintain the relationship with the other.

The word "sides" is purposely vague, so that it can refer to opposing intrapsychic pushes and pulls (wishes, fears, values, etc.) or to the conflicting agendas of individuals, groups, or organizations. Whatever the sides, when a dispute is resolved in dominant-submissive fashion, one side wins and the other loses. Subjectively, the submissive side has felt powerless and has given up on attaining something desired. Thus, a dominant-submissive pattern implies that the interaction has been structured as a zero sum game in which one side wins the other side loses. The dominant side, at least in the eyes of the depressed individual, is the winner. The depressed yielding side may have succeeded in ending the fighting and keeping the relationship going, but on at least some crucial dimension has given up and lost.

CASES ILLUSTRATING DEPRESSOGENIC COMMUNICATION PATTERNS

The following cases illustrate several types of depression. In each case the road to cooperative resolution of a conflict has become blocked, giving way instead to a dominant-submissive pattern and a depressogenic outcome. Treatment of many of the cases discussed in this chapter and the remaining chapters of Section II is discussed in Section III, in Chapter 12 on reducing symptoms.

Reactive depression: Walking on tiptoes

Reactive depressions typically occur in response to a dominant-submissive settlement to a specific conflict. The couple in the following case generally handle disagreements with mutual sensitivity and bilateral agreements. In response to one specific problem, however, similarity of this problem to a dilemma in the wife's family of origin resulted in use of a dominant-submissive manner of settlement.

Clara, in her third year of marriage, was generally a happy and productive person, pleased with her marriage, with mothering a first child, and with a gratifying career.

SYMPTOMS

Clara sought help because of persistent feelings of self-reproach of several weeks duration. She was disturbed by her uncharacteristically hypercritical thoughts about herself and by the cloud of negativity that seemed to have descended over her life.

CONTENT

Clara was not consciously aware of any troubling conflicts or problems. In treatment, however, she began to realize that she had settled into a household routine that she resented. Each afternoon she tiptoed around the house, maintaining silence and keeping the baby hushed while her husband, who had been ill, took a daily nap. As she thought about this routine, Clara became aware that she felt angry about the tension of having to "be on tiptoes" instead of being able to act normally and spontaneously. The conflict was in part with husband, who needed frequent naps because of a health problem. At the same time, the conflict was intrapsychic. That is, Clara's high standards of quiet were essentially self-imposed, a response to her own "shoulds" rather than her husband's explicit requests.

PROCESS

With respect to her pattern of conflict resolution, Clara had assumed that she had no choice but to accommodate to her husband's need for restorative sleep. During his naps she felt that she had to keep herself and her young child as silent as possible, and therefore she would expend considerable energy in complying with what she thought were her husband's and the situation's inexorable demands. The compliance involved no discussion with her husband, simply submission to what she felt was a justifiable situation. She had never thought to question the mandate that she maintain quiet in the household.

Given that Clara and her husband were accustomed to talking over problems and finding mutual solutions, why had Clara never raised this problem for discussion? A cooperative decision necessitates that one person raise the issue. Since her husband was oblivious to the strain that his sleeping was triggering in her, Clara was the only one who might have been able to launch the topic. But Clara's husband was not the only one who was unaware of the strain; Clara herself had not realized the extent to which the tiptoeing bothered her. Her distress had never reached a level of conscious awareness. Rather than emerging as anger at her husband, her irritation simmered subconsciously and emerged only as self-criticism, the negativity which she eventually labeled as depression.

Exploration of the family-of-origin foundations of this conflict uncovered why the anger had never surfaced into Clara's awareness. Clara was reacting to her husband the way both Clara and her mother had handled Clara's father, i.e., by trying to ignore their irritations at him and do whatever was necessary to avoid provoking his angry and sometimes violent outbursts. Clara did not usually respond to her own quite mild-mannered husband in this way, but a point of similarity had allowed for slippage between past and present, for confusion (psychodynamic thinkers would call it transference) between father and husband. Both men took afternoon naps. From this point in common, Clara had mistakenly assumed, though unconsciously, that her husband, if awakened, would then roar like a threatening lion as her father used to. Anticipating the pattern from her early life experience, Clara dared not risk making noise. Futhermore, just as her mother seldom risked her father's bullying responses by trying to discuss issues of difference, Clara yielded to what she felt she had to do with never even a thought of raising the question.

Awareness of the conflict and its dominant-submissive resolution enabled Clara to seek alternative solutions. She talked about the problem with her husband and to her surprise discovered that it made no difference to him how much noise she and the baby made. His "dominance" in this instance had been quite inadvertent. Subsequently Clara experimented with going about her days without cautious quiet when her husband napped. To her relief, when noise did awaken her husband he would open his eyes looking slightly disoriented, mumble hello, and then immediately slip back into sleep.

Chronic depression: Only others' needs count

When depression is a frequent event in a person's life, instead of reflecting submission in a single conflict, yielding may be a pattern of response in many interactions. These interactions can be intrapsychic, e.g., a dominating conscience may frequently overpower a person's sense of what s/he wants to, as opposed to should, do. The interactions can be interpersonal, as when one spouse's preferences consistently dominate the other's. And often they are both.

Patty, a 28-year-old woman, had been married a year and eight months and was pregnant when she first sought psychotherapeutic help. An airline stewardess, she was a tall and stunningly attractive red-haired woman who conveyed an aura of quiet poise and grace.

SYMPTOMS

On her intake form Patty described her present problem by writing, "Can't cope with personal problems right now. Seeking long-term solutions." In her initial consultation session she appeared discouraged. She described herself as restless at home, yet slowed down in her ability to get things done.

Interpersonally Patty projected a child-like, eager-to-please quality, and described a pattern of over-giving. She described having given money to her husband to support his drug habit. She also gave him the travel bonuses she had earned from her airlines work, bonuses she would have preferred to use herself. She said, "I tend to jump in and take care of everything, even though he's a real jerk."

Patty's husband's history of affairs and steady cocaine use had discouraged her about their relationship, but she was even more upset by his frequent derogatory criticisms, especially about her body (e.g., "You don't have a nice tight little ass"). Patty was also concerned about her increasing pattern of withdrawal from friends, noticing that she isolated herself even at work. In addition, Patty was bothered by intermittent nightmares and by persistent negative thoughts about her appearance, her self-worth, and her future.

CONTENT

Patty's primary conflict centered on whether or not to leave her husband. In addition, a multitude of daily conflicts frustrated her. If her husband wanted money, she gave it to him and then felt cheated. Their sexual interactions left her feeling exploited. The outcome of every couple decision, from what to do on the weekends to what hours she should work at her job, left her feeling deflated.

PROCESS

Patty handled virtually all of her conflicts in a dominant-submissive pattern. In interpersonal conflicts Patty gave in to whatever others asked of her, regardlesss of her own preferences. She was sometimes angry at herself afterwards, but when someone said "give me," she seemed to know only "yes" as an answer. Moreover, taking did not seem to be in her vocabulary; expecting nothing from others, she asked for nothing for herself.

Patty's pattern of unending nurturance of unappreciative loved ones, an asymmetrical give-get pattern, necessitated ignoring her own needs in favor of continual response to her husband's preferences. In many instances ability to nurture others is a sign of high level functioning. When someone plays the role of nurturer it suggests that s/he has strengths enough to share with others. Yet Patty, the nurturing individual in this marital relationship, was the submissive one. When nurturing occurs to the detriment of self-care, the balance between self and other becomes warped. Others' wishes take on the quality of overwhelming demands. Patty was powerless to resist such demands; she gave nurturance like a slave commanded by a master.

The pathology of this pattern was exacerbated by Patty's husband's drug habit, as well as by his narcissistic mode of using people, of continually participating in taking relationships with others. No matter how much Patty gave, it was never enough for her husband.

Having become locked into a dominant-submissive relationship, Patty ceased to judge herself by her own or objective standards, deferring instead to her husband's critical views. For instance, he complained that her body parts, though objectively attractive enough that she could easily qualify for a fashion modeling carrer, did not conform precisely to the shapes he most liked. As Patty listened to her husband's evaluations instead of relying on her own, the dominant-submissive power imbalance was perpetually reinforced and she became more and more convinced of her worthlessness.

In response to internal conflicts, Patty consistently gave in to whatever she felt she "should" do. When she was asked to verbalize a dialogue between what she wanted and what she felt she should do, the should voices spoke out clearly but the wants remained silent. Patty's wants seemed to be situated in her blind spot, inaccessible to her awareness and hence to her ability to speak.

Patty's conflict resolution patterns were functional in the context of her family of origin. Patty grew up in a family in which there was survival value in assuming that only others' needs count. Her self-absorbed and chronically depressed father was highly volatile as well as morose. Though Patty often felt angry at him, she knew that showing attentiveness to him minimized his moodiness. Patty's mother experienced life as all drudgery and stress, modeling a "should-based" existence. She had abdicated her role in the spousal relationship when Patty was in her early teenage years, leaving Patty to take care of her father. Mother was probably chronically depressed, expressing her negative feelings as continuous criticism of the children; father, on the other hand, alternated between withdrawn states and violent outbursts toward Patty's brothers. Patty's subjective experience, perhaps objectively accurate as well, was that her family only kept going to the extent that she took care of everyone, to the detriment of her own needs.

Patty recalled feeling, as a child of about six, little and vulnerable and thinking, "What's going *on* here?" intuiting that the collapsed hierarchy was somehow not how things should be. Later, in response to sexual advances from her father (an extreme of non-consideration of a child's needs), Patty tried to open the family's problems to discussion. Her parents united against her, promptly putting Patty into a psychiatric facility. This event strongly reinforced Patty's long-held belief that terrible things would happen if she did not ignore her own feelings and respond instead only to what others seemed to want and need.

Patty's chronically nurturing role in her family of origin may in fact have had great survival value in so needy and dysfunctional a family system. Perpetuation of this self-denying role into adult life, however, put Patty into a state of depression, carrying on the family depressive tradition. As she began to stand up for what she wanted instead of yielding immediately to others' wishes, the depression ceased.

Grief plus depression: Victim of a unilateral decision

Slippage from grief to depression in response to the ending of a relationship is a common phenomenon. If a marriage or boyfriend-girlfriend relationship has been terminated mutually, both former partners go their our own ways, saddened and yet enriched by having shared the chapter that is ending. If, instead, one person unilaterally chooses to end the relationship, the dominant-submissive interaction is likely to cause the recipient of the decision to experience a much more painful and depressive grief reaction.

Rick was a 36-year-old single man, an artist who sought therapeutic assistance in the wake of the breakup of a relationship with a woman he had been dating for four and a half years. He described himself as "wanting help with all phases of my life."

SYMPTOMS

Rick cried frequently at home and copiously during the initial session. He spent much of his time in hopeless ruminations, slept poorly, was eating inadequately, and carried himself in a depressed, slow-moving slouch.

CONTENT

Rick wanted his girlfriend back. She would not return and seemed to have made an alliance with another man.

PROCESS

For years Rick had controlled the relationship with passive withholding. His girlfriend had wanted them to marry, but he had said, "No, let's wait and see." Now suddenly his girlfriend had seized control by ending the relationship and finding someone new. She was now in the dominant position, and he was the victim of her unilateral decision.

A loss can always trigger grief and mourning, but a relationship loss with a dominant-submissive ending can add depression. Mourning accounted for Rick's feelings of initital numbness, then sadness, anger, and loss. However, the presence of Beck's cognitive triad of negative thoughts about self, others, and the future suggested that depression as well as grieving was involved. Rick was accustomed to wielding power in the relationship; his loss of power was as depressogenic as the loss of the girlfriend.

Over time Rick realized that the loss of the relationship was for the best. He recalled his girlfriend's quick temper and frequent bouts of raging. Remembering this and other factors that for so many years had made him reluctant to marry her, he began to shift from feeling like he was submitting to a dreaded fate to feeling that he was actively choosing to find a better mate. With this cognitive move from surrender to active choice, the depression lifted.

Eventually, Rick took the initiative again in the relationship. He phoned his former girlfriend, said a gracious goodbye, and wished her good luck in her new relationship. As he took charge, Rick felt the last depressive clouds disappear. Within a year he met and married another woman.

Psychotic depressive episode:
Biochemically induced dominant-submissive interactions?

Endogenous depression seems to involve the same dominant-submissive pattern of conflict resolution as has been illustrated in the reactive depressions described above. It is never clear which comes — or leaves — first, the pattern or the depressive functioning, but again the two clearly coincide. The two emerge simultaneously, and as medications ease the physiological state of depression, patients typically begin to deal more actively with the problems that hitherto had been met with hopeless surrender.

Karen was a frail-looking woman in her mid thirties who suffered greatly from ever-present struggles with depression. While on medications, Karen was able to function with adequate energy at work. She was also able to maintain some social contacts, interacting with her family, her therapist, and people at work, as well as talking with fellow hikers on occasional trips with a mountain hiking club. During these relatively functional periods Karen still experienced chronic depression, but at manageable levels. However, these periods were punctuated by episodes of severe depression, often with psychotic features.

SYMPTOMS

One of these episodes began shortly after Karen decided to cease taking her antidepressant medications (at that point, a combination of lithium and imipramine). Within days Karen showed distinct increases in depressive symptomatology, with radical increases in her usual sense of worthlessness and self-hatred. There was a loss of reality-testing with respect to how others saw her and her views of herself became increasingly negative. She called herself a "worthless scum" and was unable to see the overreaction in her zealous self-criticisms. The self-hatred eventually consolidated into a fixed delusional system about her badness.

Although she continued to go regularly to work, at home Karen spent a good deal of time in agitated pacing accompanied by pounding her fist into her arm as if she were punching herself. She was preoccupied with thoughts of self-mutilation and suicide.

CONTENT

Karen wanted a better job, more extensive social contacts, the opportunity to build a family, and better housing. The content of Karen's concerns tended to be more or less the same whether Karen was mildly or psychotically depressed. What varied with the depression level was the intensity of distress and the severity of hopelessness.

PROCESSES

During her healthier periods of functioning Karen could be guided through a process of listening to her very real concerns and exploring possible solutions. For example, one partial resolution of the wish/fear for a more challenging work situation had been to do volunteer teaching in an elementary school. Similarly, her longing for and fear of more social contacts were eased as she began hiking with a mountaineering club and participating in a swimming class.

Once Karen was off her medications and submerged in depressive thinking, she no longer could listen to wishes or fears. Instead, her self-hating voice would aggressively dominate. In order to force her wishes and fears to silence, Karen would belittle her wishes and herself, e.g., "How can I talk about wanting better work when I am such a total failure. I'm just lazy and stupid; that's why I have this job I hate." The intense self-criticisms squelched any focus on what she wanted or feared or on steps she could take to improve her life.

The dominant-submissive pattern would also occur as a should/don't-want-to battle. Karen would embellish on what she (sometimes unrealistically) felt she *should* do until the "should" would loom large and terrifying. "I *have* to do that paperwork," she would insist, as though some terrifying fate depended upon it. Or, "I *have* to move to Pittsburgh and live with my mother," although in fact mother seemed to be reasonably well cared for by two of Karen's siblings. Or, "I *have* to kill myself so that I will not be a burden on others."

The depression may have been precipitated by the cessation of medications. Or Karen may have chosen to end her medication as a part of a depressive self-punitive pattern. Within a reciprocal paradigm, both can be assumed to be true. As Karen began decreasing her medications in order to reduce its sedative side effects, the depression increased. As her thinking became increasingly depressed, she felt increasingly self-destructive and lowered her medication intake further to punish herself, much as an anorectic decreases food intake as depression increases. As Karen became increasingly depressed, the "should" superego voices became increasingly tyrannical, making increasingly unrealistic demands, tolerating less and less dissenting information in the way of wishes and fears, and raining down virulent self-criticisms. The dominant-submissive pattern that was always there in mild form became a relationship like that of a vicious dictator to a rights-less peon.

Even in her periods of highest functioning, several patterns in Karen's conflict processing were striking. First, like other individuals who are particularly prone to depression, Karen had difficulty feeling that her wishes were ever legitimate. Helping her to hear herself was always a central therapeutic necessity. Linehan (1988) points out that validation is both difficult and the sine qua non of effective therapy with more distressed patients. As she suggests, such patients expect and create in the therapist a likelihood of oppositional rather than empathic listening responses. They inadvertently cue the therapist to respond with at least a mild version of the "yes, but" that they generate in their own inner dialogue. For instance, they take outrageous or extreme positions that predispose a therapist to respond by countering with the opposite opinion. The therapist needs to find some way to agree, to find the core of truth in everything a patient like Karen says. Validating responses help the patient to keep his/her conflicts intrapsychic, not interpersonalized into adversarial interactions with the therapist. And validation or empathic listening responses to patient statements enable the patient to begin to hear and take seriously his/her own feelings and wishes. Otherwise the first step in conflict resolution, the expression and hearing of wishes, never reaches completion.

Second, Karen's problem-solving attempts were typically characterized by all-or-nothing thinking. Karen reasoned that she needed to be married or she could have no relationships with men at all. Either she had to adopt a child or she could have no relationships with children, thus excluding more realistic options such as teaching and tutoring, foster care, Big Sister, or expanding her role as aunt with her nieces. Such all-or-nothing thinking and consequent win-lose solutions readily lead to submission, hopelessness and depression.

DOMINANT-SUBMISSIVE PATTERNS: AN INTEGRATIVE MODEL

A number of psychological theorists, each using slightly different terminology, have described various aspects of the dominant-submissive interactions characteristically associated with depression. Dominant-submissive conflict resolution provides an overarching model that can integrate these perspectives within one comprehensive conceptualization.

Psychoanalytic views

Freud (1917 [1915]) observed that negative views of the self are character-istic in depressive states, as opposed to grief states. "The disturbance of self-regard is absent in mourning, but otherwise the features are the same" (p. 244). Abraham's (1948) classic formulation of "aggression turned inward," that is, of the presence of angry feelings toward the self, captured a similar observation. Both of these theorists felt that understanding this self-critical stance was the key to understanding depression.

Freud proposed a process that can be seen as the opposite of paranoid projection. Paranoid individuals read their own attributes on others, seeing others as selfish when they themselves are acting selfishly and others as angry when they themselves are angry. Depressed individuals, on the other hand, take the negative affect they feel toward others and experience it as applying to themselves. If a depressed person is asked, "Toward whom do you feel most angry?" the answer will usually be, "Myself." If the person then is asked, "And if you were not angry at yourself, who would be another candidate?" it is likely that someone else has indeed evoked his/her ire, and by some form of dominant-submissive interaction.

Anger emerges, though it is not necessarily expressed, in dominant-submissive interactions because anger is a mobilizing response evoked, like frustration, when we want something that we are not getting. This aspect of the dominant-submissive process is important to note because helping patients to become aware of angry feelings can be a key to alleviating depression (see Chapter 12 on symptom reduction).

Arieti's dominant other

Why would someone be reluctant to express anger and instead refocus it on him/herself? As suggested above, anger tends to emerge spontaneously when a person is not getting what s/he wants. Like other feelings, anger tends to be expressed only if the angry person is not worried about the recipient's reaction. If the angry person is concerned either about hurting the other's feelings or about antagonizing the other and thereby causing damage to the security of their relationship, the sensation of anger may be suppressed. Strong feelings of needing a given relationship may make a person particularly reluctant to risk anger.

Silvano Arieti (1962) addressed this latter case at some length. He posited that a significant relationship that consists of a submissive attachment to a dominant other is a common concomitant of depression. The dominant other is most often the spouse, but might also be a parent, a romantic attachment, a sibling, or an adult child. Alternatively, the other can be a dominant goal, around which a person's life is focused, structured, and preoccupied. The relationship with a dominant other, as opposed to a more mature love attachment to a significant other, is characterized by emotional dependence and by the childlike assumption that the relationship is not only life-enhancing but essential to life. Arieti (1978) described this kind of attachment as follows:

> The relation between the patient and the dominant other is not just one of submission on the part of the patient and domination on the part of the other. With this attitude are feelings of affection, attachment, love, friendship, respect, and dependency, so that the relationship is a very complicated one. The dominant other is experienced by the patient not only as a person who demands a great deal, but also as a person who gives a great deal. And as a matter of fact, he either does give a great deal or is put by the patient into a giving role. The patient can no longer accept himself unless the dominant other accepts him, and he is unable to praise himself unless the dominant other praises him or is interpreted by the patient as praising him. (p. 140)

Arieti implied that a dominant-submissive relationship can be mutually gratifying for long periods of time and for both partners. What then triggers depression? Arieti posited that severe depression can be triggered by any precipitating event that causes the submissive partner to switch from seeing the dominance of his/her partner as benign and protective to seeing the domination as authoritarian or exploitative.

> The patient has denied many aspects of living because she wanted peace and approval at any cost. She has been excessively compliant, submissive and accommodating. By always doing what the husband wanted and by denying her wishes, she has not been true to herself. . . . The new evaluation of her husband—the kind of dominating person he really is—is not easily accepted . . . new patterns of interpersonal relationships are due, but she is not able to implement them; and this is her predicament. (pp. 144-145)

Death of the dominant other or failure to obtain a dominant goal are the other two precipitants posited by Arieti as potential triggers for severe depressive episodes. If we look at the depressive episodes described above, Arieti's hypotheses seem to fit some but not all. Patty did have a classic "dominant other" relationship with her spouse. Similarly, Karen became depressed in response to dominant goals. When obtaining a job commensurate with her abilities or having a marriage and children looked impossible, depression ensued. On the other hand, depression also occurred in relationships with equal power distribution (Clara) or with a dominant-submissive arrangement in which the depressed person was the dominant partner (Rick). While these examples might seem to contradict Arieti's theory, in fact, the key is to look at the interactions specific to the problem triggering the depression. A couple that is accustomed to either-or decision-making may generally operate with one partner in the dominant role, but on any given issue their positions may switch. In that specific instance the customarily submissive partner will fight for his/her position, and the other will be the one who feels powerless and gives in. Likewise, a member of a couple that generally functions with egalitarian decision-making can from time to time feel strongly enough on an issue to insist upon his/her way regardless of the other's concerns. In sum, it is the importance and resolution pattern of the *specific* problem, rather than of the relationship as a whole, that determines the likelihood of reactive depression from a given interaction.

Clara illustrates a variant of this situation. Although she generally shared power with her husband, she took a submissive role on a specific issue because of her own internal "shoulds." In that case the "should" had been established by parents who had typicallly interacted within a dominant-submissive framework. A dominant-submissive decision made in the prior generation operated tacitly, curtailing the patient's freedom to express her own concerns and hence evoking depression.

Perfectionism and depression

Baker, Cohen, Froman-Reichmann, and Weigert (1954) observed that a disproportionate percentage of their seriously depressed patients came from families that placed extremely high expectations for good behavior and performance success on their children. They theorized that:

> These attitudes on the part of the parents–chiefly the mother—inculcated in the child a strict and conventional concept of good behavior, and also one which was derived from an impersonal authority—"they." The concept seemed to carry with it the connotation of parents whose own standards were but feebly held and poorly conceptualized, but who would be very severe if the child offended "them." (p. 100)

If an individual has unrealistically high performance expectations, these expectations create ongoing tension between what the person feels s/he "should" be doing and what s/he is actually able to accomplish. To the extent that the individual feels that s/he must, nonetheless, attain these impossible standards, depression decends. The submission is to the belief

"You must do x or else you are a failure." Submission to the message of failure evolves the depression.

Karen routinely believed that every situation demanded a performance level above her abilities. On the WISC intelligence test, for instance, she would overproduce, giving exceptionally prolific responses. After such responses she typically felt depressed. She had given less than she had defined as necessary. Her expectations were unrealistic relative to the actual standards of the test but evoked a sense of failure nonetheless. Similarly, her performance at an office meeting had earned special commendation from her supervisor, but her personal assessment of her performance evoked a depressive reaction. Karen consistently felt unsuccessful because she unconsciously defined success as the level of performance just beyond what she was able to accomplish. Consequently, virtually every attempt to perform a task was followed by a depressive aftershock.

Seligman's concept of learned helplessness

Seligman's learned helplessness model (1975) focused on behavioral elements in the submissive process. He noticed the decrease in response initiation characteristic of depressed individuals; that is, depressed individuals believe that they are helpless and can do nothing to improve their lot. They therefore decrease their efforts or cease altogether to try to accomplish anything.

Seligman (1975) coined the term learned helplessness to describe a state of surrender to the assumption of powerlessness to improve a painful situation. His initial work demonstrated how learned helplessness develops among animal subjects in no-win situations. Seligman placed animals in a cage in which they were subjected to an uncomfortable electric shock. Most animals made efforts to escape. If escape were not a possibility, however, most animals at some point would simply lie down and give up. When escape was subsequently available, the animals who had developed learned helplessness would no longer attempt to exit. In order to get them to leave the cage that caused pain, the experimenter would have to physically walk them through the escape solution. Even then, some dogs would need repeated walk-throughs of the new escape route before they would again try on their own to leave the situation they had learned to define as hopeless.

(Note that in the chapters on treatment, use of the term "walking through," describing the resolution of specific distressing conflicts under a therapist's guidance, is derived from this phenomenon in Seligman's research. Although this component of treatment is similar to what analytic therapists call "working through" conflicts, I prefer the connotations from Seligman's work.)

Once a state of learned helplessness had been attained, the animals ceased to make efforts to improve their situation. In behavioral terms this phenomenon is called lowered voluntary response initiation. The animals gave up, seeming to submit to what they saw as their fate, and becoming blind to even relatively simple solutions to their problems.

Hiroto's experiments (1974) with college students extended Seligman's animal experiments, further clarifying how habits of submission and chronic susceptibility to depression can be learned:

> College student volunteers were assigned to one of three groups. In the controllable noise group, subjects received loud noise that they could terminate by pushing a button four times. Subjects assigned to the uncontrollable noise group received noise that terminated independently of subjects' responding. Finally, a third group received no noise. In the second phase of the experiment all groups were tested on a hand shuttle box. In the shuttlebox, noise termination was controllable for all subjects; to turn off the noise, subjects merely had to move a lever from one side of the box to the other. The results of the test phase were strikingly similar to those obtained with animals. The group receiving prior controllable noise as well as the group receiving no noise readily learned to shuttle, but the typical subject in the group receiving prior uncontrollable noise failed to escape and listened passively to the noise. (p. 259-260)

The more an individual has been exposed to no-win situations, the more readily he assumes that other situations cannot be changed for the better. As a consequence, such individuals put out less effort to try to control new conflictual situations.

Beck's cognitive triad and cognitive blockade

Beck (1967) has clarified cognitive concomitants of learned helplessness. Writing on depressive cognitive functioning, Beck posited:

> The content of depressive cognitions is predominantly negative in tone and self-referential in direction; the individual is preoccupied with self-derogatory and self-blaming thoughts. Moreover, the depressed patient projects into the future his or her notions of real or imagined loss. He or she becomes pessimistic and hopeless and believes that the current discomfort is unending and unalterable. (Kovacs & Beck, 1986, p. 244)

Beck coined the phrase *negative cognitive triad* to refer to this set of negative views depressed people hold toward themselves, the world, and the future. Unlike mood, which a clinician may intuitively sense but mainly must assess by relying on the patient's subjective description, cognitive set can be quickly and objectively assessed in the course of clinical interviewing by noting the number and intentsity of negative views expressed. This measure can be especially useful for a clinician who is looking to monitor depression levels as they fluctuate in a given session, to assess a patient who minimizes or denies depressed feelings, or to assess the severity of a depression in a new patient. The manner in which patients express their negative thoughts can also be a diagnostic clue. Less severely depressed individuals are likely to express their negative thoughts as "it seems like" or "I'm afraid that . . ." More severely depressed individuals read their negative thoughts as absolute realities, e.g., "My future *is* hopeless." "I am scum."

A number of cognitive theorists have delineated cognitive processes that accompany depression and maintain the negative triad. These processes, which Beck (1985) calls a "cognitive blockade," feed submissive responses in conflict situations. To the extent that they are relatively enduring patterns of perception and thought, these processes may make a person depression-prone; once a depression occurs these habits of mind may perpetuate the depression. Such habits include:

- Selective recall of material with negative content at the expense of neutral or positively toned material (Lloyd & Lishman, 1975; Lishman, 1972, Nelson & Craighead, 1977).
- Assignment of global and personalized meanings to events (Kovacs & Beck, 1986).
- Selective attention to negative data in the environment and ignoring of salient positive cues (Kovacs and Beck, 1986).
- Drawing of arbitrary negative conclusions in the absence of, or contrary to, other evidence (referred to as arbitrary inference) (Beck, 1976).
- Excessive use of "should," "must," and "have to." Kovacs & Beck (1986) write,

   > Compared with the "shoulds" of nonsymptomatic people, the depressed patient's directives are generally unreasonable, rigid, and unyielding. . . . This finding parallels the psychoanalytic observation that depression-prone individuals have loftier ego-ideals (expectancies for their own performance) and more pervasive, restrictive, and critical superego responses. (p.247)

- Regarding oneself and situations as "either-or." As soon as depressed individuals notice that a behavior or event is dissonant with a positive image of themselves, they switch to a wholly negative self-view. The part becomes the whole. They view themselves as either excellent students or failures; lovable or unlovable; attractive or unattractive, etc.

With respect to the process of conflict resolution, this so-called cognitive blockade prevents people from attempting to find solutions that would incorporate their concerns along with concerns of conscience or others' concerns. Excessive "shoulds" put a person in continual conflict, as immoderate demands from conscience (superego) inevitably come into conflict with what a person wants or feels. And the "either-or" mode of thinking is a framework within which small signs of not winning convince a person that s/he is losing. Any and all of these cognitive attributes make a person more vulnerable to depression.

Systems perspectives

The theme of power distribution in family systems has been developed most persuasively by Madanes (1981), who views symptoms as metaphors. "For example," she writes, "a wife who vomits compulsively may be expressing disgust with her husband" (p. 32). The loss of energy and sense of hopelessness and helplessness of depression can be a metaphor for the very real power relationship between the depressed person and someone or something in that person's life.

A family therapist, Madanes looks first to the spousal relationship for a power imbalance. She points out that the power imbalance is two-sided, symmetrical in a sense, in a couple with a depressed partner. That is, the depressed individual feels subordinate and submissive with respect to a specific conflict with the spouse; on the other hand, the spouse is powerless against the patient's depression. Madanes's conclusion is that the depression can be resolved when the hierarchical relationship in the marriage is changed to a shared power distribution.

Hierarchy can be maintained comfortably between spouses (and is essential between parents and children) under certain conditions. The spouse or children on the lower rungs of the hierarchy must not feel that decisions made from above are unilateral. For instance, if a dominant spouse listens and takes into account the more dependent spouse's concerns, the dependent spouse is likely to feel nurtured rather than neglected, exploited or powerless. In contrast, hierarchical interactions which are unresponsive to the subdominant individual's concerns are likely to produce depression. Similarly, as the case of Clara illustrated, a couple that generally shares decision-making may resolve a single but important issue in a powerful/powerless mode. This one instance can engender depression in the submissive spouse, regardless of a generally egalitarian atmosphere.

Feldman (1976) looks at the interactive patterns between spouses that reinforce depression. Feldman's pattern, based on an assumption of reciprocal causation, describes the dominant partner as oversolicitous and yet innocently undermining. The other, who is the depressed partner, frequently acts helpless and self-deprecating. This depressed functioning in turn makes the nondepressed partner all the more oversolicitous. At the same time, the nondepressed partner subconsciously is becoming annoyed at always having to take the giving role. The asymmetry of give and take makes for irritation, which periodically emerges, generally as "helpful" criticism, which is given in relative innocence but with an undermining impact.

Although Feldman describes this pattern as an interpersonal pattern, a similar pattern seems to occur intrapsychically. The parent or superego voices of a depressed person will sometimes sound harshly critical and sometimes voice pity and concern; but the pity and concern tend inevitably to be followed by more criticism, so the potential nurturing is ignored while the person waits for the other shoe to fall.

In sum, viewing depression as a symptom or by-product of dominant-submissive conflict negotiation clarifies a common element in the multiple forms of depression. It unifies psychoanalytic, cognitive behavioral, and family systems perspectives on depressive phenomena. And, as Chapter 12 will illustrate, this conceptualization indicates quite helpfully what steps a therapist can take with depressed individuals to ease them from their stance of surrender into constructive problem-solving and alleviation of the depression.

CHAPTER 6

Anxiety:
The Immobilization Route

THE PATTERN OF CONFLICT PROCESSING associated with extended anxiety is *immobilization*. Anxiety is an unpleasant emotion that alerts a person to impending threat. When anxiety lingers, it indicates a stalemated conflict, a standoff between at least two competing elements. One of these elements is likely to be (but is not necessarily) a feared situation, and the other an impulse to go ahead and do something. If a person perceives that movement in any direction will lead to a negative outcome, no movement may become the strategy of choice. With this immobilization comes perpetuation of anxiety. The anxiety may occur in brief, persistent, or episodic form, depending on the extent to which the conflict situation is brought to or held in awareness.

OVERVIEW

While depression tends to occur after the fact ("I've lost it") but can be anticipatory ("There's no way I will be able to get what I want"), anxiety is generally forward-looking. Anxiety alerts people to a conflict between something or someone perceived as likely to attack and the desire to remain physically and emotionally intact. Anxiety arises in response to awareness of a potential danger—to a threat to physical or emotional well-being, to bodily integrity, to self-esteem, or to key attachments.

Ideally, anxiety serves like a blinking yellow light. It is a cautionary signal that warns, "Slow down and check out a potential danger." After evaluation of the problem, people are expected to proceed. The evaluation

93

can lead to attack against the object of danger, to escape, to yielding or giving up, or to problem-solving. Any of these modes of dealing with the conflict may dissipate the anxiety.

If, however, a person regards anxiety as a red stoplight instead of a cautionary look-and-decide indicator, the initial halt becomes ongoing inaction. Without any movement—attack, escape, yielding or problem-solving—the sense of danger remains, evoking continued anxiety. Immobilization perpetuates anxiety. To the extent that a person feels that the options for responding to a conflict are "damned if you do, damned if you don't" choices, inaction and anxiety may be especially likely to continue (Wolfe, 1989).

Recurring anxiety needs to be understood in terms of both the fears and the concerns that keep someone in the feared situation. For instance, people often feel anxious in response to potential censure from others, such as prior to a job evaluation or a stage performance. The fear of impending criticism battles against the necessity to perform or the wish to receive applause. If there were no such conflict, the anxiety aroused by performing could easily be resolved by avoiding performance situations. Similarly, not only other external threats but also internal thoughts and impulses—for example, sexual or angry feelings—can evoke anxiety if countered by a conflicting thought or concern.

Anxiety is an unpleasant feeling. People generally try to avoid it, although mastery of low doses of anxiety seems to be part of the thrill of scary movies and frightening "amusement" park rides. Most often anxiety impels people to *do* something. Anxiety is a shaping force in that it impels a person to mobilize, to move in order to eliminate the uncomfortable anxious feeling, hopefully by solving the problem. As will be illustrated in the subsequent case examples, anxiety remains to the extent that a person has become immobilized, frozen in stalemated ambivalence.

Varieties of anxiety:
Worrying, fear, panic, phobia, and nonfearful panic

Worrying works like the spinning wheels of a stuck car. It is a cognitive activity in which awareness of problems is sustained without accompanying problem-solving. Whereas problem-solving entails gathering information, exploring concerns, and moving forward to conclusions, a person who is worrying repetitively reiterates fears without moving forward into action. When a person looks ahead and anticipates problems, the "what ifs?" that emerge may be experienced as genuine questions or as end-statements. Addressing "what ifs" as real questions and seeking genuine answers constitutes foresight and planning. When "what ifs" are treated as end-statements instead of initial questions, the mental activity constitutes worrying rather than problem-solving.

Individuals who persist with worrying habits generally believe "If I am thinking about it, it won't happen." This magical thinking assumption perpetuates worrying. The replacement of effective information-gathering, thought, and action with ruminative immobilization makes anxiety persist. Worriers need to learn that future events can best be influenced by gathering information, taking whatever action they can to solve the problem, and then putting aside thoughts of the problem until new data emerge.

Fear and anxiety are emotions which can be somewhat difficult to differentiate from one another. Distinctions between the two may be more semantic than real. Certainly the two terms are used with varying connotations in the clinical literature. One common distinction is that fear refers to an arousal response to specific threatening elements, whereas anxiety may or may not have a specific object. One might, for instance, feel general anxiety about health problems, but a fear of a specific surgery. In fact, however, most people are attributional beings. They attribute some cause or another to their feelings. Hence people rarely experience anxiety without assigning some object to their apprehension.

Beck, who has focused on the cognitive aspects of anxiety, uses the term *anxiety* to refer to the emotional state of physiological arousal, and the term *fear* to stress the cognitive appraisal of danger (Beck & Emery, 1985). Thus, feelings of foreboding would be called anxiety, and the specific images or thoughts that arouse these feelings would be the fears.

In common parlance anxiety connotes lower intensity autonomic arousal and fear connotes a more intense reaction. In clinical usage high intensity anxiety is referred to as panic. Another important clinical distinction is between fear and phobia. A phobia is a fear that impels a person to avoid feared situations, constricting life activity.

The intensely anxious person who is experiencing panic has physical sensations similar to the asthmatic's feeling of being unable to get enough breath and to the heart ailment sensation of choking. Many patients who present to emergency rooms fearing shortness of breath and heart attacks are in fact suffering from attacks of anxiety (Beitman, Basha, Flaker, DeRossear, Mukerji, & Lamberti, 1987). Moreover, sometimes in these instances the somatic sensations of autonomic arousal occur without the cognitive label of anxiety, a syndrome termed nonfearful panic (Beitman, et al, 1987).

Why would someone react with immobilization?

The term "dynamics of inaction" is used by Gilbert (1988) to explain why people who experience anxiety about the threat of nuclear war do not necessarily become anti-nuclear activists. Gilbert summarizes research that suggests that activists are characterized by a high level of awareness of the nuclear threat, a sense that political action will be effective, and a perception of social support for their actions from family, friends, and important role models. By contrast, he hypothesizes, people who do not take action are characterized by a low level of awareness of the problem, a sense of inefficacy, and a perception of nonsupport for action from significant others.

Summarizing the research of Kiesler (1971) on reasons why individuals may not act in a manner consistent with their attitudes, Gilbert goes on to say that action is less likely if it may have restrictive implications for the future. For example, if action forces people to defend themselves to others, produces negative views in others, or causes a sacrifice in time, money, or other scarce resources, action is less likely to occur. A high degree of certainty regarding the correctness and consequences of their actions is required for most people to justify performing them.

It is possible to generalize from these anti-nuclear studies of these dynamics of inaction. First, individuals are likely to become immobilized in response to a problem to the extent that a feared situation feels uncomfortable but not immediately threatening. Second, they may be more prone to do nothing about a problem to the extent that they believe that their action will be ineffective. This supposition suggests that people who generally lack confidence in their abilities to handle life's challenges may be more inaction- and anxiety-prone. Third, when individuals expect self-criticism or criticism from others if they take action, immobilization and perpetuation of anxiety are likely. Criticism is the antithesis of social support for action.

Passivity in response to problems may also be a learned response. Like language and grammar, the tendency to take action or to remain immobilized may to some extent be learned in the family of origin and in the culture. Americans, for instance, are in general highly action-oriented, with an if-there's-a-problem-let's-fix-it attitude toward life. Many other cultures are less action-oriented.

I was once stranded with my husband and a Pakistani family in isolated mountains near the border of Afghanistan. When our car ceased to move, our Pakistani host put in a long-distance telephone call from the nearest telephone to a far-off city for help. He then settled us into the car so we would be comfortable while we waited. Our friend's calm faith that external forces would eventually extricate us was impressive. His mellow and philosophic response was reassuring to me and to my husband, but we nonetheless felt quietly anxious in this unfamiliar wait-and-see position. As time went on with no evidence of change, my husband responded in typical

American can-do fashion. He climbed out of the car, lifted the hood, looked over the engine, and began shaking wires and moving parts. Eventually something he did caused the engine to start humming and, to all of our delight, we were off again on our journey.

Cultural differences accounted for the two men's different responses to the dilemma. In any culture, the key to a non–anxious life orientation seems to be to take whatever action appears possible on a given problem and then to have faith that things will work out. I'm certain that our Pakistani friend was correct in assuming that help would eventually come our way; and our American do-something mentality also took care of the problem. Because of the different cultural perspectives, their relative passivity did not yield anxiety for our Pakistani friends because, from a Pakistani point of view, all that could be done had been done with a phone call. Anxiety emerges either from non-action, or from having taken action but then being unable to let go of the matter with trust that somehow the problem will be resolved for the best.

Predisposition to anxiety

Since many anxiety reactions come from competing fears and wishes, a person who has many fears or who reacts with relatively strong fear to common situations is likely to experience anxiety states. What might predispose a person to fears?

Clearly, physiological responsiveness varies from person to person. Some horses are "high-strung"; they respond anxiously to minor stimuli like a fluttering leaf or an unexpected sound. People, from their first days of life, have similar in-born differences in reactivity. Some children are born "shy" (Kagan, Reznick & Snidman, 1988). The tendency to experience panic attacks seems to run in families, which may in part reflect a genetic predisposition to excessive spurts of the biochemicals involved in anxiety.

Trauma can increase sensitivity. Individuals who have experienced a frightening situation will tend to be "high-strung" for a subsequent period of time. Ordinary situations may arouse symptoms of post-traumatic stress syndrome—irritability, concentration difficulties, disturbed sleep, exaggerated startle response, and physiological reactivity. In addition, anxiety is particularly likely to emerge in situations that bear some resemblance to the trauma. Individuals who have been in a plane crash, for instance, are likely to experience intense anxiety in subsequent flights, and all the more so if sudden noises or unexpected movements of the plane occur.

The quality of parent-child attachments in early life and the development of what Erikson (1950) referred to as basic trust seem to be other significant factors in determining an adult tendency to immobilizing anxious reactions. Bowlby (1973) conceptualized the fundamental relationship of a person to his caregivers as attachment. Harlow (1961) detailed the components of attachment with his famous monkeys and terrycloth surrogate mother monkeys. Whatever the language used to describe the nature of the bond between parent and infant, certain ingredients in this relationship can predispose an individual to feel more or less secure in the world, and hence prone to calm or to anxiety. Guidano and Liotti (1983) detail the parent-child interactions characteristic of individuals who later develop agoraphobia as follows:

1. Continuous warning from hyperprotective parents on the dangers of the outside world and therefore on the difficulties in dealing with it.

2. Insistence on the child's presumed physical and/or emotional weakness, which makes him or her particularly exposed to the world's dangers.

3. Modeling on the agoraphobic parent who, fearing loneliness, keeps the child with him or her.

4. Threats of desertion or family scenes that make the child insecure outside of the home. (cf. Bowlby, 1973, Chapter 19) (p. 107)

Beck describes a similar phenomenon, the anxious individual's sense of vulnerability, defining vulnerability as "a person's perception of himself as subject to internal or external dangers over which his control is lacking or is insufficient to afford him a sense of safety" (Beck & Emery, 1985, p. 67).

   Adam, an entrepreneur in his mid thirties, sought treatment for panic attacks, fear of flying that prevented him from traveling long distances, fear of doctors and dentists that kept him from obtaining necessary medical treatments, and agoraphobic fears of being home alone. Adam's mother had been a worrier. His father had seemed fearless, almost daredevil-like. In their different ways both parents had conveyed vulnerability to their son. From his mother Adam inherited a general sense that the world is a dangerous place and that anticipating troubles could magically prevent them from occurring. From his father he learned to brush away feelings of anxiety by charging into fear-evoking situations.
   As a teenager Adam had imitated his father's counter-phobic style. To his parents' distress he spent his time with a street gang. He acted tough, admired gangsters, and hung out in pool halls. As he approached a middle-class middle-age, most of his counter-phobic strategies for feeling safe were no longer options. Car racing was the only counter-phobic activity he still pursued. Moreover, his father's death from a heart attack a year prior seemed to decrease his faith in his father's way of keeping physical harm at bay. The strategies he then relied upon to maintain a sense of personal saftey in what

he continued to read as a frightening world were his mother's anxious worrying and multiple life-constricting phobias.

In addition to family interactions, any experiences with rejecting, critical, or otherwise hurtful others can induce increased tendencies to anxiety. For instance, children's peer relationships can spawn adult expectations and beliefs about the self and the world.

> Josie, a very attractive college freshman, was terrified of meeting people. When she was in junior high school, Josie and her family had moved from their farm to a city. At the new school Josie never felt accepted by the other children, some of whom teased her for being a country farm girl. Josie had concluded from these painful peer experiences that she was only minimally attractive and that others would not want to include her in their friendship circles. With these beliefs, she entered into any situation that involved meeting new people with understandable trepidation.

People generally expect the future to repeat the past. Psychodynamic theory posits that on the basis of these expectations people continue to act as if the present were the past. As discussed in Chapter 4, by acting in their old ways, people actually increase the likelihood that others will reciprocate by acting much like people in their past (Wachtel, 1977). That is, transference behaviors actually cause the present to repeat the past.

> Josie believed that she was unattractive to people. As a young child in a new school she expected them to reject her, and therefore turned away and clammed up as she was introduced. Potential new friends, reading her behavior as rejection, then responded in kind. These rejections confirmed and reinforced her worst fears. The traumas of her past kept repeating themselves in her present.

Assessment issues

Beck and Emery (1985) suggest useful criteria for determining when anxiety is clinically significant, as opposed to just a part of the ordinary and expectable flow of emotions. They define anxiety as a clinical syndrome to the extent that (1) the degree of anxiety exceeds the danger objectively evident in the situation, and/or (2) the anxiety interferes with ability to function.

Anxiety that is uncomfortable enough to lead people to seek therapy can be either chronic or episodic. Frequently it is both, that is, a pattern of ongoing low-level anxiety punctuated by specific episodes of intense panic. Thus the variables to be included in assessing patients' anxiety symptoms include both the pattern of occurrence (ongoing, episodic, or both) and the emotional intensity (from low-level anxiety to panic).

When panic attacks are triggered by specific predictable situations and a pattern of avoidance of these situations develops, the syndrome is considered a *phobic reaction*.

Many people experience panic attacks without developing a phobic or avoidance reaction. When phobic or avoidant reactions do develop, the diagnostic label usually includes the triggering event. *Social phobias*, for instance, are fears that a panic attack will be induced by situations of public scrutiny, such as meeting new people or speaking in groups.

The specific triggering event included in the diagnostic label represents the stimulus situation but not necessarily the actual fear. *School phobia*, for instance, is a misnomer. Children with so-called school phobia resist going to school, but not generally because they are frightened of school per se. Rather, the anxiety is usually aroused by patterns of interaction in the family that make leaving home appear threatening. For instance, a parent suffering from chronic anxiety may consciously or unconsciously retain the child home to be a companion. Alternatively, the child may fear that something may happen to the parent(s) when s/he is away and may remain at home to prevent that from happening (Bowlby, 1975). Although the problematic behavior is that the child does not attend school, actually the child is caught in a conflict between a desire (and necessity) to attend school and a fear that problems may occur at home if s/he does.

Conflict-based assessment of anxiety begins with clarification of the pattern of symptoms, specifying the triggering stimulus and the frequency, duration and intensity of the anxiety. The elements of the underlying conflict then need to be delineated. The more precise the details obtained regarding these conflicting fears, wishes, values, needs, longings, etc., the more effectively they can be brought to satisfactory resolution.

CASE ILLUSTRATIONS

The following cases are presented more fully to illustrate the presenting picture—symptoms, content of conflicts, and patterns of conflict management—that can accompany various types of anxiety states. Although the symptoms and the conflicts vary, all of the cases demonstrate the same response to underlying conflicts, namely, immobilization. Treatment of most of these cases is discussed in Chapter 12.

Generalized anxiety: Worried sick

Individuals who experience so-called generalized anxiety typically feel the sensations of anxiety most of the time, but have only one or several specific conflicts that are generating the anxiety. This specificity of the stimulus conflict is in contrast to individuals who worry chronically as a personality style. Also, whereas generalized anxiety connotes an ever-present anxious *feeling*, worriers engage in ever-present anxious *thinking*. In both cases, however, awareness of problems does not lead to explicit thinking, problem-solving, or action.

Marlene, a married woman in her 40s and the mother of Josie (described above in this chapter) came from an extended family in which there had been multiple cases of cancer, including her mother and two sisters.

SYMPTOMS

For the prior several months before seeking psychotherapeutic consultation, Marlene felt always anxious. Although sometimes more and sometimes less intense, the feeling never went away.

CONTENT

With questioning, Marlene expressed that her central concern was a fear that she had cancer. Neither negative findings on laboratory tests nor her doctor's reassurances seemed to diminish the persistent anxious feelings. She feared that her doctor was wrong, but she also feared antagonizing him by seeking out a second medical opinion.

Marlene reported that she had always tended toward worrying and fears. As a child she had felt particularly awkward at school. This anxiety in social situations had persisted into adulthood and been passed on into the next generation in her daughter, Josie. Marlene's fears that people would not like her were less pressing at this point than her anxiety about her health, but impinged on her ability to obtain medical help. Her fears that her doctor would not like her if she sought a second opinion were holding her at a standstill.

PROCESS

While Marlene was always subliminally aware of what was making her anxious, the worrisome problem tended to hover in the background. Without emerging into the foreground of her thinking, the fear was not converted into constructive problem-solving. The resulting immobilization perpetuated her anxiety, and vice versa. She was unable to make any movement toward information-gathering or action.

Social phobia: Frozen in fear

Many individuals seek therapy to overcome their immobilization in specific situations such as flying in airplanes, going to school, test-taking, or performing in public. To understand these phobias it is important to clarify what specifically about these inherently somewhat anxiety-producing situations evokes the patient's fear.

Josie, introduced earlier in this chapter and the daughter of Marlene, described above, was a very pretty college freshman who sought psychotherapeutic help because of a social phobia. Her manifest fear of social situations had emerged in response to multiple, barely conscious, latent concerns.

SYMPTOMS

Josie was withdrawing from social interactions because every time she met new friends on campus she experienced immobilizing anxiety which she described as feeling "frozen." In high school Josie had tended to be shy about initiating interactions with peers other than her close friends. In college her discomfort with making new friends reached panic proportions. Her intense blushing, loss of the ability to speak, and submergence into a disorienting cloud of anxiety embarrassed her in front of her dormitory friends and inhibited her from expanding her friendship network beyond her roommates.

CONTENT

Caught in a classic approach-avoidance conflict, Josie eagerly wanted to meet the very people who triggered her intense fears. She wanted to meet the most popular of her fellow students. Yet she was afraid that these intelligent and good-looking young men and women would find her dumb and unattractive. She feared they would reject her, not wanting to pursue a friendship with her.

PROCESS

When Josie became anxious she felt both muscularly and cognitively immobilized, a sensation she described as "freezing." The muscles in her head and neck became tense and stiff. If she forced herself to try to talk in response to direct questions, her voice came out abrasively loud or inaudibly soft. She was unable to hear what others were saying ("like going deaf"), to see clearly ("Everything goes cloudy; I can't look at them, can't focus"), or to think ("I blank out"). She was aware of what she wanted, aware of what she feared, and unable to take action.

Josie's preconscious thoughts in social situations revealed patterns of thinking that clearly exacerbated her fears, which in turn exacerbated her immobilization. She manifested the four cognitive patterns characteristic of anxious patients (Beck & Emery, 1985).

1. *Minimization*: Underestimation of the positive aspects of one's personal resources. Josie underestimated her attractiveness, her intelligence, and her natural personal charm.
2. *Selective abstraction*: Focusing primarily on weaknesses. Jackie focused on her moments of mental blocking, rather than her overall intelligence, and concluded that she was "dumb."
3. *Magnification*: Viewing each small flaw as as gaping hole. Every out-of-place hair or wrinkle in her shirt seemed to Josie to make her total appearance sloppy and unacceptable.
4. *Catastrophizing*: Seeing a minor problem as a major catastrophe. Blushing, which can be a minor handicap when meeting new people, loomed for Josie as a total block, a grossly unacceptable phenomenon.

Self-concept distortions tend to flourish in response to these cognitive patterns. Josie's self-concept was markedly discrepant with objective realities. She saw herself as plain when to others she was strikingly attractive. She saw herself as having little personality and nothing to say though she appeared quietly charming, interesting, and highly intelligent.

Panic attacks: The restaurant syndrome

Panic attacks are discrete episodes involving a sudden surge of the biochemicals associated with fear. A relatively common phenomenon, a spike in autonomic arousal can be triggered by performance situations, realistic dangers, and a multitude of threatening everyday situations. Often the panicked individual is not aware of any specific precipitant. In these instances a smell, sight, sound, feeling, or thought in the present situation has evoked an association to a prior anxiety-inducing experience. When the threshold for resistance is lowered, such as by fatigue or hunger, vulnerability to panic attacks may increase. Some people refer to panic attacks as "the restaurant syndrome" because the lowered blood sugar of a hungry person waiting for a meal seems to increase vulnerability and likelihood of panic experiences. The following example illustrates biologic vulnerability interfacing with a visual association to trigger a panic episode.

Wanda was an unmarried woman in her late twenties who was referred by a hospital emergency room for consultation after a first panic attack.

SYMPTOMS

While waiting for her lunch in a restaurant, Wanda had experienced a sudden panic attack with shortness of breath, rapid heartbeat, sweaty palms and light-headedness.

CONTENT

Thinking back on the episode Wanda recalled, first, that she had not eaten breakfast and felt fragile from hunger. Second, revisualizing the incident she noted that a bright swatch of red in a painting on the wall had flashed an association with the bright red dress her mother had worn during their most recent, and highly provocative, conversation. The color association brought to mind the conflicting feelings she had experienced toward her mother the prior evening. She had raged internally at her mother's insensitive comments and had been aware of an impulse to shout and strike out at her. Fearing that this rage might explode and ruin their tenuous relationship, which she still wanted to maintain, she had quickly changed the topic.

PROCESS

Wanda's mother had long evoked enormous anger in her daughter. Wanda resented her intrusive and commandeering manner. Fearing her mother's reactions, however, she had never confronted her. The urge to express her anger was inhibited by a fear of her mother's potential retaliation, as well as by Wanda's fear that she would explode hurtfully but accomplish nothing. The result was a perpetual standoff. When the red color association brought the conflict to mind, anxiety of panic proportions arose.

Agoraphobia: Double trouble

Agoraphobia is a fear of being in places or situations from which escape might be difficult (or embarrassing) or in which help might not be available in the event of a panic attack. Although the term is sometimes used to refer to a fear of open spaces, common agoraphobic patterns include concerns about being outside the home alone, being at home alone, being in a crowd, standing in a line, or traveling. Agoraphobic avoidance is generally a secondary consequence of an unexpected panic attack (Barlow, 1988; Klein, 1981). Panic is viewed as so potentially catastrophic that the patient subsequently avoids situations that are possible locations for another similar episode.

    Foa (1989) has researched this critical aspect in the development of agoraphobic syndromes. Whereas individuals with simple phobias are afraid only of the manifest specified situation and the dilemma that this situation may symbolize, agoraphobic individuals also fear fear. They fear having panic attacks. Even the thought of a quickened heartbeat or other sign of anxious feelings yields the autonomic arousal we associate with anxiety responses.

Panic attacks are inherently uncomfortable, but they are not overwhelmingly painful and hence need not be all that distressing in and of themselves. The fear of panic attacks may be a response to concern that the panic attack may result in something worse. Male agoraphobic patients generally believe the outcome will be a heart attack; female patients usually fear "going crazy" or "losing control." Panic attacks also may raise a social fear, that is, a fear that others will regard the patient critically in the panicked state, which would then evoke embarrassment, shame, and humiliation. If the panic attacks do not become infused with such frightening meanings they remain an uncomfortable inconvenience but do not seem to affect a person's life beyond the specific instances in which they occur.

Interestingly, individuals who develop agoraphobic patterns typically fear both independence and relationships with others. When they picture themselves leaving relationships they long for connection; when they see themselves connected to others they long for self-sufficiency. Wolfe (1989) characterizes these conflicting desires as longings for freedom, which seems to connote both autonomy and isolation for agoraphobic individuals, versus security, which connotes being cared for but also controlled. Individuals with agoraphobic reactions typically are experiencing difficulty sustaining a relationship and simultaneously enjoying a sense of independent functioning. Both either-or solutions—staying in the relationship and leaving—look threatening.

Symptoms such as panic attacks and agoraphobia, though life-constricting in many ways, do provide at least partial solutions to very real dilemmas. In the following case, episodes of anxiety provide the thread that holds a couple together and the few moments of affectionate support that the spouses share.

Scott and Kelly-Ann were a married couple in their late twenties with two young children.

SYMPTOMS

Both Kelly-Ann and Scott experienced panic episodes and agoraphobia. Scott's episodes, which emerged first, took the form of severe anxiety with chest pain and heart attack symptomatology. Subsequent to these attacks, Scott became fearful of being alone. Kelly-Ann would be comforting and affectionate, holding him at night for long hours.

As Scott's attacks gradually abated, Kelly-Ann began experiencing panic attacks which then developed into a full agoraphobia. Kelly-Ann's attacks involved a sudden rush of panicky sensations and thoughts. She feared that the attacks meant that she was going crazy. Furthermore, she visualized that her particular form of going crazy would involve uncontrolled aggressive behavior, namely, grabbing knives and stabbing her husband and children. She soon developed a fear of being in the house alone, particularly around knives. Her main relief from these fears came when her husband was home and could be affectionate and reassuring. When her husband had to go to work, she depended on her mother to stay at home with her and the children.

PROCESS

In an initial individual consultation session Kelly-Ann had described her marriage as a good one and said little more about it. Kelly-Ann was joined by her spouse in the second session. At first the couple seemed to relate in a stiff and distanced manner. Their "good" relationship was held together by inaction. Once they began interacting, chronic conflict emerged. Neither spouse could say more than a sentence before the other would disagree. Then, rather than pursue arguments, discussion was stifled.

CONTENT

Kelly-Ann was dissatisfied with her husband's preoccupation with his work, his minimal expression of physical affection, and with the division of labor in the household. Because any attempts to discuss these problems evoked immediate sparks, the topics were only raised and then left to smolder. Scott was experiencing extreme job dissatisfaction, but was not able to address these problems without Kelly-Ann's criticizing him. He resented her lack of sympathy and would jab at her frequently on this point.

Both Scott and Kelly-Ann were distressed by personal issues as well as by their couple conflicts. Like the couple issues, these conflicts were never squarely addressed. Kelly-Ann had been at home mothering full-time and felt claustrophobic about so much confinement and so little contact with other adults. She longed to return to the playful environment of her former work in a large and quite sociable office, but she was reluctant to admit this wish. To her, wanting to return to work meant she must be a failure as a mother. Scott felt pressured by a negative and demanding boss and discouraged by a workload which felt excessive and never-ending. He would have liked to change jobs but was reluctant to appear a "quitter." He also feared that he would not be able to earn as much money in another position.

Subsequent sessions revealed that in response to their frustrations at home and at work both spouses had been silently thinking of divorce. Their fears of "being alone" were well-founded, as their tenuous relationship at any point could have been severed and neither of them relished living as single people. In their tension-fraught marriage, the few quiet and affectionate times occurred when one or another spouse was attempting to soothe the other's panic episode.

The marital dysfunction underlying many agoraphobic reactions cannot be overstressed. The couple's interactions typically make the individual's fears of being excessively dominated or criticized in relationships quite understandable. At the same time, living independent of the relationship looks equally unpleasant, as the agoraphobic individual typically lacks confidence in his/her ability to live self-sufficiently. Early experiences of abandonment, rejection, or premature self-reliance from parental neglect can lay the foundation for these fears (Wolfe, 1989).

Post-traumatic stress disorder:
A moment of moral ambivalence

Post-traumatic anxiety reactions seem to be triggered when memories of a traumatically stressful incident in the past are stirred up. Survivor guilt involves a similar post hoc reaction. In that case the response to the conflict in the painful situation is one of depression and guilt. The patient feels that s/he did the wrong thing in the earlier traumatic situation, or that someone else was more deserving of survival. When the post-trauma reaction is anxiety, the patient has continued to respond with acute ambivalence toward the painful memory. Post-traumatic stress syndromes can include both guilt and anxiety components.

Hank was a handsome, strong, and intelligent 34-year-old farmer who had fought as an officer and a gunner in the Vietnam war. After the war Hank had returned to a Kansas farm and a wife with whom he soon had two children.

Approximately ten years after his Vietnam experience Hank took an airplane flight to Denver, feigning business, to seek out a therapist. He asked for consultation for what he described as "stress in my marriage and stress in general."

SYMPTOMS

With a pattern characteristic of the delayed stress reactions so commonly experienced by veterans of the Vietnam war, Hank complained of irritability, loneliness, inability to connect with family members, sleep difficulties, and a feeling of chronic worry. He had developed an ulcer and felt that his marriage consisted primarily of bickering.

CONTENT

To help Hank connect his ongoing anxiety with its originating experiences in the war, I structured a visualization exercise: "Close your eyes . . . (in a quiet voice with ample pauses). Take a slow deep breath to clear your mind and your lungs. . . . Allow an image of Vietnam to come up before your visual screen. . . . Notice who is in the scene . . . what is happening . . . what each person in the scene seems to be feeling and thinking . . . how the scene ends."

Hank recalled a powerful emotional moment. He had been aiming his artillery as he did on a daily basis in Vietnam. As a child he had spent untold hours out wandering in the fields near his house, carrying his BB gun, hunting groundhogs. He had always enjoyed taking quick but careful aim, confidently hitting his target. That day in Vietnam he was aware of the similarity with his boyhood. He took careful aim at the faintly moving tall grass in the distance that indicated a Vietcong soldier. Just as he was about to pull the trigger, the grasses parted. The soldier stood up. It was as if the soldier had seen Hank in the distance and knew that Hank was targeting him to be killed. The soldier stood fully upright. He looked straight at Hank. His face was contorted in a silent, wordless plea that leapt across all language barriers. "I'm a man, just like you," the face seemed to say. "My wife and children need me. Don't kill me." Hank's exquisitely trained reflexes instantly pulled the trigger, precisely at the moment that Hank's thoughts were exploding with a terrifying realization. This was not shooting groundhogs. What was he doing?

PROCESS

Hank's main way of coping with recurring thoughts that disturbed him was to brush them aside. In Vietnam he had refocused on the work at hand and concentrated on the struggle to survive, to kill before being killed. Back in the U.S. after the war, he busied himself with raising his family and running his farm. He consciously tried to exhaust himself physically during the day so that he would be able to sleep at night.

Hank's interpersonal process for dealing with conflicts was similar. On the few occasions when he tried to share any of his current concerns or his haunting memories of Vietnam with his wife, her attitude seemed to him to be: "That's dumb! Why worry about it? It's no big deal." Whether Hank's wife was responding supportively to his own attempts at suppression of the upsetting thoughts or was simply responding in her own characteristic style to her husband's anxiety, the outcome was that Hank's thoughts never became fully aired. He had never talked through his conflicting feelings to the point of digesting and resolving his intensely painful dilemma. Consequently, the overwhelmingly powerful ambivalence that had beset Hank in that intense moment in Vietnam, symbolizing his conflicting feelings about the war and his participation in it, remained to haunt him. The moment remained firmly etched in Hank's memory, like an eternal and always frightening tableau. The angst, agony, and indecision of the moment, though physically resolved by his reflexive finger on the trigger, was never resolved in his mind. Did he want to shoot this man or not? Should he or should he not? No fear was involved in this case, but rather a torturous moment of absolute ambivalence. Should he treat the faraway soldier as the enemy and shoot him? Was the enemy a fellow man, toward whom he should put down his weapon? Or should he continue to perform his soldier's work? Ten years later his haunting questions remained unanswered. The persistent anxiety evoked by this unprocessed, unresolved dilemma left Hank with irritability, sleep disturbance, chronic marital friction, and unending loneliness.

Most of the above examples of anxiety have involved approach-avoidance dilemmas in which a want is conflicting with a fear. Hank's ambivalence, on the other hand, involved the concurrence of a need to do something and a moral imperative not to do it. Any pattern of interference between seemingly opposite impulses may be able to trigger an anxious feeling, even if fear is not a component.

Perhaps anxiety without fear is evoked by what Bateson, Jackson, Haley and Weakland (1956) labeled the "double bind" mode of communication characteristic of schizophrenic families. If a parent is telling a child, "Come here and let me hug you," while his/her tone of voice is indicating reproach or disgust and thereby carrying a message of "don't come near me," the child gets anxious. Which message should be attended to? How can both be true at once? Ambivalence, one of the hallmarks of schizophrenic and also of obsessional anxiety states, is understandable in this context. Two messages compete for one person's attention like two radio signals jamming the airwaves. Intense ambivalence characterized Hank's situation as his finger rested on the trigger in a field in Vietnam.

Anxiety is associated with immobilization in response to conflicts. Doing nothing about a problem perpetuates anxiety because the troubling situation continues to exist. The reverse can also be true. Anxiety can yield immobilization, as in a social phobia, when the conditioned fear response blocks physical and cognitive functioning. By contrast, making underlying concerns explicit and taking action that responds to these concerns can lead to resolution of the conflict and anxiety reduction.

CHAPTER 7

Anger: The Coercive Route

IN SPORTS LIKE FOOTBALL and basketball the best defense may be a good offense, but in real life a person who is frequently on the attack does not necessarily fare well. The attacking individual equates domination with resolution, perhaps believing that coercion brings satisfaction, complaint brings rectification, and blame neutralizes mishap. The reality, however, is that coercion is likely to engender resentment, complaints may create defensiveness, and blame is more likely to perpetuate bad feelings than to bring unfortunate situations to closure.

In spite of the havoc that inappropriate or excessive anger expression can wreak, many people in many different circumstances certainly do attempt to get what they want by becoming angry. Perhaps this frequency is because, while depression and anxiety are painful emotions to experience, anger and the attack modes of conflict resolution can be painful to receive but satisfying to express. If others have not been responding to what one wants, a frontal attack can feel energizing, and certainly more so than submissive acceptance of "no" for an answer. Righteous indignation can be invigorating. Raging can feel positively exhilarating, though also draining and often embarrassing after the fact.

THE MANY FORMS OF ATTACK

Whether it takes subtle forms like quiet barbs and indirect criticisms or explodes in violent rages, attacking behavior in response to a problem generally includes some predictable components. For one, the focus is generally on winning by overpowering. It is assumed that conflicts inherently are zero sum games yielding a winner and a loser. Winning equals

110

getting the other to do what one wants, regardless of the other's preferences. Domination, i.e., satisfaction of one's own desires to the exclusion of hearing or doing what the other wants, is equated with resolution.

A person who utilizes attack as a conflict resolution behavior is typically focused on someone or something outside of the self. The attacker considers himself as having little or no responsibility for, or power to improve, the problem. The other is at fault. The attacker also assumes that improvement will come only if s/he can somehow force the other to change. Demands, accusations, blame and criticism feel like the only ways in which leverage over the other, and therefore over the problem, can be exercised.

As a result of this other-directed set of assumptions, attacks usually involve communications in which the subject is "you" rather than "I," creating an aura of aggressiveness rather than assertiveness. Any statement about the other, as opposed to a reading of one's own feelings or thoughts, tends to have an attacking quality. Consequently, even a mild-mannered statement beginning with the pronoun "you" immediately sets a listener defensively on edge, expectant of a potentially painful evaluation. In contrast, conveying similar information with the focus on the self instead of the other is far less threatening and eliminates the sense of attack. "You hurt me" conveys attack; "I feel hurt" does not. Because "you-statements" focus on the person instead of the problem (the phraseology used by Fisher and Ury, 1981), the recipient of a you-statement generally feels compelled to respond with a self-defensive counterattack. The argument then switches from the problem at hand to whether or not the discussants have done this or that or are manifesting this or that bad trait.

Argumentative couples sometimes develop a pattern in which each habitually speaks for the other, often wrongly describing the other's viewpoint but seldom expressing one's own. "You think that I . . ." is followed by, "I do not! You just say that because you think. . . ." This pattern (described in its most benign form in Chapter 9 as "mind-reading," an aspect of boundary disturbance in a system) sorely inhibits the forward flow of discussion. Each partially wrong statement about the other is followed by a correction. Because of the "you" form of the mind-reading, the person who has been spoken for feels attacked. The corrective response is then experienced as criticism by the initial speaker. These attack-attack sequences create eddies of irritation, with neither participant experiencing any sense of movement toward resolution.

The words "always" and "never" are frequently signals of attack or defense. "I never . . ." and "You always . . ." imply a black-and-white, dichotomous, all-good or all-bad view of the other person (or of the self), and consequently almost inevitably engender a defensive response.

As Pruitt and Rubin (1986) point out, as conflict escalates, views of the self and of the other become increasingly polarized along good-bad dimensions. The other becomes the enemy, and is viewed with increasingly harsh distrust and dislike. Negative traits are attributed to the other. As the intensity of a conflict continues to rise, adversaries' beliefs about one another can become dehumanized, deindividuated, and even diabolical. Because there is also a tendency in these circumstances to be increasingly unwilling to communicate with the adversary—as young children say, "I'm not going to talk with you anymore!"—these misperceptions are increasingly unlikely to be corrected by disconfirmatory data. In intense conflict, available communication channels tend not to be utilized (Deutsch, 1973).

All-or-nothing zero-sum-game thinking increases in other ways as well as in the image of the opponent when people get angry.

> It's either victory for them or victory for us. Positions become rigid, there is little room for compromise, and there is a dearth of imagination and creativity. Emphasis is placed on proving how tough and unyielding one is, so as to persuade the adversary that one cannot be pushed around. (Pruitt & Rubin, 1986)

As determination to defeat the enemy is increasing, internal cohesiveness on each side increases simultaneously. The decrease in capacity for empathy with the adversary seems to be accompanied by a corresponding increase in internal closeness. Third-party bystanders will be put under increasing pressure to take sides. (Pruitt & Rubin, 1986)

Anger expression and attack are not necessarily synonomous. Attacking does not always include emotionally intense expression of anger; underlying angry feelings may be contained, with the attack conveyed in quietly restrained critical comments. Likewise, anger can be expressed in non-attacking forms, with emotional intensity but in I-statements, for instance, or toward someone's behavior rather than toward the person per se, e.g., "I don't like when you do x!" Nonetheless, expressing anger without conveying attack is challenging. It requires a focus that is explicitly on one's own feelings rather than on the other person, and on behaviors rather than on personal traits. Consequently, although expression of angry feelings can be intended simply to call attention to the significance of a problem, expression of anger can easily appear to be an attack because anger and attack differ only in subtle ways and so frequently occur together.

Anger often inherently conveys disparagement of the other, in some way communicating that the other person is "not OK." We are not angry in a vacuum; we usually experience anger toward an external other or thing.

Anger thereby tends to result in the opponent's feeling either wounded or defensive. Both recipients and bystanders are likely to feel threatened in some way, regardless of the manifest content of the message. The more intense the anger, the greater the implied threat of harm.

Since anger tends to be generated when an individual is experiencing difficulty in obtaining what s/he wants, continued frustration can evoke escalating anger. As the intensity of the anger increases, the goal of the attack tends to shift. The original issue ceases to be relevant; instead, dominating or hurting the opponent becomes the goal. Winning becomes redefined as hurting the other more than s/he can hurt you, as outlasting the other through the painful battle, or as striking the blow that causes the other to give up.

Just as armies can fight with guerrilla warfare, lined-up troops, guns and rifles, or atomic weaponry, attack styles in personal disputes also include considerable variance in weaponry and style. Table 7.1 suggests the particular flavor, structure, and typical underlying concerns of two common styles of attack behavior. These two styles align with what Shapiro (1965) labels hysteric and paranoid. The differences also coincide with common male-female styles. Few individuals are pure types. Many people attack in different ways at differrent times.

EIGHT ANGER PARADIGMS

Anger seldom comes out of nowhere. Table 7.2 lists common types of conflicts that engender fight responses, clarifies some of the objectives toward which anger is directed, and suggests circumstances that can increase the anger intensity. The listing is meant to be illustrative rather than exhaustive.

The first and perhaps most common of these conflict paradigms involves situations in which two people want different things to occur, and one or both become angry in order to be heard, to be taken seriously, and to obtain what they want. The following example of a family argument illustrates this kind of paradigm, as well as a number of the aspects of attack conflict strategy described in the earlier pages of this chapter.

> Suzanne shouted at her adolescent son, Spencer, to wash the dishes. While Suzanne was a mother who strongly preferred talking to shouting, in this instance she angrily raised her voice volume. Suzanne wanted Spencer to do something that he did not want to do, namely, to wash the dishes left over from lunch. She strongly wanted those dishes washed, and soon, so that she could prepare dinner.

TABLE 7.1
Attack Styles

	STYLE A HYSTERIC	STYLE B PARANOID
Quality of attack	"But you said . . ." Effusive Reactive Defensive Self-protective Complaining	"You're mean. It's all your fault." Pointed Experienced as reactive, but seen by other as unprovoked
Tone	Likely to be highly emotional	May be tightly controlled, but with restrained anger; or may express anger
View of the other	Sees other as critical, disapproving; wants approval	Sees other as at fault and believes other wants to hurt and blame
Wants from the other (underlying concern)	Wants approval, and to be heard	Wants respect Wants safety from blame, criticism
Transference expectation	Expects to be ignored; angry in response	Expects to be blamed, shamed and punished; angry in response
Cognitive style	Global, diffuse thinking; scattered and unfocused Thoughts may flow with twists and turns, linked by associations rather than logic Overly permeable to new information; too suggestible	Narrow, like a laser beam, zeroing in on one idea Rigid, black-and-white, either/or thinking Difficulties taking in new information that disconfirms old ideas Withholds information from others, as information can be used for power
Interpersonal focus	Attention focused on other to get other to like and listen to self Does not listen to self, to own needs and feelings. Worries instead about the other's evaluation of self	Attention focused on other to prevent other from hurting self Does not listen to self; instead projects own feelings onto the other

TABLE 7.2
Common Uses of Attack

CONFLICT	GOAL OF ATTACK	EXACERBATING FACTORS
Battle between individuals with *conflicting wants*	Coercion	Intensity of desire Importance of goal Nonresponsivity of other Sense of entitlement Time pressure or fatigue Negative images of the other Other gives no evidence of having heard what one has said
Strikeback reaction to having been hurt	Retaliative counter-attack	Territorial invasion or bodily harm from other Blame or criticism from other Egocentric misinterpretation of other's intentions, imputing harmful intent
Inner battle between *fears* and belief that expressing fears is *not acceptable.* Anger is expressed at bystanders	Cover for anxiety	Intensity of fears plus intensity of belief that expressing fears is not acceptable.
Inner conflict between *fear of humiliation* and assessment of having made an error. Anger is expressed at potential humiliator	Ward off shame	Expectation that others will attempt to humiliate you for mistakes
Anger from conflicting desires or strikeback reaction is directed at an innocent but *available third* person	Displacement	Inability to express anger or discuss the disagreement with the person involved
Variant: Fears of expressing actual wants; bickering instead about peripheral issues		Displacement can be of the topic instead of the person who receives the anger
Anger from conflicting wants or strikeback reaction *expressed "to"* not "at" an available *third person*	Ventilation (may be a prelude to effective problem-solving)	Inability to express anger at the conflictual other. Availability of sympathetic person to serve as a listener

(Continued)

TABLE 7.2 (continued)

CONFLICT	GOAL OF ATTACK	EXACERBATING FACTORS
Real conflict is hidden by *manufactured conflict*	Purposive distraction	Keeping secrets as a part of a manipulative lifestyle. Relationships based on taking from, not living with, others. Willingness of other to be pulled into petty arguments and distracted from confusing facts
Content-irrelevant fighting between members of a group	Establishment of status	Ambiguity re status or membership in a group
Task overload	Expression of frustration	Multiple simultaneous demands that overload a person's coping abilities. Can be exacerbated by time pressure or fatigue
Unacceptable thoughts and feelings	Projection	Inability of recipient to understand the projection, and consequent angry or defensive responses

Angry shouting may start as a way to be heard, as if the problem is that the other person is deaf and that amplification will help to overcome the deafness. A loud voice can also be used as a tool for coercion, a cudgel that is wielded to bully or force someone to do something. Anger escalates all the further when what we want and are not getting is something of importance to us, and to which we feel entitled.

Suzanne experienced Spencer as "deaf" to her words when her request was not acknowledged by Spencer. She increased the volume and intensity, shouting instead of discussing the more she thought about how her children were supposed to wash the dishes, and that Spencer should be more responsive to her need to prepare dinner.

Spencer was experiencing similar factors. He wanted his mother to do something she did not want to do, i.e., allow him to go play baseball. He experienced her as unresponsive to his concerns, and the concerns regarded something of importance to him. He felt entitled to what he wanted to do, i.e., to play baseball between school and homework, much as Suzanne felt entitled to a clean kitchen.

The angrier Spencer became, the angrier Suzanne became, each reciprocating the other's irritation. Shouting, Suzanne crescendoed to her boiling point. She threw down her dishtowel, turned, and stomped out. Spencer stalked off to his bedroom, opened the window, and "ran away" until dinner, too upset to play baseball after all. The mutual attack had concluded, with neither of them winning. There was no dishwashing or baseball.

Additional circumstances exacerbated this quarrel. Both Suzanne and her son were tired, exhausted after a full day of school and work. Furthermore, both of them felt time pressure. They had too much to do and too little time to do it, intensifying the sense of urgency with which they experienced their respective demands. The fatigue shortened their fuses. The time pressure fanned the initial sparks of irritation into flames of anger. Lastly, negative images of each other further fueled their self-justifications about the rightness of their positions.

Suzanne was thinking of Spencer as obstinate and as unwilling to do his share of work to keep the family going. Spencer was thinking of her as the bossy mom who orders people around. He resented her interference in his life and was convinced that she never listened to what he had to say. In fact, in calmer moments Suzanne knew that her son was unusually responsible about chores, trimming the bushes and taking out garbage without need for reminders. Likewise, in calmer times Spencer appreciated that his mother often listened with empathy and flexibility when he wanted to renegotiate work assignments or talk through personal decisions. However, the angrier each of them felt, the more their negative stereotypes of one another came to the fore. The more they focused on negative images, the angrier they felt.

When people feel hurt, or feel that their territory or integrity has been infringed upon, anger is a common *strikeback* reaction. Tit for tat seems to be an inborn defensive reaction in many of us; we reflexively return kindness with kindness and harm with harm. Attacks which seem "out of the blue" sometimes are responses to having felt criticized, bullied, or trampled upon. That is, the angry person believes s/he is counterattacking against perceived provocations by the person at whom s/he is expressing anger.

Sometimes the anger retaliates for an *anticipated* hurt. Prior interactions may have convinced someone that others (or a specific other person) are likely to hurt his/her feelings. Anger arises in expectation of the first blow. The individual who has a "chip on his shoulder" demonstrates this kind of chronic belligerence.

The attribution of intent to another's actions feeds angry strikeback responses. If I bump into you and you think that I'm just a bumbling kind of person, you are unlikely to experience very much anger. If you think our collision was because I wanted to injure you, then the likelihood of your reacting with anger is higher.

Certain individuals have hypersensitive areas that hurt when even lightly touched. The more hypersensitivity, egocentricity, and poor reality-testing, the greater the individual's likelihood of misinterpreting others' ambiguous actions as having been intentionally hurtful. The content of the attribution to the other may reflect the hurt individual's vulnerable issues.

For instance, a man might prepare dinner for his wife, who is then late returning home from work. He explodes with anger at this perceived hurt, which will be interpreted differently depending on his personal concerns. If the man is sensitive with paranoid leanings, he might interpret his wife's lateness as an indication that she has been deceiving him. A man with hysteric tendencies may feel that his wife's late return means she doesn't really love him. A husband whose vulnerable issues are more classically obsessive may feel that the tardiness means that his wife lacks self-control; he may be angry because she *should* have been home on time. Someone with narcissistic tendencies may be furious because his wife has spoiled his perfect dinner creation. A man whose personality features include sensitivity to issues of abandonment may see the lateness as a sign that his wife is thinking of leaving the marriage. That is, in ambiguous circumstances, sensitive individuals may read unintentional hurt along predictable thematic lines, and then strike back with anger.

So-called "hot reactors" (McKinney & Whitte, 1985) habitually read others' ambiguous actions as hurtful and intentional. Like young children, anger-prone individuals tend to read situations egocentrically, with themselves at the center. Thus, in the above example, each of the angry husbands interpreted the wife's late arrival home as a message about her feelings toward him. In fact, if he were to ask about the situation from her perspective, he might have been surprised to discover that her lateness had nothing whatsoever to do with him or with her feelings toward him. Perhaps an office emergency or traffic jam slowed her return.

Another kind of anger-generating conflict centers on anxiety. Some individuals experience conflict between feelings of anxiety and the belief that it is not acceptable to have such worries. Their solution is to mask their anxiety with a show of anger. In this case the conflict occurs primarily in the intrapsychic realm, although the anger is expressed toward whomever is nearby.

This kind of anger confuses others. What the angry individual wants is not clear, so the anger seems insatiable. When others try to comply with the angry person's wishes, the response is not appreciation but more angry complaints that the other should have done it differently or sooner. The anger still smolders because the underlying anxiety has not been addressed and soothed.

> Dee had seemed "grumpy" to Jeremy all week. Jeremy had tried his best to please her, to be fully responsive to everything she asked of him, but the grumpiness continued. In a marital therapy session, I asked Dee to look under the anger at her fears. Dee burst into tears. She was terrified of the impending foreclosure on their home and of the uncertainty about where the family would live next. In these situations it is important to make expression of anxiety acceptable. When individuals express their fears, soothing responses are more likely to be forthcoming from others. Moreover, with the intrapsychic conflict between anxious feelings and fears of expressing anxious feelings resolved, the real life dilemmas can be faced with more likelihood of finding positive solutions. The intrapsychic resolution occurs as patients realize that in the past expressions of anxiety may not have been acceptable, but that within their current relationship such expressions will be met with reassurance and support. Coaching the anxious individual's significant others so that they do in fact respond in a helpful manner therefore can be essential.
> Once Dee's underlying anxieties had been expressed, Jeremy was able to reassure her by explaining the several housing options he was anticipating. After a foreclosure they would still have money to rent a house, rent an apartment, or move out of state. This information quieted Dee's fears. She and Jeremy agreed upon a plan of action for exploring these options, and the anger abated. Once they had actually moved to the new quarters, Dee relaxed even further, and her quickness to anger decreased.

Yet another kind of dilemma that often produces anger occurs when an individual senses that s/he has made a mistake and then anticipates feeling shamed or humiliated. Angry blame may then be fired out to fend off self-criticism or humiliating comments from others.

> Clive had been raised in a home in which severe physical punishment coupled with humiliating comments constituted the parents' main way of controlling their children. As an adult, Clive would respond with anger toward his wife any time she raised an issue as a problem for them to discuss. Joint problem-solving would have required his admission that what he (as well as his wife) had been doing was not working in their choice of doctors, in their handling of their daughter, in the care of their dog, etc. Instead of accepting a measure of responsibility for the difficulty and then finding better solutions to a problem, Clive would anticipate stinging criticism (from himself and his wife) and blitz angry criticisms at his wife to fend off the humiliating onslaught.

Anger stimulated by any of the kinds of circumstances described above can be displaced, that is, expressed onto a target other than the person or situation that engendered it. Displacement onto a third party usually develops in situations in which an individual who experiences anger believes that it would be unacceptable to express the feeling to the person who has evoked it. This kind of triangulation, involving person A who expresses his/her anger with person B by getting mad at person C, is frequently seen in families with a symptomatic child. In these cases the child may be the recipient of anger that one spouse feels toward the other. A related phenomenon occurs when an inherently stressful situation causes family members to be brittle, reacting angrily to one another over minor provocations that in other circumstances would not elicit angry retorts.

> Lawrence reacted to virtually all problems, all conflicts between what he had wanted and what actually occurred, with anger, criticism, or finding someone to blame. Lawrence was often angry at his first wife, Alice. Prior to their divorce, displacement had been a regular feature of Lawrence and Alice's marriage. Lawrence had a frustrating job at the time. Instead of expressing his anger in some fashion at his employer or problem-solving with his employer to find better solutions to work problems, he would come home feeling short-fused and, in response to a minimal provocation, would blow up at Alice. After Lawrence and Alice became divorced, daughter Joyce became the substitute target of Lawrence's anger at his ex-wife. This displacement was a factor in Joyce's subsequent depression.

Ventilation is another form of anger release that can evolve within a three-person triangle, but in this case with generally benign impact. When an individual is angry at someone and does not feel able to deal directly with that person, s/he may instead air the anger with a disinterested third party. The third party is treated as an ally; the object of the anger remains the initially provocative individual. Consequently, instead of feeling threatened by the angry person, the listener may experience a sense of special alliance as confidante. When the confidante is appropriate — someone like a spouse, good friend, therapist, or religious leader — ventilation can be helpful.

Ventilation can become detrimental, however, if the confidante is ill-chosen — a child, or someone who becomes an extramarital intimate. In these instances the resulting triangulation can undermine the closeness of husband and wife, build inappropriate intimacy between parent and child, or unfairly burden a child with parents' problems. These patterns are explored further in Chapter 9 in a discussion of conflict processes and alliances within family systems.

Anger can be used as a distraction device. If an individual is in conflict with others but does not want others to see that the conflict exists, anger can be utilized like a squid's black liquid to obscure the problem. Individuals who interact with others in this kind of manipulative and self-serving manner are likely to be what Restak (1982) describes as "self-seekers." Blum (1972) suggests that relationships with this kind of deception require a deceiver and one who is willing to be deceived. The latter must be willing to live with confusion without demanding clarity, perhaps in exchange for the lure of mystery or a sense of importance from association with someone regarded as powerful, though hurtful.

> Kurt was a charming and financially successful fellow who did not want his wife to know about his gambling and womanizing. Each day when he returned from work he would find something about which to blame or criticize her. By picking a fight he was able to distract his wife from discussions about his late hours, discussions that might have led to exposure of his illicit activities.

Attacking behaviors can be used in contending for status. Some individuals rely on their ability to put down others to establish dominance. School-aged children often manifest this pattern as they jostle one another to establish the playground pecking order. Siblings may be particularly likely to bicker toward this end in families where there seems to be too little love to go around, where parents do not recognize the relative age status of their several children, or where the parents in some way favor some siblings over others.

> In the Martin family, verbal skirmishes among the four teenagers erupted incessantly. Attempts at problem-solving ran up against an unending countercurrent of dispute about who was really right. Thus, a comment by Monica would be followed by a statement from her older brother Jim establishing that he was right and she was wrong. "Yes, but . . ." began his response; the rest was an attack that pointed out what was wrong about what Monica had said and what was right about his alternative viewpoint. Even when there was no subject of contention, the bickering was frequent, particularly between siblings who were closest in age. These arguments constituted the family's mode for establishing hierarchy and pecking order. In addition, family members seemed to assume that there was an in-group and an out-group. The siblings fought for inclusion. Pushing out others by showing how they were wrong was a way to make a place in the in-group for themselves.

Angry outbursts can occur when an individual feels overwhelmed by too many pressures in too short a time span. When a system goes on overload, sparks may be emitted. The premenstrual, postpartum, or fatigued mother who has minimal coping energies, for instance, can become quickly overwhelmed by demands from too many children all asking for her attention at once. Like the old lady who lived in a shoe, she may whip them all soundly and put them to bed.

Individuals who are minimally prone to anger outbursts may attack only in one or two of the above kinds of situations, perhaps most probably as a strike-back or overload response. More perpetually angry individuals may attack in response to the full panoply of life's dilemmas. Individuals who manifest the characteristics that are labeled borderline personality, for instance, typically react with anger to virtually every emotionally evocative situation, and also tend to escalate rapidly, with minimal ability to modulate their anger or to self-soothe (Westen, 1987).

CASE EXAMPLE

Angry patients can present therapists with major difficulties. To some extent therapists always get "pulled into the system," i.e., begin to interact in the manner of family members. Angry patients can begin to get the therapist angry; utilizing these feelings toward therapeutic ends takes practice and skill.

The following example describes a couple who demonstrate most of the anger paradigms described in Table 7.2 and also the two anger styles delineated in Table 7.1. Because both husband and wife automatically reacted with anger to so many situations, creating an ever-thickening jungle of antagonistic dialogue, working with this couple was extremely challenging.

An angry man with diabetes and his distraught wife

Steve and Molly were both highly intelligent professionals in their late twenties. They came to treatment for help with their marriage. The couple argued with quiet antagonism in the waiting room prior to their first session. Within the therapy room, their verbal exchanges escalated quickly and frequently into loud hostilities.

STEVE'S SYMPTOMS

Steve suffered from serious diabetes with multiple medical complications. A major medical problem such as this must virtually always be presumed to have psychological ramifications, although in this case neither spouse raised the diabetes as a presenting problem. They complained primarily of Steve's "moodiness." Steve described his moods as very hot and very cold. He experienced himself as swinging from extremes, "without a lot of transitional or moderate weather." In his cold phases he felt "very still, but a stillness that's like a prelude to volatility. I reach a point where I no longer keep my feelings or thoughts bottled up. They get released in explosions of tension, anger, and sadness—almost exclusively negative emotions." This self-description corroborated my perceptions of Steve as always angry, sometimes in a cold, controlled manner, often irritated, and sometimes furious.

STEVE'S CONCERNS

Any incident in which Steve did not get what he wanted or expected could trigger an anger outburst. For instance, if he wanted to meet his wife for lunch at noon and she preferred 12:30, he would get angry until she backed down and agreed to his timing. If his wife had planned to pick up the dry cleaning on the way home from her office and then, because she was late leaving work, decided to postpone the errand a day, Steve was furious. Likewise, when I interrupted a lengthy, counterproductive explanation he was giving in the therapy hour, Steve was angry at me for cutting him off. Much of the anger in these situations expressed his frustration when others did not do precisely as he wanted, with the anger intended to rectify the situation by *coercing* others to do his bidding. The frequency of these coercive attempts reflected the inappropriate expectations that he held about what others should be doing for him.

Other underlying concerns triggered angry outbursts as well. For instance, an ongoing question for Steve was, "Do people really care about my needs?" Steve had grown up in an angry and chaotic family. As an adult, any time he did not get what he wanted he interpreted this lack of response as a sign that the person who was countering him was just like his unresponsive parents. This *strikeback* anger was retribution toward those who seemed to ignore his needs.

Another ever-present underlying concern was, "Am I really not OK?" This concern probably grew out of having been the recipient of perpetual anger and vituperation within his family of origin. This concern was exacerbated by his physical condition. "Am I not OK medically, ill with the diabetes flaring up again? And am I unacceptable as a person because of the diabetes?" These questions proved to be sources of perpetual underlying concern, concern experienced as *anxiety* and *expressed with a cover of anger*.

Steve harbored secret shame about his illness. His family had never accepted the diabetes, and he had continued to feel disgraced by it. When topics were raised that related to the illness, such as his sexual functioning or the likelihood of being able to have a healthy child, Steve would quickly go on the attack, *warding off anticipated shame and humiliation*, even though Molly tended to be quite tolerant and knowledgeable about the medical realities.

Another frequent trigger for outbursts of anger was a change in routine. "I don't like surprises. If I know there *may* be changes, I'm OK. But I don't adjust well on the spur of the moment." This brittleness may have had a neurological basis, like the fragility of young children who have difficulty handling transitions. An alternative explanation is that changes reminded him of the unexpected disasters that kept occurring from the diabetes, changes affecting his vision, limiting his sexual functioning, and threatening his life.

STEVE'S PROCESS

These poignant underlying concerns were never expressed in the marriage. Instead, to every feeling, every evidence of an underlying concern, Steve reacted with angry outbursts directed toward his wife. The symptom, i.e., the perpetual anger, was utilized as a multi-purpose solution for getting things he wanted, for striking back when he felt hurt, displacement, warding off shame, masking anxieties, cushioning the shock of the unexpected, and, most of all and least effectively, for maintaining the marital relationship. Steve feared that his illness might cause his wife to leave him, though he desperately wanted her to stay. He was trying to keep his wife in the marriage by intimidation, by keeping her in continual fear of his temper, just as he tried to get her to pick up the dry cleaning by intimidation.

MOLLY'S SYMPTOMS AND CONTENT OF CONFLICTS

Molly, Steve's wife, radiated confusion. Molly didn't know if she wanted to stay married. She worried about whether she wanted to stay at her job or return to school. When she wasn't immobilized in her confusion, she was angry.

MOLLY'S PROCESS

Molly felt, "afraid to be me, because if I do anything it will make him mad, send him into a rage." Instead of being forthright about what she wanted, Molly alternated between anxious immobilization (e.g., making no decisions regarding the marriage) and defensive anger. Rather than choosing her own path, she would counter whatever Steve said. "You did!" "I did not!" "You *did*!" was their typical interaction. Reactive rather than proactive, Molly experienced herself as having no independent control of her feelings. Instead she felt controlled by her husband's moods, mirroring his anger when he was angry, his sadness when he was sad, his tension when he was tense. Molly and Steve could identify problem areas. With their mutual attacking, however, they seldom moved from accusative listing to resolving problems. The pattern left both of them chronically dissatisfied, hurt and ready to battle again.

INTRAPSYCHIC ATTACK PATTERNS

People sometimes get angry at themselves, actively calling themselves names, iterating and reiterating their errors, criticizing themselves for their shortcomings, and even cutting themselves or hurting themselves with head-banging. These evidences of negative inner dialogue and physical self-harm indicate that people are utilizing attack as part of an intrapsychic conflict resolution process. Self-criticism and self-blame are verbal forms of attacking oneself; self-mutilation is the physical escalation. The intent may be to solve a conflict, but the result is to hurt the self.

In the intensity of tournament tennis, for instance, players often complain aloud to themselves, "That was a stupid mistake! What did you do that for!" The conflict is between how they are hitting the ball and how they want to be hitting the ball. Instead of attacking themselves, they are better advised to respond to the conflict with problem-solving. Players who think over how they made their error and determine how to prevent that error from recurring can then reprogram themselves. Visualizing and even going through the physical motions of this better way of handling the shot increases the probabilities that they will handle similar shots more successfully in the remainder of the game. Berating themselves instead of problemsolving may be intended to get themselves to "shape up," but often leads to repeated errors and demoralization instead.

> When Karen (introduced in Chapter 5) was mildly depressed, she habitually undermined her fragile self-confidence by focusing on her shortcomings, and frequently berated herself with admonitions that she should have done this or that better. The depression perpetuated her negative thinking and her negative self-descriptions perpetuated her depression. When the depression was in its psychotic phases, Karen engaged in more vituperative and adamant self-excoriation. She was certain that the cause of all her problems was the fact that she was "lazy." She was preoccupied with self-hatred, self-abusive name-calling, and thoughts of self-mutilation and suicide.

Individuals who react to a problem or conflict by blaming may chastise themselves (the depressive solution) or may project the fault outside onto others. This projection outward creates a paranoid-style solution. Although paranoid individuals may feel that others are "out to get" them, their own behavior tends to be attacking. Thus, their reading of others' desires to hurt them and the resultant suspicious stance come from a projection onto others of their own stance of being always ready to attack. In addition, their readiness to attack sets up a high probability that strikeback aggressive behavior will be returned by others. Their anger and expectations bring about a self-fulfilling prophecy and can trigger a cycle of attack-attack interactions.

When attacking is pervasively utilized by a severely disturbed individual, depressive self-accusations sometimes coincide with paranoid delusions in which blame is assigned to someone or something outside of the self.

> Dolores felt enormous guilt and berated herself continuously. Her guilt and incessant self-criticism were depressive. At the same time Dolores was preoccupied with the belief that others were talking about her, especially about an abortion she had had many years prior. She believed people were rejecting her to punish her. She also believed that her problems with her teenage daughter were punishment for the abortion. She blamed the priest to whom she had once confessed and whom she believed had told "everyone."

In paranoid pathology the blame is pinned on someone or something outside of the individual, though the conflict may be primarily intrapsychic. Dolores's projection, ideas of reference, and fixed delusional thinking were hallmarks of a paranoid disorder. From a conflict resolution perspective, however, the predominant feature in Dolores' functioning was the pervasiveness of attack, blame and criticism, evident in both the intrapsychic and the interpersonal realms. She berated herself. She blamed the priest. And she exchanged a steady stream of complaints, criticism, accusation and blame with her husband and teenage daughter. Furthermore, all three members of the family communicated primarily in negatives. Attacking rather than discussing was the systemic mode of communicating. Hence problems mounted instead of being solved, decisions were seldom made, and toxic feelings abounded.

Self-attack does not always produce full-fledged depression. It may produce only feelings of guilt. In healthy functioning, an action that has evoked feelings of guilt is followed by restitution and then reprogramming so that similar situations are handled in a different manner in the future. For instance, I might feel guilty after having forgotten to send presents on my nieces' and nephews' birthdays, all of which occur over a brief period in the spring. The guilt, it is hoped, would motivate me as quickly as possible to find presents to send belatedly (restitution). Ideally, the guilt also would lead me to think through the problem and devise a solution (reprogramming). I might then write in my appointment book reminders that warn me when the birthday season is coming so that in future years I send gifts before the birthdays. Or I might decide to bring all the relatives their annual birthday gifts when we get together in the summer.

Unhealthy guilt, by contrast, occurs when an individual has internalized a process of blame and punishment rather than problem-solving and prevention in response to mistakes. Thus, if I react to my error by telling myself how stupid and thoughtless I am, the nagging unpleasant feelings of disappointment in myself will persist, my errors will continue, and my negative self-regard may be even further ingrained.

Sometimes attack in inner dialogue is met with inaction or escape rather than depressive submission. An attack-inaction (fight-freeze) pattern seems to characterize the intrapsychic conflict associated with procrastination. The more an inner voice cracks the whip insisting "I *must*. . . ." or "I *have* to . . . ," the less likely it is that the procrastinating individual will take action. The interpersonal version of this pattern is nagging from one person and passive-aggressive behavior from the other (see Chapter 4, Table 4.4). An attack-escape intrapsychic pattern can take the form of an alcoholic (or other drug or addiction) episode.

Self-battering can be met with return attack, resulting in a sense of ongoing inner turmoil. Instead of a calm and forward-moving process of gathering information, formulating options, and choosing optimal solutions, these individuals barrage themselves with negative messages. "I don't want to do this!" "Well tough, you idiot, you have to do it!" "What's wrong with me that I can't do that?" This kind of internal battle parallels the chaos and anger prevalent in families in perpetual crisis and is characteristic of families that produce individuals with borderline character disturbances.

Thus, attack can be a response to conflict within or between people. Depression, paranoid functioning, guilt, procrastination, and inner turmoil all can be indicators of a pattern that includes anger in response to intrapsychic conflict. Criticism, sarcasm, accusation, complaint, name-calling, blame, and escalations into shouting, verbal abuse and physical violence are evidences of attack in response to interpersonal conflict. When whole societies resort to not only verbal but also physical fighting to solve their problems, war can be the unfortunate consequence.

CHAPTER 8

Addictions and Other Escape Routes

CONFLICT CAN BE THOUGHT OF as an obstacle one might meet on the road of life. The problem-solver finds a way to ease past the obstacle and then continues on down the road. By contrast, depressed individuals give up on going where they have been heading. Anxious individuals stand by the obstacle without figuring out what to do. Angry people attack anyone associated with the obstacle. And those who are avoidant escape, turning away from the problem altogether.

When an animal senses danger, escape is accomplished by physically fleeing. People have multiple options when they choose a flight route. One is physical departure. "Run, run, as fast as you can. Can't catch me, I'm the gingerbread man," quoted a patient who left for a weight-loss resort, a foreign land, or a visit to her mother each time her marriage became too upsetting. Looking away so the problem is no longer in view accomplishes the same objective. Averting awareness of the dilemma puts the obstacle out of sight and out of mind, so that the disturbing situation seems no longer to exist. Cognitive, as opposed to physical, escape can be accomplished via a change of topic; by repression, denial, or out-of-body experiencing; by distraction via the use of alcohol or drugs; by preoccupying activity such as excessive work, exercise, or TV viewing; or by obsessive-compulsive habits like repetitive hand-washing, excessive eating, or self-starvation.

In moderation, escape maneuvers can have positive aspects. When a conflictual issue that makes someone uncomfortable comes up in a discussion, a simple solution is to change the topic. In more stressful circumstances, walking out of a room, and even punctuating the departure with a firmly closed door, can distance someone from a conflict that feels unproductive. More extreme flight behaviors, such as denial, obsessions, addictions, and even psychosis, can reduce the tensions induced by a conflict, offering at least a solution to the problem of how to feel better. When used as a form of strategic withdrawal, flight can bring reprieve — time-off from the battlefield to regroup, rest and heal, and then return to the fray.

A simple example of positive use of a tension-modulating escape habit is thumbsucking. This versatile children's habit can offer self-soothing in response to upset and self-stimulation in the face of boredom (Heitler, 1985). Upset or bored children may put the thumb into action, briefly retreat into a meditative state, and then, as they feel more comfortable, begin to look around the room for a new activity. The rhythmic sucking engenders a comfortable mood and promotes constructive thinking. For many preschoolers, a momentary retreat into reflective thumbsucking leads to a fresh view of the situation and a renewed burst of activity.

Under what circumstances does a withdrawal behavior become problematic? Two primary considerations are critical.

- *Does the withdrawal incur costs that outweigh its gains in making the individual feel better?* If the escape mechanism, for instance, involves a drug that stimulates anger outbursts, dangerous behavior, or addiction, the costs may well outweigh the benefits.
- *Does the withdrawal lead to rejuvenation and an eventual reengagement with the initial problem?* The retreat may be a refueling stop or a perpetual detour.

UNDERSTANDING ESCAPE
RESPONSES TO PROBLEMS

People who broadly utilize avoidance in response to intrapsychic and interpersonal conflicts are generally unaware of how, when, or to what extent they flee from conflict.

Because Leslie had grown up in a household with a cantankerous alcoholic father, she was determined not to bring either alcohol or antagonism into her adult family. When problems developed between Leslie and her husband, she utilized avoidance to keep up appearances of zero conflict. To show the world a happy face, she hid her anger at her husband by taking prescription drugs.

Leslie reacted with similar avoidance to her own intrapsychic arguments. Although she was trained as a nurse, Leslie decided not to work outside the home while her children were young. While she felt she should be available for her youngsters, she hated housework and cooking and had minimal patience as a parent. Again, rather than squarely facing this conflict, Leslie occupied herself full-time with thoughts of where the next pill could come from, when she would take it, and how. This escape solution meant that she neither satisfied her supposed objective of being a homemaker for her family nor engaged in work or leisure activity more suited to her actual interests and talents. Though somewhat physically gratifying, the escape into drugs provided a lose-lose solution to Leslie's real life concerns. "I wanted to change how I felt without putting in the time or energy to work through the problem," she later observed.

Young children believe that if they cannot see something it does not exist. Perhaps this magical thinking is at the root of the response of turning away from uncomfortable situations. One long-time alcoholic, the father of one of my patients, refused to see a doctor for what appeared to be obvious signs of cancer. Like Leslie, this man believed, "If I don't look at it, it will go away." Similarly, a 14-year-old boy, Tom, withdrew into autistic preoccupations when asked to talk about his father. The father, an intermittent alcoholic with a history of abusing Tom, was bringing a custody suit to force his son to live with him. The topic of his father evoked overwhelming emotional distress, to which psychotic escape was Tom's desperate response.

One outcome of the belief that if you don't talk about something it doesn't really exist can be an emphasis on keeping secrets. As Seixas and Youcha (1985) write,

> Come into the house where alcoholism lives. Open the front door. There's the living room. Everything is in perfect order. It looks ready for a photographer, or, perhaps, a funeral. On the far side a door swings open for a glimpse into the kitchen. This, the heart of the house, reeks of dirty dishes left in the sink, food-encrusted plates on the table, overflowing garbage. . . . The public facade is maintained in the living room, while the private chaos is hidden from view.
>
> This orderly-disorderly house is the outward evidence of an extensive denial system that began with the alcoholic (who is both the subject and the main keeper of the secret) and that by now has implicated the whole family.
>
> Hiding becomes a way of life that goes unchallenged and unquestioned as the lives of those who keep the family secret are twisted, knotted, and distorted. (pp. 3-4)

Weissberg (1983) and also Fossum and Mason (1986) stress the prevalence of this ban on talking about emotionally painful experiences, not only in families with alcohol and drug problems, but also in families in which child abuse, spousal violence, and incest occur. Patterns of avoidance create overwhelming stresses for their victims, since traumas that are "unspeakable" cannot be dealt with contructively.

Abusive behaviors, born of stress, often occur in combination with avoidance maneuvers. Sometimes problems can be ignored only up to a point. Eventually the avoidance ceases to work, the distress comes to full awareness, and the emotions explode in violent behavior. That is, when escape mechanisms no longer suffice, attack strategies often supplant them. Instead of attacking the problem, the abusive person erupts violently toward nearby individuals.

> Charlotte and Clive, both successful business executives, had a marriage torn apart by periodic anger and violence. Clive's episodes of verbally and physically abusive behavior toward his wife occurred when he felt overwhelmed by problems—harassment from his ex-wife, pressure at his workplace, or provocative loud noise from neighborhood teenagers. When he was at home he would try to escape thoughts of these difficulties by keeping televisions on loudly in several rooms. The pressures would still mount, eventually erupting in a violent episode directed toward his wife. Such episodes would release some inner tension and typically were followed by a period of calm, unless Charlotte attempted to engage her husband in a discussion of either the preceding problems or the abusive incident. Clive sometimes viewed explicit discussion of problems as almost as threatening as the problems themselves. Counterproductive elements in the dialogue patterns that Clive and Charlotte had developed reinforced his sense that discussion would add more harm than good.

Avoidance of problems may prevent battles. In families where addictive behaviors or other escape patterns are prevalent, productive direct discussion of problems is often nonexistent. If fight or flight are the only alternatives that family members perceive, and if their fights have a history of escalating to violence, flight may be an preferred mode of reaction to conflict. Avoidance does prevent, or at least postpone, arguments and violence in these families, but at a cost of letting problems go unaddressed and unresolved.

In families where escape responses are prevalent, conflict often is seen as a prelude to shaming and blaming. When something goes wrong, people can react by trying to fix the problem or by trying to affix blame. A family that responds to upsets and mishaps with fault-finding or punishment by humiliation propels its members toward escape maneuvers. The belief that attempts to deal with problems may simply open one up to criticism and humiliation provides a strong disincentive to taking effective action when problems arise. As Ginott (1965) pointed out in the context of parenting skills,

Constructive criticism confines itself to pointing out how to do what has to be done, entirely omitting negative remarks about the personality of the child. When things go wrong is not the right time to teach an offender about his personality. When things go wrong, it is best to deal only with the event, not the person. (p. 44)

Emotional overreactivity can further increase the impulse to avoid rather than deal directly with problems. If the cognitive reaction to an error is to catastrophize (Ellis & Bernard, 1985), emotional reactions will become more intense. In these circumstances, individuals are less likely to feel that they can effectively rectify the difficulty, and hence will be more prone to respond with an escape, with anxious immobilization, or with counterattack. As Ginott (1965) wrote,

A child needs to learn from his parents to distinguish between events that are merely unpleasant and annoying and those that are tragic or catastrophic. . . . A lost glove need not lead to a lost temper, a torn shirt need not serve as a prop for a do-it-yourself Greek tragedy. (p. 47)

Clive was raised in a household in which verbal humiliation and physical beatings were routine responses to children's errors. His anticipatory anguish when he felt he had done something wrong was understandable in this context.

One of the most striking aspects of communication patterns in avoidant families is the agility with which family members learn to detour problematic topics. Topic changes are gracefully executed, so that disturbing topics are left for either more comfortable or more emotionally evocative alternatives. A safer topic offers high ground on which to escape the unpleasantness of conflict, while a more emotionally charged one also works to deflect conversation from the conflict at hand.

Clive was reluctant to discuss the problems in his marriage with his wife. When an interaction between them was raised for discussion, even in the most gentle fashion, Clive would change the topic to how poorly Charlotte treated her mother. Although this change of focus could be interpreted as an attempt to verbalize indirectly how he felt that Charlotte treated him, it also effectively sidetracked the discussion of their relationship.

The extreme of the avoidant communicator is the psychopathic liar who says whatever needs to be said to keep others off the scent of what is really happening. Overt lying also tends to develop in individuals who are masking an addiction. The addiction can be to food, a drug, work, an extramarital relationship, obsessional thoughts, compulsive rituals, or any diversionary activity. Even an addiction to watching television can produce habits of lying (about whether the TV has been on, or for how long) in children who normally can be trusted to be truthful. Escape-prone individuals who do not lie explicitly may avoid the straight truth by evasion of touchy topics, by errors of omission rather than commission, or by understatement. Minimization of the extent of the addictive behavior is a particularly common form of avoidant communication. Experienced alcohol counselors, for instance, know that patients routinely grossly understate their actual frequency and quantity of liquor consumption.

Yet another way to use language to avoid real discussion of conflict is to say the right words with no intention of backing those words up with action. Trust is frequently an issue in alcoholic families, for instance, because the drinking individual so frequently fails to follow through on verbal commitments. A phone call home to say, "I'm on my way; I'll be home in just a few minutes," is likely to be followed by another extended period of drinking. The primary loyalty is to the liquor, not to the other individuals in the family. When there is a conflict between drinking and carrying out a plan of action to which the drinker has voiced commitment, the drinking tends to prevail. Moreover, this use of language to fend off criticism or dissent often generalizes, so that even when alcohol is not an issue the same pattern of saying one thing and doing another may occur.

When avoidance is achieved via such patterns as obsessive thoughts and compulsive rituals like hand-washing (which may also have a strong neurochemical component), the main mechanism of escape seems to be distraction. Whenever the painful conflict comes to mind, e.g., a wishful or angry impulse that encounters a "That's not acceptable!" self-retort, a repetition of the distracting thought or habit crowds the conflict out of conscious awareness.

Addictions often (but by no means always) begin in a similar manner, as a distraction maneuver. However, because the addictive substance is pleasurable, the habit becomes self-perpetuating. The new father who begins to drink because he feels left out of the intimate twosome between mother and child may continue to drink even after he has become integrated into the new baby's world. The positively reinforcing characteristics of the habit, as well as the substance's chemically addictive properties, perpetuate the addictive solution.

> George began going to bars after work in response to feeling exploited by his boss. He was attempting to self-medicate, to put out his feelings of burning rage rekindled daily by his employer's excessive demands and insulting attitude. Gradually George's work changed and he had less contact with his provocative employer. The pattern of extended drinking after work had become established, however, and continued in spite of the decrease in conflicts during his workday.

CLINICAL MANIFESTATIONS

Not only do individuals who develop addictive patterns or who have grown up in families with an alcoholic or otherwise addicted parent utilize avoidance in response to many of life's dilemmas, but their addiction is in itself an avoidant response to life. That is, people who choose to spend life controlling their emotional states by ingestion of substances rather than by real-life love, work, and leisure experiences may not be escaping a specific conflict but are escaping from life itself. Addictive, obsessive-compulsive, avoidant, schizoid, and schizotypal personality disorders involve lifestyles based on avoidance. Afraid of their feelings and afraid of others' feelings as well, individuals who live in these ways live on perpetual detours from real life.

Long-standing patterns of avoiding contact with other people because of fears of rejection typify people labeled "avoidant personality disorder." Avoidance is a solution to the fear, but a solution which brings forth chronic longing for more human contact. Whereas hostile conflict resolution strategies yield satisfaction to one side at the expense of the other and are based on overly forceful expression of one side's desires, avoidant strategies tend to give voice to neither side. Such individuals often live in chronic frustration, disappointment, and sadness. Their fears of conflict and of rejection are so powerful that all other human desires, such as desires for loving contact with others and for successful development of their individual potentials at work and leisure activities, become subordinate. The avoidant lifestyle is a solution to this one fear, but a solution that leaves all other needs perpetually unrequited.

Schizoid individuals share the social isolation seen in people labeled as avoidant but seem to lack their intense desire for affection and acceptance. Feelings may be avoided via depersonalization as well as by staying away from provocative situations. Escape from the relationships that make life meaningful and rich for many people seems to be a relatively successful solution for these individuals. They may experience an emotional coolness and distance from others, becoming confused and overwhelmed if they do become involved with individuals who demand an emotional responsiveness from them that is not within their capability. Remoteness from other individuals seems to stem in part from an inability to understand what others want from them, as if they do not experience the same needs for human interaction as others. Because of this difficulty understanding others' needs, these individuals tend to be most comfortable spending time alone or interacting with machines, computers or pets, which they find less demanding and more comprehensible than people. In this regard, schizoid isolation and avoidance of interpersonal encounters of all kinds (not just conflictual) can be a positive pattern of adjustment for some individuals.

Schizotypal personalities display similar patterns of social isolation as schizoid individuals, but have an additional dimension of oddities of thought, appearance or behavior. Their feelings of disconnection with themselves and with others suggest an inability to integrate. Whether this lack of meshing occurs because of a fear that conflicting elements can never be integrated or because of an inherent inability to put parts into wholes is unclear. In any case, these individuals avoid ongoing interactions with other people that would require them to negotiate their own and others' needs, both of which tend to confuse them. Either impulsiveness or indecisiveness tends to characterize their decision-making, as integration of seemingly disparate options does not occur and only either/or or no solutions are possible.

Many other escape maneuvers for dealing with conflicts show up in clinical practice. The following cases suggest a few representative examples.

Travel: Run, run as fast as you can . . .

A vacation or a trip can offer a rejuvenating break from the challenges of our daily routines.

Eleanor carried this refreshment strategy to a detrimental extreme. Her life had become organized around taking trips, which she even referred to as "retreats," designed in large part to soothe her disappointment over a malnourishing marriage. Because of all her travel, continuity with friends and involvement in meaningful work had become so diluted as to leave her life empty and chronically unsatisfying, which in turn perpetuated the travel urge.

Carrying a potentially healthy conflict response to an extreme, an extreme that makes satisfactory problem resolution less rather than more likely, is the hallmark of detrimental use of fight, immobilization, and submission, as well as flight.

Television addiction: Too late

Sometimes addictions take forms that at first appear to be conventionally acceptable behavior. A hardworking executive, for instance, may be a highly motivated employee; he may or may not be using work to avoid conflict at home. Perhaps because television viewing is so widespread in our culture, television addiction is a common escape habit in contemporary households. Instead of interacting with each other or engaging in work or leisure activities, family members escape into the fantasy world of TV programs. With this escape they may be able to maintain pleasant moods in spite of perpetual tension from lingering disputes and ongoing irritations, and in spite of a lack of personal interests or interactional nourishment from one another. The reverse can also be true. Television viewing can sap the time and energy that family members might otherwise utilize to engage with more vitality in their own and one another's lives.

Television watching was a central problem for Doris and Nolan, who sought therapeutic consultation after Doris had announced that she felt more attracted to men at work than to her husband. In fact, Doris and Nolan had been emotionally divorced for several years. They maintained isolated lives within the household by minimally interacting. Nolan watched TV during virtually all his time at home, experiencing more emotional investment in his favorite sports teams' performances than in his interactions with his wife or child. Doris sometimes yelled at her husband for choosing the TV over her, but most of the time she busied herself with her own activities.

The resultant disengaged family system, while holding little attraction for either spouse, felt "normal" to them. Although neither Doris nor Nolan reported using alcohol excessively, both had grown up in families with an alcoholic member. Their communication style, as well as Nolan's television addiction and Doris's codependency (avoidance of problems), perpetuated the dynamics of an alcoholic family.

Early in their marriage Doris and Nolan had attempted to deal with the differences of opinions and habits that newly married spouses inevitably face. Who would be responsible for which household responsibilities? How would they manage their finances, and who would spend how much for what? How much time would they spend, and how, with each of their extended family relatives? Instead of discussing these questions, however, Nolan and Doris criticized one another. As their disagreements grew more heated, neither Nolan nor Doris wanted to escalate the fighting, so they both withdrew to their respective corners. Gradually they ceased entering the ring of dispute. This ended the fighting but left hanging all the issues that need resolution to bring two individuals into a team relationship, into true marriage.

This couple's treatment exemplified a common problem with patients who practice escape. By the time Doris and Nolan began therapy, Doris had already become more invested in her escape into new relationships at work than in her old marriage. She expressed interest in understanding the pattern of avoidance, but showed little inclination to change the pattern. After three therapy sessions Doris admitted to her husband that her mind was made up on a divorce. Escape to a new situation can look more appealing, and sometimes is realistically more feasible, than trying to rectify old relationships. Nolan readily chose to move the TV out of their house. This change led to rapid improvement in his relationship with his daughter and to a healthier lifestyle, as he began exercising every evening. With respect to saving the marriage, however, it was too late.

Eating disorders: Malnourished and malnurtured

Eating disorders have much in common with addictive and obsessive-compulsive disorders. The common element in these syndromes is the pattern of avoidance of conflicts via preoccupation with a substitute conflict. Preoccupation with food provides distraction from troubling personal and interpersonal conflicts of real life.

Nancy, who was borderline anorectic and bulimic, binged periodically. When she binged, she would stay home in her apartment all evening instead of socializing. This pattern offered escape from her conflicts about obtaining social nourishment. Nancy longed for more friends yet feared that she would lose a sense of being a separate individual if she did reach out and make social connections. Preoccupation with food, with how much she was and was not eating, offered potent distraction from the potentially more gratifying but also more upsetting arena of social interactions.

Manifest conflict may express metaphorically a deeper underlying concern. For instance, conflicts about taking in food can be an expression of conflicts regarding nurturance. Patients with eating disorders may long for nurturance but fear that nurturance from others will compromise their independence.

Bruch (1973, p. 269) postulates that individuals with eating disorders have as their primary concern "the urgent need to be in control of their own lives and have a sense of identity." Concern for independence and identity separate from others coexists with the seemingly conflicting longing for connection with others, just as anorectics' obsession with controlling food intake coexists with an urge to eat.

Striving for perfection is another hallmark of individuals with eating disorders. A belief in perfection rests on good/bad, all-or-nothing thinking. The individual with eating disorder (or with other engrained avoidance patterns) typically sees every conflict as necessitating extreme solutions. The options are either indulgent eating or fasting. Comfortably moderated eating is inconceivable.

Because either/or thinking is antithetical to integrative problem-solving, conflicts are especially painful for individuals who think so rigidly. They believe that they can be *either* independent *or* connected with loved ones, *either* controlling *or* controlled in relationships. Without both/and options—to be independent *and* connected, and to share rather than have or give up control—the many paradoxes all of us juggle in daily life become overwhelming. Life becomes a series of uncompromising struggles.

Suicide preoccupation: Escape from living

Suicide offers the ultimate escape from life's challenges. Most individuals consider suicide only when no other options to a critical life dilemma look feasible. Thinking about suicide can actually offer a relieving distraction from preoccupation with a seemingly overwhelming problem.

Karen (introduced in Chapter 5) typically became anxiously immobilized in response to life decisions such as whether or not to change jobs or to purchase a home. At other times she fell into despair, resigning herself to her inner belief that she would never be able to have any of the personal relationships or work satisfactions that she really wanted. One of her primary modes of relief from conflicts, anxiety, and despair was to fantasize about suicide.

Karen's visualization of suicide options, down to the last detail, were so emotionally engaging that they distracted her from the upsetting conflicts in her life. Like any addiction, however, this mode of escape acquired its own power and danger. Repeated visualizations tend to increase the likelihood that a behavior will actually occur. Moreover, the time and energy that went into these lengthy visualizations depleted the time and energy left for living, contributing to Karen's sense of her life as barren and unfulfilling. The reverse was also true. The more unsatisfying her life, the more Karen escaped via suicidal preoccupations. This reciprocal causation perpetuated Karen's chronic unhappiness, avoidance of direct dealings with the frustrations in her life, and wish to utilize the ultimate escape, death.

Gambling: Compelled to win

A similar reciprocal interaction can occur between other compulsive activities and real life problems. The more overinvolved an individual becomes with an inherently highly compelling activity such as exercise, athletic competition, sexual adventures, or gambling, the more these activities exert their own pull in addition to serving as escape routes from other problems. At the same time, the more real life problems are ignored, the more they fester and become incentives to further avoidance.

Kurt would leave for a gambling club when conflicts arose with his wife; sometimes he even provoked fights as an excuse to be able to leave. Once he was at the gambling table, he would become wholly absorbed in the gambling, playing all evening and taking drugs to enable himself to stay awake as he gambled throughout the night. Although he sometimes won for a while, eventually he would lose large sums of money. These losses would then spur him to further gambling, as he attempted to regain his money, much as an alcoholic takes yet another drink to take the edge off a hangover.

Kurt's initial conflicts with his wife gradually disappeared from his awareness, supplanted by preoccupation with winning and with winning back his losses. Over time, as interest in his spousal relationship faded by comparison with the intensity of the gambling experience, the marriage became even more unpleasant, the absorption in gambling further intensified, and the cycle of both worsening family relationships and a deepening gambling addiction escalated.

Intertwining of addictive habits is not uncommon. Excessive pursuit of multiple satisfaction-inducing activities could be accounted for by assuming that such individuals have a high need for stimulation. Interestingly though, the same intertwining occurs with individuals with eating disorders and other obsessive-compulsive patterns, whose distracting activities are not even pleasurable.

Kurt drank and smoked steadily when he played cards and then often concluded his evening activities with an extramarital sexual encounter. Sometimes, particularly if he was losing at the gambling table, the drinking was further enhanced with other drugs. Cocaine, marijuana, or whatever else was available augmented the basic conflict strategy, i.e., to feel better by doing something other than addressing the problem that was evoking the initial unpleasant feelings.

This chapter concludes the presentation of the five primary styles of response to conflict. Like primary colors, each of these response styles comes in multiple hues and intensities. Also like colors, the five styles can be blended with one another or sequenced. Each individual, couple, and family develops characteristic blends and sequences of these conflict responses. Individuals who enjoy robust emotional health routinely engage in cooperative problem solving when they are faced with conflict. Serious disturbance, by contrast, can be indicated by extreme or rigid use of one or several of the oppositional conflict modes. Severe psychopathology can also be indicated by a breadth of poor responses to conflicts, as exemplified by individuals with borderline features, for whom anxiety, depressive episodes, raging, and addictive behaviors all intermix, creating an emotionally chaotic way of life.

CHAPTER 9

Negotiation Patterns and Family Structures

THE CRITICAL DIMENSION THAT differentiates healthy and dysfunctional families is the ability of family members to talk with each other about problems. In a nurturant home environment, family members express what they feel, listen responsively to each others' concerns, and find solutions that work for everyone involved. Maintenance of this kind of climate requires communication and negotiation skills. These skills rest on a base of respect. In a well-functioning family the adults respond respectfully to their own needs and desires, to their spouses', and to the concerns of each of their children.

CONFLICT AND TRANSITIONS

Family theorists have pointed out that family difficulties tend to erupt at transitions (Carter & McGoldrick, 1989). The family life cycle requires adaptations from everyone as singles become a couple, the couple learns to raise children, the children become adolescents, the nuclear family contracts back to just a couple, and the couple becomes a lone survivor. Each individual family member's personal development also requires family adaptation. The growth of children, for instance, necessitates periodic structural and attitudinal shifts from parents and siblings. Infants, toddlers, school-aged children, and adolescents have different needs and can contribute in different ways to the family.

Transitions often are marked by entrances and exits from the family (Carter & McGoldrick, 1989). Marriages, births, adolescents' leaving home, extramarital affairs, deaths, divorce and remarriages change the composition of the family and hence affect the roles and relationships among family members. Transitions also can be precipitated by what Pittman (1987) calls "bolts from the blue," i.e., unexpected changes such as financial reversals, moves to a new community, and injury or illness. Whatever their causes, these changes often precipitate family crises. Previously satisfactory family structures may become outmoded in the new conditions. Customary family routines governing closeness and distance, division of labor, hierarchy, and alliances may no longer suffice. To adapt to new situations, although family members need to be able to problem-solve together, to exchange viewpoints regarding the changed circumstances and to find commonly satisfying solutions, this adaptation process does not necessarily require that someone say explicitly, "Let's sit down and talk this over." Brief but honest exchanges of information often suffice. In one form or another, however, the affected individuals need to accept the new conditions and find new patterns of behavior that work well for them and for the rest of the family.

The critical factor in a well-functioning family is not the presence of stresses, change, or trauma per se but whether the system's conflict negotiation capabilities are adequate to the task. Can the family assimilate ever-changing data about each member's needs and adapt to each new set of circumstances? Healthy families continue to function as a cooperative team through even the most stressful circumstances:

> All the attributes of a healthy couple come to fruition in the skill of negotiating problem solutions that meet both people's needs. To see a healthy couple or family work on a task is a systems researcher's delight: Boundaries are clear, mixed feelings are resolved, caring is expressed, goals are defined and decisions are made. (Beavers, 1985, p. 82)

On the opposite end of the continuum, severely disturbed families cannot assimilate new realities. Distressed couples have noticeably poor communication skills (Gottman, 1979; Jacobson & Holtzworth-Munroe, 1986). Unable to problem solve about even the simplest problems, they may live in perpetual turbulence or shatter into isolated fragments via separation or divorce.

Most families from time to time utilize all five of the primary responses to conflict—fight, submission, immobilization, flight, and problem-solving. Resentment, blame, and criticism may fester until tempers heat up into explosions. At other times one person may dominate and others give in. The family may sustain a state of tension as awareness of a problem hovers over the household with no one clearly addressing the issue. For a while everyone may avoid talking about a dilemma. But the bulk of conflicts in a healthy family are handled, eventually at least, with constructive information exchange and solution-seeking.

Sometimes individuals, pairs, or the whole family may develop a rigid use of one conflict processing style. Families seeking treatment have usually reached a point where constructive talking is minimal and at least one of the four self-protective response styles has become predominant. Rigidity develops as reciprocal interactions reinforce one another over time. For instance, spouses may get irritated at each other and exchange complementary criticisms. Faced with a problem that is not becoming resolved, they may then interpret the situation as needing more of the same, in this case more anger and criticism. Such "more of the same" thinking—if I just get angrier, wait a bit longer, give in just one more time, take one more drink— exacerbates the problem. The real life dilemma can get lost as fallout from the anger, depression, anxiety, or addiction increases. Consequently, by the time couples or families seek treatment, they may no longer even recall the circumstances that required adaptation in their family structure. Instead, they see only the havoc wreaked by their misguided attempts at solution.

> Leroy and Lucinda were locked in chronic antagonism. The angry interactions had begun in response to Leroy's emotional involvement with a female work associate. This extramarital intimacy had been a response to growing distance between the spouses. They had evolved a strained and increasingly disengaged relationship as they avoided addressing and possibly fighting over the many little issues raised by having children.
>
> The original conflicts involved financial decisions and allotment of responsibilities for childcare. Sidestepping the tension around these perpetually unsettled conflicts, both spouses absorbed themselves in work outside the home. Gradually the disengagement in their marriage and overinvolvement in work led to a new set of problems, the extramarital relationship. Instead of directly discussing their differences with soul-searching and information exchange, Leroy and Lucinda took what they experienced as the defensive, self-protective route, i.e., attacking one another with criticism, blame, and raging.
>
> By the time Leroy and Lucinda sought therapy they were both seriously considering divorce. Lucinda was infuriated by Leroy's incessant criticism and Leroy was no longer willing to tolerate his wife's frightening bouts of explosive rage. The initial differences of opinion about children and money had long since been buried under the difficulties caused by the poor conflict communications.

REGRESSION ON THE HOME FRONT

Many people address their spouses in derogatory, sullen, or antagonistic ways that they would never use toward work associates or friends. Usually people do more of what works. Since cooperation works, why don't family members always cooperate? Why do rifts and battles emerge? One obvious answer is that family members live with more interdependence than work associates or friends. Family members' actions impinge on one another because they share the same physical space, financial and emotional resources, etc. More issues arise which therefore need a common plan of action.

A cooperative pattern, with niceness begetting niceness and both spouses feeling optimally satisfied, is evident in many marriages. Partners learn that if they try to be responsive to one another, both will benefit. These couples develop patterns of solution-building that feel fair to both spouses. Such patterns needn't be highly sophisticated to yield a sense of ongoing cooperation. For instance, solutions can be win-win because of a pattern of sequential rather than fully integrative satisfactions; that is, "We'll do it your way on this issue and mine on another issue that's more important to me" can suffice to maintain harmony. But, overall, these spouses learn that cooperation works; by trial and error they learn to settle disputes with sensitivity to both of their needs.

The natural learning situation provided in a marriage, which should gradually teach and reinforce cooperation, tends to be undermined by the presence of strongly felt issues. Intense fears, resentments, and longings can override goodwill, stimulating self-protective responses instead of cooperation. When differences arise on issues that evoke strong feelings, when too many issues arise at one time, or when one spouse is routinely self-focused and nonresponsive to the other, then self-gain-only interactions may emerge. Danger lurks if the spouses then become locked into cycles of dominance-submission, attack and counterattack, fight-flight, or mutual avoidance.

The tit for tat model suggests that forgiveness pays. That is, rigidification of mutual "defections" can be prevented if one participant from time to time offers a cooperative move to break the pattern. If the other is able to respond to a generous gesture with a similar gesture, cooperative interactions can be resumed. But when spouses are in conflict over issues whose costs and payoffs feel extremely high, they may be extremely wary of risking generous moves, even after a period of distressing lose-lose interactions. Just as tennis players are apt to interact with cooperation when playing for exercise and fun, but with more intensity and self-interest when playing in a high stakes money tournament, family members may become more self-oriented when they feel intensely threatened or wanting. Less emotionally healthy individuals tend to feel more intense desperation about what they want. As Angyal (1965) writes, "It is not "I would like to do this or that," but "I must do it *or else*" (p. 82).

Psychodynamic and behavioral theories share a second explanation (also discussed in Chapters 3 and 4) for why so many people handle conflicts less well at home than outside of their families. Home is where we feel we can let down our hair, slip off our shoes, and slip into a more natural, less controlled way of being. Alas, what comes naturally, as the insightful Haim Ginott once observed, is the pattern we learned in our families as we grew up. Whether we call these patterns Piagetian schema, psychoanalytic transferences, or learned habits, the reality is that family-of-origin patterns tend to be carried over into families of procreation, even when the same individuals function markedly more cooperatively at work and with friends.

Thus, individuals who enter marriage with a personal history of emotional difficulties start with two disadvantages. First, they may have accumulated a greater reservoir of unmet needs and intense feelings about getting what they want, making cooperative negotiations more risky and generous moves less likely than purely selfish actions. Second, because they typically have come from families that did not model cooperative problem-solving, they may lack skills in this area.

Nonetheless, modes of negotiating conflict play a pivotal role in determining a family's well-being. Negotiation patterns determine to what extent the family will succeed in resolving questions from sexual life to child care and from who does the laundry to what movies they see. The quality of the solutions to all of these decisions tends to be a function of the extent to which family members are able to express what they want, to listen to one another, and to seek mutual solutions. And family conflict resolution patterns determine family climate. How the individuals go about getting what they want determines if the household will be turbulent, heated with frequent controversy, icy with cold resentment, frozen in tension, dark with hopelessness, or brightly warmed by the glow of caring, listening, cooperative responding, and affection. Individuals whose concerns are not heeded in the family will almost inevitably experience the home climate—and thereafter the world—as frightening, toxic, or depriving.

CONFLICT PERSPECTIVES ON FAMILY STRUCTURES

Poor solutions to family members' conflicting wishes can yield (and stem from) defects in the family's structure—the family's shape with respect to solidarity, hierarchy, division of labor, boundaries, alliances, and so on. Such defects can be regarded as analogues of symptoms in individuals. All individuals experience, and need to experience, positive and negative moods, anxiety to signal difficulties, irritation when they are not getting something they want or when others seem provocative, and the impulse to take a break from challenges when they are feeling "burned out." These normal and healthy emotions can be well-managed. If instead they become unbalanced and extreme, they can become clinically significant symptoms, such as depression, anxiety, excessive anger, and substance abuse. Similarly, all families need to negotiate closeness and distance among members, to establish appropriate hierarchy between generations, to distribute responsibilities for accomplishing the tasks that are required to keep a family functioning (housekeeping, child care, food distribution, financial input and management, etc.), to maintain boundaries that clarify who is in and who is out of the family unit, and to foster intimacy between family members. These structural patterns become symptoms of family dysfunction when developed into excessively disengaged or emmeshed family bonds, rigid or collapsed hierarchy, poorly defined or inappropriately allocated division of labor, impenetrable or overly permeable boundaries, and inappropriate alliances.

Suboptimal family structures generally need to be addressed early in treatment and noted every time they surface. Like individual symptoms, structural defects in a family system may emerge as a result of poorly resolved conflicts, and also can interfere with resolution of conflicts.

Problems in regulation of closeness and distance: Enmeshed and disengaged families

Families need to offer each member developmentally appropriate degrees of freedom, as well as the security of a nurturant home environment. Angyal (1951) posits that these seemingly contradictory needs, for independence and for belonging, constitute essential paradoxical aspects of the human condition.

> The overall pattern of personality function can be described from two different vantage points. Viewed from one of these vantage points, the human being seems to be striving basically to assert and to expand his self-determination. . . . This tendency which I have termed "the trend toward increased autonomy"— expresses itself in spontaneity, self-assertiveness, striving for freedom and for mastery. . . . Seen from another vantage point, human life reveals a very different basic pattern. . . . The person appears to seek a place for himself in a larger unit of which he strives to become a part. . . . In the second tendency he seems rather to strive to surrender himself willingly to seek a home for himself in and to become an organic part of something that he conceives as greater than himself. (p.131)

A healthy family manages to provide *both* autonomy and a sense of belonging for each of its members, rather than either/or solutions. Healthy couples and families, for instance, develop a rhythm of together and separate times. These relationships breathe in and out, accordion-like, with periods of intimacy alternating with periods of individual identity. The in-and-out rhythm flows daily, typically with morning and evening together times and mid-day independent functioning. A larger cycle flows similarly through the week, with more separate time during the week and an increase in shared activity during the weekends. The flow through the year may also develop a rhythm, with couple and full family vacations punctuating longer periods of school and work.

Closeness and distance are also a function of the degree to which family members care about, try to influence, and help one another. Siblings or spouses who are "close," for instance, interact more frequently than those who are "distant", not only because they share more common time but also because they are more interested in one another's lives. They enjoy hearing about each others' separate experiences and try to be helpful to each other. Family members who are optimally close pursue individual interests, capabilities, and friendships; they then bring these individual experiences home, enriching the full family and sometimes also drawing on the resources of other family members for emotional and practical support.

> The Hillander parents and their four children, who ranged in age from 10 to 17, were all involved in activities outside of the home until supper time. At dinner, beginning with preparing the meal, the family enjoyed time together as a family. Each family member typically related experiences from his/her day and shared the others' joys and disappointments. Dinnertime also included heated discussion of family matters, laughter over new jokes, exploration of religious and political issues, occasional bickering, and general camaraderie. Dinner ended with everyone clearing the table and washing dishes, usually to the accompaniament of fairly loud rock or folk music.
>
> After dinner the siblings worked separately, some retreating to their rooms and some remaining in the kitchen or family room to complete homework and practice musical instruments. These hours also involved considerable interaction as they discussed with one another how a snag in the science fair project could be overcome, how to improve a song, or what they each thought about the latest boy and girlfriends. The parents helped their children with school-work, chatted with each other or the children, and sometimes worked on their own household or individual projects. Early the next morning everyone again went their separate ways for school and work.

To a large extent, cycles of together and separate times develop naturally. At other times, individuals' agendas seem to conflict so that explicit negotiations become necessary. When these negotiations are ineffective, balancing closeness and distance can become a source of repeated hurt or controversy.

> On Friday evenings the Hillander family concluded the week with an elaborate dinner, often including dinner guests. Once they reached high school, Sally and Annie, the two older siblings, began to find that these family dinners conflicted with parties with their peers. They wanted to join their friends; the parents sympathized but felt that the relaxed time together at the end of the week was critical to maintaining the warm atmosphere at home.
> When party/family conflicts came up several weekends in a row, tensions began rising, launching a family discussion. The girls stressed the importance of going out on Friday nights in order to maintain their sense of belonging with their friends. They added that the parties lasted until midnight, beginning to get lively at about ten o'clock. The parents emphasized the high value they placed on family unity, and the importance of a full evening together on Friday nights to sustain that sense of family togetherness. They noted that the critical hours from their point of view began at about 5:30, when everyone set the table and finished the cooking, and ended by 10:00, by which time the adults and younger children were usually tired and ready to retire. Everyone agreed on the importance of family time and of teenage socializing time. By adapting the schedule so that dinner began somewhat earlier, they were able to sustain the leisurely Friday evening meal and relaxed family time, and then for the girls to go out.

As this above example illustrates, closeness and distance issues spark many family disagreements because of the frequency with which these patterns must be renegotiated. Each developmental change may require readjustment of the routines. Young children need an adult nearby all the time. Adolescents want to spend as much time as possible with friends. Newlyweds need much shared time to consolidate their relationship. Older married couples may prefer to use more of their leisure time in independent activities. Each of these modifications in circumstances necessitates adjustments in the together/apart arrangements.

> When their children were younger the Hillander parents, Bill and Stacy, had had time to sit and talk every night after the children were in bed. Now the adults went to sleep before all but their youngest child had even finished their homework. Although their family felt warmly interactive, Bill and Stacy felt that as a couple they had grown too far apart. With so little time left after work and children, they both jealously guarded occasional moments when they could pursue their own individual interests. Couple time seemed to have become a last priority.
> The extent to which the situation was becoming problematic showed up in both Bill's and Stacy's feeling ignored by the other. As they discussed their mutual sense of emotional malnourishment, they each expressed their own feelings rather than accusing the other. They sought to describe the problem

in "I" and "we" rather than "you" terms. Rather than, "You have time for everyone in the family but me," they each in different ways expressed, "I want more time alone for the two of us."

Agreeing that, "We are having trouble including couple time in the family routines," they were able to define their predicament in terms of the family's development instead of either spouse's fault. With this systemic view they were able to brainstorm together on changes that could help. They thought of several small alterations in their routines that could give them the needed time to rejuvenate their relationship without sacrificing too much of their availability to the children or of their brief times for personal projects. They could take some extra time in the morning together before they left for work. Instead of being so available to the children in the evenings, they could routinely slip away for at least a brief time after dinner by sequestering themselves together in their bedroom out of sight of their always-eager-to-talk sons and daughters.

The Hillander family was able to regulate closeness and distance by making continual adjustments and readjustments in their routines. Many families, however, have difficulty negotiating changes, lurching toward the polar extremes of disengagement or enmeshment instead of managing subtle modifications. In certain circumstances these extreme structural arrangements can be appropriate. For example, in times of external threat, such as war or economic disaster, greater interdependence is necessary; in times of plenty, less interreliance and more personal freedoms tend to develop. In most circumstances, however, more moderate positions are needed.

Families also tend to drift toward these structural extremes to the extent that they have been unable to resolve conflicting needs with cooperative discussion. When family members fear to address differences because they sense that voicing conflict will evoke angry interactions, they move toward the disengaged end of the continuum. They would rather interact less with one another than risk the eruption of fruitless angry confrontations. Families who are not intimidated by the expression of anger and who express their thoughts and feelings readily may tend toward the enmeshed end of the continuum. Their communication difficulties tend to be exacerbated by inability to hear one another's individual concerns, as anger begets defensive retorts, more anger, or depressive surrender.

Thus disengaged and enmeshed families are similar in that both have difficulties constructively handling conflicts between family members. The specific skill deficits and communication errors tend to differ somewhat. Avoidance and anxious immobilization tend to be primary response styles in disengaged families. Enmeshed patterns, by contrast, tend to evolve in argumentative and depressive families. Criticism, demands, and accusations generate (and emerge from) blocks in listening, angry fights and, for the losers of fights, depression. Because both disengagement and enmesh-ment stem from poor conflict processes, a given family can function in either mode at different times. Periods of fighting and distance can alternate.

> George developed problems with alcohol during his first year of marriage. His wife Leona expressed initial distress, especially when he would say he would be home at a particular time and then show up intoxicated several hours later. Leona's complaints were greeted with counterattacks. "You always are complaining, always nagging at me," he shouted. When Leona persisted in objecting to the drinking, the subject generated threats from George that he would leave her. Gradually Leona ceased to bring up the problem. Instead she gradually became overcommitted at work and began to look with interest at other men. The marriage then developed in the direction of disengagement. By the time they sought counseling, both George and Leona had considered hiring divorce lawyers, which would have consum-mated the trend toward disengagement with severance of the marital relation-ship.

The labels clinicians give to families may be a function of their negotiation styles. Families that show dominant-submissive and attack-attack patterns of conflict tend to be highly interactive, as individuals strive to get what they want by asserting their dominance. Because of their high quantity of interaction, these families are generally labeled enmeshed by clinicians. Less expressive families may be labeled disengaged irrespective of the actual intensity of emotional involvement.

As members of conflict-avoidant families become a collection of mini-mally interconnected individuals, they may give up caring as well as fighting. On the other end of the continuum, families who fight continu-ously or who persistently lock into dominant-submissive interactions often show enmeshment in the sense of overinvestment in one another's lives. A cost of this intense caring is that an individual in this environment can feel smothered by what other family members think s/he should do.

Asthmatic families typically show this kind of conflict resolution pattern coupled with overly intense caring about one another (Ford, 1983). Symbiotic parent-child or spousal relationships reflect an extreme of overinvolvement in one another's lives; one individual lives through another or is inappropriately reliant on another for some aspect of functioning.

Interestingly, however, the frequency of communications does not necessarily correspond to the intensity of family members' actual emotional involvement with one another. Some families are superficially argumenta-tive without a deep level of caring. In other families, the members appear disengaged because of the sparsity of their interactions, but actually experience profound feelings toward one another. In these instances, in contrast to their apparent distance from one another, certain individuals may be intensely emotionally preoccupied with others.

> Peter realized that he reacted to virtually everything his wife said by saying the opposite. They bickered whenever they were together. As he described it, every time she said "white," he said, "black." In retrospect, Peter realized that the bickering was intended to produce distance. He felt trapped in the relationship and wanted to extricate himself. Although Peter respected his wife, the depth of caring in this relationship was minimal even though the interaction level was high and intense.

> By contrast, Brian and Ellen came to therapy to seek help with "communication problems." They each related to their one daughter, but communication between the spouses had reached a virtual total impasse months before. As the therapist encouraged a reopening of communication within the safety of the therapy session, the floodgates opened with a surge of pentup hurts, resentments, and love.

Families locked in either/or thinking have difficulty conceiving of mutually beneficial solutions. They therefore can be particularly vulnerable to movement toward the extreme ends of the disengagement-enmeshment continuum. Their decisions may overvalue the individual at the expense of the group, or the group (or one member with special status) at the expense of individuals. Either of these directions of imbalance is likely over time to be less satisfying for family members than decision strategies that are able to generate integrative both/and solutions.

The terms enmeshment and disengagement, though cornerstones of systemic thinking, may frustrate the clinician because they seldom refer to discrete phenomena. Although occasionally families clearly do seem to fall on one or the other end of the continuum, most families show attributes of both enmeshment and disengagement depending on the criteria and the situation. Consequently, it is understandable that these terms tend to be used loosely, and to refer to different behavioral indicators for different therapists and with respect to different cases.

> When the Martin family first entered treatment no one said a word. The family seemed dead, and I felt like I was doing artificial respiration, forcing breath into members to get them to speak to one another. Once they began to breathe again, I felt as though my attempts to breathe life into the family had fanned the last embers of energy into flames of a conflagration. Everyone spoke at once, interrupting everyone else with angry introjections. I had to fight multiple brushfires in order to calm the family enough to engage them in productive discussion.

The Martin family then continued to show attributes of both enmeshment and disengagement. Sometimes the family members dealt with conflicts by fighting. Sometimes they were afraid to bring issues up at all. In general, the less dominating members (the mother and the three daughters) tended to remain silent, to refuse to talk, and/or to isolate themselves when issues concerned them. The more dominant individuals (the father and the son) did raise issues that concerned them, but in an overly strong manner. These conversations quickly became angry and argumentative.

In sum, families with conflict resolution difficulties tend to migrate toward the extremes on the disengagement-enmeshment continuum. If a family is having difficulty making decisions cooperatively, one tendency will be to avoid controversial issues via escape or immobilization responses. These strategies move family members further and further apart. When conflicting wishes and needs are handled by argument and coercive attempts, family members may tend toward enmeshment, excessive concern, and overinvolvement with each other.

Boundaries

Boundaries define permeability of a system or subsystem. External boundaries around a family group can be described as excessively thin or thick to the extent that people and information are allowed to pass from outside the group to within or from within to outside. Boundaries and enmeshment-disengagement are related but different aspects of family cohesiveness.

When the external boundaries are thin, family members are likely to invest more energy in interactions with nonfamily individuals than with one another. Such a family may be unable to bring all its members together for family therapy sessions. The external boundaries may also be excessively diffuse in the sense of not yielding clarity about who is in and who is out. Extramarital affairs may be more likely to occur. Children may derive little sense of security or identity from their family unit, feeling more solidarity with nonfamily groups such as gangs, peers, or religious groups.

At the other end of the continuum, a family may interconnect only minimally with outsiders, holding members closely within the family unit for most of their time, energy, and social needs. Holocaust survivor families, for instance, tend to hold closely to one another and to permit few nonfamily members (unless they are also survivor families) to become friends.

Paradoxically, families with thick or rigid external boundaries may have thin internal boundaries, and vice versa. That is, families that interact minimally with the external world may simultaneously have thin boundaries around the individuals, with individuals overly involved in one another's personal spheres. Likewise, a family system with fragile external boundaries may maintain thick and rigid boundaries separating individuals within the system. In these families, each individual experiences considerable autonomy and is relatively minimally influenced by others in the system.

One way to assess the boundaries around a family system is to look at how much time and what activities family members share with one another versus with nonfamily members. Families with thick external boundaries interact primarily with one another. Members of families with thin external boundaries interact mainly with people outside of the system, seldom sharing time or activities with one another. When they are together physically they may share common space with minimal interaction; e.g., he works on the lawn while she does the dishes, or he reads his newspaper while she takes care of the children, with neither spouse paying attention to the other.

> Charlotte and Clive (introduced in Chapter 8) developed the kind of thick external and thin internal family boundaries that are quite typical for an abuse-prone family. Clive was periodically physically abusive and chronically verbally abusive. Charlotte suffered from the depression characteristic of a battered wife syndrome. For the most part family members were overly preoccupied with one another and only minimally involved with others outside their emotionally intense family unit. Their involvement with one another was not over joyful shared activity. However, hostile encounters, such as the verbal and physical violence in this family, can be enormously absorbing.

Another indicator of external boundaries is information flow. Families with thick external boundaries sometimes develop a distrustful or disinterested relationship with the world outside their family group. By contrast, families with thin outer boundaries can be excessively influenced by information from outside the family. Children in these families may be more prone to influence from outsiders. By adolescence, for instance, having received less positive identity-forming input from parents, they are likely to be more receptive to religious cults, extreme political movements, the lure of drugs, and the appeal of peer culture than youngsters who have grown up in more cohesive and interactive families.

The strong influence of outside factors in families with thin external boundaries makes parent-child conflict resolution all the more difficult. The conflicts are triadic rather than merely dyadic, with the third leg of the triangle being the peer group. Extramarital relationships pose the same problem for couples, particularly if one spouse's outside emotional attachment has become as strong or stronger than the attachments within the family.

Boundary disturbances can be manifest in family members' habits of speaking up for themselves, speaking for each other, and interrupting one another. When individuals do not speak their minds at all, never venturing onto the first step of the conflict resolution road, excessive boundaries develop. Disengagement is likely to be a concomitant structural problem and conflict resolution may be nonexistent. On the opposite end of this continuum, when family members speak for and/or interrupt one another, these patterns signal enmeshment and overly permeable boundaries between individuals.

Nonexpression of feelings and, on the other extreme, interruptions and "mind-reading" are aspects of boundaries, evidenced in dialogue, that are strongly influenced by cultural norms. For instance, family members with ethnic roots in northern Europe are likely to expect a pause of several seconds to signal availability of air time between speakers. They see interruptions as rude. More emotionally expressive Mediterranean cultures, by contrast, may regard interruptions as normal, as signals of caring about the topic in question. Speaking for others can likewise signal a caring relationship to some and a discounting to others. When spouses interact with different cultural assumptions, one individual is likely to feel impinged on by the other, who in turn is likely to feel that his/her spouse is too distant and the boundaries between them too wide.

Even when family members all share the same rules, poor boundaries can hamper the smooth exchange of information between individuals that is necessary for cooperative problem solving. When family members do not speak their minds, for instance, sufficient details about problems are not exchanged, inviting misunderstandings from inadequate flow of information and halting the flow of discussions before a point of resolution. Discomfort with verbalizing thoughts, excessive talking, interruptions, passivity toward other speakers who continue too long, and speaking for others instead of saying what is on one's own mind all are aspects of boundary disturbances in dialogue patterns that can interfere with forward flow from conflict to resolution.

A particularly common and counterproductive boundary disruption, referred to by some as "mind-reading," occurs when one person says what s/he thinks another person thinks or feels. Individuals who speak for one another in this fashion often think that they are adding clarity to the discussion. If the statements about the other's thoughts and feelings ascribe negative attributes they will engender defensiveness and counterattacks, a pattern described in Chapter 7. Without negative attributions, mind-reading interferes with constructive dialogue by producing confusion. One person says, "You think that I . . ." The other tries to correct the misunderstanding by answering, "No I don't; I think that you, . . ." Family members' feelings and thoughts become increasingly muddled. Instead of pooling data and moving forward in problem-solving, the discussion detours into discussions about what each person *really* thinks. This side road detours participants and seldom leads back to a resolution pathway.

Furthermore, because each misreading of sentiments puts the misinterpreted individual on the defensive, considerable tension can be generated in such discussions. Consequently, the format, though seldom dull, is likely to lead to battles. The task switches from problem-solving to fending off others' misinterpretations of one's thoughts.

> Candy and Timothy came to treatment because of chronic arguments. One centered on golf.
>
> Asked to discuss this problem in the first session, Timothy began, "Well Candy, you think that I always want to play golf all day Saturday and all day Sunday."
>
> Candy, clearly miffed, hastily defended herself, "You are always telling me what I think, and what to do, and bossing me around." She concluded with a return mind-reading comment, "You think I'm your child, not your wife."
>
> As the therapist I felt myself drawn in, listening closely to make hunches about what each spouse really thought. I found myself guessing aloud that Timothy was worried that if he relented at all to his wife's concerns he would never have time for the sport he adored. I suggested that Candy feared she couldn't interact adult-to-adult with her husband. Then I realized that I had been pulled into the family pattern. I too was mind-reading.

Mind-reading is a kind of trespassing. It involves crossing the boundaries between one person's thoughts and the thoughts of another. Invasions of personal territory inherently provoke self-protective responses. On the other hand, if individuals do not open up and verbalize their own thoughts, they invite mind-reading from others.

Hierarchy

Hierarchy, another fundamental parameter of family structure, refers to relative power and status. This definition can be further refined by understanding the vague term "power" in terms of conflict resolution patterns. Power can be seen as the extent to which one individual's views influence the behavior and decisions made in conflicts between that individual and other family members. So-called power struggles are, in this view, attempts to be heard and thereby to affect decisions.

Several weeks after JoEllen's teenage son Morris had been hospitalized in a psychiatric unit for assessment of his rage outbursts and violent behavior, a hospital staff member described JoEllen to me as involved in power struggles with them. The hospital had been making unilateral decisions regarding Morris's length of stay and privileges to come and go from the hospital. In response to the hospital's disinterest in JoEllen's input, JoEllen began seeking unilateral power herself, demanding that her son be released immediately. Once the hospital staff scheduled time to sit and discuss their concerns with JoEllen, and asked about and heeded her concerns, a more cooperative atmosphere developed and the so-called "power struggles" ended.

Authority and responsibility are additional crucial dimensions of hierarchy. In a healthy family, at least by American cultural standards, spouses function as a team, and parents maintain authority over their children. Parents teach bilateral decision-making to their children by expressing their own preferences (wishes, values, etc), listening closely to their child's wishes, and then selecting solutions that will take both into consideration. In this manner they exercise authority and responsibility within a cooperative environment.

For example, the young child may say "I want to play more," and the parent may feel that it is naptime, that the child needs the rest and the parent needs a break. It is up to the parent to structure a mutually acceptable solution, and to implement this solution in a firm but kindly manner. Saying, "Let's bring a puzzle onto your bed, and you can play until you get sleepy," the authoritative parent takes the child's hand and begins walking toward the bedroom. Although the solutions are determined by the parent, what the child says s/he wants is considered important. The parent considers the unspoken needs of the child as well as those the child is able to verbalize. The parent's own needs are also relevant data in the decision.

As children mature, and especially as they approach their teenage years, they become increasingly able to share responsibility for decision-making. They learn to articulate their desires effectively, explaining rather than shouting or complaining. They grow increasingly less egocentric, becoming less exclusively focused on their own perspective and better able to understand their parents' concerns. They become creative at generating sensible solutions. If parent and child have been developing habits of mutual listening in the earlier years, by adolescence there is likely to be minimal battling, much dialogue, and only rare instances in which parents overrule teenagers' decisions.

Thus, although conflict resolution between parents and children ideally includes full consideration of both the parents' and the children's concerns, modifications in the form of the decision-making are necessary for different developmental periods. For win-win solutions to occur between parents and young children, the parents must be in charge. They guide the process of problem solving and bear responsibility for the decisions. Young children are developmentally egocentric and consequently are unlikely to seek out information about their parents' concerns. Effective conflict negotiation with this age group requires authoritative parental guidance. On the other hand, parents who retain too hierarchical a structure as children mature into adolescence will meet resistance from the children. While younger children can be encouraged to articulate their views within a context of parents making the actual decisions, adolescents need increasing responsibility in family decision-making, and broader realms in which they handle their own decisions.

Dysfunctional hierarchy is characterized by asymmetrical (win-lose) conflict resolution with winners and losers. Power in the wrong hands or too much power differential can both be factors. Whereas in a well-functioning family the parents are in charge, poorer functioning families often have collapsed hierarchy. Children control parents. Parents are overly influenced by their children and do not attend sufficiently to their own needs and judgments. Authoritarian parents can err on the opposite extreme by holding the reins too tightly and to the detriment of their children's needs. They may enforce their own preferences coercively, demanding that children comply with their unilateral decisions. "Do it because I said so!" is the parental response when differences arise. Data input is asymmetrical, so the parents are more aware of their own concerns than of the children's. Inadequate consideration is given to the needs and wishes of the child in settling parent-child disputes.

Neglect can be regarded as another form of hierarchy disturbance. Whereas collapsed and authoritarian hierarchies both suggest dominant-submissive forms of conflict resolution, neglect implies turning away from parent-child conflicts. Children's needs are ignored as parents abdicate from their responsibility for providing care for their offspring.

Lastly, conflicts between the wishes of parents and children can be handled in an inappropriately egalitarian mode. If there is too little power differential, particularly with younger children who are not yet developmentally ready to negotiate with equal power and responsibility for decisions, families become stressed by each and every small and large decision, from what to eat at breakfast to establishing bedtimes. In these families, for instance, bedtimes may have to be renegotiated nightly. Anxiety and/or continuous tension are likely to emerge because nothing is ever settled. Constant bickering may also occur, especially if every little decision activates the underlying question, "Who's really in charge here?"

Division of labor

Division of labor, allocation of the work that is necessary to sustain a system, connotes both a verb, reflecting the process of division, and a noun, reflecting the outcome of the distribution of jobs.

The process by which a family decides who will do what in the family can be authoritarian and dominant-submissive, with some people telling others what to do regardless of the others' concerns. The process can be conflictual, with ever-lasting battles about who will do what and how. It can be avoidant, with no clear decisions about who will be responsible for what. Or the process may be more sanguine, based on a cooperative pooling of information about what needs to be done, who prefers to do what, volunteering, and then clarity about who is responsible for which tasks.

If the process has been an open and cooperative one, the outcome will be responsive to the actual interests and abilities of each family member. If the decision process was poor, the outcome is more likely to be unfavorable for some family members. One family member can become Cinderella, assigned excessive responsibilities. Another can become Peter Pan, never expected to grow up, or an exploitative king, queen, or prince whom others are expected to serve without reciprocation. Division of labor can also err by being too vague, with certain family functions never accomplished because no one has clearly taken responsibility for them. Good division of labor implies that responsibilities for each aspect of family functioning are clearly delineated, with all family members contributing in a manner that is optimally matched with their abilities and interests.

Alliances

Alliances are subsystems within the family. Alliances often are productive. For example, when spouses form a close alliance, this couple subsystem enhances the emotional life of everyone in the family. Siblings thrive when they share a sense of solidarity as a group and know they can count on one another for support. By contrast, a lack of solidarity, reflected in spousal disaffection and sibling jealousies, can be disruptive to family (as well as to individual) functioning. Whereas rivalrous spousal or sibling relationships can undermine family members' self-esteem and form the template for uncooperative interactions with colleagues and marital partners in adult life, supportive relationships give life joy and give family members emotional resilience vis-á-vis life's challenges.

Sometimes, however, alliances can have a negative impact. If family members resolve conflicts by battling for dominance, each member may look to bolster his/her power by forming coalitions with others. These alliances are negative in the sense that they serve negative (fighting) ends and can have a toxic effect on family members. On the other hand, such alliances are understandable when family members cannot get their concerns heard without amplification from others. Wilmot and Wilmot (1978) point out that coalitions often are formed expressly to increase the power of one or more of the participating parties. Coalition formation consequently can serve to escalate conflicts.

> Coalition formation is escalatory because it (1) highlights the disparity of power between the conflict participants and (2) demonstrates an attempt to shift the power balance. Whether a small child is saying "my big brother is going to beat you up" or a political leader is discussing "cooperation between us so that we can overpower the opposition," the fact that coalition formation is a power move is apparent to all. (p.127)

> The Martin family exemplified shifting fighting alliances. The choosing of allies followed some consistent patterns and some issue-dependent patterns. Lila and Jim, the two eldest children, had virtually always aligned with each other until Lila as a teenager developed a close boyfriend. Jim then felt abandoned and switched to an antagonistic stance toward Lila. Monica, the middle sister, was often the outcast against whom the whole family teamed up. On the other hand, she and her youngest sister Mandy might join together on an issue of shared concern like borrowing the older teenagers' clothes or insisting to their parents that they be allowed later curfews. From time to time both Dad and Mom sought allies among their children to bolster their positions against one another. Dad and the only son, Jim, tended to back up one another against the females.

Alliances in this family were critical because issues were won or lost on the basis of being able to overpower the other side. Also, the outcome generally involved a winner and a loser rather than two winners. Enlisting allies who could amplify demands was a sensible strategy in this context.

Triangulation refers to a special kind of alliance—the involvement of a third person to alleviate problems between two people. For instance, a parent may confide his/her grievances with the spouse to a child. Triangulation can make the alliance of parent-child stronger than the marital alliance, an arrangement which is seldom desirable. An overly close parent-child relationship can become burdensome for the child, especially to the extent that the relationship serves the parent's needs to the detriment of the child's.

Sometimes parents develop an overinvolved relationship with a child that deflects negative feelings away from their spouse, a process Minuchin

(1974) calls detouring. Detouring relieves the tension from conflicts between the spouses by focusing negative attention on a child. The child's problems serve to maintain illusory harmony between his/her parents, as the one thing they agree upon is the deficiences of their child.

> The parents' detouring may take the form of attacking the child, defining him as the source of family problems because he is bad. In other families, the parents may define the child as sick and weak, then unite to protect him. (Minuchin, 1974, p. 102)

Triangulation can also occur in the form of two individuals' looking to a third to mediate their disputes. Third-party mediation can sometimes be helpful. For instance, when children are arguing, a parent may intervene effectively as negotiator. The ideal is probably for siblings to learn to resolve their own differences constructively. Until children are old enough to do this, parental mediation can offer a way to deescalate fights, maintain a sense of fairness and cooperation, and gradually teach cooperative conflict resolution skills. A mediator's role is not to be a judge who allocates blame. The parent who intervenes in sibling disputes by saying, "You are right and you are wrong," may be doing the children a disservice. Rather, the mediator's role is to facilitate effective problem-solving.

The flip side of alliances is chronic antagonisms, which can impede the flow of family problem-solving. Sometimes the chronic antagonism is simply habitual. Family members may be unaware of the negative tone in their voices when they address one another. Even if they are aware, they may talk in an antagonistic manner as a family style.

> Monica, the 16-year-old daughter in the Martin family, had chronically antagonistic relationships with all three of her siblings. Expecting negative responses from them, she had learned to talk in a provocative/defensive manner. She deprecated her siblings' concerns and expressed her own in a hostile manner that insured that others' responses would be unsympathetic. Her siblings likewise spoke in a derogatory manner toward her, and seldom took her concerns seriously. Each round of the interactions further reinforced the mutually hostile pattern.

After a period of hostilities over a specific dispute, negative reaction to anything the other person says or does can become reflexive. At other times antagonism emerges because the problem being discussed is contaminated by a countercurrent of emotions from another long-standing battle. If the ongoing antagonism is between siblings, for instance, the underlying issue may be dominance. Who is better, stronger, more likable, etc., may be chronically at stake.

As the Hillander and Martin families illustrate, closeness and distance, boundaries, hierarchy, and alliances affect how conflicts are handled. At the same time, conflict-handling patterns influence these structures. The relationship is reciprocal. The following chapters, on psychotherapeutic treatment, show the importance of attuning to both in order to help distressed families resolve their differences.

SECTION III

Treatment

CHAPTER 10

Overview of the
Therapeutic Journey

VIEWED FROM A CONFLICT perspective, the purpose of therapy is to help patients resolve their current troubling conflicts and, in the process, develop more constructive ways to deal with future challenges. Whatever the specific presenting problems of individuals, couples or families, treatment generally needs to include the following components:

- *Symptoms*
  a. Assessment of presenting symptomatology and, if necessary,
  b. Interventions to reduce symptoms
- *Content*
  a. Clarification of the content of the troubling conflicts
  b. Resolution of these conflicts
- *Process*
  a. Clarification of the characteristic patterns for processing conflicts
  b. Development of healthier resolution patterns

This chapter and the following, Chapter 11, clarify how these components can be arranged in a treatment and suggest criteria for making critical treatment decisions.

The specific goal of treatment at any given time determines the therapist's role. When working toward the first objective, symptom management, a therapist functions like a ski instructor who fixes any injuries and repairs malfunctioning equipment adequately enough to be able to proceed with a class from the top to the bottom of the mountain. Symptom alleviation interventions, in which the therapist serves essentially as a repairman or healer, are discussed in Chapter 12.

With respect to the second objective, resolving specific conflicts, a therapist functions like a ski instructor whose goal is to guide the skiers in his charge safely down a difficult trail. A therapist guides patients via leading questions and other active interventions that produce the communication patterns, depth and detail of understanding, and generation of options that will yield resolution. Chapters 13, 14, 15 and 16 elaborate on the kinds of interventions that facilitate these therapist-as-guide sessions.

By contrast, when the focus is on the third objective, improving patients' processes for handling conflict, the therapist becomes like a ski instructor whose intent goes beyond getting the skiers down a specific slope to teaching them the elements of effective skiing. The goal of this coaching is to enable the skiers to learn to ski down difficult slopes without an instructor. Chapters 17, 18, and 19 detail techniques useful in these therapist-as-coach therapy sessions.

Beitman (1987) has suggested that virtually all effective psychotherapy has four basic stages: engagement, pattern search, pattern change, and termination. In the initial stage, engagement, the presenting problems are clarified, and patient and therapist get to know one another well enough to form a cooperative working relationship. Research on the ingredients of a successful engagement indicates that teaching the client about him/herself, plus conveying kindliness, compassion, and warmth, constitute key ingredients in convincing patients to return to therapy after the initial intake session (Tryon, 1989).

With respect to termination, toward the end of treatment virtually all effective therapy concludes with a wrap-up debriefing phase. These final sessions generally include a review of treatment gains, exploration of feelings about ending therapy, and expression of appreciation and good-byes. Treatment within a conflict resolution perspective relies similarly on establishment of an effective therapeutic alliance at the outset of treatment and closure in a positive manner at the termination of treatment.

The following chapters focus on the treatment events that occur between engagement and termination. Beitman delineates dual therapeutic tasks — pattern recognition and pattern change. Psychodynamically oriented theorists typically emphasize techniques for obtaining insight, i.e., pattern recognition. By contrast, the usual emphasis of behavioral treatments is pattern change. A conflict resolution treatment plan includes both recognition of patterns and change in these patterns.

This dual emphasis is, in fact, common to most effective therapy. In a case study exploring differences between psychodynamic and behavioral approaches, Messer (1986) describes a man who entered treatment with concerns about sexual identity. A psychodynamic therapist would explore patterns in the man's feelings toward women, his homosexual impulses, and the roots of those feelings and impulses. A behaviorist might focus sooner on facilitation of changes, helping the man build a new lifestyle firmly based on one or another sexual orientation. However, both treatment approaches, if conducted by skillful practitioners, would include insight into current problematic patterns plus development of new and more sanguine patterns of behavior, cognition, and feelings. As David Ricks (1974) has shown, good therapists are more alike than different. Or as Wachtel (1987) writes, both insight and action are important in the process of change.

The following chapters illustrate how insight and action, i.e., pattern recognition and pattern change, are interwoven with a conflict resolution focus.

CASE EXAMPLE: GIFTS

The following case illustrates one basic layout for the main elements in a conflict-focused therapy. I present the case initially with the raw data emerging as it might in an initial consultation session.* I then show how this raw data can be rearranged into a conflict-focused format to provide a clear diagnostic map that can serve as a guide for treatment. Lastly I circle once more through the data—organized now into the three conflict arenas of symptoms, content and process—to summarize intervention options.

The assessment and treatment techniques described briefly in this case will be elaborated more fully in subsequent chapters. The case presented here is for readers to use as a kind of baseline to first clarify the formats they customarily rely upon for assessment, and then to augment these formats with the conflict-focused perspective. To obtain this kind of baseline it may be helpful for readers to pause after the initial case presentation and at that point to assess the case on their own prior to reading on.

This particular case involves a married couple. The same assessment and treatment model pertains, for conflict-focused treatment with patients in

---

*This portion of the case was written up by Nolan Saltzman for the Clinical Exchange section of the *Journal of Integrative and Eclectic Psychotherapy*, Spring, 1989. New York: Brunner Mazel.

individual treatment and for families. It is assumed that individuals, couples, and families all need to deal with conflicts in all three realms — i.e., intrapsychic, interpersonal, and systemic.

This potentially quite complex map is less intimidating than it might at first appear because of the number of reduncies in both content and process in the three realms. Also, the conflict is usually most salient in one arena. Furthermore, fortunately, resolution of a conflict in this salient arena often suffices to resolve the issue in all three arenas. In this respect, the ability of the human mind to generalize understandings generated in one life arena to multiple realms of experience is truly remarkable.

The raw data

Judy and Paul have been married for 12 years. She is 37, he is 41. Each blames the other for day-in, day-out discontents. Judy has climbed the executive ladder in a large advertising firm. She describes herself as always being frazzled, but not letting anyone know it. She "has shitty feelings" about herself. Paul is a medical researcher. Two years earlier he was promoted to a position he now describes as glorified note-taking. He feels trapped, because he cannot afford to go back to his low-paying research lab job, and there seems to be nothing opening up above him. He despairs, "There has to be more than this," but he doubts there is for him.

JUDY'S COMPLAINT #1.

I have no time for myself. Everyone in this family likes to eat and needs clean clothes. Everyone expects me to prepare meals, do laundry, and take care of the children. I work from six in the morning until Lisa's bedtime around ten. All I ask is 20 minutes for myself, in bed at the end of the day to read a book — before we make love. Paul, you're either grumpy because I keep you waiting, or you fall asleep even though I've just told you I put my diaphragm in. Why can't you wait 20 minutes?

PAUL'S RESPONSE AND COMPLAINT #1.

I always find myself defending this. Judy makes me feel like a panting dog. It's not that I want sex all the time, I want to feel Judy wants sex with me. You used to, Judy, or was I fooling myself? Now, it seems like another one of your chores.

JUDY'S COMPLAINT #2.

Maybe I would be more interested in sex if I felt you were interested in me. You're involved with your work all the time. If you hate it as much as you say, you should leave it at the office. You even forgot my birthday until I reminded you. Then you ran to the supermarket and bought me my favorite chocolate ice-cream pop. Cute, but I always get you a real present.

PAUL'S RESPONSE AND COMPLAINT #2.

Here we go again! I didn't forget your birthday, but it came after a long weekend, and I lost count of the date—I thought it was the next day. And I *did* get you a birthday present, a month before—the video camera. I gave it to you early, in the summer, so you could tape the kids.

JUDY: Some present—I paid half of it!

PAUL: I didn't want your money, but since you offered it, I thought you were saying that half [of the price of the camera] was enough.

JUDY: Oh! But it was our anniversary, and you'd given me earrings, so I thought this was another anniversary present, and you were spending too much. So, I gave you half—we both bought the video camera for both of us, I thought, for the family.

PAUL: No, the video camera, all of it or half of it, if that's what you wanted, was supposed to be your birthday present. I bought the camera first for our anniversary, but before I could give it to you, you dropped a big hint that you wanted earrings for your anniversary. . . .

BACKGROUND

Judy and Paul have a nine-year-old daughter, Lisa, and a five-year-old boy. Lisa's adjustment problems in school appear to reflect the conflict between her parents: She literally does better when they have a good weekend.

At the beginning of one session the therapist noticed that Judy drank a glass of ice tea all in one gulp. "You must be awfully thirsty," he said. That led to a remarkable clue to Judy's early life. She reported a lifelong tendency to drink a whole glass at a time, along with a feeling that she can't breathe until she finishes. She modifies the behavior for very hot or alcoholic beverages, but the panicky feeling is the same. She completed college in three years and zipped through her M.B.A. in one academic year and a summer term. The therapist asked Judy who was the first person who liked her doing things double-quick. Judy recalled her aunt relating that her mother, having been too "skittish" to nurse her daughter at the breast, bragged to a group of young mothers about bottle feeding Judy in record time; apparently she jammed the bottle into the baby's mouth, making her feeding into a kind of race.

In between her lightning accomplishments, Judy says she was, "the laziest person in the world." Before her first child arrived, she would often spend an hour soaking in a hot tub. However, when faced with a challenge, she would feel she was not allowed to breathe until she had overcome it. She is a perfectionist, which she traces to her mother's finding a minor fault in everything she did. She is pained and frightened by the praise her work earns from the president of the firm and her colleagues.

Judy's parents divorced when she was six. She remembers a few idyllic moments with her father while mother was away "for a rest," apparently a step away from a mental breakdown. Then, after the divorce, her father turned on her; she could never please him, he threatened to whip her for "sassing" him, and did whip her legs with his belt a few times. He did not seem so antagonistic to Judy's younger, more docile sister.

As a single woman, Judy alternated between one-night stands with "cool" sadistic men and longer involvements with passive, doting men. One man dated her for a year without making a pass. When she finally decided to seduce him, he proved to be homosexual. Judy suspects she had dated several homosexuals without realizing it. Paul is unassertive sexually, but lately she resents whatever appetite he shows.

Paul is a study in sabotage. He usually appears to work hard and comply with his obligations. Yet he feels trapped in his work and in his marriage, and he is angry about it. One clue is a grudging tone that creeps into his voice while he is being compliant. He cannot express his needs or his rage. He can only try harder, subtly screw things up, and withdraw.

Paul admits that he has always felt helpless against "the system." He does not work at a high enough level to design his own projects. At work, as at school, he has always taken what fell his way. He is afraid that if he were to stand out by asking for greater scope and independence, he would be fired.

Paul is angry at Judy for what he sees as her sexual and affectional holding-out. She makes him feel guilty about his sexual desires, which he finds intolerable.

Paul's father was a financial adviser to major underworld figures. A shift in gangland power compelled father to retire abruptly. He became morose, lived as though under house arrest, and consoled himself with his hobbies, cooking and baking. Perhaps partly as a result of overindulgence in his own creations, he suffered a fatal heart attack. Paul was then 13. Paul's father was proud of him, but in calling him "the professor" was also showing his doubt that Paul would ever make a great deal of money. Paul recalls his father shushing him out of concern for his mother, who may have been a cyclic depressive. A pretty, genteel woman, she never took a stand against her husband or asked questions. Her depressions and chronic headaches required quiet, kept her from working, playing with Paul, or enjoying anything except going to parties "all dressed up," or serving as hostess, when she was surprisingly lively and talkative.

Paul was an only child. Because of his father's secrecy and his mother's illness, he was never permitted to invite his friends home. He remembers hours waiting outside his mother's room to be allowed to come in. She would be in bed, sometimes weeping. When she embraced him, her arms lacked strength, her delicate fingers were cold, her smile wan.

Paul's father left enough savings and life insurance to support his family and put Paul through graduate school. Paul was a tense, studious young man, a loner. He rejected opportunities to make friends because he did not feel comfortable with others; he did not know what people wanted from him.

Assessment: Organizing and drawing conclusions from the data.

How we organize raw data determines and is determined by the therapy to follow. The raw data presented by patients can be organized around the three aspects of *conflict*:

- *Symptoms*: The solutions to, symbolic expression of, or by-products of poorly resolved conflicts.
- *Content*: Actual personal, family and work problems, and the underlying feelings, needs, and values that cause these problems to feel conflictual.
- *Patterns*: The processes (as opposed to the content) by which conflicting wishes, feelings, and thoughts are handled.

SYMPTOMS

The primary individual symptoms in "Gifts" are Paul's mild depression, Judy's anxious and overwhelmed "frazzled" feeling, Judy's anger, and the daughter's school adjustment problems, presumed to be secondary to her parents' marital difficulties. The main couple symptom is continual bickering. It is generally useful to assess each symptom with respect to when it first emerged, how frequently it occurs, and how disruptive it is to functioning.

The diagnosis, based on these symptoms, would be Adjustment Disorder. Paul and Judy have inadequately coped with the transition from single to family life. In addition, both are experiencing difficulties adapting to transitions in their respective careers.

CONTENT

Although conflictual issues can be listed as topics, delineation of the conflicting tugs and pulls is more illuminating. The "laundry list" of conflicts that cause Paul and Judy tension, distress or arguments includes:

- *Paul*: Wanting to change his work situation and fearing to attempt to bring about these changes; wanting to experience more sexual activity and fearing that his sexuality would make him seem "like a panting dog."
- *Judy*: Wanting sexual pleasure, appreciation and soothing, yet rejecting them; wanting to be successful at work and at home with her family, and yet not liking the way she feels "frazzled" at work and with "no time for myself" at home.
- *Couple*: Division of labor in the household, specifically, with respect to laundry, meals and child care; presents, what is given and how received; sexual activity, when, how frequently, and with what attitudes.

Note that this list expresses the manifest content of the conflicts. As each conflict is dealt with, the latent underlying issues will need to be explored.

While additional personal and couple issues are likely to be added as therapy progresses, making an initial list accomplishes several objectives. The list (1) provides an outline for treatment; (2) indicates how far along in treatment patients are at any given point; and (3) clarifies when treatment will be complete, namely, when all the conflictual topics have been brought to comfortable resolutions *and* when a more cooperative and effective mode of negotiating conflicts has been learned.

PROCESS

Paul manifests the passive, submissive (to a dominant other or superego) response pattern to conflict characteristic of people who experience depression. When Paul does fight back against Judy's criticism, he fights weakly and ineffectually. He despairs of getting his needs met, either at work or at home.

Paul will need to explore where he learned this pattern. The data thus far suggest that Paul learned submission from his parents' modeling and from his powerless position vis-á-vis both parents. Now, as an adult, instead of effectively voicing his concerns at work, Paul waits to be let in the door of a better situation, much as he helplessly waited "for hours outside his mother's room to be allowed to come in." And just as his waiting as a child led to only wan smiles and weak, cold-fingered embraces from his mother, waiting for his wife's sexual attention or for a better job leads to no genuine satisfaction.

Judy's attack-until-the-other-feels-like-shit response to conflictual situations is characteristic of people whose dominant emotion is anger. From her father Judy learned blaming and fault-finding instead of cooperative problem-solving. Judy's father "whipped" her both verbally and physically. She continues to whip herself with self-statements about being "shitty" and "lazy." She whips her husband with incessant blame (regarding their sexual life, "Paul, You're either grumpy . . . or fall asleep"), or sarcastic criticism (about the present he gave her, "Cute, but I always get you a real present").

Paul and Judy's conflicts involve interlocking of their personal patterns of submission and attack. The more Judy blames, the more Paul retaliates with ineffectual counter-accusations and feels hopeless about asserting his own needs. Paul's weak responses exacerbate Judy's frustration and resentment, evoking reiterations of her angry complaints. The cycle continues indefinitely, with Judy's complaints maintaining Paul's sense of hopelessness and inadequacy, and Paul's helpless responses in turn fueling Judy's anger. Framing their interaction in terms of reciprocal causation makes both partners equally responsible for changing the pattern.

Paul and Judy utilize the same patterns for handling intrapsychic conflict as they use in interactions with each other, with similar poor results. Paul has difficulty acknowledging to himself what he feels and wants. He suppresses these voices with domineering "facts" of why he can't get his wants met. "You can't afford to go back to the job you liked because it doesn't pay enough" and "Nothing better will ever open up" are indications of this kind of dominating, suppressing pseudo-ego responses to his impulses and wishes. As to Judy's pattern of inner dialogue, she might try to say nice things to herself, but then she probably negates these self-accepting thoughts like her response to her husband's attempts to express positive feelings to her with his gifts. The outcome is her chronic "shitty feelings" about herself.

In sum, assessment of the conflict *process* begins with identification of each family member's predominant patterns of response to conflict situations. As the individuals' patterns become clear, how their tendencies fit with one another needs clarification. Lastly, uncovering the roots of these patterns in the family of origin gives important depth to both the patients' and the therapist's understanding of the existing conflict processes. Discovering who in the family modeled this behavior (and why) and with whom the patient(s) developed the current pattern gives patients a more empathic view of their foibles, opening the way to change.

Treatment: From conflict to resolution

With the initial diagnostic data organized into symptoms, content, and process of conflicts, treatment can proceed in an orderly, systematic, and yet flexible and creative fashion. Additional assessment data, of course, will continue to be gathered throughout treatment, but the above picture provides a map for planning a treatment strategy.

TREATMENT OF SYMPTOMS

The symptoms in this case all seem to be of manageable proportions (not incapacitating, life-threatening, or likely to interfere with treatment). They also seem to be by-products of poor handling of conflict rather than biochemical dysfunctions or conditioned responses. Therefore, initial symptom reduction via medications or behavior modification is not necessary.

TREATMENT OF CONTENT

The "laundry list" of conflictual topics provides a treatment agenda. The therapist helps Paul and Judy air and iron out these issues one by one. The three steps in effective conflict resolution guide resolution, leading to new solutions that satisfy both sides in each conflict.

Expressing conflicting wishes. The first step is to delineate the two (or more) sides of a conflictual issue. Regarding sex, for instance, Paul and Judy each want to be convinced that the other really wants to make love.

Exploring underlying concerns. The second step in conflict resolution would be to help Paul and Judy explore their underlying concerns. These explorations must be symmetrical, with equal time and depth given to both spouses.

Judy's concerns in the sexual arena have both immediate and deeper psychological aspects. On the conscious and practical level, Judy feels depleted by the time she gets to bed and wants time alone to recharge. The division of labor in the household leaves her feeling overburdened and resentful. She is reluctant or unable to pace herself in a more self-responsive manner; after hurrying herself all day, she is exhausted by bedtime.

On a less conscious level, Judy longs for and yet deprecates pleasures from others, whether physical gifts or sexual attentions. When they are given to her, she has trouble believing that Paul's gifts and affection are heartfelt. She also misperceives Paul as demanding that she hurry up about sex. "Why can't you wait 20 minutes?" she complains, misunderstanding his fears that being kept waiting means that he is not wanted.

If these explorations are facilitated by brief and focused dives into relevant family-of-origin data, the therapy will have more depth and meaning. For instance, in discussing conflicts regarding their sexual inter-actions, Judy will need to explore her concern that her husband is not genuinely interested in her. Were the roots of this belief in her father's initially loving and then subsequently critical attitude toward her? Is her sense that she needs to hurry up for sex with her husband transferred from her mother's bottle-feeding attitude?

To help Judy discover these connections, when she is talking about one of these feelings, the therapist can suggest that she close her eyes and picture a time in her youth when she had experienced similar feelings. Since memories are often filed by feelings, the relevant parent-child interactions usually will come to mind with this depth-diving technique for accessing early memories.

Paul's sexual concerns are less evident, which is understandable given his pattern of nonexpression of his needs and wishes. Paul would need to be encouraged to articulate more fully what changes he would like in their sexual relationship. The data thus far suggest, however, that Paul's underlying concerns center on wanting to feel desired. Is this feeling a transference of his interactions with his depressed and cold mother? With his self-preoccupied father? Paul also needs reassurance that his sexual impulses are acceptable. His inhibition of spontaneous expression of impulses may derive from his youth when he was not allowed to express or satisfy normal childlike impulses to make noise and to have friends.

Again, as Paul's feelings in the current marital conflict (in this case, about lovemaking) emerge, he can be asked to close his eyes to explore into the associated family-of-origin memories. Once the origins have been uncovered in this emotional context, the therapist can ask, "What is the same now, and what is different with your spouse from how it was with your parents?" This latter question is critical for loosening the hold of old cognitive schemas on a patient's current perceptions.

As their underlying concerns emerge, Paul and Judy can begin to clarify how the concerns of each trigger and are triggered by the other's. By keeping busy with her household responsibilities Judy inadvertently sug-gests to Paul that his needs do not matter to her and that she does not really love him. Feeling as he always has, that his emotions should be suppressed and that his needs do not count, Paul makes little attempt to obtain a satisfying sexual life, inadvertently confirming Judy's beliefs that she ought to invest more effort in her household work and that her husband is not really sexually interested in her.

Choosing mutually satisfactory solutions. The third and last step in resolving each of their specific conflicts would be for Paul and Judy to devise new solutions cooperatively. With respect to their sexual activity, for instance, maybe Paul could handle the children's bedtimes, giving Judy time off earlier in the evening. Then Judy would hopefully feel more responsive and appreciative toward her husband, which would meet Paul's concern. The goal would be for Paul and Judy to create an evening routine that would make sexual activity more likely, safe, and gratifying for both of them.

TREATING THE PROCESS

As Paul and Judy begin to experience relief and renewed optimism from resolution of some of their conflicts, the emphasis can gradually turn to their conflict-handling patterns. The assumptions about themselves and about each other that have blocked cooperation need to be transformed. The cognitive habits and communication behaviors that have blocked problem–solving need to be eliminated. The negotiation skills missing from the problem-solving repertoire need to be added.

As Paul hears that his wife is thirsty for his affection rather than cold to him like his mother, he will be better able to express his tender feelings openly. As Judy realizes that Paul has been depressed and despairing, not intentionally depriving, she may feel less angry at him, be able to hear his needs, and begin to express her own in a more kindly manner.

Still, this softening in attitude may not be enough to change long-standing communication patterns. Paul and Judy may need explicit coaching, Paul to learn to express what he wants, and Judy to use positive and self-focused "I feel" and "I would like" statements rather than negative you-focused criticism and blame. Brief exercises would help convey and ingrain these new communication skills.

Paul and Judy can be encouraged to discover the well-intentioned ends which their seemingly self-defeating communication habits have been meant to accomplish. Even the most counterproductive conflict patterns generally emerge as solutions to real concerns. Paul, for instance, perhaps believes that his nonassertive, grudging compliance may prevent total rejection (job loss or divorce) even if it does not yield improvements in the work or family system. Judy may criticize in part because that was her family's mode of discussion, and also in part because she believes that being the first to criticize softens the criticism she expects from others. To evoke these legitimate intentions, patients can be asked to picture the positive outcome that they at some level envision their counterproductive behavior will bring about.

Once Paul and Judy have learned to open up areas for discussion with frank statements of opening positions and constructive "I messages" instead of attacks, they will probably need guidance in developing empathic listening skills. Paul and Judy also will probably need to learn to generate new solutions, to ask themselves, "So what can we do about this problem? What kinds of solutions can we come up with that will satisfy both of us?" They may need to learn to make explicit summary statements that insure that they conclude with similar understandings. Lastly, they will need to learn to ask, "Are there any pieces of this problem that still feel unfinished to either of us?"

Conflicts are the focal element of diagnosis and of treatment. By the end of treatment, Judy and Paul should find that their symptoms have been eliminated because their conflicts have been settled. Instead of bickering and blaming they should find that they are enjoying one another's companionship and affection. Moreover, they should be able to approach subsequent conflicts, which life inevitably will continue to provide, with deeper understanding of themselves and of each other, and with more effective cooperation.

CHAPTER 11

Essential Treatment Decisions

WHO SHOULD BE INCLUDED IN treatment sessions? When should the therapist serve as a healer, a guide, or a coach? When should the focus of treatment switch between symptoms, process, and content? This chapter suggests a number of principles that therapists can utilize in exercising responsibility for these treatment decisions. A first important issue, however, is *who* should be making these decisions.

Therapists can let patients decide which family members should be included in treatment and in what sequence problems should be addressed. A therapist can follow the lead of patients' assumptions about who should attend treatment sessions and patients' flow of thoughts. Many therapists, particularly those trained primarily to do individual treatment, tend to assume that the individual who initially requests treatment should be the primary participant. And "Go where the energy is" is certainly a time-honored principle of gestalt therapy. However, excessive therapist passivity with respect to these decisions can create a kind of collapsed hierarchy between therapist and patient, with the patient exerting inappropriate control or assuming excessive responsibility for treatment decisions. Similarly, therapists can err by too rigidly adhering to preconceived ideas about what should be discussed in treatment and who should attend treatment sessions.

A sculptor may begin by drawing a sketch of what s/he is trying to create from, say, a block of stone. Once the carving or chipping away has begun, however, the piece of material has its own peculiar demands. The demands of the sketch must be integrated with the lines and textures that emerge in

176

the stone. The artist responds simultaneously to internal images of what s/he wants to create and to each individual characteristic of the stone. The process, even with an inert piece of stone, is one of mutual and reciprocal creation. Psychotherapeutic treatment likewise emerges as a mutual creation in which patient(s) and therapist interweave and reciprocally respond to one another's agendas and plans for growth.

Therapeutic decisions thus are best resolved via a process of integrative conflict resolution. Therapists can err either by too passively following the lead of patients or by assuming that they know what to address without asking patients what they feel is most pressing. However, although the therapist must solicit patients' input, just as the decisions of a sculptor lie with the artist, not the rock, and just as parents must accept responsibility for directing their children's growth, treatment decisions are the therapist's responsibility.

WHO SHOULD BE SEEN IN TREATMENT?

To a man with a hammer, the world is a nail. Alas, this saying can be applicable to therapists. Too often, therapists decide whether to utilize individual, couple, or family treatment on the basis of their particular therapy training rather than on the nature of the problem. This mode of deciding who participates can lead to inadequate assessment and inappropriate treatment.

Misconceptions about how an individual (child or adult) is functioning can occur when the therapist has not assessed the identified patient both alone and in the context of his/her interactions with other significant family members. Someone who appears to be calm and delightful alone can present rigid stubbornness or raging fury in a different context. Likewise, hearing about other family members only through the patient's viewpoint can lead to misjudgments about them. For instance, individual therapists must guess whether the spouses of their patients are being accurately described if they are relying only on the data that has been filtered through their patient's perspective.

Moreover, individual therapy has a definite, but not always beneficial, impact on the patient's family. This unfortunate reality has been studied particularly extensively in the case of agoraphobia. Goodstein and Swift (1977), reporting on the individual treatment of three agoraphobic women, found that one resulted in divorce, one led to the husband's developing severe depression (which lifted with conjoint marital therapy), and the third was precipitating dissolution of the marriage when conjoint therapy was initiated to ease the marital strain. Hafner (1977) studied the husbands of 30 married agoraphobic women before, during, and after their wives' individual treatment. He discovered that a significant proportion of the husbands reacted adversely to their wives' symptomatic improvement, with several developing serious psychological problems.

Similar evidence that progress in individual therapy often negatively impacts spouses and marriages has been found with other emotional disturbances (Hand & Lamontagne, 1976; Marshall Neill, 1977; Mayo, 1979). The emergence of spouse and marital problems as a side effect of individual therapy appears to be far more than an occasional phenomenon.

Several studies have indiciated that marital distress is associated with a greater likelihood of treatment failure or relapse (Milton & Hafner, 1979; Rae, 1972). For instance, Rounsaville, Weissman, and Prushoff (1979), looking at individual treatment with 22 depressed women who reported marital disputes, found that two-thirds of the marital relationships did not improve during the course of treatment, and these women remained depressed or worsened. Sims (1975) found that poor marriages were a predictor of poor therapeutic outcome irrespective of the diagnosis of the individual in treatment; that is, the impact of the family system was stronger than the impact of therapy.

Such results, while disturbing, are understandable. If emotional disturbances arise when an individual does not have better options for negotiating the conflicts with significant others, improving the emotional state must go hand in hand with changing the ways in which conflicts have been and will be handled. To change conflict patterns, all parties involved in the conflict need to make changes.

Given these research findings, how should decisions be made with respect to individual, couple and family treatment? Martin (1977) and Dare (1986) suggest that the critical factor to consider is the patient's current social system. They propose that, with only a few exceptions (delineated nicely in Martin's landmark paper), virtually all married people should be treated in a couple format. Children are best treated with the full family system except, perhaps, when they are responding to a trauma or developmental crisis wholly unrelated to the family (which is rare). Unmarried adults, in the life stage transition between the family of origin and the family of procreation, can be appropriately treated in individual (or group) therapy. Adolescents, because they should be differentiating from their families of origins, may best be seen in a combination of individual and family sessions.

With these guidelines in mind, I routinely ask new patients calling for an appointment if they are single or married. If they are married, I suggest that both spouses should plan to attend the initial treatment session and that both spouses will probably be involved in some fashion in the ongoing treatment. If the individual with a presenting problem is a child, the entire family is included at the first session. At various points in the subsequent treatment, sessions may include the full family, the child and parents, parents alone, the sibling subsystem, and/or the child alone.

When symptoms are conceptualized as consequence of poor interactions over conflictual issues, it becomes understandable that treatment of individuals without their spouses, or children without other family members, vastly decreases the therapist's leverage. Like a coach trying to work with only one side of an athlete's body or with only half of the team members, the therapist who treats only part of the family system works under severe constraints.

Furthermore, as the research confirms, the patient in individual treatment and the patient's family system are put under iatrogenic (treatment-induced) strain. At home the patient must become the therapist, the change agent, and the spouse must be willing to become the recipient of his/her marital partner's new change agent role, in order for the couple to adapt to the growth initiated in the therapy office. Resilient individuals and couples sometimes can manage this challenge. For a couple whose relationship is already characterized by avoidant or antagonistic communication patterns, this additional challenge can become overwhelming.

> Lily sought help for low self-confidence. She described herself as never trusting her own opinions. Lily's husband Jim agreed to join her in therapy. Jim's attitude toward his wife, which clearly reinforced Lily's attitudes toward herself, was, "I know and am right, and you, poor thing, just don't understand." If Lily had been in treatment alone, Jim might have experienced her growth as threatening the stability of their marriage. Lily also would have found herself swimming against the current; maintaining a more positive self-image in the face of her husband's ongoing belittlement would have been difficult. Understanding and altering Jim's attitude and behavior were as critical to Lily's growth as her own self-explorations. Treatment in a couple format avoided defining Lily as the "sick" one. Instead Jim could mutually explore the reciprocal ways in which they triggered one another's superiority-inferiority stances, and together they could enjoy building a more sanguine pattern of mutual respect.

The strategy of routinely treating married adults with couple therapy must, however, be applied flexibly, with patients' concerns about couple or family involvement taken into consideration. When the steps in conflict resolution are applied to treatment format decisions, therapists can integrate their own rules of thumb with patients' specific concerns to find format solutions that are satisfactory all around.

On the telephone requesting treatment, Renalda expressed strong reservations about bringing her spouse to the initial consultation session. Her husband had been ill with cancer, and she did not want to add additional emotional stresses to those he was already struggling to handle. I proposed that we schedule an individual session for the initial consultation, suggesting that the husband might need to join subsequent treatment sessions. In fact, the single session proved to be enough to ease Renalda through her impasse to a resolution of the conflicts that had troubled her, and the spousal relationship was open enough that Renalda could implement these changes cooperatively with her husband without further therapist assistance.

Many married patients benefit from augmentation of the marital format with a brief series of individual sessions. Four circumstances in particular suggest that scheduling one or several individual sessions may be indicated. First, when one partner seems to be moving more rapidly in treatment than the other, individual sessions can facilitate the slower partner's growth. Although it is generally preferable to maintain symmetry with respect to the numbers of individual sessions for both partners, symmetry of learning speed is also important to monitor. This aspect of symmetry is addressed by giving the slower partner booster sessions so that s/he can keep up with the spouse's growth.

Lawrence and Alice had been divorced for eight years but still fought incessantly over child custody issues. Their battles were taking their toll on their children, one of whom was frequently depressed, so a therapist was engaged to help them learn to negotiate their child-related decisions in a more reasonable and cooperative fashion. Although Alice progressed rapidly, Lawrence was unable to let go of his angry mode of interacting. Additional individual sessions enabled him to understand more fully toward what end he maintained his anger, where this strategy had been learned in his family of origin, and how he could reduce his volatility.

Second, if one partner is unable to tolerate the self-exploration necessary to obtain therapeutic movement and refuses to continue in therapy, the stronger partner can benefit from individual sessions to learn to make the best of a difficult situation. Gaining a more accurate and sympathic view of the nonparticipating spouse can enable the spouse who continues in treatment to stabilize the marital interactions instead of falling into escalating conflicts.

Paula functioned well in many arenas of her life, but harbored rage at her husband that was of psychotic delusional proportions. The psychotic nature of her beliefs about him became evident when we tried to discuss her anger more dispassionately during the therapy hour. She was unable to tolerate disconfirmatory data, and after several sessions refused to continue in treatment, refusing medications also.

Paula's husband Joseph continued in treatment. Joseph was able to accept that a psychotic process was blocking Paula's ability to handle the conflicts underlying her rage. We discussed how he could keep peace in the household by skirting the topics that agitated his wife. Over a period of months and with this more detached stance from Joseph, Paula's rage subsided, but the delusional thinking never gave way to fully rational thought. After several years, Joseph eventually decided to obtain a divorce.

Third, sometimes an acutely troubling side issue arises for one individual while the couple is actively addressing an important couple issue. Scheduling an individual session for resolving the side issue can prevent breaks in treatment continuity.

> Bart and Jeanne were in the midst of a series of productive sessions. Bart suddenly faced a difficult and emotionally distressing problem with a business partner. Rather than lose the continuity in their couple sessions, we scheduled an individual session for Bart. In this way Bart's individual needs were responded to without sacrificing the couple's progress on their shared issues.

Fourth, the initial couple evaluation may reveal that there is minimal spousal interaction in the presenting problem or potential for the spouse to be part of the solution. Some issues that individuals may benefit from exploring in sessions without their spouse include work-related conflicts, difficulties with members of the family of origin, or personal problems of long-standing origin—perfectionism, anger control, tendencies to shame and guilt, chronic self-doubt, or healing the wounds from early life traumas such as early parent loss, incest, or child abuse. Spousal attendance at sessions, however, can be valuable even when these seemingly individual issues are addressed.

> Hannah asked for help learning to deal with her mother. Each time she spoke with her mother on the phone she was upset for the subsequent several hours. Pregnant with her fourth child, she was dreading her mother's visit to see the new family member. The key intervention was to help Hannah understand that the mother suffered from chronic paranoia. However, the fact that Hannah's husband participated in the session with his wife added several dimensions.
>
> First, Hannah's husband added information, as he had been concerned about the mother for many years and had a more objecive perspective on her. Whereas Hannah saw her mother's paranoia as a relatively new problem, her husband was able to add examples of the illness from way back, suggesting that what was new was Hannah's ability to step back and see her mother's problems more clearly.

Second, as they built a mutual view of the mother, the couple could discuss how to handle Hannah's mother with a shared understanding, rather than returning to the pattern of argument that had characterized most of their prior discussions about this sensitive topic.

Sometimes exceptions to the couple treatment format must be made because work demands make one spouse genuinely unable to participate in the ongoing treatment. In this case, one option is to tape-record the sessions for the absent spouse to listen to and discuss with the in-treatment patient. Although full participation of both partners is definitely preferable, this strategy can work.

The caucus: When should the therapist meet alone with individuals in the midst of a couple or family session?

In political and business negotiations, large meetings are broken into smaller group formats when an impasse is blocking progress (Pruitt & Rubin, 1986). In particular, Pruitt and Rubin point out, caucuses provide an opportunity for excessive angry emotions to be ventilated without damage to the other negotiation participants.

> People in escalating, competitive struggles typically experience a great many angry, irrational feelings. Although these feelings may sometimes reflect deep-seated concerns that are not easily brushed away, at least as often they constitute "hot steam," the venting of which permits the principals to work more effectively toward a settlement of their differences. . . . Heavy venting, involving heated accusations and insults, should ordinarily not be allowed in the presence of the adversary, because that might poison the relationship. The third party should allow such venting only in private "caucus" sessions. (p.177)

In the context of couple or family therapy, smaller subgroup meetings can occur within the therapy room. These caucuses can be conducted within the hearing of other family members if the therapist simply focuses temporarily on the one individual or subgroup (e.g., siblings) whose emotional intensity has increased beyond the range for constructive inter-action. At other times, the therapist can ask the rest of the family to leave the therapy room for a few minutes. With the others out of hearing, the therapist and upset patient can sometimes more easily clear the emotional blockage and make way again for productive explorations and resolutions.

Margaret and Michael had been in therapy for several months when, in the midst of a quiet but intense couple therapy session, Margaret suddenly erupted into agitated shouting and rage. Her behavior looked angry. Her subjective experience, reported later in reflecting back on the incident, was of panic.

Simplification of the environment can be a first priority in moments of acute behavioral disorganization (see Omer & Spivak, 1987) such as Margaret was manifesting. I immediately asked Mark to step outside into the waiting room. I could focus exclusively that way on soothing Margaret, who soon calmed down. Once she was out of her panic state, Margaret was able to reflect back on her episode. She recalled that she had suddenly come into contact with an issue that made her feel furiously angry at her husband. Simultaneously, she had felt terrified that her anger might burst out, hurting her husband's feelings and threatening the security of their tenuous relationship. She was sensitively attuned to her husband and wanted to protect him from the pain which she feared these revelations might cause him. At a less conscious level, she also feared that his distress could cause him to abandon her. The intense conflict, thus, was between an urge to express what she felt and terror about expressing the feeling. Once the intense affect had abated and Margaret understood what had happened, we invited Michael back into the session and productively discussed the episode with him.

It is always a concern that family members excluded from the caucus (as well as from individual sessions within an overall couple treatment format) will worry about what is being said about them in the private sessions, particularly if they tend toward paranoid features. My own experience, however, is that appropriate reassurance that the private session is in their best interests suffices and that the gains of an occasional caucus are well worth this risk.

A related problem with caucuses and individual sessions within a couple treatment format is the issue of confidentiality. Should information divulged in individual sessions be aired in the couple and family format? Although different positions are possible on this issue, my own preference is to be willing to share the burden of secrets but to encourage patients to share whatever is troubling them with their spouse or family to the extent that this is possible or appropriate. The privileged information also can help the therapist know what to probe for in subsequent sessions.

Sondra confided in an individual caucus that her overflow of tears in the session was really from upset because her husband had slapped and kicked their son during the prior week. She had been unable to confront him about this incident in the therapy session, and he had made no mention of it. As a result of this brief caucus, in subsequent sessions I looked for leads that could allow me to ask the husband to talk more about how angry he gets at his son. Supportive questioning enabled him to describe the incident without either his wife or I having to "tell" on him.

In sum, unmarried adults may need to be treated in individual therapy. Virtually all other patients can be treated with more leverage in couple or family treatment. Adolescents benefit from some of each format since individuation from the family of origin is one of the developmental tasks at that age. Asymmetries, blocks, side eddies, or excessive turbulence in the flow of treatment progress can be indicators that an individual caucus, session, or series of sessions will productively augment the couple or family treatment.

BEGINNING THE SESSION

Establishment of continuity, review of homework, and determination of the agenda constitute important initial therapy tasks in each session.

A brief review of the prior session can be a routine and positive way to launch a session. Asking patients to recall the main points of the prior session makes for learning as opposed to insight and then forgetting. The review also adds a sense of continuity to a process that is inherently discontinuous.

In addition, an occasional overview of where patients are in the overall treatment process is sometimes appropriate. When patients begin the session by asking, "How long is this going to go on?" or "How do we know if this is helping?" an overview of the therapy strategy and a line showing the therapist's perception of where the patient is thus far can be extremely helpful. This kind of orientation makes patients feel more positive about the journey thus far and more confident that their guide knows the way to their destination.

If patients were assigned homework in the prior session, a review of homework is critical. Reliable debriefing of homework experiences encourages patients to take their assignments seriously, and the discussion of what happened generally provides lush grounds for learning.

Nevertheless, determination of the agenda for the session is probably the most critical task at the start of each treatment session. Asking patients what they want to focus on is a direct way to obtain agenda input. In addition, listening closely to first comments as patients enter each session can clarify the central issue.

> As Bart and Jeanne entered one session, Bart saw that the two chairs in which he and his wife usually sat in were slightly out of place. "Let's set up the dueling chairs!" he chuckled, whistling "Dueling Banjos." The focus of the session became exploration of why and how Bart and Jeanne slip so quickly into antagonistic positions when they discuss any problem.

In addition to aiding in clarification of the session's focus, patient(s)' opening musings can offer useful information for concluding the session. At the end of the session, the therapist can summarize by referring back to the initial comments, creating a neatly tied-together package.

In general, establishing the session's agenda requires that patient(s) and therapist each articulate their goals for the session and then move ahead with a plan that incorporates both parties' concerns. For this mini-exercise in conflict resolution to be effective, both therapist and patient(s) must have done some preparatory thinking. In this regard, taking a few moments prior to the patient(s)' entrance into the therapy room to review a patient's chart and clarify the likely next step can be helpful. Likewise, patients can be encouraged to think over what they want from the session prior to their arrival. If they did not clarify their agenda preferences while they were traveling to the session or sitting in the waiting room, a first activity in the session can be for patients to close eyes, take a deep cleansing breath, and allow a picture of their concerns to emerge.

When patient and therapist offer different bids for agenda, the solution may be sequential or integrative. For sequential solutions patient and therapist need to determine an order and time frame for addressing each issue. For example, if the therapist wants to review homework and the patient wants to discuss an upsetting event that occurred during the week, patient and therapist may choose to allot the initial portion of the session to the recent event and to save the last 15 minutes of the session for homework review. Integrative solutions allow more than one item to be addressed simultaneously.

> Karen said that she wanted to work on being able to look for a new job. Seeking continuity from session to session and wanting to bring unfinished work to closure, I suggested that we continue exploring Karen's family's input into her current self-image, an area of exploration that Karen had begun investigating during the prior session. Together we concluded that we would begin by exploring Karen's current concerns regarding job-hunting. We could include a continuation of the last week's work by exploring the messages Karen had received from her family regarding her work-related attributes and expectations.

Conflict resolution with large family groups can become complex. One practical way to keep all members' agendas in mind is to write them down as they are spoken, minimizing the likelihood that some family members' concerns will get lost in the tumult. Setting the session's agenda offers the family a weekly example of the new conflict resolution process. For this example to be a positive one, the therapist needs to play an active role so that the agenda decision-making does not become frustratingly time-consuming and so that all participants' input is included.

> A session with all six members of the Martin family typically began with everyone voicing different preferences for topics. In one session Mom wanted to discuss her changing needs for everyone to pitch in on housework since she had just started a graduate school program (a specific problem to be resolved). Dad wanted to see that all the children talked to him more openly and were more open to what he had to say (a process objective). Son Jim wanted to discuss how he wished his parents would give, and refrain from giving, advice. And Monica and Mindy wanted to talk more about their sister Lila's suicide attempt.
>
> To integrate these preferences into an efficient and a mutually agreeable plan, I suggested that the family delay Monica and Mindy's agenda to the following week when Lila would be joining the session. That way they could talk with, not about, her. Everyone agreed. I suggested that family members begin to accomplish Dad's objective (more open discussions) by discussing Jim's concerns about advice-giving and Mom's concerns about division of household labor. When, in fact, time ran out before both of these topics could be covered, I assigned homework to complete the remaining agenda. The family was to conduct a family meeting in which they would utilize their improved skills in talking openly to address how to redistribute cooking, laundry, and cleaning responsibilities given Mom's new time commitment outside the home. The next session began with assessment and completion of this assignment.

ADDRESSING SYMPTOMS

Under what circumstances do symptoms need direct intervention? When is a therapist well-advised to focus on symptom relief? Symptoms need attention when they

- create excessive discomfort,
- interfere with patient(s)' functioning,
- interfere with treatment, or
- pose a danger to patient(s) or others.

Symptoms can emerge at any point in therapy, prior to treatment, or while treatment is in progress. When symptoms—depression, severe anxiety, excessive anger, addictions, marital affairs, etc.—pose severe discomfort or interference in patients' daily lives, symptom relief may be imperative. As a practical matter, patients need relief from troubling symptoms to be willing to continue treatment. Trust in the responsiveness of the therapist can be eroded unless presenting problems are addressed.

Until intense presenting problems are sufficiently under control, the system (be it individual, couple, or family) may be too chaotic or distressed to resolve any issues in a thoughtful and purposeful way. Symptoms that interfere excessively with ego functioning, with ability to think clearly enough to pursue insight and modify behaviors, preclude work on conflicts. Depression, for instance, may leave patients with too little energy to register what has transpired in a treatment session or too negative and pessimistic to assimilate new insights. Intoxication, poor reality testing, delusional thinking, and other forms of thought disorder can render conventional talking cures impotent.

In addition, control of symptomatic aspects of presenting problems that are dangerous — self-destructive or destructive to others — is mandatory. If suicidal or homicidal ideation is present, appropriate plans and contracts must be established to reduce the danger. Abuse of alcohol and other drugs or self-destructive eating patterns generally need to be halted prior to addressing other issues. Medication may be necessary for severe depression or thought disorder. Similarly, extramarital affairs generally are toxic to a family system and must be concluded before meaningful therapeutic attention can be paid to internal family problems.

Medications, behavioral therapies, and paradoxical techniques often can offer relatively rapid relief from worrisome symptoms. These interventions need to be a part of the repertoire of every therapist or therapist team (social workers and psychologists, for instance, work in conjunction with a physician for handling psychotropic medications).

Reframing symptoms in terms of their positive contributions can aid other techniques of symptom reduction. Explaining symptoms in the context of the larger family system, for instance, can reduce a family's focus and fright of the symptom, thereby detoxifying it. Because a reframe can refocus attention from the symptoms of a problem to the underlying conflicts, it is a particularly important intervention within a conflict-based treatment.

Chapter 12 suggests additional conflict-based interventions for alleviating depression, anxiety, anger, and addictions.

SEQUENCING PROCESS AND CONTENT

When should treatment focus on content, on process, or on both content and process? Conceptualizing these options as "laundry list" and "the process is the problem" strategies can be helpful.

The Laundry List: "Walking through" Conflicts

The case of Gifts in Chapter 10 illustrates a laundry list strategy. The therapist begins by gathering a list of problematic issues, which then form an outline for the remainder of treatment. The issues are walked through one by one, as Seligman (1975) walked his dogs (see Chapter 5, p. 88), with the therapist guiding the way from conflict to resolution.

As several of the most pressing issues have been resolved, and the core conflicts brought to awareness, the therapist begins to focus on process issues. How the couple has dealt with conflict in the past and how these patterns can be altered in the future become of concern to patients once they have seen that there is another way to address problems.

In the author's experience this gradual switch of focus from content to process typically occurs after the first several issues of the laundry list have been resolved. This timing can vary considerably, with some patients ready to shift the focus from content to process more rapidly than others.

Eventually both content and process concerns can be addressed in each session. Once patients have settled into the therapy process, resolution of at least one conflictual issue plus identification and practice of at least one new communication or negotiation skill in every session is a realistic goal.

The Process is the Problem

When a patient, couple, or family is chronically argumentative, explosive, asking explicitly for help with "communication problems," or complaining of difficulty making decisions, an immediate focus on the medium, on the conflict resolution patterns per se, may be in order. Again, the need for symptom reduction must be assessed first. Once patients are quieted enough to focus productively on issues, the process rather than the content of conflict may emerge as the appropriate foreground of treatment.

> Jeanne and Bart spent a series of sessions early in treatment analyzing a disagreement they had had about how to get their three dogs over a fence. The problem itself was incidental, of minimal import in and of itself. The focal issue was instead the rapid movement into contention that characterized their relationship. Any little dilemma immediately precipitated irritation, anger, and resentment in both of them.

Exploration of the conflict process involves elucidation of communication and negotiation patterns to clarify the specific errors and detours that have been making patients' attempts to deal with problems so unsatisfactory or turbulent. Beliefs about one another that hinder cooperation are also critical to uncover. As the old patterns and attitudes become increasingly clear, new patterns may gradually need introduction. These coaching interventions are described in Chapters 17, 18, and 19.

As more constructive conflict patterns become established, patients can be asked to clarify what topics remain that are ongoing or current sources of friction and blocked communication. At that point the laundry list of conflictual issues can be generated. These issues then can be aired one by one, with a dual focus on content and process so that resolution of the laundry list issues provides opportunities for practice of the new resolution skills.

Note that these two strategies eventually cover the same territory. They differ primarily in the order in which process and content issues are addressed. Whether the initial focus has been on the content of issues (the laundry list model) or on how conflicts are processed (the process is the problem), sessions later in treatment are quite similar, with a dual focus on process and content (see Table 11.1).

By the end of treatment in either strategy, patients should feel that their painful, repetitive, and chronically uncomfortable issues have been resolved. They should feel also that they can deal effectively with whatever subsequent problems may come up in their lives because they have learned to resolve conflict effectively on their own.

INTEGRATING PSYCHOTHERAPIES: FITTING TOGETHER THE PIECES OF THE THERAPY PUZZLE

Most experienced therapists develop a full repertoire of therapeutic interventions. A conflict resolution perspective can help an integrative or eclectic therapist to clarify which interventions are appropriate in each phase of treatment. Tables 11.2 and 11.3, offer suggestions regarding how various therapeutic interventions fit together into one picture. Table 11.2 categorizes commonly used interventions in terms of their focus on symptoms, on content, or on process. Table 11.3 considers some of many interventions that focus on content in order to facilitate resolution of a specific conflict. Clarifying whether the objective of the technique is to express the conflict, explore the underlying concerns, or create and implement new solutions makes clear at what stage in the resolution process the use of each of these techniques may be indicated.

HOW DOES THERAPY END?

I like therapy sessions to end with a sense of closure, perhaps from resolution of a specific conflict, perhaps with a summarizing statement

TABLE 11.1
Summary of Treatment Overview

LAUNDRY LIST STRATEGY	PROCESS IS THE PROBLEM
Symptom reduction	Symptom reduction
Generate a list of conflicts.	Generate clarity about the process currently being used to resolve conflicts and its family-of- origin sources, and the beliefs about one another that foster poor communication habits.
Resolve them one by one, initially by the therapist walking patients through from identification of conflicts to resolution.	Coach improvements in the process; teach an alternative, healthier conflict resolution process.
Clarify the repeated underlying concerns, i.e., the core conflicts, and their family-of-origin sources	Construct a laundry list of long-standing and current conflictual issues.
Gradually add a focus on the process issues; identify the current process and its origins, and the beliefs about one another that perpetuate it.	Gradually use the improved conflict style to iron out, one by one, the issues on the conflict list
Teach an alternative, healthier conflict resolution model, and coach the specific skills need to implement this process.	Address the underlying core conflicts and implement new solutions to these conflicts.
Utilize the remaining issues on the laundry list to practice the new conflict resolution process.	Utilize the remaining issues on the laundry list to practice the new conflict resolution process.

providing the final stamp of completeness. Alas, not all sessions end so cleanly. Nonetheless, even with incomplete progress toward resolution of a conflict, or with a session that has focused on process issues, the session can end with more or less of a closure feeling. The key is to leave adequate time for summary statements. To the extent that a patient can step back from the issues and reflect on the session's accomplishments, the session can end with a sense of completeness. Closure can come from feeling, "I have done what I have done, and feel satisfied with it," as well as from being able to say, "The job is now finished." There is a maxim, "The wealthy man is he who feels satisfied with what he has." Similarly, satisfaction after a session is

TABLE 11.2
Pieces of the Therapy Puzzle:
The Three Foci of Treatment

WHEN THE FOCUS OF TREATMENT IS:	AND THE TREATMENT PHILOSOPHY IS:	SOME TREATMENT TECHNIQUES ARE:
Symptoms	Cognitive/ behavioral	Cognitive restructuring Behavior modification (response blocking and contingency management) Conditioning (flooding, desensitization, etc.) Emotion-control techniques (e.g., relaxation training; anger inhibition)
	Physiological	Psychotropic medication
	Systemic/family	Direct, paradoxical, and strategic interventions Structural therapies
Content (Identifying and resolving specific conflicts)	Psychoanalytic	Free association Dream analysis Identification of core conflicts, including conflicts evident in the transference
	Gestalt	Exploration of polarities, via dream role-playing, empty chair technique, here and now explorations, etc.
	Ericksonian	Hypnosis and story-telling
	Systemic/family	Genograms Structural reorganization Reframing Homework prescriptions Identifying "vicious cycles"
Process (Identifying and improving *how* conflict is handled)	Social-learning	Communication skills training Parenting skills training
	Psychoanalytic	Analysis of defensive maneuvers
	Systemic/family	Identification of reciprocal interaction patterns

TABLE 11.3
Pieces of the Therapy Puzzle:
The Three Stages in Resolving Specific Conflict

WHEN THE OBJECTIVE IS:	AND THE TREATMENT PHILOSOPHY IS:	SOME TECHNIQUES ARE:
Clarification of *positions*	Social-learning	Assertiveness and active listening training
	Gestalt and Jungian	Identification of polarities
	Psychoanalytic	Identification of transference phenomena or defenses
	Family	Identification of life-cycle issues
Exploration of under-lying *concerns*	Psychoanalytic	Transference explorations Exploring resistances Free association
		Explorations of family-of-origin events, dreams, etc.
	Gestalt	Exploration of here and now feelings and thoughts (or past via role-playing)
	Jungian	Dream and archetypal analysis
	Cognitive-behavioral	Clarification of beliefs, fears, goals.
	Systemic/family	Exploration of family history and life-cycle events.
Choice and implemen-tation of *solutions*	Crisis intervention	Contingency planning
	Systemic/family	Strategic inteventions Prescriptions Paradoxical interventions
	Behavior therapies	Behavior modification Conditioning

contingent on the extent to which patient and therapist have focused on what they have accomplished and allow themselves to feel pleased.

If therapist and patient have timed their session well, they will have left time not only for the summary but also for one last question, the question recommended as the last question in the conflict resolution process: *Are there any pieces of what we have done that feel unfinished?* Unfinished agendas do have the benefit of keeping patients simmering on their therapy session as the week between sessions unfolds. This Ziegarnik effect (Lewin, 1951), the remembering of unfinished work, may be less productive than other solutions to the dilemma of how to keep the work of therapy cooking during the six days or more between sessions. Assignment of homework tasks, for instance, can be a productive way to end a session and lay the conditions for productive growth in the real world outside of the therapy hour.

> Ralphine made considerable headway during a session in exploring the underlying concerns that were subconsciously pushing her to reject a boy-friend whom she loved and wanted to marry. The session was running out of time, but several aspects of her behavior remained mysterious. I commented, "I still don't understand completely why you 'could care less' when Mike gets affectionate."
>
> "Nor I," Ralphine answered, so I suggested an assignment. Ralphine, with Mike's understanding and consent, was to observe her feelings and thoughts as she tried several alternative responses to his affection. She was to try a paradoxical experiment, consciously going cold and pushing him away and tracking her feelings and thoughts as she did this; she was to experiment with consciously making an effort to try taking in the affection he offered; and she was to try living out her fantasy of how she could find his affections endearing, namely, if first she had to beg and plead for them.

The grand separation at the end of a full course of treatment deserves a similar but much more ample summary of what has been accomplished. To the extent that patients can recall how they felt at the outset of therapy and compare this state with their subjective experience at the end, treatment is likely to conclude with a subjective experience of closure.

One strategy for accomplishing this comparision is to suggest to the patient, *"Close your eyes. Picture yourself interacting with me in our first session. Notice how you were feeling. Notice what was troubling you, and what you thought about those problems. Notice what you wanted from me. Notice how you experienced me."* Once these visualizations seem to be clear, the therapist can suggest, *"Notice how you feel here in this room now. Notice how you feel about yourself. What still seem to be problem areas in your life? What thoughts come up as you think about those problem areas? Notice also how you experience me, how I seem to you, and how we seem to interact."* These questions generally evoke images of personal or family distress at the outset of treatment, and of dependency on the therapist. Images at the conclusion of treatment, by contrast, usually include images of optimism, confidence, and of a more egalitarian relationship with the therapist.

A second means of obtaining closure is to review the patient's initial laundry list. Patients almost always express major surprise and pleasure when the list that seemed so lengthy and overwhelming when they entered therapy appears brief and almost trivial by the end.

> Margaret and Michael, whose relationship prior to treatment had been overwhelmingly stormy, said in their final session, "Now that we can talk with each other, the problems on our list that felt insurmountable when we started here just don't sound like big problems anymore. Even if we don't yet agree on a solution to some of them, we know we can handle them."
> Likewise, a clear assessment of the initial conflict processing patterns (see Chapter 17) sets up the possibility of a clear contrast with the process that has become automatic at the end of treatment. Patients frequently bring in a new problem just as treatment is ending. This problem can serve as a kind of final exam, that is, as an opportunity to clarify to themselves and to the therapist the way they have learned to handle life's inevitable conflicts on their own. Explicitly delineating the contrast between this new competence and the former blockages or turbulence can be extremely gratifying.

Most of our separations in life are not absolute but gradual. As healthy children gradually disengage from healthy parents, they retain and even strengthen family ties while at the same time reaching out to live their own adult lives. The relationship with their parents is not severed but simply involves less frequent and less dependent contact. Likewise, as patients no longer need their therapist, regular sesssions can be tapered off and then discontinued, and the invitation to return as needed can remain open.

Decisions regarding the issues raised in this chapter—who should be included in treatment sessions; when symptoms, content or process should be the focal issues on the agenda; how to determine which specific conflicts to address in a given session; and how to begin and end sessions—are practical matters that every therapist faces in every treatment hour. Once these matters have been settled, techniques for progressing along the pathway from conflict to resolution become essential. The remaining chapters map specific interventions for each step of treatment—for reducing symptoms, for guiding patients through to resolution of conflicts, and for coaching improvements in their conflict patterns.

CHAPTER 12

Symptom Relief

SOMETIMES A THERAPIST NEEDS TO focus treatment on the reduction of symptoms. As discussed in Chapter 11, explicit symptom reduction generally needs to occur when a symptom may be harmful to the patient or others (e.g., suicidal intentions), is disturbing to the patient or others (e.g., depression), or interferes with treatment (e.g., thought disorder). At these times, treating the symptom takes priority in the therapy hour over attention to conflicts and conflict-handling patterns. This principle applies to symptoms that emerge during the course of treatment as well as to symptoms that are presented at initial consultation sessions.

> Sheila was referred for outpatient evaluation and treatment by her physician for what the emergency room had treated over the weekend as panic attacks. The picture in fact was of a woman overstressed by challenging work demands; saddened by a gradual loss of closeness that had occurred over the years in her marriage; physically vulnerable from excessive use of wine (a bottle a day), coffee (a full pot daily), and cigarettes (two packs a day); and showing cognitive and emotional signs of a manic episode. Psychotherapy would have been impossible given the cognitive dysfunction (racing thoughts, difficulties concentrating, poor judgment) caused by the mania. Equally important, the manic and the substance abuse syndromes were endangering her physical well-being, evidenced in heart rate and blood pressure abnormalities.
>
> Hospitalization for Sheila's personal safety and medications to control the manic state were the first treatment priorities. A substance abuse treatment program could also best be initiated under the medical supervision available in the hospital setting. Once the mania and multiple addictions were under control, the conflicts involved in Sheila's work and marital difficulties could be addressed in outpatient psychotherapy.

Symptoms pose a dilemma similar to that caused by pain in medical treatment. Both pain and symptoms provide vital clues about the existence and nature of underlying difficulties. There is therefore always some danger that alleviating symptoms will cut off this essential information source. At the same time, empathy with the patient and concern for patient safety mandate that therapists try to reduce suffering as rapidly as possible. Symptom reduction also is vital in building the trust between patient and therapist. Despite insights and changes, patients seldom feel fully positive about treatment when symptoms are bothering them.

Fortunately, resolution of conflicts and improvement in conflict-handling patterns eliminate many symptoms that have been by-products of, or solutions to, the poorly handled conflicts. Nonetheless, identification and treatment of conflicts per se, though broadly effective, has clear limitations. Individuals with schizophrenic episodes, major affective disorders, or other psychotic reactions are likely to require medication. Individuals with post-traumatic stress responses need multiple retellings of the traumatic incident to integrate the experience and to extinguish the aftermath anxiety (Foa, 1989). Addicted individuals may need strong confrontation and behavioral contracting, as well as supportive self-help groups such as AA, to overcome the pull of the habit. Families with collapsed hierarchy need behavioral coaching to teach parents to handle their children more authoritatively.

Conventional cognitive, behavioral, paradoxical and medication symptom-reduction treatments that have been extensively written up in the psychotherapy literature will not be covered in detail here. The following pages illustrate additional strategies based on the principles of conflict resolution. Interventions are suggested for reducing symptoms associated with each of the four non-cooperative conflict patterns. Note that most of the cases used to illustrate these symptom-reduction strategies have been introduced in Chapters 5 through 9.

DEPRESSION

Because depression reflects a dominant-submissive solution to a conflict, the therapist treating depressed individuals can make rapid progress by addressing the power imbalance. The depressed person needs to experience either equality or dominance over the dominant other. This reallocation of power can be accomplished in a number of ways. The patient can be empowered, the power of the dominant other can be decreased, or the submissive side (intrapsychic or interpersonal) can be encouraged to speak up while the domineering side is encouraged to do more attentive listening. In individual treatment these changes can be induced via visual imagery or gestalt empty chair dialogue. Couple treatment makes real life intervention feasible.

Treatment with individuals

Visual imagery offers a particularly efficient way to alleviate depression when only the individual client is available. To lift depressive symptomatology, visualization techniques uncover the conflict, correct the power imbalance, and move the depressed individual from a position of submission to a stance of problem-solving.

Anger, the feeling that arises in at least subtle form when a person does not get something s/he wants, can be utilized to access dominant-submissive interactions. The depressed patient is asked to close his/her eyes* and visualize someone toward whom s/he feels or could feel angry. My clinical experience has been that the person who comes to mind is the dominant other in the depressogenic conflict. If no one comes to mind, or if the patient insists s/he is angry only at her/himself, the therapist responds, *"That's OK. If you were going to be mad at someone, or had to imagine being mad at someone, someone other than yourself, who could that person possibly be?"* Depression-inducing conflicts most often involve some other person. If the conflict is purely intrapsychic, the person can picture an interaction between parts of him/herself. I usually press first, however, for the interpersonal aspect.

The next instruction is for the patient to visualize some interaction between him/herself and the visualized person. *"Note what each of you is doing . . . what each of you feels as you do this . . . what thoughts come to mind . . . what you want . . . and how the interaction ends."* A moment characteristic of the interaction that gave rise to the depression is visualized and reexperienced. It is usually helpful at that point to have the patient open his/her eyes and describe what s/he observed, heard, and felt.

After the debriefing, which will typically bring up angry as well as depressed, helpless feelings, the patient is instructed to resume the visualization, again with eyes closed: *"Picture yourself handling the situation differently this time. Picture yourself being effective. . . . Stay with the image until you have done something that gets you what you want. . . . How does the other respond? . . . Do you feel satisfied? . . . Stay with the scene until you have done something that makes you feel completely finished . . ."* The patient's facial expression usually indicates when the visualization has been satisfactorily completed subsequent to this visualization. The patient, with eyes open or closed, describes what has occurred.

Patients may be reluctant to see themselves acting in ways that violate their norms of how they *should* behave. To remove inhibitions the therapist

---

*Individuals with contact lenses sometimes feel more comfortable focusing upon a spot on the floor.

may need to suggest, *"Picture yourself doing whatever you need to do to make yourself heard, including things you might never want or be able to do in real life."* This additional instruction is especially necessary if the depressed individual is harboring violent thoughts. A visualization of violent reprisals can be particularly effective in lifting depressive affect. The typical image is of stabbing, punching, or in some other way injuring and deflating the powerful other. Some patients are too severely depressed, discouraged, or overwhelmed by the power of the other to picture an effective response. The therapist may have to suggest options, including violent options that would be suitable only in fantasy.

Lastly the patient is asked, with eyes open, to discuss how s/he feels now toward the visualized person. Having vanquished the other, even just in fantasy, patients typically feel more powerful, less angry, less depressed, and more in control. From this emotional vantage point they then can discuss real life options for dealing with the person and situations that have frustrated them to the point of depression.

I am frequently amazed at the power of this intervention. Most patients leave the therapy hour genuinely free of depressive affect. Moreover, they begin to interact more appropriately, from a less submisssive position, in real life with the visualized person.

> Jenny, a single woman in her late twenties, did not know why she was feeling so depressed, so disgruntled with herself. She described herself as feeling "defeated, like an underling, like there's nothing right about me."
>
> Asked to visualize an interaction that angered her, she pictured a moment in which her boss, an officious older woman, was treating her like a neophyte or an inadequate child rather than a competent fellow professional.
>
> Jenny's visualization of an effective response began with initial meek attempts to tell her boss not to treat her so critically. She saw her boss ignoring these feeble pleas. I suggested that she try another strategy that might be more effective. She then switched to a highly aggressive style. She pictured herself "punching out" her boss, "giving her a kick in the pants." As she continued to see herself punching and kicking, Jenny became increasingly enthusiastic, beaming with satisfaction when she reached the point of visualizing her supervisor totally crushed by her blows.
>
> From this more powerful emotional position Jenny, now with her eyes open, was able to explore new options for dealing directly with her boss. She visualized and then role-played a series of realistic assertive options, options that lay between the old passive or pleading options and the new aggressive fantasy. During the subsequent week Jenny did not in fact confront her supervisor openly. She did find, however, that as she felt more equal to her boss and interacted without her prior depressed self-downing stance, her boss treated her with more respect.

Sometimes visualizing physical domination of the dominating other does not suffice.

Peter was a college tennis player who usually loved the game. Lately, however, he was not winning his matches. Instead of playing with his usual confidence, he was doubting himself and criticizing himself incessantly both on and off the court.

Asked to visualize someone toward whom he felt irritated, Peter immediately pictured an interaction with another tennis player, Andy. In this interaction Andy had arrogantly snubbed him, refusing to practice with him and treating him as if he didn't belong with the rest of the varsity squad at the courts. At the time Peter had said nothing in response to Andy's belittling remarks and demeanor. The visualization brought to his conscious awareness, however, the extent to which he had felt infuriated, pushed outside by Andy's attitude.

In this case, Peter expressed wanting to punch Andy, but a visualization of fighting him did not seem to change his sense of the power loss. What helped instead was a reframe of Andy's behavior. Peter had been seeing Andy's behavior as a statement of his position high above Peter, who was low man on the tennis totem pole. As he was visualizing the scene again, Peter could see that Andy's behavior might indicate the extent to which Andy felt threatened by him. Peter, though less experienced, was in fact the more talented athlete. The idea that Andy was acting out of fear and jealousy rather than out of strength shook Peter out of his submissive and self-critical stance, and his usual enthusiasm and self-confidence returned.

Treatment with couples and families

If both individuals involved in the depressogenic interaction are present in the therapy session, the therapist can work in vivo rather than via mental imagery. The therapist then has leverage over both the dominant and the submissive members of the interaction and can direct interventions at both. The therapist can increase the effectiveness of the depressed individual by encouraging assertive behavior and decrease the dominance of the other person by facilitating more genuine listening.

Systems therapists use reframing techniques to readjust power relationships. A therapist, for instance, might look at a depressed man with a domineering wife and suggest to the husband, "You clearly have the power in this family, because your moods control the whole family. No one can act normally for fear of upsetting you." And to the wife who is in the dominant power position, "You must feel terribly helpless in the face of your husband's depression. Nothing you do seems to have any impact, no matter how hard you try to help him by suggesting this or that."

Reframing alone, however, probably induces only transient mood changes. The key intervention is to help the family to renegotiate the issue(s) around which the dominant-submissive interactions have occurred. If the depression is a function of an ongoing interaction pattern rather than a by-product of a specific conflict, then the ongoing pattern must be explicitly altered. Techniques therapists can use to coach these kinds of changes are elaborated in Chapters 17 through 19.

Sometimes a therapist attempts various interventions to eliminate a dominant-submissive interaction, but does not see rapid alleviation of the depressive symptoms. Although therapist skill deficits may be a problem, physiological factors may be causing the persistence of the depressive state. Psychotic depressive states are likely to need antipsychotic as well as antidepressant medications, and may also need evaluation for shock treatment. Even with milder but chronic depressions, however, medication use is always important to consider, especially if sleep is being disrupted. Antidepressant medications can be used either in conjunction with the above interventions or subsequently. Behavioral regimes that keep depressed individuals physically active rather than vegetative can also be an important adjunct to treatment that shifts the dominant-submissive power arrangements.

ANXIETY

For anxiety to be diminished, the competing issues, e.g., the threatening situation and the objectives that keep the individual in a threatening situation, need to be addressed. The conflicting elements need to be clarified as precisely as possible. Once these concerns have been brought to full awareness, a response needs to be formulated. These are the same steps involved in any conflict resolution, i.e., exploration of underlying concerns followed by choice and implementation of a plan of action.

Clearly articulated fears can be ameliorated in a number of different ways — by reality-testing, obtaining information, reframing, skill-building, repeated desensitizing exposures, etc. In addition to focusing on fears, the opposing wishes need clarification and plans for fulfillment. A full understanding of all the conflicting fears and wishes opens the possibility of an optimal resolution, that is, a resolution that satisfies the concerns on both sides of the conflict.

In general, information is one of the best antidotes for anxiety. Information-gathering mobilizes patients, giving them something to do about the problem, and may simultaneously yield a new view of the problem that offers more potential for resolution. Sometimes, however, anxious patients are reluctant to take in disconfirmatory data which would otherwise be reassuring.

Adam appeared to be seeking appropriate information by consulting cardiologists with regard to his fears that his panic states were in fact heart attacks. Unfortunately, he was unable to hear the information given to him. If the cardiologists did not confirm his fears, he discounted their input by disparaging their knowledge and credentials. Interestingly, after going from cardiologist to cardiologist, and emergency room to emergency room, Adam eventually contacted a cardiologist with an exceptionally paternal and reassuringly authoritative style. This cardiologist enabled Adam to relax his guard in the office visit. They were able to build a soothing trust relationship, within which the cardiologist was able to convey the necessary information. Nonetheless, although this information about the health of his heart did reduce Adam's chronic anxiety about having a heart attack, the information did not curtail the agoraphobia or affect his belief that each panic attack, while it was occurring, was a heart attack.

Generalized low-level anxiety: Too busy and Too worried

When anxiety is ongoing and the intensity low to moderate, the therapist may find that the fastest anxiety reduction technique is to focus immediately on identification and resolution of the stalemated conflict rather than to utilize relaxation or medication interventions. Whereas these latter treatments are directed at the anxiety per se, resolution of the immobilizing conflict addresses the problem at its source.

> Dr. Sporen, a physician who was writing a book, experienced pervasive low-level anxiety during his first several days back in his office after a two-week vacation. He was eager to return to writing. Yet mail, phone calls, and clinical work kept him busy. Anxiety nagged at him, interfering with his concentration on the work that had to be done.
>
> To reduce the anxiety I suggested that Dr. Sporen stop for a few minutes and focus on identifying precisely the conflicting pulls giving rise to the anxious feeling. Dr. Sporen identified many small immediate tasks, clinical and office administrative responsibilities that had to be attended to, plus a fear that he might never free enough time to write. I encouraged him to continue to gather information. Dr. Sporen focused on the office commitments that required his attention, assessing how much time they would require. He determined from his calendar specific times might be freed up for writing.
>
> Having gathered this data, Dr. Sporen was able to chart a plan of action. He resolved that the backlog of clinical and office work could be completed by the following Monday and Tuesday, that most of Wednesday could be set aside for writing, and that henceforth a full Wednesday and half a day on Mondays and Fridays could be devoted to his book. With this time-partitioning solution, conflicting impulses to work and to write no longer barraged him simultaneously, his fears of never proceeding with his book were alleviated, and the nagging anxious feeling disappeared.

Sometimes identification of the competing concerns and information-gathering are critical initial steps which must then be followed by decisive action.

Marlene came to treatment presenting with chronic anxiety. Identification of the fear was relatively easy. Marlene feared that she had cancer, and her doctor's reassurances left her unsettled. The conflicting wants included the obvious wish for health, plus a desire to remain on good terms with her doctor. Wanting the doctor to like her felt incompatible with her distrust of his diagnosis.

The obvious way to relieve the cancer anxiety was to seek more information, but Marlene had several underlying competing fears that were keeping her immobilized. She was reluctant to do anything too assertive, such as speaking up about her anxiety or obtaining a second opinion, for fear that this assertiveness might alienate her doctor. Therapeutic reduction of this fear involved reframing the importance of trusting her own intuitions as a way of helping her doctor to be genuinely successful. The wish to obtain a second medical opinion was also reframed. Instead of indicating lack of confidence in her doctor, requesting a second opinion was framed as an aspect of handling illness in a medically responsible fashion. Role-playing the dialogue in which she would tactfully explain to her initial doctor that she had sought a second opinion also helped reduce Marlene's fears.

Another fear-inducing thought holding Marlene back was terror of finding out that she might indeed have cancer. Marlene felt panicky at the prospect of facing death. In any conflict resolution, obtaining detailed understanding of the specific fears and wishes is critical to finding solutions. I asked Marlene to close her eyes and allow an image of the scene that most scared her when she thought about dying to come to mind. Marlene pictured the heroically calm demeanor her mother had maintained when she was fatally ill. She feared that she would be unable to attain this high standard, that she would be unable to handle pain with dignity. Mapping out a plan of relaxation training plus discussing pain-killing medications reassured Marlene that she would be able to find a way to handle death in a way that would maintain her self-esteem.

Lastly, Marlene was reluctant to contact the physician she most trusted as a consultant for a second opinion because she had left his practice for other reasons several years prior and was embarrassed to recontact him. I offered to telephone him myself, feeling that fostering dependency was a less relevant consideration in this instance than obtaining the medical consultation. This offer relieved Marlene of her last immobilizing concern. With her permission, I phoned the gynecologist immediately, during the therapy session. Since his office is in the same medical building as mine, he agreed to fit Marlene in for a brief medical evaluation as soon as our session was over.

The outcome of this case was particularly dramatic and poignant. The second physician decided that, in spite of negative findings on laboratory tests, his clinical evaluation substantiated Marlene's intuitions. He recommended immediate surgery. On his insistence Marlene underwent surgery that afternoon. She did indeed have cancer, in advanced stages. Radical surgery plus chemotherapy brought the cancer into remission.

Treatment of Marlene's generalized anxiety began with delineation of the specific wishes and fears yielding stalemated immobilization. Information-gathering, reframing, exploring the family origins of the concerns, and even direct therapist assistance enabled Marlene eventually to respond with action instead of immobilization, both with respect to the immediate cancer crisis and then to her overall pattern of anxiety.

Social phobia: Farm girl

Josie (daughter of Marlene, described above) had multiple fears and wishes underlying her intense blushing and anxiety in certain social situations. As each of these fears and wishes were identified, practical solutions were found to alleviate the fears. This approach, in conflict negotiation terms, involves "chunking." The initial global panic is broken down into the component sub-fears and wishes. These mini-objectives can then be addressed with varied mini-solutions.

For instance, Josie feared having nothing to say and appearing dumb. Practicing several topics for social conversation boosted her confidence in this area. Josie also wanted to look like she "belonged." Arranging to go places with her roommate gave her this sense of belonging and greatly enhanced the confidence with which she was then able to meet new friends.

Reduction of the multiple fears was further enhanced by investigation of the childhood origins of the frightening images. Severe peer rejection when Josie was a farm girl who went to school in a nearby city had left Josie feeling chronically like a frightened outsider. Thus behavioral, psychodynamic, and cognitive interventions were integrated by understanding the panic in terms of the immobilizing conflict, exploring the multiple underlying concerns, wishes, and fears, and then finding solutions that were directly responsive to each underlying concern.

Panic attacks

When anxiety occurs at panic levels of intensity, people can become so frightened by the physical sensations that they severely constrict their lives in order to avoid repeated panic episodes. In this case, the therapist first needs to address the symptom per se by offering tools for managing these states. Once patients feel calmer about the attacks, the underlying conflicts and conflict handling patterns can be addressed.

Many victims of panic attacks are immobilized by the conflict between wanting to continue with normal life activity and fearing the recurrence of panic sensations. This fear can be decreased by reframing the meaning of the attacks so that they are no longer viewed as terrifying events and by teaching a self-observation response to them. Patients can be taught that the panic state is a simple physiological overreaction that will subside naturally, rather than an initial sign of impending heart attack or "nervous breakdown." This approach addresses the underlying concern that feeds the panic reaction, i.e., the fear that the panic episode is a sign of something worse to come. When this concern is met with new information, the old solution to physiological signs of arousal — a massive panic episode that calls for help — can be replaced with new reactions.

For instance, when patients understand that panic is a physiological overreaction to an underlying conflict, they often find that they can distract themselves from the panic sensations by attempting to figure out what underlying concerns triggered the response. Some patients also learn to soothe themselves with the calming technique of self-observation, a cognitive intervention that teaches adoption of an observer stance toward panic. Patients are instructed to respond to panic episodes by focusing their attention on specific anxiety sensations, such as heart pounding or rapid breathing. They can visualize a curve graphing the symptom, which generally rises abruptly and then subsides more gradually. They can notice when the curve seems to be peaking and which panic sensations decrease at what rates and in what order.

Self-observation calms panic sensations by giving patients a task that occupies their minds and substitutes observation for panic-exacerbating thoughts. Recognition of these thoughts, e.g., "I'm going to die!" "I'm going crazy!" "This is going to give me a heart attack!" or "This is so embarrassing!" and recognition of the inflammatory as well as erroneous nature of these thoughts are also useful. As patients substitute task-oriented for anxiety-increasing cognitive activity during their panic states, the attacks cease to constrict their life functioning. The panic episodes become intriguing phenomena and minor inconveniences instead of disabling events.

> The initial intervention for Kelly-Ann's panic attacks was information-giving. Kelly-Ann was reassured to hear that panic is unrelated to "going crazy" and that losing control of herself during a panic attack was simply not likely to happen. Once Kelly-Ann understood that her panic attacks were not first signs of something worse to come, Kelly-Ann learned to handle them in a new way. When they occurred she sat back, relaxed, and mentally mapped the curve of the rise and fall of the anxious feeling. This observing ego response gave Kelly-Ann something to do during the attacks. In addition, it enhanced her new belief that the attacks were a harmless biochemical irregularity about on the same order of dangerousness as a strong sneeze.
>
> After Kelly-Ann felt secure about managing her panic sensations she was ready to look at the conflicts that immobilized her and triggered the anxious reaction. I validated the periodic anger that Kelly-Ann sometimes felt toward her children, as she was cooped up with them too much for her stamina level. I further suggested that the feeling was worth taking seriously and using as

data for making changes. With increased self-acceptance of her feelings, Kelly-Ann hired more babysitters and took some time to pursue personal interests, which greatly alleviated the anger and claustrophobia she had been feeling toward her children.

The fact that this solution seems so simple and obvious is another indication of the manner in which anxious immobilization halts thought in response to a conflict. As soon as Kelly-Ann had become dimly aware that what she and her children needed might be in conflict, anxiety had clouded her thought and brought problem-solving to a total halt. The therapist's role is to encourage the patient to express the conflict and think about it instead of repressing the conflict and feeling anxious.

Agoraphobia: Mutual marital misery

Agoraphobia treatment involves two elements. First, reduction of the panic attacks is critical. Medications as well as cognitive-behavioral treatments can be useful toward this end. Second, the very real underlying conflicts to which agoraphobia provides a solution must be addressed.

As in treatment of low-level anxiety and panic attacks, careful delineation of patients' specific underlying fears and concerns is critical to symptom reduction with agoraphobic patients. Individuals with this diagnosis, however, may pose a particular problem in this regard. They are ofttimes strikingly unaware of their troubling underlying issues. With these patients in particular, a therapist's familiarity with the usual dynamics (concerns and fears) is very important in anticipating which issues will need to be uncovered.

A clue can usually be found in the agoraphobic's manifest fears, which often metaphorically express the real life conflict. A fear of leaving home, for instance, may reflect fears and wishes about leaving a marriage. A fear of being home alone may reflect fears and wishes that a spouse is going to leave the marriage. Understandable concerns generally underlie these conflicts. For instance, poor conflict processing between the couple may be evoking desires for more power in the relationship, increased autonomy, and paradoxically, more intimacy. The poor problem-solving patterns also may be evoking multiple fears. Intimacy, for instance, may be feared because of the assumption that closeness would bring submergence under the spouse's control. Increased autonomy may be feared, as it may be associated with helplessness, loneliness, or inability to cope.

As these longings and worries come to conscious awareness, agoraphobic individuals generally need help in restructuring their relationships to more satisfactorily meet these concerns. In most instances couple treatment gives the therapist the most leverage for inducing changes in both spouses and in their interactions. Couples with an agoraphobic member typically deal with differences by bullying one another (attack), caving in (submission), walling themselves off (flight), and/or tiptoeing tensely around touchy topics (freeze). They need to learn to discuss disagreements cooperatively in order to develop both intimacy and autonomy. The same poor conflict patterns hinder the agoraphobic individual's ability to deal with inner conflicts. Conflicts in both arenas are likely to need to be openly addressed.

Given the poor communications that usually occur between with agoraphobic individuals and their spouses, the agoraphobic syndrome can be seen as bringing at least some benefits. Some therapists refer to these as benefits as secondary gains, but that term has unnecessarily negative connotations for what are generally well-intended if not ideal solutions to real concerns. For instance, agoraphobic limitations may evoke emotional support from a spouse in a relationship that is otherwise barren of warmth and affection. As these problems become understood, the individual and couple hopefully can find better solutions.

> Scott and Kelly-Ann both were suffering panic attacks, and Kelly-Ann had developed a full agoraphobic reaction about being home alone and about going into the kitchen where there were knives (which she feared she would use to kill her children). The treatment plan included conjoint sessions for working out the marital disagreements, along with individual sessions to reduce the frightfulness of Kelly-Ann's panic attacks and to help Scott make decisions about handling his boss and changing jobs.
>
> Prior to therapy both spouses had reacted to marital and/or personal conflicts with a standoff followed by anxious tension and no further discussion. Gradually both spouses learned to take their own concerns more seriously, to listen to each other's perspective, to cease their antagonistic "you shoulds" and "yes, buts," and to pursue discussions to the point of mutual agreement. These negotiation pattern changes, plus the use of these new skills to redecide troubling issues, such as how often they would go out together for fun evenings and whether Kelly-Ann would return to work, enabled the marriage to regain its vitality.
>
> As Kelly-Ann began to feel less stifled in the couple relationship and by her children, she no longer experienced desires to leave the marriage or to kill her children. The couple began going out dancing on weekend evenings; Kelly-Ann resumed employment part-time; and Scott changed jobs to a position with less stress, a more supportive work climate, and more money. Scott's anxiety attacks, Kelly-Ann's fears of being alone, her frightening anger at the children, and her fear of knives disappeared.

ANGER

Viewed from a conflict resolution standpoint, expression of anger can be helpful to the extent that it illuminates the presence of an underlying conflict. In these cases, the emotional explosion may release pent-up (frozen, suppressed, avoided, or denied) sentiments. Airing them at least puts the cards face up on the table, where they can then be processed. Anger also can indicate the intensity of feelings associated with a conflict. Like a fire alarm, an angry tone of voice insists, "Pay attention to me!" Once the alarm has been heard, however, continued anger can interfere with subsequent resolution of the conflict. Expression of anger therefore needs to be carefully managed and gradually transmuted to more effective negotiation strategies.

When working with patients who utilize attacking strategies toward parts of themselves (who are self-critical, self-negating, or self-blaming), toward others, or toward the therapist, therapists need a good deal of savvy. The anxiety evoked by intensely aggressive comments made by a patient toward a family member or toward the therapist can make it difficult for the therapist to sit back and think calmly. In these instances it can be helpful for the therapist to bear in mind short- and long-term objectives.

In the short-term perspective, anger expression needs to be blocked and/or converted so that it does not derail patients from the track that leads to effective conflict resolution. Virtually all attack behavior leads off the resolution pathway. To ease an angry person back onto a more constructive track, the techniques are the same for therapists responding to angry patients and for individuals who confront anger in themselves or others in their daily lives. Table 12.1 lists responses that have a calming impact on anger.

With respect to long-term goals, therapists' responses to patients' anger serve to model anti-attack maneuvers for the sake of both the attacker and the attacked. Patients with attack habits need to learn to problem solve instead of to attack, and they need to learn to compensate for their inadvertent attacking comments with neutralizing, cooperation-resuming actions. Attacked individuals need to learn to hear anger as a problem of the angry individual rather than as a phenomenon that should be taken personally; at the same time, they need to understand that they are responsible for how they respond to others' anger. Their responses can soothe the angry person, perpetuate fighting, or swing the discussion around onto cooperative dialogue. Viewing anger as evidence of a problem rather than as a personal attack, individuals may more easily learn to listen to the angry person's underlying concerns. They then, hopefully, can respond helpfully to the underlying concerns instead of continuing to respond defensively to the anger per se.

Thus, the immediate steps that a therapist takes toward getting patients back onto the path of cooperative conflict discussion serve to launch

TABLE 12.1
Effective Responses to Anger

STRATEGY	VERBALIZATION	CIRCUMSTANCES
Defuse the anger by validating the content	(In empathic tones) "What you are saying makes sense. I agree that . . ."	When other is escalating in an attempt to get heard
Detoxify the situation with an apology	"I'm sorry. I didn't mean to hurt you. What upset you in what I said/did?"	When anger has been a strikeback to a perceived hurt
Detail the situation, adding one's own point of view	"I understand better now what you're upset about. Let me add what was going on with me when x happened. I . . ."	*After* a detoxification or defusion. When a "hot reactor" has experienced a strikeback reaction because of misinterpretation of other's actions
Define the objective	"I hear you're angry. What would help you feel better? What do you want?"	When you-messages— blame, criticism, and complaints—are obscuring what someone wants and a switch to I-statements is needed
Describe the anger and *deescalate* or *disengage*	"We're fighting. This is not constructive." Followed by alternatives, e.g., "Let's discuss this in the morning (after dinner, etc.)"	When anger levels make information exchange impossible
Delete the inter-action	"We're getting agitated. Let's back up and start this discussion again."	When excessive voice volume or accusatory attitudes flare, but participants know how to discuss conflicts better
Delve under the anger	"If you weren't feeling angry now, what would you be feeling? What feeling is *under* the anger?"	When anger covers fear or shame
Dead end the anger by escalating over it and insisting on a halt.	(In a firm voice) "Stop! That's enough! We'll talk again later." Followed with disengagement from the situation or distraction onto another subject.	When anger is escalating into potentially destructive interactions

(continued)

208

TABLE 12.1 (*continued*)

STRATEGY	VERBALIZATION	CIRCUMSTANCES
Dominate	Take charge of the situation, using authoritative verbal or physical action as needed in order to establish control over angry other.	When other is unresponsive to empathic or cooperative attempts to curtail his/her/their aggression, and the situation could become dangerous

movement toward the therapist's long-term objective, teaching better conflict resolution habits. Initial therapist modeling provides a foundation for later more explicit teaching of skills to transform attacks and anger into more constructive actions.

Effective responses to attack.

Table 12.1 summarizes various constructive ways in which individuals, including therapists, can respond to others' angry or attacking behavior. To facilitate recall, the various alternative anger responses have been labeled to begin with the letter d. Leisurely reflection is not an option in attack situations, so developing several of these as reflexive responses can be helpful.

A shift from attacking to mutual problem-solving can occur if the recipient of the attack listens for what the attacker is trying to achieve, to what s/he wants, rather than listening to the deprecating "You're not OK" message conveyed by the anger. Therapists generally are trained to react to their patients' anger in this manner. Instead of feeling personally threatened, a good clinician can sit back emotionally, tease out the patient's underlying concerns, and respond empathically to these rather than defensively to the criticism or accusations. To the patient who asserts, "You just sit silently in your chair and don't really listen to me. You don't even care about what upsets me," a therapist might respond, "My silence seems to give you the impression that I don't listen and don't care. Being heard and being cared for must be very important to you, as they are to all of us."

Hearing the attacker's anger and commenting empathically on the feeling can be another soothing response. For instance, "I hear your anger. Our interaction was clearly very upsetting for you," can be a soothing response that sidesteps the question of who is to blame for the upset and at the same time validates the painfulness of the feeling.

A combination of anger responses will be necessary, i.e., defusion of the anger by validating the angry person's concern, detoxification by clarifying that there was no intention to cause harm, and then definition of what it is that the angry person wants in order to solve the problem.

Most of the responses summarized in Table 12.1 are meant to calm or block the anger and to induce cooperative problem-solving. The last is designed to stand firm and win. If the other party in the conflict is a determined aggressor, unwilling to cooperate, aggressive counter-responses may be appropriate, a la tit for tat.

One of the lessons the allied countries learned in the Second World War was that counterattack, or a strong blocking response of some form, can be essential at times. The Tit for Tat studies lend credence to the idea that a strong countering show of force is a necessary response to an individual who is fixed on attacking. If aggression cannot be defused by discussion that addresses the underlying concerns, aggression tends to continue unless met with some clear form of strength. In this case, attack may need to be matched with an equally strong or stronger force if domination by the self-gain-oriented, competitive opponent is to be blocked. When the attacker is convinced that attack yields no gains, a switch to a cooperative strategy may eventually become a possibility.

ADDICTION AND OTHER AVOIDANCE PATTERNS

Many therapists go by the rule of thumb that treatment of addictions generally must precede other therapeutic assistance. Confrontation and then a behavioral change of the escape pattern, particularly if the escape involves an addiction, certainly needs to be a first priority.

Sometimes, however, treatment moves more effectively if conflictual personal and marital issues are treated first or simultaneously, reducing the need for escape. With couples, a simultaneous treatment approach decreases asymmetrical assignment of responsibility for marital problems to the addicted partner allowing the spouse's co-dependency issues to receive helpful intervention along with other marital problems that may have been perpetuating the addiction. Taking the focus off the addiction can give the addicted individual face-saving space within which to make changes. Nonetheless, immediate cessation of the avoidant behavior is an essential first priority if the escape route takes the form of a self-destructive addiction or compulsion, or has severely toxic impact on other family members.

Key ingredients in terminating addictive behavior include a breakthrough of the denial surrounding the behavior, an increase in motivation to end the behavior (by a new view of the costs and increased appreciation of the rewards), and some form of response blocking. Rewards for success usually emerge spontaneously, e.g., in more gratifying family interactions. It is helpful for the therapist to draw attention to these rewards, as awareness of these reinforces the changes.

It is easy for spouses and therapists as well to feel angry at an addicted individual. The problem is the intoxicant, not the person, however. The therapist may need to keep clarifying and reclarifying this point so that spouses can work as allies against the addictive substance rather than fight each other.

Therapists sometimes need to be especially alert to catch subtle versions of flight behavior. For instance, patients who utilize avoidance may simply not raise crucial but delicate topics for discussion. Easier to note are quick shifts in the focus of discussion when sensitive topics do emerge. But the avoidance may begin prior to the treatment hour; a patient who is coping by avoidance is likely to be reluctant to enter therapy. Premature termination can also be a sign of this pattern.

> Miriam came to therapy because she was exhausted from trying to hold everything together in a household with a severely disturbed husband. Although she herself was not addicted to any substances, she had grown up in an alcoholic family and had learned avoidance as a primary response to problems. Therapy required her to face her husband's disturbance squarely and to begin to think about options for dealing with it instead of trying to cover it up. After two sessions, she ceased coming, saying that financial problems were interfering.
>
> Six years later Miriam returned to treatment. Her husband's psychopathology had worsened steadily over the years. His paranoia had deepened into a fixed delusional system focused on their daughter's boyfriend. His behavior included compulsive obscene telephone calling and exposing himself to women on the television. At that point I realized that by allowing Miriam to drop out of treatment on the financial excuse I had let myself be taken in by Miriam's avoidance instead of confronting it.

The above techniques can augment a therapist's bag of tricks for alleviating troubling symptoms of emotional distress. The meat and potatoes of most treatments, however, consist of guiding patients through troubling conflicts and coaching them so that they develop more effective conflict resolution patterns. The next eight chapters focus in detail on these two objectives, suggesting the kinds of interventions that can make a therapist an effective guide and coach.

CHAPTER 13

Guiding: Expression of Troubling Conflicts

WHEN THE GOAL OF A TREATMENT session is resolution of a specific life dilemma, the therapist serves as guide along the three-phase passage from conflict to resolution. The therapist's role can be thought of as shepherd-like, i.e., pointing out safe paths and helping patients stay on these paths. This chapter and the next three explore when shepherding is necessary and what kind of guidance is useful in each of the three main conflict-processing steps: (1) expression of initial positions, (2) exploration of underlying concerns, and (3) determining optimal win-win solutions and launching effective action. Many of the techniques described, which by no means constitute an exhaustive listing, should be familiar to experienced therapists. The goal is to bring clarity to why specific therapy techniques are useful for processing conflicts, and when. With a conflict resolution map, a therapist can choose treatment pathways with precision, knowing which specific segment of the resolution journey each intervention is meant to facilitate.

When the goal is promoting resolution of a specific conflict (as opposed to coaching resolution skills), the therapist's first objective is to clarify the initial positions in the conflict. Clarification involves constructive expression of both sides of the issue, plus some kind of response to each side that indicates that the initial positions have been heard and taken seriously. In guiding this expression, a therapist wants to circumvent poor communication habits so that they do not block the initiation of problem-solving. An active therapist can structure the discussion format and monitor the communication style to maintain constructive expression. At the same time,

212

the therapist needs to avoid undue attention to patients' communication errors which might distract from a clear focus on the problem to be resolved.

When patients begin to work on a conflict using inadequate—vague or negative—openings, how can a therapist reform these into constructive communications? The following examples illustrate various options for accomplishing this reformation with individual clients, with couples, and with families. The examples illustrate typical problems and potential solutions in this stage of therapeutic work. Effective guidance in this earliest phase establishes a format for constructive problem-solving.

EXPRESSING CONFLICTS IN INDIVIDUAL THERAPY

Clarification of specific conflicts can be somewhat elusive when the conflict is intrapsychic rather than interpersonal, particularly when the conflict is outside of the patient's awareness. Individuals do not generally come to treatment saying that they have "a conflict." They describe symptoms such as panic attacks, feelings such as anger or sadness, behaviors such as alcohol abuse or violent episodes, relationship problems such as marital fighting, or developmental crises such as difficulties deciding to get married or to have children. The therapist's challenge is to utilize these presenting complaints as a gateway to the troubling dilemma.

Without such clarification, therapy may be interesting, but can be a meandering exploration rather than a focused passage to resolution. Although such exploration can be intriguing, it does not necessarily yield growth, change, or resolution of conflicts. In contrast, once the patient's presenting problem has been defined in terms of conflict and the conflicting initial positions have been clarified, the therapy session can flow directly into probing underlying concerns and choosing new solutions.

How does the therapist guide the patient toward a clear statement of opening wishes? Sometimes the nature of the presenting problems suggests which interventions would be suitable. Therapist preference and training also play a role. In general, techniques utilizing mental imagery seem to be particularly efficacious for a wide range of presenting problems and can be added relatively easily to most therapists' repertoires. Two mental imagery techniques, as well as several other structuring interventions, are described below.

Visualization and metaphor

A number of researchers have suggested reasons why mental imagery works so well in helping individual patients identify and then work through their conflicts. Anees Sheikh (1984) points out the power of imagery to focus patients immediately and vividly on the heart of the upsetting matter, bypassing irrelevant issues and other layers of defense that can obfuscate the conflict. Other research indicates that "free imagery," which is analogous to free association, is highly effective in circumventing even stubborn defenses and bringing to light repressed material (Jordan, 1979; Klinger, 1980; Reyher, 1963). Interventions that utilize imagery may catch the patient by surprise in their direct expression of the central issues (Singer, 1974).

To switch from verbal discussion to mental visualization, the therapist can begin by listening for a metaphorical expression in a patient's words. A colorful verb or adjective can suffice, but an actual simile or metaphor gives an especially strong foothold. When patients describe feeling "boxed in," "under the gun," "like a pinball being bounced back and forth," etc., they can be asked to close their eyes and to describe the image that they see.

> Renalda had presented for treatment because of intense feelings of distress that she did not understand and could not seem to alleviate. From the outset of the session, Renalda spontaneously used multiple images and vivid verbs, any of which could have launched clarification of the conflict, e.g., "making fertile ground for everyone," "moving forward," "running on positive energy," and "trying to make it all go smoothly when it just can't." Renalda's language was so replete with imagery that I felt I could take my time and pick an image that sounded particularly concrete and evocative. When she said she "felt a weight of responsibility for everyone's welfare," I responded by encouraging her, "Close your eyes. Sit back in a comfortable position, and take a deep cleansing breath. Using your closed eyes like a television screen, allow an image to come up of the weight you feel like you are carrying."
>
> When Renalda's facial expression indicated that she was satisfied with the clarity of the image, I continued, asking her to describe the weight and what she wanted to do with it. Renalda said that the weight was like a large bundle of snow. She wanted to set down the big snow load, but she was reluctant and, without knowing why, kept holding it. The basic conflict had been expressed in a visual and concrete form that could be sustained for the exploration of concerns and the selection of a resolution.

Visualizations provide a medium through which the conflict not only can be identified, but can also be worked through to resolution. Often it is possible for a patient to explore the underlying concerns and find a resolution while working entirely within the metaphor.

> Renalda explored her concerns about setting down the burden she was carrying in her marital relationship by experimenting with visualizations of setting it down and then discovering what consequences she feared. As her

awareness of her underlying concerns grew, she was able to visualize additional options. Visualizing these options to clarify what worked and what was problematic with each option, she eventually found a satisfying solution—all by watching herself carrying and setting down her heavy load. At that point Renalda opened her eyes and we discussed how the metaphorical solution could be translated into her actual life dilemma.

As this example illustrates, visualization techniques offer many clinical advantages. The most important from a conflict resolution perspective is the rapidity and clarity with which they crystallize the troubling conflict. Even patients who cannot consciously describe their conflictual issues may immediately express the essential conflict in their visualization.

Visual metaphors, as opposed to abstract verbalizations, seem to be particularly easy for patients to access after the therapy hour. If the format involves only words, patients may appear to be confused at the end of the session and may soon forget the main points. Mental imagery seems to leave more memorable impressions. I have often found that in follow-up sessions months or years after treatment, patients who have forgotten much of what we talked about still vividly recall visual images that they explored.

Lastly, visualizations are gratifying. They tap into creative talents, talents that patients may have been unaware of possessing. The unveiling of this creative talent, which makes patients feel good about themselves, provides an added treatment bonus. Moreover, the intriguing images that come up in visualizations make therapy more playful for both patient and therapist.

Visualization of relationship moments

This intervention compensates for the absence in treatment sessions of the other party in a conflict. Patients are asked to close their eyes and allow a moment to come to mind that includes the significant other person. The scene that emerges will virtually always depict the central troubling conflict, a phenomenon which gestalt thinkers account for by the notion of "unfinished business." By visualizing the other person and imagining interactions with him/her, the patient can deal more or less directly with the other, talking *with* instead of *about* the other person. (This gestalt-type intervention, with slightly different instructions, was described in Chapter 12 as a technique for altering depression.)

This intervention can be begun by asking the patient to close his/her eyes and take several relaxing mind-cleansing deep breaths. The following instructions then can be given, with pauses between each suggestion: "Picture a moment, real or imaginary, that includes the two of you. . . .

Notice what you do and say. . . . Notice how you feel as you interact. . . .
What does the other feel? . . . do? . . . and say? How does the incident
end?"

This scene can be followed up with a second scene that lays the
groundwork for subsequent exploration of concerns and resolution of the
conflict. Ask the patient, "This time visualize the same beginning scene, but
have the interaction turn out differently. Have it turn out the way you wish
it would occur, with a new ending that you like better."

> Nancy, a single woman in her thirties who had completed a course of
> treatment several years earlier, returned to therapy complaining of depression
> with no understandable origin. Asked to close her eyes and picture someone
> she was annoyed with, she visualized her husband Gary. She saw Gary
> radiating negativity, with a scowling face and a steady stream of complaints.
> Encouraged next to look at her own participation in the scene, Nancy related,
> "I absorb the negativity. I try to be the cute, nice child, trying to make it
> right." The interpersonal conflict underlying the depression pitted Gary
> against Nancy, with Nancy trying to curb her husband's dour manner and
> meeting with no success.
>
> Asked to associate to similar interactions in her family of origin, Nancy
> recalled with bemusement, "He's just like my mother used to be! He has that
> same depressive outlook on the world: 'Life is to suffer through; you can't
> change anything.' And I'm reacting just the way I used to as a kid. I swallow
> my angry reaction and get cute in order to make *some* kind of relationship. He
> harbors feelings of anger toward just about everyone, but I absorb it
> personally. I feel like I need to do something to make it right."
>
> Nancy had difficulty visualizing an alternative reaction to her husband's
> negativity. In a subsequent visualization, as she was encouraged to describe
> her thoughts and feelings in more detail, Nancy identified an intrapsychic
> conflict. She wanted to be able to deflect instead of absorbing the negativity,
> but she was afraid such a response might be inconsistent with her image of
> herself as a caring person. With these concerns understood, Nancy was able to
> visualize several options, each of which might offer a satisfactory resolution
> in different circumstances. She could express caring in other ways, but
> confront Gary firmly but politely when he was taking his negativity out on
> her. She could have a quiet discussion of the problem with him. She could
> react playfully to reduce the tension but without feeling so personally
> responsible for her husband's bad moods. Or she could express her caring by
> allowing Gary to deal with issues in his own way, while she distanced herself
> patiently until his negative episode was over.

Empty chair dialogue

Another productive technique for expression of an intrapsychic conflict is
the gestalt empty chair technique. This technique is particularly appropriate
when a topic or specific decision, as opposed to a feeling or a relationship,
has been posed as the presenting problem. Training in gestalt treatments

definitely enhances a therapist's ability to use the empty chair most effectively (and visualization techniques also).

Joen Fagen describes the essentials of empty chair interventions as follows:

> The empty chair, probably the best known and most widely used Gestalt technique, is one with tremendous power. In the hands of an expert it looks very simple: the patient is instructed to move back and forth between two seats or positions which represent two different aspects of himself or the relationship between himself and another person and engage in a dialogue. . . . (Fagen, 1976, p. 647)

> Karen felt she should move to Los Angeles to live closer to her aging mother. One chair represented the voices that said "move." In this chair Karen worried about how her mother would be able to take care of herself and her large house as she aged, especially as her health had deteriorated since her husband's death. Karen then switched to the other chair. There she spoke from the parts of herself that wanted to stay where she was, make no changes, and keep her life as it had been. She voiced never liking changes. She treasured the independence she had earned by becoming financially self-sufficient and by settling geographically far enough away from other family members to make her own decisions and live a lifestyle of her own choosing.
>
> Continuing with this empty chair format Karen was able to find a resolution that satisfied both chairs. She would phone home more frequently to make certain her mother was remaining well and would encourage her mother to take on household help. These two changes would satisfy the concerns from the one chair; meanwhile, she would be able to remain where she was currently living, which would satisfy the concerns from the other chair.

Toward what end?

When patients present with ego-dystonic behavior (behavior that is unacceptable to themselves), the therapist needs to help them understand what is motivating the seemingly "bad" behavior. It is helpful in these instances to suggest that the patient view the behavior as a solution, and then backtrack from the solution to an understanding of the problem. Resolution then involves finding an alternative solution to the initial problem that is consonant with the person's values.

> Boris knew that his angry and hypercritical outbursts toward his wife antagonized her. He realized that these mini-rages had been a significant factor in propelling her into an extramarital relationship, yet he could not seem to cease his provocative behavior.
>
> Asked to look at what, if seen in the best possible light, these angry outbursts were meant to accomplish, Boris realized that they were meant to

prevent his wife from mistakenly continuing her affair. He feared that unless he raged periodically, she might think he didn't mind if she continued her extramarital relationship. He wanted to stop acting so aggressively. And, he wanted to communicate to his wife that he could and would not tolerate a continuation of her extramarital connection.

Once these two conflicting agendas were explicit, Boris found an alternative behavior that would accomplish both. He sat and talked quietly with his wife instead of raging. He poignantly explained to her how vulnerable he felt and how devastating the thought of her further involvement with the other man was for him. This strategy felt ego-syntonic to him. Eliciting his wife's empathy also proved far more effective than his prior bullying tactic in ending her extramarital involvement.

Tevya's Scales

Tevya in "Fiddler on the Roof" models another technique for clarifying the oppositional elements in an intrapsychic dilemma. Whenever Tevya confronts a challenge, he holds his hands out to either side, palms up, like scales, as if balancing weights on each, saying "On the one hand (looking at one palm), . . . and (looking at the other palm) on the other hand. . . ." Unlike Tevya, who then chooses one side *or* the other, patients then can be encouraged to find solutions that satisfy the concerns on both sides.

> Ralphine was self-critical with respect to her distancing behavior with her new boyfriend Mark. She began the session with a potpourri of insightful statements about a smattering of aspects of the problem. Her intelligence and insight made these statements intriguing, but the insights were not leading to a productive line of thought. We needed a structure to clarify the central conflict.
>
> Before I had launched a restructuring, Ralphine shifted from associational musings to complaining, berating herself for her tendency to pull away from Mark and to push him away via nagging and criticism. Complaints, criticisms and other negative statements are particularly counterproductive ways of defining the elements in a conflict. They block rather than open the resolution process. Ralphine's earlier serial comments had been seductively intriguing though unfocused; the complaining was clearly unproductive.
>
> The Tevya technique immediately yielded a more positive expression of Ralphine's conflict. "On the one hand," Ralphine contemplated, looking at one uplifted palm, "I want security. Caring and concern. The kind of unconditional acceptance Mark gives me." Looking at the other palm, Ralphine continued, "On the other hand, I'm fearful of losing him because I'm not able to be as affectionate as he is." This clear statement of the opening positions in her conflict enabled us to proceed efficiently toward understanding and resolution.

Therapist-patient dialogue

Patient-therapist dialogue, i.e., discussion in which the patient talks about his/her problems while the therapist asks guiding questions, responds empathically, and encourages problem-solving, can be a productive conflict resolution format. However, while it is probably the most frequently used therapeutic format, it is replete with pitfalls and requires highly developed therapist skill. Mere dialogue looks easy; after all, conversations about problems with friends and family are everyday events. However, discussion in the context of therapy has multiple risks and requires sensitive therapeutic maneuvering.

What are the difficulties in encouraging a patient to talk about problems in dialogue with the therapist rather than structuring the exploration so that the patient is in dialogue with him/herself? First, in verbal discussion the problem is seen only from conscious and intellectualized perspectives. Astute questioning is needed to lead into material that the patient has not been aware of before the therapy session.

There is also a risk that the therapist will lose the position of neutral sounding board against which the patient bounces his/her own ideas. Patients can slip into verbalizing just one side of their intrapsychic conflict, with the therapist reflexively articulating the other, inadvertently interpersonalizing the intrapsychic conflict. If the therapist espouses one side of the conflict and the patient the other, therapist and patient become falsely pitted against each other instead of the patient experiencing both sides of the intrapsychic struggle as his/her own.

> Danny was trying to decide whether or not to attempt one more time to pass a real estate broker's licensing exam after three demoralizing failures. He talked about all the reasons why he should not try again. In response to his unbalanced presentation, I found myself verbalizing reasons why one more try might be worthwhile. The format was setting us against one another, with Danny and I conflicting with each other instead of joining against the problem. Danny was struggling against what he felt I wanted him to do, rather than owning the two sides of his own inner conflict. Furthermore, this structure was inadvertently making me sound like I was espousing a position that in fact I did not even believe. Worse, had I remained in the trap and continued to voice one side of his ambivalence, Danny might have followed my suggestions. He then would have felt justified in blaming me if he failed the exam a fourth time, instead of accepting responsibility for his own decision.

Keeping internal conflict from being interpersonalized is particularly difficult with more disturbed patients as they tend to expect and provoke invalidating responses. When patients take extreme positions, they stimulate contradicting responses from the therapist and others in their world (Linehan, 1988). In response to one-sided comments, most people—

therapists included — reflexively try to balance what they have heard with the opposing perspective.

> During a period when she was particularly depressed, Karen worried aloud, "It's too late for me. I can never have friends or a better job." My normal human instinct was to try to mitigate Karen's despair and buoy her hopes, particularly when the despair seemed ungrounded in reality. If I succumbed to this impulse, however, Karen would experience my reassuring comments, comments that offered data contradicting her extreme view, as invalidating. Responses that try to add the other half of the story inadvertently set up an oppositional relationship between patient and therapist. Because Karen interpreted my more optimistic viewpoint as invalidating her bleak subjective perspective, reassuring comments from me actually buttressed her insistence that life is hopeless.

On the other hand, a Rogerian empathic response does not necessarily help either. Validating comments sometimes encouraged Karen to continue elaborating on how hopeless her life was without having the intended paradoxical effect of leading to Karen's voicing, eventually, the other side of the conflict. When her depressions were in severe phases she tended to take comments I might make to empathize with her negative views of her self, her present, and her future, as confirmations of the hopelessness of her life.

An therapeutic skill, the ability to validate a patient's subjective experience without necessarily agreeing objectively, can help in these instances. This kind of "Yes, and . . ." responses agrees and then adds an additional perspective. However, expression of the conflict via visualizations or empty chairs can bypass this sensitive task of validating the subjective validity without confirming the objective validity.

Patient-therapist dialogue can lead to other difficulties as well. Inexperienced therapists in particular can be drawn into discussions in which patient and therapist concur in their assessment of a third person and then proceed with an "ain't it awful" conversation. Instead of facilitating either interpersonal or intrapychic conflict resolution, this kind of joining maintains stasis. Again, a visualization technique that forces the patient to interact with the significant other, albeit only in imagination, can prevent this kind of triangulation, of coalition building that pits patient and therapist against the absent third party.

Even if a therapist remains a relatively blank screen by asking questions instead of stating his/her own viewpoint, discussion may not lead to delineation of the various sides of a patient's conflict. Conflicting elements may remain entangled, particularly if the patient's natural flow of thoughts is associational or chaotic rather than systematic and goal-oriented. If the intent of the session is resolution rather than mere viewing of a conflict, disentanglement is imperative.

Lastly, even if the therapist carefully tries to prevent the patient from interpersonalizing the intrapsychic conflict, some patients still project one side of their inner conflict onto the therapist. Considerable skill is necessary to recognize and work with such transference and projection. Interventions that rely initially on other techniques for clarification of conflicts are simpler. Interpretations of transference and projection can be used as a backup.

> One week Karen was particularly depressed and socially isolated. She announced that she had given up on ever making any friends or having any social life. All of my attempts to help her discuss the issue, even with seemingly nonpositional questions, were interpreted as expressing dissatisfaction with her decision. Worse, any comments or questions from me were interpreted as confirmation of her transference fears, namely, that I held expectations of her that she could never possibly meet, and that therefore I would be angry and disappointed in her.
>
> These transference issues were tempting to explore. At the same time, they were clearly secondary to, merely a small aspect of, the immediate problem. Karen's fears and desires about moving out of her isolated existence were reaching crisis proportions and needed to be addressed. Discussing transference fears at this time would have been a sidetrack that could lead away from, rather than closer to, resolution of the loneliness conflict. I decided to switch from discussion to visualization techniques to bypass the transference issues. With the change in format, we were able to refocus productively on the immediate crisis, that is, on clarifying what during the week had triggered Karen's fears that she would never succeed in making friends, and what could be done to improve her chances.

Realistically, patient-therapist discussions do occur in treatment and in fact are often productive. What are the characteristics of these more productive discussions? Rogerian-type responses can validate and thereby encourage expansion of what the patient says. Once a person feels that what s/he has said has been heard, the next thought typically flows spontaneously. That next thought may add more weight to the same side of the conflict. However, once a person has fully verbalized one side of his/her ambivalence and feels that it has been heard and accepted, there seems to be an internal see-saw that then says, "So what's the other side of the picture?"

Perhaps a therapist's active listening serves also to pattern the patient's internal responses to his/her own verbalizations. That is, as the therapist verbalizes acceptance of what the patient has said, the patient accepts his/her own thoughts and feelings more fully. In this way a Rogerian-type accepting and echoing response pattern may foster movement toward conflict resolution by facilitating the patient's ability to express and listen to his/her conflictual inner thoughts and feelings. For instance, if a patient in distress says, "Ouch!" and the therapist answers, "That must hurt," this acknowledgment facilitates the patient's acceptance of his/her own state- ment of pain, and thereby readies the patient to express the other side — "Yes, and it will be fine in a few minutes if I just treat it tenderly for a bit."

Many other interventions are commonly used to foster articulation of conflicts (see Table 11.3). Jungian therapists note polarities, using data from dreams or from behavior within the session. Gestalt therapists attune to breaks in the flow of talk, to discrepancies between words and nonverbal messages, and to behaviors that patients experience as other than what they want to be doing (reflecting a "topdog/underdog" conflict). Therapists trained in psychodynamic short-term treatment approaches enter the central conflicts through cues in defensive behavior and/or through evidence of transference reactions to the therapist. Any of these techniques can launch a productive conflict resolution process.

EXPRESSING CONFLICTS IN COUPLE AND FAMILY THERAPIES

When helping couples and families to process a conflict, as in work with individuals, the therapist's initial task is to open the dispute constructively. Expressing initial positions involves both sides saying what they want and both sides giving evidence of having heard what the other side wants.

Alas, the human proclivity for tit for tat is nowhere so evident as in the launching of couple or family dispute resolution. A dispute begun with an attack is likely to yield a counterattack. Criticisms beget counter-criticisms, complaints engender counter-complaints, blame invites blame in return. If tit for tat warfare does not ensue after a negative opening to a dispute, submission or avoidance are likely alternatives, neither of which leads to deeper understanding and long-term optimal solutions. On the other hand, a constructive opening statement that says what the person wants rather than dwelling on what the person doesn't want (which is the essense of a criticism, attack, blame, or complaint) invites a cooperative response. The following techniques are essentially behavior-shaping procedures designed to begin the conflict on a positive track by getting participants to express their initial positions and to listen cooperatively to their counterpart's initial positions.

Asking

A time-honored therapist as well as conversational tool, a good question can prompt constructive statements of initial positions. When the therapist asks a question to structure a statement by one spouse, it is helpful to suggest that the response be directed to the spouse rather than to the therapist, so that the interactions transpire primarily between the spouses, not between the therapist and one or the other of the patients. In the following rather emotionally explosive situation, a two-step questioning intervention worked well to launch a productive dialogue between antagonistic spouses.

> Eric launched a discussion of an upsetting couple incident with a pseudo-question that was really an attack. "Why didn't you listen to me last night when I told you I wanted my friend to come in to use the bathroom?!" he angrily asked/complained to his wife, Vicki. The tone of voice and the "you" focus conveyed his aggressive posture.
>
> I intervened immediately to block a defensive counterattack from Vicki. The intervention consisted of asking Eric a question designed to help him rephrase his opening. "What are you trying to tell your wife you were wanting last night?"
>
> "I'm trying to tell her that I was very upset by not being able to let my friend in to my own house," he responded.
>
> "Now I understand," I replied. "Let's start again, and this time say to your wife what you said to me."
>
> The question refocused Eric on himself instead of on his wife. In addition, it created a calming break while he and I conferred, a few moments for de-escalation of feelings before the discussion was resumed.

Preparatory suggestions

Sometimes therapists err by being reactive rather than proactive. Explicit prompting can set patients on a positive track. Most patients would rather be prepped so that they can communicate effectively than repeat the same unproductive interactions that they have at home. This kind of prompting differs from coaching in that the therapist does not dwell on how or why to communicate in one way or another, but simply suggests, "Now do this."

Eric's distress could have been handled with prompting prior to Eric's first statement. "Hold on a minute. Let's begin with your telling Vicki what you felt and wanted last night."

Eric hopefully would have responded with something to the effect of, "I was very upset. I wanted my friend to use our bathroom before he rode his bike on home. I want to feel like I can treat my friend hospitably in my own house."

Translation

Sometimes a patient is too agitated and locked into his/her anger to cooperatively state the problem. In that case the therapist can intervene by restating the opener less provocatively. A movable chair (on rollers) is useful for these situations. If the therapist moves next to the upset patient, the patient feels a sense of support. At the same time, if the therapist is sitting adjacent to the speaker instead of forming the third point in an equilateral triangle, the translation feels to the spouse more like it is coming from the original speaker. However, because this position moves the therapist out of a position of symmetrical relationship with the arguing individuals, it is a good idea to remain next to one spouse as briefly as possible.

In the situation above, the therapist could interpose a translation between Eric's attack and his wife's response. The restatement would be designed to elicit concern instead of an angry rebuttal from Vicki.

"Vicki, Eric is trying to tell you that he became quite upset last night. He wanted to invite his friend into the house to use the bathroom, and he was hurt and angry when you said no."

Modeling

After a translation of a hostile explosion has been offered, the hostile patient can be given the opportunity to express the upsetting feelings again. By reiterating what the therapist has just said, the patient learns by imitating and practice. There are several additional benefits to this format. When discussion is too hot to be productive, slowing down the interactions in this manner turns down the heat. At the same time, the modeling provided by the therapist's translation enables the spouses to feel that they are talking with one another even though their interactive style may be radically new.

Oppositional clients are sometimes unable to allow themselves to rely on the therapist's modeling. With such patients, the therapist may find that translation and questioning are the best options. However, most patients who grew up in households where argument or avoidance were all they saw and heard seem to appreciate the therapist's modeling of more constructive ways to communicate.

Eric could be offered a translation of his angry opening statement and then asked to try to express himself in this new manner. Thus, after the above restatement, I would turn to Eric and suggest, "You try a second draft, something like I just did. Try to express yourself in a way that is informative instead of attacking."

Eric would look somewhat anxious, and then mobilize with a genuine effort to use his own words to convey his feelings with a tone that conveyed cooperation rather than accusation.

Second draft

Sometimes therapist modeling is unnecessary, particularly later in treatment or with healthier patients. Simply encouraging a second draft can evoke a more inviting opener. The therapist can interrupt with a simple calming, "Whooaa. Let's try that one again."

Many patients respond well to the implication that they can do better that is inherent in this request. With women, I usually offer the suggestion with explicit reassurance that they will be able to improve with a second attempt. With men, a more challenging, "Can you do better than that?" stance seems to yield good responses.

"OK Vicki," I might say to Eric's wife. "I have heard you sometimes stop, take a breath, and tell Eric the same information but minus the attack. Want to give it a second try?" Using playful paradoxical chiding to challenge, Eric I might suggest, "You got in a good dagger or two with that one. Is that the best you can do? Can't you add some spears, and maybe arrows too? Stabbing Vicki softens her up to be concerned about your feelings, right? Want to try it again?"

Reiteration

Sometimes blockages in expression of initial positions derive from listening problems rather than from how a topic is broached. Assertiveness trainers teach a "broken record" technique in which people keep saying what they want to communicate until the listener has given evidence of having heard. When the therapist, instead of the patient, does the reiterating, the burden of change is thrown more on the listener to open his/her ears than on the speaker to keep rephrasing his/her positions. Although both speaker and listener need to learn to be more effective, therapist reiteration directs the intervention at the specific blockage in the communication process.

> Difficulty getting other family members to listen to her wishes was a major source of frustration for Carla, the mother in the Martin family. The lack of

hearing was, in fact, a major cause of the family's rigidity, i.e., of its inability to adapt to changing circumstances, and was resulting in Carla's feeling increasingly depressed. Carla had enrolled in paralegal training in part to provide the family with a firmer economic base. Her teenage children, however, were resistant to accepting responsiblity for the housework that their mother had always handled. Whenever Carla would raise the question of who was going to wash the dishes, who would run errands, or who would do laundry, the siblings would protest loudly, listing the many reasons why they were too busy to pitch in. Carla was doing her part in raising issues, but no one was willing to listen. What could have been seen as the children's expressing their concerns was in fact a defensive tactic; they used concerns as ammunition to stave off their mother's attempts to communicate, to get the family to sit down at the negotiation table.

Because the block in the expression of wishes came in the *listening*, I intervened by reiterating that there really was a conflict here that needed to be discussed. Rather than dismiss their mother's requests, the children needed to sit down with her and with their father. Father needed to learn to listen more to Carla, and to amplify her requests instead of joining the children in ignoring them. They needed to hear their mother out and, as a full family, address how to adapt their division of labor to cope with Carla's return to work.

Once I had reiterated Carla's wish that the household tasks be reassigned, this time making certain that everyone was taking it seriously, the discussion of concerns and solutions was relatively straightforward.

Preparation for active listening

Preparation of the listener can be as helpful as preparation of the speaker. "While your husband is saying what's troubling him, your job is to listen closely. After he has finished I'm going to ask you to repeat as fully and exactly as possible everything he has said." Setting the expectation that a listener will be asked to reiterate promotes focused listening. The actual reiterations clarify what data have and have not been taken into the mutual information pool and also indicate misunderstandings.

Directing traffic

The therapist needs to note who is talking to whom and who is avoiding contact with whom. As a general rule, individuals in conflict with one another need to sort out their difficultes with one another, not by complaining to a third family member. By contrast, triangulation, or speaking to a third person about problems with someone, can detour expression of wishes in families. It is a pattern that is particularly likely to flourish if family members become defensive or show disinterest when other family members do try to address problems directly. When triangulation does occur, a therapist can gently redirect individuals to speak directly with one another. The most common triangulation in couple treatment involves spouses each trying to talk to the therapist instead of communicating directly with each other.

> Triangulation was prevalent in the interaction patterns of the Martin family. For instance, an attempt to establish triangulation with the therapist as the third party occurred midway through their treatment. Carla phoned me to schedule an individual therapy appointment. Whereas in the prior example Carla had been stymied by her children's reluctance to listen, in this case the block had occurred even one step earlier, in reluctance to begin the conflict process by raising an issue. This was understandable given the particular circumstances, but I still needed to rechannel the communication into direct interaction.
>
> Carla was worried about the extent to which her eldest daughter, Lila, might still be suicidal. She was also increasingly angry at Lila's unwillingness to discuss the suicide attempt that had so terrified all the family. Because Carla still did not understand how or why the suicide attempt had occurred, she felt hostage to Lila's every whim. At 3:00 a.m., when Lila called and woke her up quite inconsiderately, Carla was afraid to tell her that the call could have waited until morning, fearing that the rejection might yield more suicidal impulses. Instead of saying what was on her mind to Lila, Carla requested an individual therapy session to talk about the problem.
>
> I responded on the telephone first by validating Carla's concerns about Lila and then by encouraging Carla to speak up about the problem in the next therapy session. By turning down the request for a separate individual session, I was blocking the triangulation, that is, Carla's attempt to talk about the problem with a third party rather than with the person involved. On the other hand, I reassured Carla that I would watch Lila closely during the session to monitor signs of suicide potential, and would discuss this question explicitly in an individual session with Lila. That is, while turning down the request for a triangulated *solution*, I was careful to respond to the underlying *concerns* that had prompted Carla to ask for an individual session. I suggested an alternative solution, a solution that encouraged Carla (and set an example for all the family members) to say what she wanted directly to the family members involved in the problem, along with reassurances that I would note Lila's responses to be certain that the discussion did not further her suicidal potential.

In prior sessions triangulation had been discussed as a family pattern of communciation that had roots in Carla's family of origin and then had flourished in the Martin family. With this background I was able to set the context for this discussion, helping Carla see that her current request was another instance of this pattern of avoiding face-to-face negotiation between family members in conflict.

Obtaining symmetry

Expression of one person's desires and evidence that these have been heard completes half of the first stage of the conflict resolution journey. The second half entails a symmetrical repeat with participants switching speaker/ listener roles. A therapist can utilize the techniques described above to be certain that both sides' initial positions have been expressed and incorporated into the definition of the problem to be solved.

> Carla wanted to discuss Lila's suicide attempt. Lila did not want to discuss it. Lila needed the therapist's encouragement to be able to voice her reluctance. With these initial positions clear the family was able to agree on ground rules for talking about the suicide attempt that would enable Lila to feel safer about talking and would give Carla the insights she needed.

In sum, ruptures in the first stage of conflict resolution generally occur because wishes are not being expressed, are being expressed in an attacking (blaming, accusatory, or critical) mode, or are not being heard. When patients are ineffective in introducing a conflict for discussion, the therapist has multiple options for facilitating constructive expression and cooperative listening. The therapist's responsibility is to do whatever works to put — and keep — patients on the road of effective conflict resolution.

TRANSITIONAL SUMMARIZING

Stages in the resolution process are bridged most effectively with summarizing. The summary of the first stage needs to include some form of explicit statement of the conflict. Symmetry is essential. Equal weight and validation, evidenced by equal length descriptions, must be given to both sides.

The summary that effects the transition between initial expression of the conflict and exploration of the underlying concerns benefits from an additional ingredient, a change in the level of abstraction used to describe the conflict. This kind of change enables the two or more conflicting wishes to be subsumed under one conflict.

> When Carla wanted her teenagers to start handling dishwashing and other household chores and they felt they were doing plenty already, the family needed to settle differences regarding division of labor, i.e., who would be responsible for doing what in the household.

In the above example a summary of the essential positions on each side is followed by an umbrella statement of the topic or problem. With this kind of foundation, the next negotiation stage can begin with a calmer problem-solving orientation. An umbrella conflict definition enhances the likelihood that the opposing sides will cease to feel like antagonists and instead will feel like cooperative teammates working together to resolve a shared problem.

Lastly, it is important to include several key words in an effective summary, namely, the pronoun "we" and the integrative word "and." With a couple or a family, the pronoun "we" furthers the sense of a team working together vis-a-vis the problem, as opposed to individuals working against one another. With individuals, couples or families, the word "and" links seemingly oppositional initial positions, establishing an integrative and inclusive problem-solving cognitive set. By contrast, the word "but" does not belong in a summary, as it negates whatever has preceded it.

> Eric could summarize his and his wife's initial positions by saying, "I want to be able to invite my friends into our house and you are worried about protecting your privacy. We need to find some rules of thumb for whom we want to invite into our house and under what circumstances."

The therapist might raise the discussion to a higher level of abstraction, adding both legitimacy and arm's-length distancing to the topic. "Yes, boundary maintenance is a critical issue for every family. The boundaries around your family unit need to be closed enough to keep everyone feeling secure and yet open enough so that the family can maintain revitalizing relationships with friends and extended family."

CHAPTER 14

Guiding: Keeping on Pathways
That Lead to Resolution

HAVING SUCCEEDED IN DEFINING A conflict to be addressed, the therapist's next task is to guide patients through an exploration of the feelings, wishes, memories, values or other mental elements that underlie both sides of the apparent conflict. This enterprise generally constitutes the primary focus of insight-oriented therapies, including psychodynamic, humanistic, existential, Jungian and gestalt approaches. The breadth, depth and specificity of this exploration determine the ease with which solutions will arise once the exploration has been completed.

The structure that has been established for expressing the initial conflict can provide the format for exploring concerns. With individuals, this may be a visualization, the gestalt empty chair, or dialogue with the therapist. With couples and families, conflicts are more explicit and therefore format is generally less of an issue, except that discussion should proceed primarily between and among family members.

Patients who keep talking about each other to the therapist instead of about the problem to each other may be looking to the therapist to be a judge, passing judgment on who is right and who is wrong (Ables, 1977). The therapist is better off maintaining the role of guide, the one who keeps family members on the path of productive interactions.

Like most rules, this rule has critical exceptions. When participants are too angry and volatile to talk and listen without fighting, discussion can be kept cooler by channeling comments through the therapist. Also, from time to time the therapist may want to help one individual explore deeper concerns, concerns that need semi-hypnotic exploration. In these instances the patient speaks to and with the therapist rather than primarily with other family members. In general, however, the therapist's role in the exploration of concerns is to guide both sides in the conflict so that they engage in cooperative discovery. The therapist's role in the initial expression of a conflict was to define the problem and set a format that would channel cooperative problem-soving. In the second stage of conflict resolution, the therapist needs to watch that patients stay on productive pathways (Chapter 14) and cover the necessary territory (Chapter 15). Patients can go astray in many ways. In particular, the therapist-guide wants to be vigilant in maintaining an optimal emotional tone, a clear focus, symmetrical exploration of both sides of the conflict, and adequate specificity.

MAINTAINING AN OPTIMAL EMOTIONAL TONE

An open and cooperative atmosphere of exploration generally flourishes within an optimal range of emotional intensity. Excessive anger or anxiety, for instance, can constrict the flow of exploration and allow listening to give way to defensiveness. Inadequate expression of underlying feelings likewise blocks exploration, in this case by obscuring the signs that indicate which directions need to be explored. To maintain an emotional tone that lies within these extremes, the therapist must be sensitively attuned to breaches of effective communication. Nonthreatening saying and empathic listening are essential if patients are not to become lost or injured in their explorations. When ineffective or provocative interactions do occur, immediate therapist intervention can assist patients in reestablishing constructive verbalizing and empathic listening patterns.

Much of the time therapists can guide in a manner that maintains an accepting climate without undue anger or anxiety.

Nonetheless, strong emotions do inevitably erupt from time to time, and these eruptions too can be therapeutic. In these situations, the therapist needs to help patients digest the outburst productively, detoxifying the anger, decreasing the anxiety, and bringing to the fore the meaningful information that has burst forth.

Freud's original instruction about the technique of free association was that his patients must learn to say aloud whatever comes to mind without judgmental screening. A modification of this instruction is helpful to bear in mind, particularly in working with couples and families. Whereas the content of the explorations needs to be openly expressed, with the instruction to verbalize whatever comes to mind, the manner in which this content is expressed — "I" versus "you" messages, tone of voice, reiterative listening, etc. — must be carefully guided.

"Discuss the problem, not the person" (Fisher & Ury, 1981) is one principle for determining when patients have stepped out of bounds in the tone dimension, resorting to blame or attack rather than problem exploration. Satir (1972) coined the term "leveling" for the kind of informative data-sharing that occurs in cooperative problem-solving that is free of either blame or evasiveness.

> Jeanne and Bart's repetitive attack-counterattack cycles created eddies and whirlpools of destructive interaction that offered endless detours away from actual problems. Bart and Jeanne stated their concerns in attacking "you" form. To get them to say and hear underlying concerns I had to pull continuously against the current of their ongoing efforts each to prove that the other was the worst bastard. An attack by one or fear of a forthcoming attack would provoke a defensive counterattack, and they were off and dueling.

With a couple like Bart and Jeanne, keeping a very tight rein on the inflammatory comments, on listening skills, and on escape attempts is critical. How does a therapist "keep a tight rein" during the exploration of underlying concerns? In general, a therapist's most powerful tool is his/her presence, his/her way of being and interacting. As Freud once pointed out, the group takes on the personality of the leader. Family therapists similarly emphasize the powerfully calming impact of a therapist who is able to maintain a non-anxious presence in the midst of troubled families. A therapist's interested, accepting, and good-humored attitude can convey a change in rules for even the most tense, blocked, judgmental and antagonistic individuals and family systems.

A more active way to maintain a constructive tone is careful preparation of patients before they explain each concern. As in the first conflict step of stating initial positions, explicit instructions given by the therapist prior to each patient comment can detour the communication patterns that have frustrated patients in their attempts to solve their problems on their own. Instead of leaving patients to express their concerns in unconstructive ways, the therapist can structure the exploration with questions that elicit "I statements" and requests for reiteration of what has been heard.

> Jeanne had difficulty focusing on her own needs and feelings rather than on what Bart was doing wrong. When they were discussing how they fought when trying to help their dogs over a fence, Jeanne was about to tell Bart how inconsiderate he had been of the dogs' feelings. Anticipating this complaint, I asked Jeanne to tell Bart what her worry had been, what she was concerned about, with the dogs and the fence. Before her response I also turned to Bart,

suggesting, "and you see if you can listen openly so that you'll be able to express back to Jeanne what you heard. It will help if you focus on what is *right* about what Jeanne says, what makes sense to you." The point, thus, is to prompt good communication patterns step by step, *prior* to each verbal interchange.

Even with a therapist's calm presence and careful preparation, however, when dealing with difficult issues patients may still resort to the engrained communication difficulties that have caused them to need help. When sharing and empathic listening disappear in the intensity of an emotionally explosive topic, the therapist must *do something*. The therapist then functions like a referee in a basketball game, blowing a quick whistle when the discussion goes out of bounds, followed by a question or statement that gets the discussion in motion again. Certainly there are times to let poor process such as angry attacking, judgmental listening, or blocked emotional expression proceed unchecked. For instance, if the goal of a session is to understand when, how and why poor process occurs, then episodes of poor process can provide helpful data. In content-oriented sessions, however, when the point is to move as expeditiously as possible from conflict to resolution, tolerance of poor communication behaviors detours progress toward the destination of resolution. For these times it is helpful for the therapist to have a full repertoire of whistle-blowing as well as preparatory responses.

Table 14.1 outlines problems of excessive or inadequate emotional expression and suggests some helpful therapist responses. Novice therapists, in order to accomplish these interventions, may need to remember that interruptions may not be appropriate in good dinner table conversation, but they can be essential in therapy, enabling exploration to continue in a productive vein.

Emotional outbursts

If the patient's stance has been critical, blaming, or attacking, the therapist can suggest backing up and expressing the concern again, this time with the focus on the speaker's own feelings rather than on what the other has done.

"Wait just a minute, Bart. Stop, and refocus. Try to clarify more calmly what you are telling Jeanne about *you*, instead of angrily talking about *her*."

When it is evident that the listener's feelings have been hurt and/or that the attack is about to yield a counterattack, the therapist may need to do a quick cleanup, detoxifying the unconstructive comments with quick refram

TABLE 14.1
Maintaining Optimal Emotional Range

PROBLEM	THERAPIST RESPONSES
Emotional outbursts	
Criticism, blame, complaints	Validate underlying concerns and how strongly the speaker feels about these.
	Change focus from *you* to *I*
	Detoxification via reframing
	Refocus on the anger to understand what triggered it.
	See also Table 12.1
Panic or severe anxiety	Sooth by verbalizing the feeling. Offering reassurance. When appropriate, offer physical calming (e.g., hand on arm or knee).
Emotional blockages	
Frown, tears, quivering chin, foottapping, etc.	Encourage the individual to focus on the feelings, and then to verbalize what s/he feels and is aware of.
Provocative listening	
Ignoring. Listening for what is wrong with what the other says	Encourage the listener to reiterate what makes sense in what the speaker has said.

ing. A good reframe can translate the threatening comment into a constructive contribution.

> In the Martin family Monica and Jim were in conflict over his absence at her birthday dinner. When Monica accused Jim, "You always have something else to do whenever I have an important event!" I intervened by reiterating, in a gentle voice, to Jim, "Monica feels very disappointed when you are not at her special events like her birthday dinner. Your presence means a lot to her." This detoxified translation, focused on expression of Monica's feelings rather than on Jim's behavior, evoked understanding, as opposed to defensiveness, from Jim.
> Jim then replied with genuine chagrin, "Gee, Monica, I never thought it mattered to you if I was at dinner or not. I'm sorry."

Sometimes, instead of trying to diminish or delete the angry outbursts, or even to understand the underlying concern, it works as well or better to zero in on the anger to understand the context that gave rise to it. This technique is particularly appropriate if the discussion has been fairly productive and then anger suddenly erupts. If the therapist, instead of smoothing over the anger, asks the agitated speaker to introspect on the feeling that suddenly emerged, the trigger for the anger can be uncovered and rectified. For instance, sudden angry outbursts often occur when patients have heard implied criticisms in the other's comments. A slow rise in irritation may mean that the person felt like what s/he was saying was not being heard.

> When Bart responded to Jeanne's concern with a sudden defensive retort, I asked, "What happened just now that triggered your distress? What just set you off?" For Bart the answer was usually that he had heard criticism or sarcasm in something Jeanne had said. I could then validate that an implied criticism may well have been there *and* that the main point Jeanne was making was a comment about herself, not about him. Patients who routinely listen to others' comments by scanning for criticisms may frequently need this kind of help to detoxify their understandings (or rather, their misunderstandings) of others' comments.

Sometimes excessive anxiety erupts within a session. Patients cannot think clearly when they are overwhelmed with anxious feelings. Their thinking becomes too constricted or too scattered to continue with useful explorations. To calm them, both verbal and physical reassurance can be helpful. Patients may need to hear that they will be safe, that the problem can be worked out, that it is not their fault, etc. Sometimes, when appropriate, a reassuring arm around a child's shoulder or a firmly reassuring hand on an adult's knee or arm conveys the therapist's calmer state to the panicked patient. Appropriateness in this case can be a function of the degree to which the physical contact conveys parental soothing rather than sexual feelings. If the latter is likely for any reason, physical contact is a poor option.

> From time to time in her treatment Karen would experience intense waves of anxiety during which her entire frail body would tremble. She would stand up and pace back and forth in the therapy room, which seemed to exacerbate the anxiety. These episodes embarrassed Karen, further increasing her panic.
> Gradually Karen and I discovered that if I spoke to her in a soothing voice and sat next to her on the couch with my arm firmly around her shoulder, the panic would abate, leaving her thinking exceptionally clear and resulting in a period of particularly lucid therapeutic exploration.

When anger or anxiety erupts with sudden intensity, a patient may stand up and try to bolt from the room. If the patient is physically small enough and the therapist physically large enough to pose a solid and reassuring obstacle, the therapist can sometimes block the escape route and soothe the patient over the emotional wave. A quick judgment call is necessary, however, because sometimes patients obtain appropriate relief and prevent violent action by removing themselves from situations they cannot handle.

> The Whitman family, which had a history of episodic violent behavior, seemed to benefit from allowing explosive family members to exit from sessions. The father, Jeremy, bolted out of sessions from time to time, returning after several minutes of calming himself out in the hallway. On one occasion, an emotional confontation occurred between the teenage son, Jeb, and his stepmother, Dee. Jeb had been trying his hardest to maintain calm in the face of Dee's clear rejection. Eventually the intense antipathy she subtly expressed toward him broke down his ability to sustain goodwill toward her. "You're so . . . selfish!" he blurted out. He stood up and dashed from the room.
>
> As I explained to Jeb in a phone contact later that evening, parents send young children to their rooms when they are getting emotionally overwhelmed by a situation they cannot handle. Adults need to learn to send themselves to their room, i.e., to leave situations that would only lead to worse explosions if they stayed. I commended Jeb for his rapid departure. The abrupt exit had been positive for Dee as well. After Jeb had left in such obvious distress, Dee, for the first time, began to soften in her rigid scapegoating stance toward her stepson.

Occasionally, emotional intensity in the therapy session reaches a level that causes a patient's functioning to break down altogether. Omer and Spivak (1987), labeling this state "acute behavioral disorganization," suggest that in this state of intense emotions both thinking and behavior can become either fragmentary, haphazard, and chaotic or rigid and repetitive. Sudden rage, mutism (inability to speak beyond unintelligible sounds), violence, panic, and shock can be among the many manifestations of this kind of abrubt shift to a state of emotional overarousal.

> Margaret, in an episode described in Chapter 11, stood up suddenly in the middle of a session, looked about to attack her husband, swung her arms randomly, and started shouting. I immediately asked her husband to leave the room, stood up next to Margaret, looked directly into her eyes, and spoke to her in a firm but soothing voice until I had captured her attention and brought her into resonance with my (at least somewhat) calmer emotional state. I also put my hand on her arm, and walked along next to her until I could nonverbally steer her toward sitting down in a low and comfortable armchair.

Omer and Spivak detail a number of ways that the therapist can reengage attentional contact with the disorganized person and reestablish normalized thinking and behaving. Because stimulus overload overtaxes the person's capacity for integration, the therapist's first response needs to be to simplify the situation, removing the patient from the provocative stimuli or the stimuli from the person's environment. Then, to establish contact, resonance can be accomplished via pacing, imitation, modeling and distraction techniques. These techniques, illustrated briefly in the example with Margaret, are described fully in the Omer and Spivak article.

As in the cases of the Whitmans, of Karen, and Margaret, the period after an episode of emotional intensity can be one of particular insight and capacity for conceptual shifts. Although emotional overload is not necessarily a state one aims to create in treatment, its aftermath can be extremely productive if therapist and patient can then debrief, clarifying the conflictual concerns that gave rise to the emotions and seeking new solutions.

Emotional blockages

Avoidance of emotional expression signals the need for therapist intervention. Tears, a quivering chin, agitated foot-tapping or other body movement, a frown all can cue a therapist to gently probe for expression of the thoughts or feelings. An invitation to express the underlying emotion may suffice. In other instances, gestalt-type encouragement to experience the underlying feeling through repetition and exaggeration of the visible activity (the foot-tapping, etc.) can help to bring the feeling to consciousness.

The emotional climate created by the therapist is particularly crucial when patients are holding back feelings. By the kindly attitude and emotional calm s/he projects, the therapist reassures patients that expression of feelings will be met with accepting empathy. Unless emotions are intensified to the point that they emerge into consciousness and become verbalized, critical data for understanding the underlying concerns in a conflict may be missing.

Provocative listening

At least four poor listening responses commonly disrupt explorations of underlying concerns and need to be addressed immediately by the therapist to keep the discussion cooperative. Sometimes a listener moves right on to the next comment because s/he has in fact not taken in what the prior speaker has said. In this case a reminder that slower is faster is in order. Encouraging a redo of the interaction gives a second opportunity for the communication to be heard. These patients sometimes benefit from reminders that, just as throwing a ball is only half of the game of catch, saying is only half of the exploration of concerns.

Second, data may have been heard and registered, but not acknowledged. To prevent the speaker from becoming upset because s/he feels ignored, the therapist can explicitly ask the listener to recapitulate what was said. After hearing this reiteration, the original speaker will be in a better position to switch roles and hear the other person's response to his/her concerns.

Third, as suggested in the previous chapter, a judgmental listening response can mean that the listener has heard the speaker's comments but rejected them. Judgmental listeners listen for what is wrong instead of what is right in what the other is saying. They listen to criticize instead of listening to understand, as if the object of listening was to reject rather than to receive information. Generally these responses will come out with "but" as the first word, negating what the speaker has said. To avoid this pitfall the therapist can start the listener out by prompting, "And. . . ." A judgmental listener also can be guided to reiterate the speaker's comments in a more accepting manner by being advised, "Start by responding with what seems right to you about what you have just heard, what makes sense to you."

Lastly, some individuals listen with hyperalertness, straining to hear what the speaker is *really* saying. The manifest content is seen as merely offering hints of the genuine message, which often is assumed to be critical. Instead of taking words at their face value, this kind of interpretive listening looks behind the verbal screen to find the hidden message. For listening to individuals who in fact do say something other than what they really feel, this kind of interpretive listening can be useful. In most instances, however, it irritates the speaker and interrupts the flow of dialogue. I usually deal with this form of listening problem by stating a flat rule. People are responsible for saying in a straightforward manner what they mean. And listeners are not allowed to engage in guesswork. Creative listening is out of bounds; the object is to hear only what has been explicitly said. I then ask the patients to redo their dialogue, operating by the new rules. When rules, including rules of discourse, are explicit, most people want to play by them.

What if a therapist notes persistent antagonism, blocked emotional expression, or inadequate listening? The therapist may choose to turn the focus from the conflict at hand (content) to investigation of the interaction patterns (process). What is causing the interactions to be so blocked, defensive, suspicious or hostile? Certainly this side trip to "analyze the resistance" can be productive, and ultimately it is likely to be a most memorable exploration. The question is one of timing, of which agenda to pursue and when.

Interestingly, if the critical goal for that particular session is resolution of a specific conflict, successfully guided exploration of the underlying concerns can lead to a decrease in antagonism. Thus, keeping the exploration focused on one issue and tightly managing the emotional tone can pay off both by settling the issue at hand and by improving the emotional climate. This strategy, however, does not always work. If interventions to maintain a positive tone do not suffice to generate productive explorations, the therapist can switch from content to process, from the attempt to actually resolve a specific conflict to an explicit focus on the patterns with which conflicts are addressed. The content of any specific dispute may in fact be secondary to the process difficulties; poor patterns of emotional management can repeatedly create conflicts. For instance, some patients only know how to argue. They don't want to feel antagonistic, and they don't care particularly about any specific issues. If they are limited in this way in their repertoire of how to talk over problems, however, their belligerence can cause disputes over even simple mutual decisions.

What can a failure of all of the above measures mean? The most likely explanation, other than lack of therapist skill, is a resurgence of symptomatic behavior—severe anxiety, psychotic thought, major mood disorder, drug addiction, or extramarital affairs—that needs to be addressed before verbal therapies will be effective. It may be a time when treating symptoms is necessary in order to quiet down the "noise" in the system enough to productively engage in explorations and movement toward conflict resolution.

Maintaining focus

Many patients get distracted or lost when they try to explore their concerns. Some, such as those whom Shapiro (1965) describes as having a hysteric cognitive style, may become scattered in their exploration. They may make frequent quick turns from topic to topic rather than systematically exploring one question at a time in depth and breadth. Because the ideas are linked by associations, by points of similarity, instead of by relevance to the central topic of concern, this meandering thinking can make maintenance of focused exploration difficult. Other individuals, with what Shapiro labels as an obsessive pattern, may get stuck in small peripheral issues and cease to move forward toward an overall understanding. Getting lost among the trees in the forest can result in a loss of orientation toward the conflict resolution objective.

Both wandering and obfuscation can be countered by frequent reiterations of the focal conflict. Crary (1984) notes that children attempting to problem solve in groups need frequent restatements of the problem they are addressing. Their tendency to roam off on tangents causes them otherwise to lose their train of thought. Many adults have the same need. In addition, periodic summaries of the main points made thus far in the explorations enhance movement along the path. Again, "slower is faster" holds true. Slowing down to review progress with summarizing statements enhances the sense of accomplishment during explorations and consolidates gains.

A therapist can block digressions by explicitly requesting a return to the central problem. By validating that a comment has been interesting and adding that a later discussion on that topic might be fruitful, the therapist can tactfully lead the discussion back to the central issue without causing a straying participant to lose face. Tracking the association that led to the peripheral explorations also can be beneficial. This technique can rapidly enlarge understanding of the underlying concerns and at the same time refocus the exploration on the central conflict.

> Maryanne, who had been exploring why she frequently seemed to enter into battles with her two-year-old son, suddenly switched to comments about her husband and their impending move out of state. What was the connecting link? In both cases Maryanne experienced someone forcing her to do what they wanted without consideration of her preferences and needs. She felt controlled by her young son just as she felt controlled by her husband. This connection helped Maryanne to crystallize the concerns she felt regarding what therapists would call "collapsed hierarchy" and what Maryanne called "getting out of control."

Maintenance of a positive climate makes therapy more fun, a more positive experience. Some diversions are simply that, diversions for the sake of pleasure, for the sharing of time together and the consolidation of the bonds between the people involved. Therapy needn't be an altogether heavy or painful process. Joking, laughing, and sharing can enhance therapy as well as life. Still, patients are paying for every minute in treatment and may feel as if the playful time is a waste of their therapy dollars. A helpful way to integrate work and play is to conclude playful diversions with thoughts about how they bear on the session's primary topic. This strategy helps the patient to convert a brief wandering off the path into a productive side exploration.

> During a particularly serious therapy hour with Bart and Jeanne, Bart launched into a lighthearted exchange with the therapist. At the conclusion, in response to my question, "How do the last few minutes relate to what we have

been talking about?" Bart said that he realized that playful discusion such as he had just enjoyed with me were quite lacking in the marital relationship. This insight went to the heart of the therapeutic issue for that session, namely, improving the perpetually tense climate in their household. The result was a productive clarification of ways in which both Bart and Jeanne could increase the likelihood of more playfulness between them.

In sum, a therapist can deal with digressions by returning patients to the central issues, by reiterating the conflicting positions they are exploring, by offering summarizing statements of the explorations thus far, or by discovering connections between the divergent topic and the original one.

Two other practical considerations help to govern decisions about when to let patients' associations flow and when to channel their explorations more tightly. One is simply the clock. As the end of a session approaches, it becomes increasingly appropriate to limit associational diversions and to focus all dialogue explicitly on the conflict at hand.

A second consideration is the extent to which patients react adversely to interruptions by the therapist to their train of thought. Some patients appreciate the help with focusing, acknowledging that their thinking gets disorganized and unbounded. Other patients, who tend more toward the oppositional than the compliant, are hypersensitive to being controlled by others. These patients are likely to feel resentful when the therapist cuts them short or redirects their thoughts. In these cases the therapist's shepherding may need to be most tactful and reserved for situations in which diversions are clearly unproductive. A therapist must not be frightened away from confronting a patient who resists direction and wants to control the treatment him/herself. On the other hand, battles can be chosen judiciously and then must be clearly won, with kind firmness. Expressing understanding of the patient's upset and concern may help, e.g., "I can see that you do not like when I interrupt you. Sometimes I will do that. I will make it a point, however, to be sure that I understand what you are trying to say before we return to the original topic. You were saying "x," is that right? Let's return now to the topic we had agreed would be our focus for today, and perhaps as we do you can clarify for us what the link is to the thought you were just expressing."

Maintaining symmetry

Dare (1986, p. 23) points out, "The need to obtain symmetry is a consistent feature and an example of the constant need for a directive element in marital therapy." Dare further discusses the need for the therapist to "redress the balance of utterances pouring from one spouse by urging the

speaking member of the couple to get a response from the silent spouse."
Symmetry of air time is critical. Rather than thrusting the responsibility for
its maintenance on the wordier partner, as Dare suggests, I prefer to make
this a joint responsibility of both participants, as part of a general attempt
to symmetrically distribute the responsibility for making changes. Thus
quiet family members need to speak up more, learning to interrupt if
necessary. Lengthier speakers need to learn to limit themselves and to
expect more participation from others. And the therapist-guide serves as a
traffic policeman who controls the flow of cars through an intersection
giving equal time to each lane.

Dare (1986) also mentions the need for the therapist to maintain equal
alliances with both spouses so that neither feels that the therapist is more
aligned with one than with the other. Attention to this aspect of symmetry
is essential to prevent rivalrous competition for the therapist's positive
regard. Giving equal weight to the contributions of both spouses, spending
equal time exploring both spouses' concerns, being certain that both engage
in active reiterative listening, and positioning the furniture so that the
therapist's chair is equidistant from both spouses' are some of the many
specific ways in which equal alliances are conveyed.

When conflicts are intrapsychic, symmetry maintenance is equally
important, though not always so obvious. The following case illustrates this
point (Heitler, 1987).

> Todd was an attractive and intelligent unmarried man in his late twenties
> who wanted to resolve his ambivalent response to advances from his former
> girlfriend. On the one hand, he wanted to hold onto his hopes that the
> relationship might somehow be salvaged; on the other, he wanted to let go and
> be free of the troubling relationship.
>
> The conflict exploration was structured with the gestalt empty-chair
> format. I suggested that Todd explore his inner dialogue by sitting in one chair
> when speaking from the parts of him that wanted to hold onto the relation-
> ship, and in the other when he was wanting to let go. These chairs represented
> the initially expressed wishes on both sides of the conflict.
>
> From the side that wanted to hold on Todd first emitted a weak, "But I love
> her. . . ." He then moved to the other chair, where he confidently listed a
> number of compelling and sensible reasons for giving up on the relationship.
> He noted his former girfriend's emotional instability, her insistence on
> blaming him for all problems that emerged, her refusal to discuss differences,
> including their fundamental religious differences, and their sexual incompat-
> ibility. The lopsided exploration of concerns ended with Todd convinced to let
> go, but feeling resigned and emotionally distraught.
>
> I noted this asymmetry to Todd, who responded with the realization that a
> similar pattern had occurred whenever he would try to discuss issues with his
> former girlfriend. Either Todd would feebly express his own wishes and then
> resign himself to doing whatever she wanted, or she would become sullenly
> silent and go along resentfully with whatever Todd expressed.

I sensed that Todd was responding to more concerns that were underlying his impulse to hold onto the girlfriend, but that these were relatively less accessible to his conscious awareness. For accessing these deeper concerns, we used a visualization technique.

"Close your eyes," I suggested. "What do you picture when you think of holding onto the hope of returning to your girlfriend?"

Todd was surprised to see an image that he described as "salvaging the impossible." He realized that a similar theme characterized the professional work he most enjoyed, namely, rescuing public agencies from mismanagement. He realized that what he wanted was not the girlfriend per se, but the challenge of reviving an ailing relationship, of accomplishing the impossible. Todd opened his eyes (which signaled a return to more present and conscious material). He noted that his current work lacked this challenge, that he had known for several years that he had outgrown his work and needed to find new challenges. His present job was boring, unsatisfying, and unsuitable for him. Intrigued by this unexpected finding, I wanted to check if family-of-origin concerns were also feeding Todd's tendencies to keep holding onto both his girlfriend and his unsatisfying job. Again I suggested to Todd that he close his eyes. This time I suggested, utilizing the words with which Todd had described his problem, "Visualize and feel yourself *holding on tightly*. What moments from your youth does this feeling remind you of?"

Todd recalled traveling with his parents to Mexico when he was about five years old. He remembered holding intensely onto his parents' hands. They had warned him, "Hold on tight or the people here will steal you away!" Todd had felt terrified and had believed that tightly holding on was all that would save him from a terrible fate.

Again opening his eyes, Todd discussed how holding on tightly made a scary world a safer place. It was clear now that Todd had been motivated by two powerful and yet seemingly contradictory concerns. He sought challenge and excitement in the attempt to accomplish the impossible. On the other hand, he experienced the world as a scary place in which survival was contingent on holding onto others.

With this understanding of the complex concerns on *both* sides of his conflict, an understanding that came from noting the asymmetry of Todd's concerns, Todd was ready for new solutions. He decided to indulge his love of rescue and danger in realms other than relationships with women by initiating a career move into work that would in fact be considerably more challenging. Then he felt free in his personal life to satisfy his longing for security by choosing a woman who could be an appropriate match for marriage. Addressing the asymmetry and bringing equally to light the underlying concerns on both sides of his intrapsychic conflict enabled Todd to clarify what he wanted to do regarding his former girlfriend and how he wanted to design the next period of his life.

Obtaining specificity

Exploration of concerns benefits from a maximum of specificity and concreteness. Here, again, slower is faster, as more thorough and detailed exploration prepares the way for an easier slide into solutions. To obtain specificity a therapist can ask the patient to close his/her eyes and visualize the problem being explored.

> Hannah complained to the point of tears when she thought about their home, which was sorely in need of renovation. Her husband suggested they begin doing something about the most frustating area, the living room, by at least painting it. Hannah looked alarmed and said, "Absolutely not!" What was it about this proposal that led her to react so strongly? What was her underlying concern? Hannah easily said, "I'm afraid if we do any temporary solutions then we'll delay all the longer on the permanent Grand Plan renovations." Hannah's husband Craig reassured her that a delay would not occur, but his reassurance did not seem to suffice.
>
> To obtain more specific details I asked Hannah to close her eyes and picture temporary solutions. The image that came to mind was of their neighbors' house. Their neighbors had discussed renovation of their mansion for years, but the daughter's bedroom never received actual work until she was a senior in high school, and the son's had been postponed until he was already out of the house and in college.
>
> Whereas stating her concern as a general fear had yielded little sympathy from her husband, who felt confident that he was not likely to procrastinate, when Hannah articulated the specific image of their next door neighbors' home, both of them chuckled, united, and together vowed not to let that happen to them.

Guiding patients in their explorations through emotionally evocative conflicts, therapists thus must continuously monitor multiple factors—a modulated emotional tone, a clear focus on the content of explorations, symmetry, and specificity. This kind of therapeutic work is more like guiding an expedition over challenging mountains and down through treacherous canyons than like guiding a flock of sheep to pasture.

CHAPTER 15

Guiding: Exploration
of Underlying Concerns

As a therapist guides patients from conflict to resolution on a specific issue, the territory needs to be explored with sufficient scope to yield optimal solutions. As suggested at the end of the last chapter, the pathway is not a simple one. It has not only right and left turns that determine the breadth of the exploration, but also vertical factors of depth.

One might think that limiting explorations to fewer concerns would make solution-building simpler. Paradoxically, a larger number of concerns actually enhances the probability of reaching satisfactory resolution. More concerns on both sides of a conflict make for more dimensions that can be involved in trade-offs.

COVERING THE TERRITORY WITH ADEQUATE BREADTH

Breadth refers to the width or range of concerns that are explored. For instance, a broad exploration could include concerns about likes and dislikes, values, needs, fears, relationships with others, abilities, and so forth.

> Ralphine was engaged to be married to Mark, but she was experiencing doubts. Although she was embarrassed to admit it, Ralphine's fears about the marriage centered on dislike of Mark's dog. We used one therapy session as a preparation so that she would feel more comfortable discussing the problem at home with Mark. Our goal was to bring to awareness the full breadth of concerns that Ralphine harbored about her fiance's pet.

As she thought about the dog, Ralphine realized that because he was large and affectionate, he overpowered her, particularly when he jumped up to lick her, which she hated. The dog had not been to obedience school and was not responsive to her commands to stay down. His shaggy hair, which he shed all over the house, gave Ralphine a mild allergic reaction — a runny nose and itchy throat. Because the dog was allowed throughout the house, Ralphine felt she was never safe from him. When he came up to greet her, he sometimes affectionately grabbed hold of her arm with his mouth, which hurt and felt distasteful. His swishing tail endangered objects on end tables, so Ralphine felt continually on the alert, prepared to lunge for falling objects. Lastly, at night the dog slept in their bedroom and woke her with the jangle of his dog tags as he moved about.

For purposes of discussing the dog problem with Mark, this list of concerns, broad but not deep, sufficed. Ralphine and Mark discussed her concerns; Mark added his; and together they worked out a mutually acceptable solution. They decided to return the large dog to its original owner and to find a smaller, shorter-haired, and quieter animal that they could both enjoy with less distress.

Interestingly, trivial as this dilemma was in some respects, it turned out to have a pivotal impact on Ralphine's relationship. Before this discussion, Ralphine had found herself pulling away from Mark. The dog negotiation helped her to realize that her central underlying concern was whether or not she could affect things she did not like in their relationship. To the extent that she felt she could not, every mild dissatisfaction became a cue to disengage from the relationship. Having worked out a mutual solution to this one problem, Ralphine felt a renewed sense of hope. She began to think that, in contrast to her beliefs and behaviors in prior relationships, she might now be able to sustain a couple relationship and simultaneously sustain her own sense of who she is and what she likes and doesn't like. Solving the here-and-now issue of what to do about the dog radically influenced Ralphine's underlying recurring concern or, as it is referred to later in this chapter, her core conflict. And exploring the full breadth of her concerns gave her a series of repeated experiences with allowing herself to have a feeling, to verbalize it, and to have it received with understanding.

When concerns are less concrete and tangible than those of Ralphine and the dog, a visualization can offer a particularly enlightening vehicle for clarifying the multiple dimensions of a problem. Whereas discussion between patient and therapist does not always clarify how broadly the concerns need to be explored, a visual image can make explicit the range of concerns that must be considered.

Patrick, who had fallen into an intense relationship with a woman at his office, felt tortured, pulled between his wife and his new love, yet unable to move in any direction.

I asked Patrick to close his eyes and visualize who or what he felt pulling at him. Patrick responded with the following image.

"I see my wife Janice pulling in one direction, on one of my arms. Dorinda is pulling on the other arm. I see myself pulling in a third direction, and a blob of something, it's hard for me to make out what, pulling in another direction. Me and the mass of whatever are on the front and back of me."

Prior to this session Patrick had been thinking of his dilemma in either/or terms, i.e., should he stay with his wife or leave his wife for Dorinda. His decision-making see-sawed back and forth between the two women; whenever he was with one, he wanted to go to the other. By contrast, this image allowed us to determine that there were four areas of concerns, represented by the four forces pulling on him. The goal of the session then became to understand the meanings of each of these forces, and to find solutions responsive to each of them.

OBTAINING DEPTH IN EXPLORATIONS OF CONCERNS

The notion of "deeper" concerns, explained in Chapter 2, connotes variation on two dimensions, an awareness (consciousness) continuum and a historical continuum (Norcross, 1986). The awareness continuum extends from concerns that are easily accessible to those that are deeply buried. The historical continuum is based on when the concerns first emerged, ranging from a person's early family years to the present. Exploring at adequate depths requires subconsciousness-penetrating interventions to clarify the ties between current concerns and earlier family-of-origin issues. Greater depth of understanding of concerns seems to lead to greater success in eventually finding more sanguine solutions to troubling conflicts.

Metaphorical and other visualizing explorations

If expression of the conflict was structured initially with a visualization, the concerns can be explored in the same manner. The following case, introduced in Chapter 13, illustrates how a metaphor that was used to clarify the elements in a conflict can then be utilized to explore underlying concerns (and to find solutions).

Renalda had visualized herself carrying a large burden of snow. Her conflict was that she wanted to put down this burden, and she also feared setting it down. What were the concerns underlying these contradictory impulses? Renalda felt tired of carrying the heavy burden. The burden was cumbersome, and she wanted to be able to move freely about. On the other hand, she feared that the snow would disintegrate if it was set down. She feared that setting it down would mean she was not capable of carrying her load. She feared also that setting down the load would distance her too much from loved ones.

Once Renalda understood her concerns, at least expressed metaphorically, I encouraged her to experiment with various solutions. She first envisioned that to leave the snow burden she would have to sneak away from it, which made her feel quite uncomfortable about herself. This solution clarified another concern, a desire to handle the burden in a straightforward, forthright manner that she could feel comfortable with.

Solution proposals often facilitate clarification of underlying concerns. Participants sometimes do not realize all of their underlying concerns until a proposed solution has alarmed them. Cooperative problem-solving of complex problems sometimes involves considerable back-and-forth movement between exploring underlying concerns and proposing solutions.

> Renalda next pictured herself dropping the load, which scattered the snow. Although this image offered some relief, it also raised further concerns. In a third attempt at visualizing a solution Renalda set the load down carefully and it remained intact. She felt lightened and visualized herself dancing, then happily walking side by side with her husband.
>
> After we had gone through all three stages of conflict resoltuion dealing only within the visual metaphor, I invited Renalda to open her eyes and think about how these images related to her real life dilemmas. The snow load had represented the burdens on her to protect her husband from all worries so that he could utilize his energies to recover from cancer, chemotherapy and surgery. Now that his physical recovery was nearing completion and his cancer was in remission, the family roles needed reassessment. Setting down the snow load represented letting go of responsibility for protecting her husband from stress that had been necessary during this period of medical vulnerability. Now Renalda and her husband could return to a relationship as partners, freeing Renalda to pursue again her own creative endeavors.

The depth dive for family-of-origin explorations

Sometimes the concerns raised by patients make clear sense given the circumstances of their conflict. In other cases, however, the concerns have an idiosyncratic feel to the therapist or exist with more emotional intensity than the overt situation seems to warrant. The concern may be one that most people would not share. Or the concern may be one that anyone in similar circumstances would experience, but to a lesser degree of intensity. These clues suggest that occurrences in an individual's past are exerting as much or more influence as the exigencies of the present. How can these concerns be probed, concerns which are "deep" in terms of historical remoteness and also in terms of remoteness from conscious awareness.

Sensing these clues, the therapist can facilitate a depth dive. In swimming lingo this kind of depth dive is called, paradoxically, a "surface dive." The swimmer, swimming initially along the top surface of water, bends at the waist to take a near-vertical plunge into the depths, swims briefly around in the deep, and then returns with a near-vertical ascent. In therapy, a plunge directly from the present dilemma down to the past and then a rapid return back up to the present enables patients to bring to light the specific past interactions that are influencing the current conflict.

Wachtel's writings on the relationship of Piaget's concept of schemas to the phenomenon of transference (see Chapter 4) forms the theoretical basis for this depth diving technique. Wachtel (1987) writes,

> Piaget's concept of schemas, characterized by the two basic functions of assimilation and accommodation, seems particularly useful for understanding . . . transference and other . . . relationship phenomena. . . . The concept of transference was an attempt to come to terms with an extreme version of this tendency to experience events in terms of structures and expectations based on earlier experiences. . . . (p.30)

> One can readily see that *all* perceptions and behaviors are mediated by schemas which are the product of past experiences and which attempt to assimilate new input to them—as well as to accommodate to their novel features. (p.33)

To initiate a depth dive, the therapist suggests that the patient close his/her eyes and focus on the feelings evoked in the current conflict situation. Utilizing gestalt-like techniques, the therapist can suggest that the patient allow these feelings to intensify. Operating on the assumption that memories are filed and can be accessed via feelings, the therapist asks, "When in your past experience have you felt a similar feeling? Allow an image to come to mind of a time when a similar feeling has come up for you." The patient then is encouraged to describe this situation in maximum detail. The situation typically illustrates the cognitive schema that is influencing the patient's current concern.

A variation of the depth dive utilizes reactions to people rather than emotions to uncover the schema evoked in the past that is affecting the present. The therapist suggests that the patient close his/her eyes and picture the person with whom s/he is involved in a troubling interaction. "Focus on just how that person appears to you when s/he does 'x' (i.e., whatever occurs in the conflictual situation). Now allow that image to fade into an image of someone else whom that person reminds you of."

Once the situation or person from the past has been clarified, the concerns that are being evoked in the present situation become more comprehensible. Sometimes the depth dive initially brings up a person or situation that occurred at some point between childhood and the adult present. In these cases it is sometimes helpful to suggest a second round of the same exercise, so that the links to earlier childhood experiences become evident. It is likely that the concerns will be similar in both instances, but the earlier situation may explain the potency of the reaction in both the intermediate and the present situations.

> When her two-year-old son would press her to do this or that for him, Maryanne would react with a disproportionate and distressing fury. Depth diving to explore similar earlier feelings, Maryanne recalled intense anger toward a male roommate during her first post-college years. She described the situation. "He would ask me to cook or do this or that, and when I said no he would go on and on, backing me against the wall until I would scream at him to leave me alone."
>
> In response to my suggestion that she again close her eyes and allow the roommate's face to transform into someone whom he resembled, Maryanne immediately saw her father. She recalled incidents in which her father would command her to feel or do something, and the helpless rage within her as she realized that he would never listen to what she had to say about it. Verbally abusive to her and physically abusive to her brother, her father had been cruelly impervious to her attempts to voice her feelings.

Because uncovering potent early memories can evoke intense and disruptive feelings for patients, the therapist must allow enough time in the session to come back to the surface for a full follow-up debriefing. The patient returns to the present by opening his/her eyes and refocusing on the here and now. Then s/he is asked two critical questions to decontaminate the present from the past and detoxify the material that has been brought up from the dive:

- *What is the same about that past experience and your present situation* (or between the person in the past and the person in your current life)? This question yields the associative links between two incidents or people and usually reflects the central underlying concern.
- *What is different about the past experience or person and your present interaction?* Sometimes in order to respond to this latter question patients need reassurance that key differences do exist. Uncovering these differences enables the patient to discern ways in which the past and the present genuinely do differ. These new perceptions open the way for the emergence of new schemas and the discovery of new solutions to old concerns.

> Maryanne understood that the common theme in all three rageful moments was a feeling of being pressured to respond to someone else's interest at her own expense. In all three instances she had squelched strong feelings arising within her because they seemed incompatible with the demands of her father, roommate, or son.

In response to the second question, regarding differences in the three situations, Maryanne realized that her father left her no options other than to suffer silently, while with the roommate she was at least able to respond with anger, achieving some emotional release. With her own son she had far broader response options. She realized that she was the adult and he the child, so she had many degrees of freedom in choosing how to respond.

The remainder of the session involved clarification of parenting responses that would be more effective than raging when her son was excessively demanding. No longer trapped by the self-denial her old schemas had imposed and armed with new parenting options, Maryanne left the session feeling relieved and optimistic. I cautioned that practicing the new strategies would take time, encouraging Maryanne to give herself permission to experiment gradually with the new parenting skills until they became as automatic as enraged yelling.

Paradoxical explorations

For patients who are rigid and/or oppositional, paradoxical interventions are another option for facilitating exploration of underlying concerns. In these cases the concerns are "deep" in their inaccessibility to awareness.

Madanes (1984) defines *paradoxical intervention* as "a directive (an instruction to do something) or extended message (a discussion) that is apparently inconsistent with itself or with the purpose of therapy" (pp. 148-149). She distinguishes between "straightforward communications" which therapists "expect will be accepted or followed," and paradoxical interventions "designed to provoke a family to change by rebelling against the therapist" (p.7). Although family therapists propose multiple variations on the theme of paradoxical intervention, Madanes suggests that the technique always involves the following element:

> Within a context where a patient comes to therapy in order to change, the therapist asks him to produce more of the behavior that the patient wants changed, and within a context of acceptance of the involuntary nature of the patient's behavior, the therapist requests that the patient produce this behavior voluntarily. (p.8)

Family therapists who work with rigid pathological systems find that paradoxical interventions shake up the system and thereby promote faster change (L'Abate, Ganahl, & Hansen, 1986):

> Given the greater capacity of the family to resist change and maintain sameness, the methods of family therapy must necesarily be of greater intensity than those used with individuals. With families a certain degree of shock or suddenness is useful, essentially to surprise the family. (p.6)

Interestingly, the intention of paradoxical treatment may appear to be to circumvent the insight process and move directly to implementation of changes. In fact, skillful use of paradox can promote a dramatic surge to awareness of the underlying concerns that are driving problematic behaviors. Papp (1981) utilizes family therapy terminology to make this point, saying that a common error in using paradox is to prescribe the symptom "without connecting it to the system in a circular definition." In conflict terms, this error then could be described as prescribing a solution (the symptom) without explaining the concerns that the solution is meant to solve. Clarification of these concerns is what enables families to realize that perhaps alternative solutions might meet these concerns with fewer costs than the present symptom-solution. The following example by Papp (1981) illustrates this point.

> . . . an eight-year-old boy is failing in school. The therapist determines that the symptom serves the function of keeping the mother's disappointment focused on her son, Billy, rather than on her husband. The husband is failing in business and, rather than redoubling his efforts, is sinking into apathy. . . . He gives off signals that he would collapse if confronted openly with this issue, and the mother collaborates in protecting him. Whenever she becomes angry at his lack of ambition, she nags Billy to straighten out and make something of himself. . . .
>
> The therapist tells the mother it is important for her to continue to express her disappointment in Billy, because otherwise she might begin to express her dissatisfaction with her husband. This would be risky, as her husband might become depressed, and since Billy is younger and more resilient than her husband, he can take it better. Billy is advised to continue to protect his father by keeping the mother's disappointment focused on him, and the father is commended for his cooperation. The mother has an immediate recoil, saying, "You're suggesting I fight with my eight-year-old son instead of my husband, a grown man? Why should I damage my son to protect my husband?" thus defining her own predicament. . . . The conflict is refocused onto the parents, and Billy is released from his middle position. (p. 247)

Papp's paradoxical intervention clarified the family's concerns and alleviated some of their problems. The next step would be to assist the spouses in working as a cooperative team rather than as antagonists in confronting the husband's business difficulties.

Other techniques for probing deeper concerns

Free association, interpretation of resistances, elaboration of the transference, gestalt interventions, and dream interpretation are commonly utilized psychodynamic methods for pursuing depth explorations, particularly toward the goal of accessing preconscious information. Behaviorists explore underlying concerns by taking detailed information regarding thoughts and feelings surrounding troubling behaviors. For accessing concerns in terms of historical depth, i.e., concerns arising out of the family of origin and early life experiences, systemic therapists utilize the genogram. These insight-oriented techniques (listed also in Table 11.3) are well described in the psychotherapy literature.

With most of these exploration techniques, care must be taken in making "interpretations" of underlying issues. As gestalt therapists point out, therapists' interpretations are likely to be less accurate and less well-received than patients' own clarifications of their underlying concerns. Hunches and intuitions about patients' issues are inevitably influenced by projection of therapists' experiences onto the patient. A certain degree of projection seems inevitable, even when a therapist's reality-testing is quite good so that there is only minimal contamination of patients' feelings and thoughts by the therapist's issues.

Even if therapists are remarkably free of the tendency to project, they will not be able to describe patients' concerns with the precise language and imagery with which patients themselves experience the problem. Moreover, if the therapist offers the "interpretation," i.e., the plunge down to deeper underlying concerns, the patient is freed of the responsibility and learning experience of discovering his/her own unconscious motivations. For all of these reasons, it is no more positive for therapists to "interpret" patients' concerns than for family members to "mind read," i.e., to speak for one another instead of each speaking their own thoughts.

In sum, exploration of underlying concerns can be undertaken via a multitude of vehicles. Therapists need to choose an appropriate exploration vehicle, guide patients to the discovery of their concerns, and then share in the exploration by actively listening and empathically reiterating the concerns they hear voiced. Enabling patients to articulate their discoveries in their own words and with their own imagery is generally preferable to verbalizing concerns for patients.

CLARIFYING CORE CONFLICTS

Interestingly, as a therapist guides patients through several problematic conflicts, certain themes will tend to recur. Luborsky (1987, p.57) describes these themes as "redundancies in the narratives that patients spontaneously tell throughout their psychotherapy."

Luborsky (1977) developed a formalized system for identifying the wishes, responses from others, and outcome feelings and behaviors that occur repeatedly in any given patient's upsetting relationship incidents. In general, these wishes have been frustrated by others' responses, accounting perhaps for their recurrence (see Chapter 4). A person whose hunger is not satisfied with food continues to wish for food until that need has been met. Another explanation is that these incidents are selected by the patient for recall in the therapy hour because they involve a lack of closure and therefore evoke a kind of Ziegarnik effect. Gestalt theory refers to such themes as "unfinished business."

Luborsky refers to these repeated wishes and to frustrating responses they receive as transference themes. They tend to occur and recur in interactions with the therapist as well as with significant others in the patient's world. With or without the concept of transference, such repeated upsetting wishes, which Luborsky calls "core conflictual relationship themes," can be identified as recurrent, highly sensitive, and emotionally provocative underlying concerns.

A relatively small number of these concerns tends to recur for each patient, making the therapist's task in identifying underlying concerns far simpler. An individual who frequently becomes upset, seemingly embroiled in a multitude of conflicts, typically is repeatedly responding to a very small set of deeper concerns. Helping the patient to identify the one or several main underlying concerns in one incident sets the stage for more easily discovering the essential underlying concern(s) in subsequent, seemingly unrelated, incidents.

The following two cases illustrate a couple and then a family in which individuals' underlying core concerns frequently recur. Although the manifest content of the arguments is highly varied, the more deeply felt underlying latent concerns are quite consistent.

Lucinda and Leroy argued about everything from what Leroy ate for lunch to what Lucinda thought of a woman they met at a party. The triggering issue in these arguments was relatively irrelevant; the underlying concerns, always centered on the same several fears and decisions. Whereas a "laundry list" of argument-inducing topics based on manifest content would have been infinite, the core conflictual issues were quite consistent. The couple's fights virtually always involved Leroy feeling anxious and angry because he couldn't figure out what his wife wanted him to say or do, and Lucinda feeling anxious and angry because she felt brushed aside whenever she expressed a feeling.

Leroy worried about how to escape from his wife's criticism. When he couldn't understand what his wife wanted from him, he anticipated that she would then be angry at him. Lucinda, in fact, was often curious or anxious rather than critical, but transference from family-of-origin experience with a hypercritical parent fed Leroy's concern. Lucinda's core concern was that she would be cut off from dialogue with her husband. Lucinda's mother, who had suffered frequent depressions, would frequently become irrationally angry at her and then go through extended periods of refusing to talk with her daughter, as if her depression had been caused by something terrible her little girl had done. Leroy's attempts to escape from what he read as a pending onslaught of criticism felt to Lucinda like her mother's refusals to talk with her.

Families, as opposed to couples, bring considerable complexity to the identification of core concerns, as each individual family member may have his/her own repetitive issues. Identification of these issues, however, can greatly reduce the frequency and duration of battles triggered by the same concerns, day after day.

> Two-thirds of the way through treatment with the Martin family I asked the family to redefine the laundry list of remaining unresolved arguments. How many issues did each family member think they had still on deck, I asked. Each family member estimated that they had two or three issues — except Jim. Jim said, half-jokingly and half-seriously, "Oh, 165." While we went around the family circle, each listing their several remaining unresolved disputes, Jim managed to get into a fight with Monica. Monica had said that she still battled with her father over the delegation of responsibility for household chores. Jim corrected her. "You can delegate power but not responsibility!" he adamantly insisted, referencing his college sociology course with authoritative zeal. Monica, after the first several salvos from Jim, became silent, implementing her new policy of verbal restraint instead of allowing herself to get sucked into her old defensive position in these arguments. Mom effectively intervened. "Jim," she chuckled, "You have one fight that you fight over and over about everything. It's 'I'm right and you're wrong.'" Of Jim's 165 topics of conflict, 164 turned out to be variants on this theme. (The one other issue was the way his family was treating his fiance.)

THEORETICAL CONSIDERATIONS

A conceptual revolution has occurred in all the sciences. Whereas Newtonian theorizing posited that one thing leads to another, that the world consists of chain reactions of cause and effect, post-Newtonian thinking posits reciprocal causation. That is, my doing x causes you to do y, and your y makes me do more x, which in turn makes you continue or even escalate with y, and so on. My anticipation that you might do y is enough for me to do my x, and your mere anticipation that I might do x likewise can launch your y, so who started the cycle is never clear; both participants know their parts and expect and obtain reciprocation from the other. The punctuation of these sequences, that is, where the sequence begins and ends, is assumed to be arbitrary. That is, my x did not launch the interaction.

Rather, my x was in fact a response to the belief, based on prior experience or subtle cues, that you were about to do y. Hence my x, the apparent first act in the sequence, was experienced by me as reactive to an earlier or anticipated y from you.

How does such an interaction pattern come about? Wachtel and Wachtel (1986) write about what Bateson (1972) called "coevolution,"

> Parents are familiar with the fruitlessness of the question, "Who started it?" Each child says with utter conviction, "He (she) started it," and both are both right and wrong; it depends on with which act of the repeated circle one starts. (p. 5)

Reciprocal causation and interlocking concerns

When exploring the concerns on both sides of conflicts, it is critical to indicate how the concerns on each side interconnect, reciprocally triggering one another. This conceptualization counters patients' tendencies to look for someone to blame and instead distributes responsibilities for difficulties jointly among the participants in the dispute.

> Lawrence became furious and withholding in his child-custody negotiations with his former wife, Alice, whenever he felt, "She is the queen and I am the pawn." As this image indicates, one of Lawrence's focal concerns was maintenance of power in their decision-making. Alas, as soon as Lawrence withheld a payment, reneging on a prior agreement to pay for car insurance, clothing, etc., Alice felt cheated. She would lose confidence in Lawrence's ability and motivation to negotiate reasonably and follow through on his agreements. As Alice gave up on being able to trust a cooperative bilateral process, she began acting unilaterally. Lawrence's passive-aggressive with- holding of payments and Alice's unilateral actions reciprocally triggered and exacerbated one another.

Relating intrapsychic and interpersonal concerns

I have hypothesized that a given individual tends to use similar patterns of conflict *processing* in response to both intrapsychic and interpersonal conflicts. Is there also a relationship between the *content* of individual and interpersonal conflicts? If so, which causes which?

The psychodynamic literature posits a phenomenon sometimes referred to as projective identification. That is, inner conflicts can be externalized and viewed as conflicts between that person and others. This process is intensified to the extent that the other individual reciprocates by interacting in the projected manner. As Scarf (1987) writes,

The individual who is seething with unconscious hostility can, for instance, remain utterly out of contact with those feelings and experience himself as completely without anger—as long as he is assisted by a collusive, obliging mate who will act out his anger for him. (p. 178)

The reverse process can also occur. As Berman, Lief, and Williams (1981) point out, a person who has internalized a conflict with an explosive, judgmental father may internalize aggressive, critical self-statements. Thus, interpersonal conflicts can create issues that become the content of ongoing intrapsychic struggles, or vice versa.

The plot thickens further. Berman, Lief, and Williams go on to suggest that this individual can then interact with a spouse as if s/he had those aggressive and judgmental characteristics, which again externalizes the conflict. "Internal conflicts are transmuted into marital blame" (Framo, 1985). Married people can view the disowned aspects of themselves in their partners and then object to these traits in their spouse. And the complaints spouses raise about one another do tend to become the issues that individuals then feel anguished about within their own inner thoughts.

Wachtel's (1987) concept of vicious cycles suggests further that individuals' expectations for how others will act can influence the others' actual behavior. And inner conflicts over longings for more dependency, intimacy, autonomy, etc. do not necessarily, and maybe only seldom, grow out of inner conflict alone. Such inner conflicts can be engendered by actual, not just projected, deficiencies in a person's marital and family interaction patterns.

Fortunately, the therapist needn't worry about which is primary, the inner or the interpersonal conflict. Dealing with either can shed light on the other, and dealing with either seems often to take care of both. Moreover, patients generally raise whichever conflict is most distressing. If the therapist acts with sensitivity to the gestalt therapy principle, "Go where the energy is," the appropriate conflict realms eventually seem to get addressed.

CONCLUDING THE EXPLORATION PHASE

Many cases follow a complex pattern in which therapist and patient move back and forth between generation of solutions and exploration of additional concerns raised by these solution possibilities. For purposes of clarity, however, we will proceed as if the three phases of conflict resolution—expressing the conflicting positions, exploring the underlying concerns, and determining solutions—flowed in simple one, two, three order. A therapist who has been guiding patients through their exploration of concerns can conclude this phase and prepare to launch the next by looking for signs of softening and encouraging patients to summarize.

Softening: Signs of success

If the participants in a conflict can reach a point where they have listened to one another and are beginning to undertand the concerns on both sides of an issue, an easing of tensions tends to flow spontaneously. Greenberg (1984) uses the term "softening" for the increase in empathy that occurs as two people, or two sides of one person (utilizing gestalt empty chair technique), come to appreciate one another's fears, hurts and longings. Softening signals that the exploration of concerns is moving along effectively.

> The concept of "softening". . . refers to a change in the other chair to an expression of compassion, caring, or understanding. . . . Phenomenologically, it appeared as if the harsh internal critic had melted — expectations were suspended and there was a softening in attitude . . . accompanied by a shift from a poor contact, externalizing lecturing voice to a good contact, focused or emotional voice and a change to a more accepting attitude. (p. 112)

> After several months of treatment, Bart and Jeanne emerged from their session and then remained in the waiting room to chat and joke for several minutes with my secretary. After they left, my secretary commented appreciatively, "They used to come in here separately, and the tension between them made me uncomfortable. Now when they come in separately (in separate cars to go after the session to their respective jobs) they seem happy to see each other. They seem to enjoy sharing each other's company. They talk and laugh with each other."

Therapists may be tempted to hail this attitudinal shift as a sign that patients have been "cured." One of my first group therapy patients once roundly chided me for "pushing my robins prematurely from the nest." She was right. When I saw patients' improvement in morale I mistakenly interpreted this change to mean that their problems had been resolved. Improved morale signifies improvements in the patient's life experience, but it does not mean that the core conflicts have all been resolved, nor that the resolution process has been satisfactorily improved.

Softening does signify insight. Full resolution, however, requires decision-making and implementing. Insight does not constitute resolution. Creation and implementation of a plan of action remain before an issue is fully resolved. Nonetheless, attainment of "softening" does provide significant relief in patients' experience of tension and distress. The attitude shift brings with it optimism that the problem *can* be solved and motivation that raises the likelihood that it *will* be solved. As Greenberg's detailed research has indicated,

> . . . the act of softening was related to the report . . . of significantly greater relief of discomfort associated with the target complaint. This was most likely attributable to relief of the underlying sense of struggle and hence improvement in the related discomfort. (1984, p. 113)

Greenberg also reports that in his research those patients who demonstrated evidence of softening "experienced significantly greater self-acceptance, integration, and feeling of power" (p. 113). Along with self-acceptance, softening heralds a change in perceptions of the other (person or other parts of oneself). As an individual begins to understand the other's actual concerns and relinquishes his/her prior misperceptions of the other, cooperation and empathy ensue.

Summarizing: Looking back to move ahead

The transition from exploring concerns to the third and final conflict resolution stage, determining solutions, proceeds best with a backward look. A second run-through of the concerns that have been uncovered seems to consolidate understanding. The summary tends also to re-package the multiple concerns into a form most amenable to solution.

As in the summary that marked the transition between the first and second stages of this process, the therapist must be attuned to symmetry. The concerns on both sides of the conflict need to be fully included. If that happens, restatement will generally propel patients comfortably into the search for solutions.

CHAPTER 16

Guiding: Choosing Solutions

UNDERSTANDING IS ENLIGHTENING, but one more final sprint is necessary to attain the full sense of well-being that comes with completion of the journey from conflict to resolution. Fortunately, after the intense work of exploring underlying concerns, mutual solutions usually flow fairly easily. Even patients who have had difficulty framing conflicts and exploring underlying concerns sometimes cover this final territory with a fresh burst of vitality.

As Fisher points out (in Stewart, 1988), negotiation at this point involves "a search for inventive new solutions, where creativity and thoughtfulness are rewarded." This chapter begins with a look at solution-choosing in that majority of cases in which the last stretch of the journey toward resolution flows with relative ease. Guidelines are suggested for when solutions should come from the patient and when therapist input may be appropriate.

The chapter continues with suggestions for sticky cases. Some patients do not move easily through this third and final phase of mutual conflict resolution. Predictable blocks emerge, making solution-choosing difficult. Some common obstacles are listed, along with intervention options.

Therapist clarity about types of win-win solutions can facilitate solution-building. "The first goal should be to broaden things, to generate new options," suggests Ury (in Stewart, 1988). The final sections of this chapter suggest a number of solution-building principles that have been delineated in the integrative psychotherapy and the political-negotiation literatures.

GUIDING SOLUTION-BUILDING

Encouraging patients to devise their own solution options is generally the preferred way to begin generating solutions. Virtually all therapy ap-

260

proaches encourage patients to solve their own problems. Besides the philosophic issues of empowering patients and of insuring that patients feel responsible for solutions, the practical reality is that patients inevitably understand the multiple dimensions of their lives better than even the most empathic therapist. They can tailor-make solutions incorporating data that have never even been mentioned in the treatment hour. Their own solutions are considerably more likely than a therapist's options to take all of the relevant factors into account.

Some patients just need some encouragement to pursue their thinking about a problem to the point of resolution. Individuals who are accustomed to blaming and criticizing, for instance, may never have pursued a conflict to the point of finding solutions. Typically they are delighted to have obtained shared understanding and do not ask themselves to take the next step of obtaining solutions. This phenomenon is the easiest for a therapist to deal with. Questioning, "So what plan of action would take into account your various concerns?" and encouraging, "Keep going until you come up with solutions that feel finished," can provide enough intervention to yield full resolution.

> The Martin family had been fighting about the messiness of Monica's bedroom, which typically was strewn with papers from multiple homework projects. Monica wanted "the freedom to be creative," saying that she needed to make messes as part of the creative process. An underlying issue was her desire to receive more validation for her creative talents. Dad wanted the house neat, especially when he was home on weekends. Another, deeper concern was maintenance of his authority with his teenage daughter.
>
> Monica and Dad designed a plan of action that allowed Monica to let the clutter build up over the week, which was when she did homework and wanted creative liberties. She would clean her room on Friday nights so that it would look attractive by her Dad's standards on the weekends.
>
> Critical to the success of the plan was attention to the deeper concerns. Dad needed to begin expressing more appreciation of his daughter, toward whom he had typically offered more criticism than positive comments. Monica agreed to try to facilitate this change by ceasing to behave in ways that predictably would provoke her father's irritation. As to the authority issues, Monica needed to become more responsive to requests from her father instead of reflexively countering all his suggestions with "no," or "yes, but. . . ." The other half of this change required Dad to become more realistic about the kinds of authority that are appropriate to exert with a teenager. All aspects of the plan required practice. Even with good intentions, hitches typically develop in the implementation of solutions. Over time, however, the plan did decrease the incessant hostilities between Dad and Monica, particularly those triggered by her room's appearance.

For patients who are hesitant to express solution ideas, an exaggeration technique can be useful. The therapist can suggest that patients come up not with one, but with three, five, or even ten options. After initial laughter and balking, and sometimes with a little help, meeting the seemingly absurd challenge can stimulate playful and successful brainstorming.

> Fred and Sandy fought over Fred's weekend golf. The underlying agenda for Fred was to be able to enjoy his passion for golf without feeling guilty over taking time on the golf course. For Sandy the central concern was to feel that she and Fred shared a close relationship and that she was a valued part of his life. With brainstorming the two together were able to come up with several modifications in their family life that would accommodate both of their concerns. They thought of various ways in which they could increase their affectionate interactions as a couple so that Sandy would feel more appreciated. More eye contact, smiling with one another and joking together; more exchange of brief tidbits about their workday experiences; more talking together about the children; daily after-dinner walks; and more frequent evening sexual activity could provide the atmosphere of intimacy that Sandy yearned for. Within this nurturant atmosphere Sandy would feel less emotionally malnourished and could more generously encourage Fred to take time for the weekend golf he found so invigorating. His happiness with the golf opportunities, in turn, would continue to feed good-humored couple interactions. The key was the delineation of the relatively lengthy, though all simple, list of options for improving the marital climate.

After testing the limits of patients' abilities to find their own solutions, the therapist may want to add some suggestions. For various reasons patients sometimes genuinely cannot come up with constructive solutions to a problem. They may be lacking the requisite information or skills.

> Dahlia wanted to maintain a sense of authority with her young daughter Luanne. On the other hand, she wanted to eliminate their incessant fighting, particularly about daily routines such as bedtimes.
> Dahlia could come up with no ideas for bedtime strategies other than either authoritarian demanding or overly permissive bending-over-backwards followed by explosions. She found it very helpful to watch me demonstrate multiple options. We role-played each strategy, with Dahlia pretending to be her daughter. And then Dahlia practiced them at home with Luanne. Bedtime preparations became a shared race against the clock: "Let's see if you can get your pj's on before the clock says eight!" We practiced using physical action instead of just verbal instructions, e.g., taking the pj's out of the drawer and handing them to Luanne instead of saying, "Go get your pajamas." Playful rituals offered another option: "Stick 'm up" Dahlia learned to say, and Luanne raised her hands for her T-shirt to be pulled over her head. To get tooth-brushing cooperation, Dahlia learned to name each tooth after a cousin or friend: "Danny is looking clean and shiny today; I think he's dressed up for his birthday party. Look here at Lydia; she must have been playing in the sandbox; we'd better give her a good brushing." As Dahlia's repertoire of

parenting techniques expanded, she began to be able to generate solutions to new parenting situations on her own.

In other instances solutions may require psychotherapeutic expertise.

Maryanne was struggling with a conflict between always remaining serious and wanting to be able to let loose, relax, and enjoy herself in life. Visualizing her dilemma she had pictured herself enclosed in a stark, barren place bounded by a high, thick wall. She longed to get out, to pass to the other side, but could think of no way out. Since encouragement was leading to no solution attempts except repeated frustrating encounters with the wall, I began to take a solution-inventing role as therapist.

I knew that the main fear blocking Maryanne from moving beyond the wall was a fear that she would disintegrate into pieces if she allowed herself to relax. Therefore, my first intervention was to suggest that she visualize herself putting on a protective sweater, a magical sweater that would hold her together. Visualizing this sweater allayed the disintegration fear.

The other main concern had been a fear of going beyond where she had ever been. As much as she wanted to explore beyond the wall, that arena of spontaneity and happiness felt frightening. To deal with the fear, I utilized the safety provided by the therapeutic relationship, along with anxiety reduction via desensitization. Within the visualization I suggested that she picture that her therapist was right by her side, offering soothing safety. Visualization of repeated and increasingly longer visits beyond the wall gradually introduced her to the feared new place and desensitized her reaction.

"As you watch the wall, notice that there now is a big and elaborate but tightly closed door in the wall. I have the only key, and as you test it you will see that it is locked shut."

I had her test the door, describe its appearance and feel, so that I would be certain she was with me in the visualization.

"Now this time I am going to take out my key and open the door ever so slightly so that both of us can take a quick look."

Through this fantasy, I took Maryanne initially just for a look beyond the wall, then for a brief step out the door and back, holding onto my hand. Eventually she was able to go out and in from the doorway at will, to stay out and explore, to bask in the sun on a large flat rock along the brook, and to enjoy the flowers and shade trees. She became comfortable going in and out the door without me, provided she was wearing her sweater. Lastly she chose to include her husband and two children in the grassy scene beyond the wall and to imagine enjoying it with them.

We concluded with the understanding that Maryanne could close her eyes and return to this fantasy at home whenever she felt she had returned behind the wall. In fact, during the subsequent week she was able to utilize the fantasy on several occasions and was able to experience multiple relaxed, happy and tension-free periods. Within the metaphorical visualization we had found win-win solutions, solutions responsive to Maryanne's desire to try a freer mode of living and also reassuring with regard to the fears that had been holding her back.

HANDLING BLOCKAGES

As suggested earlier, generating synthesizing solutions is usually refreshingly simple. With most patients, just asking what they conclude about solutions yields satisfying new alternatives. Active choice and implementation of one or more of these alternatives bring the resolution process to a satisfying sense of closure. Sometimes, however, win-win solutions do not come from the patients, therapist suggestions meet surprising resistance, and none of the above techniques seems to lead to resolution. Some patients remain locked in their initial positions even after having explored their underlying concerns. Others may generate new solutions if pressed, but then, after having been guided through the generation of new options, are unable to commit themselves to cooperative solutions.

When difficulties in choosing win-win solutions occur, the therapist has a number of options. Chapter 20, on resistance, offers a general format for dealing with blockages in treatment. In addition, the following pages list a sampling of difficulties that can surface or re-surface at this point in spite of a therapist's relative success as a guide along earlier phases of the road to resolution.

The need to explore deeper concerns

Sometimes prior trauma or persisting personality patterns necessitate an exploration of concerns at a deeper level than were pursued thus far. Psychodynamic therapists might call this kind of exploration an analysis of the resistance.

> Lawrence and Alice, who had been divorced for eight years, were attempting to negotiate practical childcare decisions needing joint resolution. In the solution-building phase Lawrence systematically turned down any proposals that might include benefits for his former wife, even if these proposals also responded to his own requests. Before Lawrence could allow himself to agree to any win-win solutions, exploration of concerns relative to altruism toward his wife (and in general in his life) was necessary.
>
> In this renewed exploration of underlying concerns Lawrence explored his intense feelings of hatred for his former wife and his determination to give her nothing. The hatred had begun when his wife unilaterally decided to obtain a divorce. Broadening the context in which he viewed this painful event helped him to shift his understanding. Perhaps he had been less a victim of her unilateral actions and more a participant in a system in which both of them took turns insensitively making unilateral decisions. Reframing the incidents early in their relationship enabled him to view those times in a way that rankled less, freeing him from the intense hatred. As his hatred abated, he felt

less need to withhold to get back at his wife. Though still only with conscious effort, Lawrence did become better able to choose and implement solutions to the current childcare dilemmas that included benefits for his ex-wife as well as for himself.

Further explorations uncovered another concern. Lawrence was in the habit of expecting others to give more to him than he gave to them. Solutions did not feel "fair" to Lawrence unless they were favorably biased in his direction. We explored this pattern via Lawrence's transference reactions to the therapist, acted out in reluctance to pay his therapy bill. Looking at the origins of his ideas of fairness in his parents' behaviors added clarity. As he understood that his deeper underlying concern was to maximize the gain to himself, and that cooperative win-win solutions would in the long run gain him more than persistent stinginess, Lawrence began to modify his sense of what solutions were "fair."

Characterological cognitive rigidities

Some individuals become absolutely fixed on their initial position and show no interest in changing despite attempts to explore concerns and facilitate a mediated settlement. Such people become remarkably attached to a given solution and refuse to take in additional data that might challenge it. Individuals with a paranoid cognitive style, who block out disconfirmatory data, may be particularly intransigent in this regard. Those who are locked into a political ideology may display a similarly absolute set of ideas.

On the whole, patients with this kind of extreme cognitive rigidity are the most refractory to psychological treatment and are the most difficult to deal with in treatment. Beavers (1985) posits that the presence "of an overt, pervasive and disruptive paranoid orientation on the part of one partner toward the other" (p.24) is a contraindication for productive marital therapy.

On the other hand, many individuals who initially appear intransigent can become more flexible. The key seems to be for the negotiating partner to learn to augment his/her listening. Every concern expressed may need clear reiteration and explicit validation. This slower process is ultimately faster with people who need extremes of reassurance that their perspective has been taken seriously. Rigid individuals hold tightly to their view until they feel thoroughly heard. Only then can they potentially move on to constructive dialectical dialogue and solutions.

Exploring why the person maintains such a tightly closed informational system can be productive. The fear that others will not take one seriously generally has an element of projection, since the cognitively rigid individual does not take in others' viewpoints. Where was the close-minded habit learned? What could make it worthwhile for this kind of person to try listening instead of rejecting new information? Why, in the sense of "toward what objective," is the person blocking the entry of new ideas and information?

These patients can be aided by addressing their underlying conflict about maintaining a closed system versus taking in new information. Usually characterological patterns begin to change as an outgrowth of experiencing new patterns of conflict resolution. In the case of individuals who block the intake of new data and resist trying new solutions to old conflicts, the characteristically closed perceptual style sometimes needs to be addressed first.

> Arthur, visualizing this conflict, pictured himself like a robin. He pictured himself spitting out whatever worms, insects, or other foods or nesting materials were brought to him by his mother bird. Thinking about the metaphor, he realized that this habit had developed from expectations that much of what his mother said or gave to him was painful and toxic. Visualization of a new style of tasting and sometimes swallowing what other birds brought him would be necessary before he could let himself function in a less closed and paranoid manner within therapy or real life situations.

Obsessive stasis in decision-making

Another relatively common block to choosing solutions is obsessive reluctance to make choices. Some patients enthusiastically explore concerns around a given dilemma and seem to reach a point where closure on solutions should be easy. At the point of making actual decisions, however, conflicts about committing themselves to one path or another suddenly loom overwhelmingly. In these cases a visualization or other vehicle for understanding and resolving the patient's conflicts about making decisions may be necessary.

> Maryanne needed to decide whether to seek a divorce or to move to another state to rejoin with her estranged husband. Over a series of sessions spanning several months, and sometimes including the husband who had flown in to participate, Maryanne had thoroughly explored the concerns on both sides. Eventually she reached a clear decision point. Then she became immobilized.
>
> I structured the visualization by asking Maryanne to close her eyes, take several slow and deep cleansing breaths, and then "Picture yourself on the road of life. Notice the landscape. Notice also that up ahead you are coming to a fork in the road. What happens as you approach this fork in the road?"
>
> "I slow down," Maryanne answered.
>
> "And then . . .?"
>
> "I either sit down or back up."
>
> "And then . . .?"

"I ask everyone I know which way they think I should go. Then I make the choice that gets me the most approval." This behavior had been a pattern for Maryanne. Maryanne was able to articulate the difficulty with this—her usual—strategy. She felt no ownership for decisions, and would then blame and resent the people whose advice she had taken when problems later emerged.

"Now try again," I suggested, testing the limits of solutions she could come up with on her own.

"I sit down again. Making a decision is just too scary. I don't know where I want to go. All I know is that if I'm good I'll go to heaven; if I'm bad I'll go to hell. Life on earth is the proving ground."

Maryanne had had lifelong problems with making decisions. Until she resolved the conflicts about making decisions in general, which she accomplished via the above visualization, she was unable to choose and implement solutions on any given decision. This visualization marked a turning point.

Misplaced problem-solving focus

Sometimes when a solution-building phase feels frustrating to therapist and patients the wrong aspect of the problem is being addressed.

Eileen and Dirk wanted to settle the issue of what to do about their country house. After spending most of the session exploring the concerns on both sides of the problem, they listed options for keeping, renting, or selling the property, and chose which they would try and in what order. Still, as the session ended they seemed irritable and showed little sense of closure. The next session the therapist asked them each to pick up on what felt unfinished from the prior session.

Eileen said, "I still feel guilty about having made Dirk leave that house and buy one in town for us to live in. Do you still resent that decision?" she asked her husband. Dirk replied, "I do resent having been pulled away from the house and forced to give it up."

These restatements of concerns highlighted an aspect of the problem that had been overlooked in the earlier explorations. It was not the decision to move from the house per se that had disrupted the couple several years prior. It was how they had made the decision that had provoked both Dirk's long-standing resentment and Eileen's persistent guilt about the house. The current problem was not really what to do about the country house. Rather, the central issue was whether the couple was going to continue to utilize unilateral modes of making key decisions. As Dirk and Eileen readdressed the house decision in this context they experienced a sense of relief and closure. The house represented unilateral decisionmaking with a winner who would then carry about years of guilt and a loser who would harbor years of resentment. The essential decision for these partners was whether they would continue to make decisions in that unilateral manner or would both commit to learning and utilizing a bilateral win-win decision-making mode. With this decision made explicit, Dirk and Eileen reviewed the options regarding what to do with the country house and selected a joint plan of action.

SOLUTION-BUILDING ENHANCEMENTS

Sometimes a proposal that sounds appealing to all sides engenders goodwill where mistrust was still prevailing. As Moore (1986) points out, parties often adhere to fixed positions because they see no way of developing new ones. In general, however, when adversaries know they are problem-solving together, not forestalling concessions from opponents, they are more likely to think creatively (Fisher, in Stewart, 1988).

Brainstorming techniques can enhance this sense of cooperative creativity. Brainstorming is the popular term for an effective solution-generating format. Participants begin by tossing out ideas as they occur, without any attempt to screen out the bad from the good. All ideas are included on a list for later evalution, with no initial judgmental responses allowed. This proscription of potential critical responses encourages participants to maximize their creative thinking.

To enhance the sense that participants are working together against a common problem, rather than against one another, some negotiators suggest that participants sit on the same side of the table, rather than on opposite sides, perhaps facing a common blackboard on which solution possibilites are jotted down (Ury, in Stewart, 1988).

Solutions can be proposed on a practical and detailed level or on a more general formulaic level. Allyn (in Stewart, 1988) describes American and Russian stylistic differences in this regard. American negotiators offer specific plans of action, tally their bargaining chips, and look to make concrete deals. Their Soviet counterparts look for general confidence-building formulas, joint statements, and broader issues. Zartman and Berman (1982) characterize these styles as inductive—putting agreement together with piecemeal additions of specific items—and deductive—establishing general principles and then gradually working out the details. To maintain cooperation these stylistic differences may need to be bridged via solutions incorporating both levels.

> Gloria, a real estate broker, was a detail person. Her husband Jason, a policy analyst, looked at the big picture. In order to settle their ongoing disputes about their relationship, solutions needed to be expressed at both levels. Gloria needed to know the exact ways in which she could rely on her husband to be a more assertive partner. Jason wanted to understand his general pattern of passivity and to learn overall formulas for taking a more active, manly stance. Gloria's changes similarly needed to be expressed in terms of specifics for her and of principles for Jason.

As long as participants are able to engage in full information exchange about their needs, a team orientation produces more integrative solutions

(Schultz & Pruitt, 1978). The essence of a team ethos is the belief that both sides will be better off if they look out for the other's as well as their own best interests. When this attitude looks shaky, a therapist can designate one or another side as responsible for generating solutions that specifically take into account the other side's concerns.

> In spite of a cooperative exploration of concerns regarding how to structure their weekends, as Fred and Sandy began generating potential solutions, Fred again became self-protective. To counter this tendency I appointed him the executive administrator in charge of weekend planning for the subsequent month, specifically assigning him responsibility for implementing his wife's request for periods of shared couple time. With more explicit responsibility for accounting for his wife's concerns as well as his own, Fred became more symmetrically attentive to both his own and his wife's interests.

Types of integrative solutions

Most people initially think of compromise when they attempt to please both sides in a dispute. Compromise, or splitting the difference, is the most cooperative option available to participants who are settling a conflict by positional bargaining. By contrast, when parties proceed with interest-based bargaining (exploring underlying concerns and then looking for solutions that optimize what both sides want), genuine integrative solutions become possible.

Early approaches to psychotherapy integration (attempts to reconcile or resolve conflicts between different schools of therapy treatment) explored the *common factors* approach to synthesizing various systems of treatment (Arkowitz & Messer, 1984; Beitman, 1987; Frank, 1976). Applied to solution-building, this approach suggests that patients look first to what concerns both participants share. These common concerns can provide a foundation for a settlement plan, which can then be erected by adding details to accommodate the specific additional concerns of each party. This approach to building integrative solutions has the advantage of launching the process with a sense of solidarity. Participants experience more sense of cooperation and eagerness to find solutions when the concerns that they share are summarized.

A second form of solutions that put together diverse concerns is *additive*, i.e, doing what both parties in the apparent conflict want. Whether such solutions amalgamate like a compound or intersperse like a mixture, a potpourri style often works well for creating integrative solutions. In most instances the underlying concerns that need to be satisfied are complementary rather than oppositional, making additive solutions quite feasible. In the realm of psychotherapy integration, Beitman (1987) refers to additive solutions such as cognitive-behavioral therapy as hyphenated treatments.

Additive solutions are often *sequential*. If one person wants an evening of quiet talk and the other wants one of humorous entertainment, the two might go first to a movie and then to dinner, or vice versa, sequentially satisfying both objectives. In the attempt to integrate psychotherapies, Prochaska (1986) has suggested that therapies can be sequenced in a progression from symptom removal, to cognitive change, to attention to interpersonal and family treatment, and finally to depth exploration of intrapsychic conflicts. This sequence is based on attending first to the issues most contemporary in time and accessible to awareness, and then adding therapies to explore issues that are more historical and remote from consciousness as needed.

Another form of additive solution is *incorporative*. A parent confronting a child who wants to stay up and play at bedtime, might come up with an incorporative solution, suggesting that the child go to bed and then in bed will be told a bedtime story. In therapy integrations, incorporative solutions insert one form of treatment inside the structure of another. For instance, gestalt techniques might be incorporated into a treatment that is essentially psychodynamic.

Sometimes obvious additive solutions to concerns do not emerge. Instead the concerns need to be put together with a *synergistic* effect, yielding a new solution entirely. In these instances a kind of paradigm strain is at work. What is needed is an entirely *new conceptual framework*. In the arena of psychotherapy integration, for instance, Wachtel (1987) integrated behavioral and psychodynamic concepts via the new conceptual framework of cyclical psychodynamics, a framework which offers more than the sum of its behavioral and psychodynanic parts. Such conceptual breakthroughs can initially generate resistance, as people cling to their old ways of thinking while struggling to grasp the new idea, but then may generate excitement as the enlarged potential of the new paradigm becomes evident. Pruitt and Rubin (1986) coin the term *bridging* for this latter kind of solution, with the implication that understanding of the underlying concerns has enabled interested parties to invent an entirely new solution that includes what both want.

Sometimes both additive and synergistic solutions are blocked for want of scarce resources. *Expanding the pie* may be a crucial element in creating more promising options. Pruitt and Rubin (1986) offer the following practical examples.

> Our couple (she wants to vacation at the mountains and he by the seashore) might solve the problem by persuading their employers to give them two

additional weeks of vacation so that they can spend two weeks in the mountains *and* two weeks at the seashore. Another example (cited by Follett, 1940) is that of two milk companies who were vying to be first to unload cans on a platform. The controversy was resolved when somebody thought of widening the platform. (p.144)

Expanding the pie can be a particularly important function of the therapist-guide. For example, if a couple is feeling swamped by work and children and needs more time to nurture their relationship, the therapist might ask, "What other resources might you turn to in order to free up time to be alone together? Are there relatives who might spend an evening with the children, or neighborhood babysitters who could give you a night off?"

Lastly, *tradeoffs* rest on the fortunate reality that in most conflicts the issues of major import to each participant are different and complementary, even though the participants initially assume that their wishes are oppositional. The more concerns have been raised, the higher the likelihood that participants can rate these concerns in terms of their significance, and then arrange exchanges that enable each to give up low priority interests and receive satisfaction on their higher priority interests. Pruitt and Rubin (1986) use the political term "logrolling" to describe this phenomenon. Although the term sometimes has negative connotations in the political sphere, Pruitt and Rubin regard logrolling as a common and highly effective model of mutually satisfactory solution-building.

In a solution by logrolling each party concedes on issues that are of low priority to itself and high priority to the other party. In this way each gets that part of its demands that it deems most important. . . . It is possible only when several issues are under consideration and the parties have different priorities among these issues. (pp. 145-146)

All of these solution-building strategies rely for their effectiveness on careful detailed exploration of underlying concerns. At the same time, as suggested in earlier examples, solution proposals often facilitate clarification of underlying concerns. Participants sometimes do not realize some of their underlying concerns until a malfitting proposed solution has clarified them. Cooperative problem-solving of complex problems generally involves considerable back-and-forth movement between exploring underlying concerns and proposing solutions.

THE CRITICAL FINAL QUESTION

One question remains. At the conclusion of the process of mutually choosing a satisfactory solution, the therapist can inquire, "Are there any pieces of the problem that still feel unfinished?" This essential question will unveil concerns left unaddressed by the agreed-upon solutions. Also, given that almost any solution generates the seeds of new problems, this last question can help to anticipate difficulties. The importance of this final question cannot be overemphasized.

> Fred and Sandy worked out what seemed to be a satisfactory plan for parceling out golf, couple, and family times during weekends. Yet the question, "Are there any pieces of this problem that still feel unfinished?" yielded strong reservations for both spouses. Fred continued to believe that Sandy was really against his having any golf time whatsoever. Sandy continued to believe that Fred really wanted to play golf all day all weekend, with no time for her or the children.
> The therapist drew a pie, and asked each spouse to write, as honestly as possible, how s/he would ideally divide the weekend hours between golf, couple, and family times. To their surprise, their proportionate preferences were identical. Both wanted to see the weekend days divided in roughly equal thirds, with approximately five hours of each day devoted to each. This correction of their misperceptions turned out to be essential to the success of their new plan.

In sum, therapists can expect to see a relatively spontaneous emergence of solutions if the prior steps of conflict expression and exploration of underlying concerns have been successfully traversed. If this flow does not occur, a redefinition of the essential conflict, a further look at underlying concerns, or exploration of characterological conflicts that impede solution-building can be helpful. In addition, therapeutic success in establishing optimal solutions to conflicts is generally enhanced by a *detailed* understanding of the patient's specific concerns. The more specific the understanding of concerns, the more likely that well-fitting solutions can be generated. Clarification of the valences attached to each concern can help negotiating parties *trade off* issues of minor concern for satisfaction in arenas of more significance. Awareness of various *types of integrative solutions* can aid parties in generating solution options.

After solutions have been generated and agreed upon, a critical last question, "Are there any pieces of this problem that still feel unfinished?" anticipates problems and clarifies remaining unaddressed concerns. Resolution of these final elements of the problem greatly enhances the probability that a full resolution will be accomplished.

CHAPTER 17

Coaching: Creating Cooperation

SOMEONE WHO TAKES ON A coaching assignment with a tennis player or a musician, or with a group like a basketball team or an orchestra, faces at least three tasks. For one, the coach needs to instill a cooperative spirit. A second objective is to assess each individual's skills and the skills of the collective interactions of the team as a whole. Last, the coach chooses methods for improving players' skills. These are the three main coaching tasks for therapists who want to help their patients learn more effective conflict resolution patterns. This chapter explores methods of establishing cooperative interactions; the next, Chapter 18, offers techniques for rapid assessment of negotiation skills; and Chapter 19 details skill-building exercises.

In what order should these objectives be undertaken? A therapist needs to trust his/her intuitions and choose what seems appropriate at a particular time. In general, however, if a basketball coach has inherited a team with a history of bickering and criticism, the coach may need to convince the team members to call a truce and agree to commit themselves to cooperation. It may be necessary to take this step prior to proceeding with assessment and skill-training. Clear assessment of existing skills may be another early coaching priority. Note however, that the order of these two elements is not rigid. Sometimes starting with assessment gives the therapist information that facilitates the switch from competitive to cooperative, and sometimes the opposite order, building cooperation and then assessing existing skills, works fine. In general, however, establishment of cooperation and assess-

273

ment of existing skills lay the foundation for, and therefore precede, coaching on specific communication skills and negotiation strategies.

An individual's ambivalent feelings, spouses who differ, or any parties in apparent opposition can become locked in antagonistic battle. Equally problematically, they may become rigidly determined to avoid talking to each other, or stuck in any of the noncooperative interactions described in the previous chapters. How can a therapist help to make a truce? How can a therapist convince opposing sides to give up fighting against or running from one another and begin problem-solving?

Achieving cooperation among sides that perceive themselves as rivals is not a simple task. Some patients — individuals, couples and families — never accomplish this step and conclude therapy prematurely as a consequence. These cases, often our treatment failures, may end before symptoms have fully disappeared. In the extreme, individuals may decompensate instead of growing toward more cooperation, integration, and inner harmony. Couples and families may rupture, disintegrating instead of concluding with a more hospitable family system.

The following seven intervention options can enable a therapist to effect the shift from competition to cooperation. These options are not mutually exclusive; sometimes a combination works. In addition, there is plenty of room for innovation.

PRESENCE OF A THIRD PARTY

Pruitt and Rubin (1986) suggest four conditions that increase the likelihood that cooperative problem-solving will occur in response to a perceived conflict. Two of the these conditions are participants' faith in their own problem-solving ability and their perception of the other's willingness to problem-solve. These two conditions improve, hopefully, over the course of treatment.

Third is the availability of a mediator to serve as a communication link between the parties and to help develop integrative solutions. Therapists, serving as optimistic and skilled third-party mediators, can establish a new tone of cooperation and set new rules for interacting. A neutral third party has leverage over both sides that goes well beyond the influence that any of the distrustful participants can grant one another. When a therapist sets a more relaxed and less anxious tone, this new climate fosters a relaxation of both sides' tight clinging to their initial positions. Thus even if the parties in a dispute have no confidence in their own or the others' abilities to problem-solve cooperatively, confidence in the third party mediator can override their distrust.

WALKING THROUGH PRESSING CURRENT ISSUES

Pruitt and Rubin's fourth condition is what they refer to as momentum.

> Momentum refers to prior success at reaching agreement in the current controversy. The more frequent and recent such successes have been, the greater will be Party's faith that these successes can be reproduced in the future and that problem solving is worthwhile. Momentum can sometimes be encouraged by scheduling easier issues earlier in a negotiation agenda, so that a solid foundation of success has been built by the time more difficult issues are encountered. (p. 37)

Whereas psychodynamic therapists talk about "working through" issues, the behavioral therapist Seligman (1975) *walked* his dogs through the solution to their problem (see Chapter 5). That is, he physically moved his depressed dogs' legs to get them to walk out of the cages where they were experiencing unpleasant electric shocks. Seligman's dogs needed this "walking through." In their apparent resignation, the dogs seemed to believe that they could not escape their painful situation and had ceased trying new options. An analogous "walking through" can provide an antidote to the hostile stance problem, demonstrating to patients that cooperation can bring them more benefits than antagonism.

The kind of guidance described in the previous four chapters enables a therapist to lead patients through from conflict to resolution on initial "laundry list" issues that they have not been able to negotiate on their own. Having been guided through to successful resolution of one or two issues, antagonists become more willing to put aside fears and angers enough to work cooperatively. They then can begin to work together instead of against one another to resolve remaining conflicts and learn new approaches. They may not yet be able to talk cooperatively about sensitive topics on their own at home, but at least within the therapy session, under the guidance of the therapist, they continue to try working as allies instead of as opposing forces.

> Jeanne and Bart fought continuously. Initially, to build cooperation, I tightly controlled their interactions in the therapy session to guide a series of conflictual issues to successful resolution. The couple first addressed their long-standing feud over Bart's snoring. After this warm-up issue, they came to agreement about Bart's extramarital affair. Third, they came to an agreement on nose-picking, which turned out to be an issue that involved fundamental differences in attitudes toward health and sickness. And they came to a mutually acceptable plan on the sensitive issue of legacies for their children

versus their stepchildren in their wills. These issues took several months of weekly sessions resembling business or political negotiations.

Resolution of these four specific upsetting issues reduced the tension and pressure that had been crippling the marriage. Both spouses began to experience a new, though still fragile, optimism about their future as a couple. They began to sense that cooperation might get them more of what they both had been wanting than their fighting had yielded. This new belief did not yield a decrease in the battles at home. It did, however, sufficiently reduce hostilities within the therapy hour so that a coaching process could begin.

ACCUMULATING HISTORICAL INSIGHT

Instead of the "laundry list" strategy of walking patients through to resolution of current pressing conflicts, the "process is the problem" strategy can sometimes yield more rapid cooperation. To decrease hostilities when the immediate focus is on identifying and changing conflict patterns, gleaning an understanding of the origins of the current patterns of conflict resolution can be critical. With this empathy-inducing perspective, the hostile interactions can be replaced with more cooperative attitudes.

> When Maryanne began treatment asking for help with making decisions, one of the first issues she addressed was choice of careers. Her initial pattern was for one side of her dialogue (her "shoulds") haughtily to ignore the desperate pleas from the other, the side describing what she really wanted to do. The therapist's guidance through this first issue, encouraging her to listen to both sides' concerns and to take them both as serious and legitimate, effected a truce and yielded at least some internal cooperation.
>
> As we proceeded with subsequent decisions, the atmosphere of cooperation disintegrated and internal distrust reemerged. With each decision we went deeper into the sources of this internal antagonism. Harshly critical superego voices kept hampering her forward momentum each time Maryanne would begin to express what she felt or wanted. We explored the bases of this antagonism in Maryanne's interactions as as child with her intrusive, demanding, and verbally abusive father.

Historical insight seems to melt antagonism in several ways. Seeing the antagonistic behavior in her internal dialogue as a replication of her father's behavior helped Maryanne see what she was doing with more clarity. Experiencing the behavior as ego-alien, i.e., as belonging to someone else and foreign to her own values, also made it easier for Maryanne to ease her self-critical stance.

Historical perspective can enable patients to see that their given conflict strategy was quite serviceable at some earlier time in their lives, that that the strategy at present is counter-productive.

As a child, Felicia had coped with an intermittently psychotic mother by repression, by ignoring her mother's rages and odd talk. She focused her energies and attention outside of her home, particularly enjoying time spent with a kindly neighboring family and attention and support from her Girl Scout leader. Escaping in this way from the harsh realities of the lack of parental support in her own home, Felicia survived what could have been a chaotic and destructive home environment.

Years later, as a newly-wed adult, Felicia experienced panic when she faced the choice of whether to have children. Her semi-conscious underlying concern was that having children makes you crazy, a belief her mother had often voiced. Although she wanted to continue to suppress all thoughts of her mother, whom she had left at age 17 and had seldom seen since, Felicia's lack of information about her mother's illness made it difficult for her to make a clear assessment of the validity or falsity of the thought that was blocking her from having children.

Whereas avoidance of thoughts about her mother had served Felicia well throughout her childhood and adolescent years, this flight strategy was preventing an open exploration of her fears and desires at this juncture in her adult life. She needed to gather information about her mother's illness in order to determine whether having children was likely to precipitate a psychotic reaction in her. As she came to understand the appropriateness of her earlier repression, Felicia began to appreciate the need to change now from avoidance to an information-gathering and problem-solving strategy.

REFRAMING: ADOPTING A MORE BENIGN PERSPECTIVE

Battling people generally go to war because they think that the opponent is a villain, and that they, on the side of virtue, have been victimized. A reframe which enables people to see that they and their opponents are both simultaneously hurting and being hurt by each other, reciprocally interacting in a negative spiral with one another, may soften the antagonism. As the antagonism decreases, the virulent view of the other typically mellows as well.

A view which affixes blame for the problem at least in part on some external cause (instead of on each other) can further enable both sides to relax their guard and begin to cooperate. This external cause can be a situation or life circumstance. For instance, spouses who married before they were old enough to handle couple responsibilities, or who had children before their marital relationship had stabilized, can reframe their view of their difficulties in a way that blames "the situation." With this perspective, they can move from working against one another to joining together against the common problem.

Alice and Lawrence had been divorced for eight strife-torn years. Virtually every discussion about logistical arrangements regarding their two daughters quickly deteriorated into character assassinations. They came to treatment in order to reverse this pattern and learn to handle the logistical questions regarding their children with less strife.

No negotiation was possible within the volatile framework of vilification that existed between Alice and Lawrence. The first step had to be establishment of cooperation. An initial reduction of hostilities was accomplished in the first session, a two-hour session, by reframing three issues.

First, the fighting did not occur because either Lawrence or Alice was a bad person, but rather because of the court system. While clearly the couple had long had a tendency to utilize open conflict (fight-fight) strategies for dispute resolution, the adversarial structure of legal proceedings, and their divorce lawyers in particular, had exacerbated their tendencies to fight. Moreover, the one-sided settlement that ensued was misnamed "settlement," in that its multiple inequities had launched a subsequent eight years of warfare.

Second, the couple had become locked in a negative cycle, a vicious circle of demanding and passive-aggression. The more Alice "stabbed and demanded," which was how Lawrence experienced her attempts to elicit his child support payments, help with carpooling, etc., the more he felt helpless and declared he would do nothing. The more Lawrence would do nothing, striking back at Alice with passive-aggressive tactics, the more Alice felt she had to demand and stab to prod him into action. This interaction pattern left both Alice and Lawrence feeling like victims. Although neither intended to be a villain, both needed to become aware of the equal responsibility they bore for continuing the cycle. Framing their interactions as reciprocal decreased the "who's to blame" fights.

Third, fighting (both aggressively and passive-aggressively) was reframed as a poor strategy for accomplishing what were in fact two legitimate goals, i.e., obtaining fair agreements and ceasing to upset their children by their constant antagonism. Putting aside the hostilities long enough to learn cooperative strategies might possibly achieve better results toward both important shared objectives.

It is important to note that reframing did not once and forever turn this couple from battling to cooperating. It did, however, establish enough of a lull in the fighting to begin the treatment process. In the relative calm of the next several sessions it was possible to start working out some practical immediate conflicts, which further reassured both participants that cooperative negotiation could yield better outcomes than continued fighting.

REMOVE PROVOCATIONS

There is a joke about psychotherapy, that therapists teach a person to be able to live with a tack in his shoe. Common sense suggests that sometimes a better course of action would be to do whatever is necessary to remove the tack. A specific problem may be inherently provocative. Until this situation has been altered, a cooperative tone is virtually impossible.

> Eileen was referred by her gynecologist for depression. Eileen was in fact poignantly negative toward herself and toward life. The problem that had triggered and was sustaining the depression was a physical problem. Eileen was experiencing incapacitatingly intense pain (vulvadynia) for which her doctors had been unable to find an explanation or remedy.
>
> The initial two years of therapy sessions focused on finding medical resources that might be able to remove the causes of the pain. We mapped a nationwide search for information. We formed a non-profit research foundation and convinced local doctors and a medical researcher to investigate the problem. We sought out women nationwide who were complaining of a similar pain syndrome, and organized them into a mutual support network. Eileen even worked in the research lab, performing biochemical tests and mathematical analyses. This search kept Eileen active, preventing more severe lapsing into hopelessness, helplessness, and suicidal thinking (which occurred from time to time nonetheless, particularly after difficult surgeries which at first seemed to help but then were thwarted by return of the pain). Eventually, the search met with success. The researcher developed an effective medical treatment which eliminated the pain (for Eileen and also for many of the other women in our research network).
>
> Only at that point did we directly address the personality patterns that had made Eileen vulnerable to hopelessness and a depressive stance. The key and lengthy initial intervention, however, was to remove the intolerable provocation. (Although, needless to say, after such a lengthy period of mobilizing and problem-solving to find a cure for her pain, the earlier non-assertive Eileen had changed considerably.)

Marital infidelity can pose a similar chronic provocation. When a spouse is sexually unfaithful, both partners may become chronically angry. The spouse whose partner has been unfaithful is furious at the breech in the marital contract. The unfaithful spouse becomes angry because of the constant attacks s/he experiences from the other. Ending the affair tends to be a first-order priority and a sine qua non for resumption of cooperative interaction.

> Jeanne and Bart's marriage was being poisoned by his extramarital relationship. Bart's woman friend not only drained energy from his bond with his wife but also provoked his wife's intense anger. The affair had to end before Bart could be invested enough in his marriage to work cooperatively and Jeanne could cool off enough to join him in this effort.

Alcohol and drug abuse, gambling, and other addictive patterns can be similarly inherently provocative. Halting the addiction enables a cooperative climate to take hold. Toward this end, conceptualizing the addiction as

an external element that has infiltrated the family system can reduce blame
and guilt. In this case, family members can be encouraged to cooperatively
support each other against the addiciton instead of maintaining the
addiciton and fighting each other.

Children and adolescents with emotional problems often live in emotionally toxic households. Again, removal of the provocation, such as by
helping the parents to live more comfortably with one another and/or by
upgrading their parenting skills, is essential if the child is to be able to
change and heal.

UTILIZE THE PRISONER'S DILEMMA GAME
TO CAUSE A PARADIGM SHIFT

Patients may relax when they are offered a reframed perspective on conflict
and alternative strategies for achieving their goals. They may feel more
cooperative when told that they are fighting (within themselves or between
each other) to get things they legitimately want and that what they want
makes sense. They may need to hear that, while their wishes and concerns
are understandable, the particular strategy they are using to obtain their
objectives is relatively unlikely to yield success.

Power is something everyone wants and needs. People who fight
generally do so because they think power comes from acting tough, critical
and domineering. For these people, explanations of cooperative conflict
resolution need to address explicitly this fear of powerlessness. Such
patients need to hear that cooperation is a way to *increase* their power.
Fearing that cooperation implies caving in and looking weak, these
individuals may need to be informed that the purpose of the new cooperative approach is to enhance, not decrease, their power.

Axelrod's version of Prisoner's Dilemma (see Chapter 1) can be utilized
to demonstrate these ideas to patients who persist in antagonistic interactions. The game helps them to understand that they have been interacting
with a zero-sum assumption, namely, that conflicts will conclude with a
winner, who gets what s/he wants, and a loser, who gets nothing. When this
underlying assumption prevails, no amount of communication skills
training is likely to yield cooperation. Actually having patients play out the
game offers a playful way to expose this assumption and to suggest an
alternative win-win framework for conflict resolution.

The Axelrod version of Prisoner's Dilemma is structured for two-person
play, and therefore works well with couples. In the context of family
treatment (with children at least school-aged), the family members need to
divide into twosomes, but the pairings can keep switching until everyone has

had a chance to try the game with everyone else. This last option mimics most closely the actual conditions in the Axelrod experiments, where multiple rounds of the game enabled each computerized strategy to be pitted against each of the other entrants in the competition, with the winner being the entrant with the overall highest total score.

> By the 15th session of a 40-session treatment with Ron and Shelly, I began to despair of ever eliminating their chronic oppositional stance. Neither individual was particularly explosive, but they were both locked into rigid defense of their basic principle, "I'm right and you're wrong." Whatever one said, the other always disagreed. The tension between them was continuous and oppressive. Walking them through multiple conflicts had produced settlements that satisfied both on specific issues, but these settlements had yielded no general increase in cooperation. Family-of-origin explorations had added insights, but these too made no dent in their competitive stances.
> I assumed that if I offered them a conceptual explanation of what they were doing or how they could settle conflicts more constructively they would respond oppositionally to me, just as they did to one another. Instead, therefore, I had them play the Prisoner's Dilemma, hoping that as they learned about their own tendencies and experimented with the winning strategy, Tit for Tat, they might discover on their own the relative merits of competitive and cooperative interactions.
> When Shelly and Ron played Tit for Tat, they both started with cooperative moves. This generous initial period seemed parallel to the courtship in their relationship. Then, in the second round of play, Shelly defected. Shortly after, Ron defected. They both played increasingly antagonistically. After a brief series of cooperative moves, one would try to get more points by slipping in a self-gain-only move. By the last several rounds, they each had decided that there was no way they would let the other take the advantage. Both gave defection responses consistently, not so much to win points as to prevent the other from winning. This progression from initial cooperation to an entrenched stance of opposition mirrored the development of their relationship.
> At home, midway through the week between that session and the next, Ron and Shelly had a talk. They agreed that they each would hoist a white flag. They agreed to avoid "snappy comebacks and argumentativeness." Although this agreement certainly did not result in instant cure, it did provide a significant turning point, marking the beginning of resumption of the cooperation that they had gradually lost in the first years of their marriage. Considerable skill-building was necessaray to implement the new agreement, but the dedication to cooperative intentions endured and enabled constructive coaching in the therapy sessions to proceed.

ADDRESS THE IMAGES OF SELF AND OTHER

Antagonistic behavior is sustained by the beliefs one side holds regarding the other. Bringing these beliefs about one another into consciousness and reexamining them can help to ease the interactions toward cooperation.

Karen, who was almost always at least mildly depressed, experienced a resurgence in inner turmoil when she began to think about moving from her basement apartment to a brighter and airier condominium. Using the empty chair technique, Karen began to express her inner dialogue. One side described the living space she wished she could have and thought might even be affordable. The other side lambasted the wishful expressions with a critical barrage of exaggerated statements regarding her supposed stupidity, history of failures, and inadequacy as a human being.

Sitting in a third chair and reflecting on this dialogue, Karen described the wishful chair as her idealistic and unrealistically optimistic self, and the harshly critical chair as the voice of reality. Together we explored an alternative view, that the wishful chair was the voice of the real Karen, and the negative chair was the Party Pooper who kept undermining her with untruths about her personal attributes, untruths based on distortions of her experience. The Party Pooper took mistakes and blew them up into proof that she was stupid, took problems and labeled them failures, and took anxieties as signs of gross human inadequacy. As long as Karen viewed her impulses as untrustworthy and her overly harsh conscience as the true guide, cooperative interaction between the two was impossible. The hope was that as the images of the two voices shifted, each could became less threatened by the other, and they could begin to cooperate.

Family members can reinforce one another's negative views and can become rapidly locked into unnecessarily harsh ideas about each other.

Jeb, a teenager, lived with his grandparents because of volatile interactions with his stepmother, Dee. Jeb had experienced a bout of drug abuse several years earlier. Also, he had once been arrested when he and some friends entered a vacant store illegally. His grandparents, who loved him and felt protective toward him, were terrified that he was "a bad kid." They reacted by being overly restrictive and incessantly critical.

Therapist intervention, stressing Jeb's strengths as an intelligent student and a talented musician, enabled the grandparents to reestablish their view of Jeb as a capable young man striving to find a healthy route for his life amidst turbulent family situations. With this more positive view of their grandson, the grandparents were able at least briefly to relax their critical stance and resume cooperative, and sometimes even appreciative, interacting. Unfortunately, however, a series of events shook their frail positive view of their grandson. As they returned to and became locked into their image of Jeb as bad, Jeb became depressed and hostile in response. In order to change the grandparents' rigidly-held hypercritical view that their grandson was destined for evil and failure, it was necessary to find Jeb an alternative home. In the more positive environment Jeb was able to relax and to flourish.

Burton and Sandole (1986) declare a recent Kuhnian paradigm shift in the theoretical study of conflict, and indeed in worldwide attitudes toward conflict. This shift, entailing movement from a power/coercion/zero-sum game model of social exchange to one based on mutual problem-solving and win-win outcomes, is what therapists have long intuitively offered patients. Increasing our conceptual clarity about these two modes of conflict resolution will make us that much more effective in communicating this shift, from competition to cooperation, to our patients.

CHAPTER 18

Coaching: Assessing
Problem-Solving Skills

A THERAPIST CAN UTILIZE VARIOUS strategies to clarify patients' existing patterns of handling conflict. Whatever the strategy, the objectives are to identify which constructive communication behaviors are present, which are missing, which unconstructive behaviors occur, and what the overall negotiation patterns are.

To obtain these data, therapists can inquire about the details of how conflicts in general, or a specific conflict, are handled at home. They can observe how patients handle a conflict that comes up within a session. Or they can present a standardized situation as an assessment device and observe how the patients interact to resolve this problem. Inquiry about conflicts in general can yield a useful overview but usually elicits little data on specific communication skills and deficits. Having patients describe the details of a particular conflict may be useful if they are troubled at the moment by that incident. In most instances, however, live enactment within the session provides the most thorough database.

Once the raw data on conflict processing have emerged, the therapist and patients need to find a way to describe the elements in the patients' standard conflict repertoire. Although labels such as those suggested in Chapter 4 (attack-attack, attack-flee, etc.) can be useful for focusing the therapist's observations, language that is more specific to each patient, expressing that patient's unique style as well as the generic patterns, may be preferable. This language may be abstract, e.g., "A attacks and, after a brief defensive rebuttal, B caves in." Or it may be more behaviorally explicit, e.g., "A starts with quiet complaints, and then gradually talks louder and faster. B responds with attempts to explain an alternative view. As A's complaints get louder and longer, B says less and less, and then voices agreement." And the language may be metaphorical. "A and B start to talk, and then, as soon as A begins to express a point of disagreement, B begins to feel like a frail child. A turns into a locomotive, going faster and faster down the track. The frail child, B, is on the track, about to get mowed down. Acquiescing to what A says is the only thing that saves B from the on-rushing train."

ANALYSIS OF A CONFLICT THAT OCCURRED AT HOME

One alternative for assessing conflict patterns is to discuss in the therapy session a conflict that an individual or couple experienced recently outside of the therapy session. An advantage of this strategy is that the individual or couple may be able simultaneously to resolve a prior painful issue and to clarify the conflict habits. A disadvantage is that who-said-what recapitulations of a prior argument offer less clear data than a disagreement happening freshly in the therapy session. Also, rehashing the past is seldom as satisfying as interacting in the present. On the other hand, putting closure on a distressing incident can offer relief.

> In the Whitman family, teenager Jeb lived with his grandparents. Jeb and his grandmother had argued at home over how many times a day he should be allowed to change his shirts. Initially they had yelled at each other, each accusing the other of abuses. Grandma said Jeb was taking advantage of her generosity in doing his laundry. Jeb said that Grandma clearly didn't love him because she was always yelling at him for one thing or another. They separated, and then later had a calmer discussion with the help of Grandpa. Grandma at that point suggested that she could understand that now that he was beginning to have girlfriends he might want to change his shirts more often. Jeb conceded that 19 shirts a week was maybe too much washing and ironing to expect. They worked out a solution, with Jeb changing shirts as often as he wanted, but putting only a set number per week in the regular laundry basket and washing the rest himself.
> Analysis of the first and then the second rounds of confrontation helped Jeb and Grandma to understand what they typically feel, think and do when they get into an escalating argument. They also identified what, by contrast, they had done that worked more satisfactorily in their second go-round on the excessive-shirt-changing problem.

The above example was unusual in that the patients discussed a conflict that had a second and more sanguine chapter. Usually the incidents that patients want to discuss in their treatment hour are those that have gone poorly without later rectification. In general, instead of reiterating who-said-what, these incidents are better utilized for assessment purposes if patients are asked to deal with the same issue in the present therapy hour, either by reenacting their earlier argument or by picking up from where they left off at home.

ANALYSIS OF A CONFLICT THAT OCCURS WITHIN THE SESSION

A second assessment strategy is to utilize a conflict that has come up within the session. Disagreements often occur spontaneously within the course of treatment. Alternatively, the therapist can request that patients address an issue that is potentially slightly sensitive. Even a routine information-gathering topic, such as a first-session discussion of why a couple or family has come to treatment, can give the therapist considerable data about information flow and blockages in the family.

When a provocative topic is being discussed, the therapist can let the dialogue flow until the individual, couple, or family has enacted a relatively full replication of how distressing thoughts and/or interpersonal dissension are handled at home. Note that the therapist's treatment intention must be clear. If the goal is to resolve a conflict, letting poor process flow is inappropriate. Careful shaping would be more effective. If the goal is assessment, however, seeing the full distressing scenario is useful. Note also that "full" need not include escalations of shouting or violence. Once a couple or family seems to be heading in this direction, the therapist can interrupt and ask, "If you were at home now, what would happen next?" And then, "How would the scene end?"

Immediately after the conflictual scenario has been demonstrated, the therapist launches a debriefing, engaging patients in the project of describing their conflict resolution pattern.

In their first session David and Laura were asked to discuss with each other (not directing their comments to the therapist) why they had come for treatment. David articulated his concerns about their lack of sexual contact and emotional closeness. He also admitted that he felt pressured to spend time with Laura that he really wanted to keep for himself. As he expressed his distress, Laura said nothing.

I began the debriefing by observing several asymmetries in the couple's communication pattern. David had done virtually all the talking. And when she did offer a comment, Laura had spoken slowly, hesitantly, and softly, whereas David, a lawyer, had spoken fluently and with a loud and self-assured tone.

> Both David and Laura were surprised at these observations. They had somehow missed the obvious.

It is often helpful to ask patients in what ways these elements are similar and different from how sensitive communications would be handled at home.

> Once these differences became explicit, many aspects of their mutual withdrawal from one another began to make sense to both David and Laura. They each added details of other aspects of their lop-sided dialogue pattern and gave multiple instances of discussions at home that had succumbed to this format. They also became engaged in understanding the series of phases by which this pattern had developed in their relationship.
>
> "Initially I was the yeller," David said. "Then Laura was the yeller. Now we don't talk."
>
> Invited to add her perspective, Laura said, "I'm afraid to say things now, and David probably is too. We've had such terrible arguments in the past. I get tired of feeling rejected. We never seem to match up, so I quit trying."
>
> Interestingly, the total treatment with this couple took only three sessions. Once they understood their verbal pacing differences and their cultural origins, David and Laura were determined to override the old patterns. They both made conscious efforts to communicate with equal air time and volume. The resultant burst in communication led to relatively rapid resolution of their backlog of conflictual issues and a renewal of the relationship bond.

Debriefing can be accomplished via metaphor, a technique commonly used by family therapists (Papp, 1981). A metaphor does not specify the exact communication and negotiation habits that need improvement. On the other hand, it provides a vivid image that can be used to guide patients toward a visualization of how they would like to improve their communications.

> Maryanne and her husband George had an exceptionally argumentative relationship. During an early session they quickly flared up into a fight. After several minutes I sensed that the fighting could continue indefinitely, and asked them to pause, close their eyes, and visualize their interaction as that between two animals.
>
> George visualized Maryanne as a wildcat with all four claws bared. He felt like a dog, bigger than the cat but still very afraid. He wanted to run, to get away, to protect himself.
>
> Maryanne visualized George sitting on an ice cube. She saw herself as something without arms, like a seal, because she felt so incapacitated. She felt like she kept running up into the ice, a huge and slippery block of ice with no cracks or toe-holes.

Usually patients enjoy visualizing how their imagined scene could be altered so that they would be pleased with the interactions. Patients' responses to this assignment can indicate a great deal about their willingness or ability to make changes and about what the eventual outcome of treatment will be.

> When asked to visualize the dog and cat or the seal and ice block acting in a more satisfying way toward one another, neither George nor Maryanne was able to envision mutual solutions. George expressed skepticism. He said that he had thoughts of a lion and a lamb lying down together, like on a Christmas card. "I don't know what will happen when they wake up though," he said, suggesting that he had little faith in the relationship's changing in anything but their wishful thinking.
>
> Maryanne envisioned herself, "struggling up atop the ice and taking a shit. The defiance is satisfying. I got up, and there was nothing worth having, so I'm leaving. I go on to a group of other seals, a more friendly environment with things to eat and sunshine and creatures of my own kind, accepting and approachable."
>
> This couple eventually decided to obtain a divorce.

A STANDARDIZED CONFLICT RESOLUTION TASK: THE DINNER DILEMMA

This option is the least threatening assessment strategy and consequently particularly useful with highly explosive or severely disengaged couples and families. The idea is to assign a decision-making problem and then observe as patients attempt to resolve it. By utilizing the same problem with many patients, a therapist becomes sensitive to subtle variations in patients' ways of dealing with the assignment. Furthermore, aspects of the assigned problem can be adapted to gather information about how patients respond in less and more stressful situations.

In the situation I usually pose, "the dinner dilemma," I instruct the patient(s), "Pretend that it is getting close to suppertime, and decide what you are going to do for dinner. Where and what are you going to eat?"

This diagnostic exercise works on the premise that people utilize relatively consistent communication and conflict resolution patterns in the multiple interactions they face in everyday life. In particular, a given pair of individuals, such as a husband and wife, will develop a relatively finite repertoire of conflict and decision-making interaction patterns that may escalate and deescalate in intensity but are relatively stable from day to day. Radical changes in conditions can cause changes to such patterns. More stressful issues, or a weakened physiological state (e.g., tired, hungry, ill), can also result in pattern shifts. Overall, however, the basic elements and deficits in the patterns will be apparent even in a simple conflict situation.

For uncovering intrapsychic conflict patterns, two chairs are set facing one another and the patient is asked to verbalize aloud a dialogue of his/her inner thoughts on the dinner dilemma, moving from chair to chair as different internal voices speak. Often the intrapsychic dialogue will pit wants and fears against shoulds, that is, desires and inhibitions against values. Sometimes the dialogue is between competing wishes, between wishes and fears, or between competing value beliefs. With a couple or a family, patients should face each other (as opposed to facing the therapist). Most couples and families launch into the assigned discussion relatively easily. This is the dinner dilemma structure in its simplest form.

The basic initial task will generally indicate the decision-making pattern utilized in less threatening conflict situations: who typically initiates suggestions and how, who speaks how much and in what verbal style, who explicitly says what s/he wants and who blames or criticizes, how much listening is occurring, and the extent to which the basic stance is cooperative or oppositional. It also suggests whether the discussion stays on the level of positional bargaining or addresses underlying concerns and generates solutions. Symmetry and asymmetry should be evident in all three stages, in the initial expression of the conflict, in the exploration of underlying concerns, and in determining solutions. The exercise will indicate whether the discussion includes adequate summarizing statements, and whether it leads to a full sense of closure or is terminated prematurely.

Even in this nonthreatening task, subtle versions of the potentially pathological patterns delineated in Part II will generally be visible. Because the situation is so benign, emotional intensity or rancor should not occur. If negative affect is present, this is an important clue about the extent of tension and hostility within the individual(s) and in the household. The presence of dominant-submissive, attack-attack, and other interactional patterns can also be detected in subtle form, even if they do not precipitate explicit depressed, angry or anxious feelings in this nonthreatening exercise. On the other hand, when one of these patterns occurs, careful questioning about the participants' emotional experiences during the interaction often yields low-level dejection, irritation, or anxiety even if these were not explicitly conscious or visible at the time. These subtle evidences of pathological patterns indicate the paths that the pair would be likely to take when dealing with more important and more emotionally charged issues.

Disengaged couples or families, or individuals who avoid thinking about conflictual issues, may give so brief a discussion as to offer very little diagnostic detail in the first run-through of the exercise. This sparsity in itself says much about the patients' conflict processing patterns. Full information exchange may be truncated for fear that discussion of conflictual issues will lead to fights or hurtful interactions.

The therapist who is alert to tiny clues can learn a great deal from minimal evidence. For instance, a partner who only voices agreement, "Well, I guess so," to the spouse's first suggestion may be illustrating, in abbreviated form, a pattern of reluctance to examine or articulate his/her own inner concerns as well as a tendency toward dominant-submissive interactions. A response that begins with the word "but" signals listening difficulties. Similarly, an individual who stops after a first suggestion, e.g., "I'll fix myself something from the refrigerator," may be indicating a difficulty listening to his/her semi-conscious wishes, values, or impulses. Instead of a flow of thoughts and self-observations there may be either impulsivity or rigidity, a fixedness of cognition. That is to say, even very brief responses to this initial part of the diagnostic exercise can be illuminating.

Stressed version

It is often helpful to ask patients to repeat this exercise in a second variation to investigate how the basic pattern is altered under stress. This time, so that rapid agreement is less possible and more tension is engendered, the instructions are modified to produce clearly conflicting initial positions. These conflicting initial positions would be the equivalent of ambivalence in an individual or of dissension in a couple or family.

The more difficult the conflict, the more decompensation in the mode and escalation in the intensity of the conflict pattern is likely. A conflict can be more difficult because of the importance of the issues, because of the degree of attachment the participants feel toward their positions, or because of the degree of apparent opposition. This following example primarily manipulates the latter, the degree of apparent opposition in the initial positions, to intensify the conflict. Importance of the issues and degree of attachment to the positions can be similarly manipulated in the therapist's instructions to patients.

To stress the conditions exploring an intrapsychic conflict I suggest, "This time the decision will be harder. You (looking at one chair) really want to go out and treat yourself to a meal that you don't have to cook yourself. On the other hand, you (indicating the other chair) feel you really should stay home and prepare something yourself."

For interpersonal conflict I suggest, "Let's run through the same decision a second time. This time I'll make it harder. You (turning to one family member) want to go eat at the fast food restaurant around the corner, and (turning to the other) you want an elegant dinner at a very elaborate French restaurant."

Again, in the debriefing phase therapist and patient(s) work as partners.

The accuracy of assessment seems to be enhanced if patient and therapist share the diagnostic task. Important data emerge when patients are asked to describe what they were aware of as they were doing these exercises. They and the therapist can together detail the conflict patterns and compare these patterns with their conflict behavior at home.

Round Three

Both the diagnostic and the heuristic value of this exercise can be further exploited if time remains in the session for a third round. Patients appreciate coaching that walks them through to mutually acceptable solutions of the dinner dilemma. This demonstration of cooperative conflict resolution enables them to leave the diagnostic session with new images of what could be, as well as new clarity about what is. In addition, this third round provides prognostic indicators of patients' openness to new learning.

The dinner dilemma assessment procedure has many advantages over less formalized clinical observations. First, it is relatively standardized. When the same example is used with many patients, including individuals, couples, and families, the observer can see how a range of patients compare. As with standardized testing, a therapist can develop a sense of the diverse ways in which people typically handle the same problem and become that much more sensitively attuned both to typical patterns and to subtle deviations.

Second, the dinner conflict offers a format for testing the limits of patients' conflict patterns. The low and high stress versions enable investigation of patients' conflict resolution repertoire under more and less stressful conditions. In addition, patients can be asked to role-play the same conflict several times, each time trying to improve on their ability to reach a comfortable resolution, another form of testing the limits.

Third, the same format can be used to assess both intrapsychic and interpersonal conflict patterns. One of the major advantages of using conflict resolution theory for treatment is that it enables the clinician to work in both arenas under one theoretical umbrella. The dinner dilemma extends that advantage to assessment, offering a simple means for diagnostic integration of intrapsychic and interpersonal patterns.

By divorcing observation of process from work on real conflicts, the dinner dilemma offers a minimally threatening and even playful way to accomplish the assessment process. A real-life conflictual issue is likely to trigger accumulated emotional reactions that could put a negative tone on the assessment session. When patients role-play a pretend conflict, intense emotions that have built up around real issues are bypassed.

TABLE 18.1
Checklist of Communication Skills and Maladaptive Habits

STAGE	COMMUNICATION SKILL	MALADAPTIVE PATTERN
Expressing Initial Positions	Saying	Suppressing thoughts and feelings and saying nothing
		Hinting
		Expressing what one doesn't want instead of what one wants, e.g., complaining, criticizing
		Blaming or accusing, starting with the pronoun "you"
	Active Listening	Answering with "Yes, but"
		Defensive, "That's not so!"
		Listening for what is wrong in what the other has said
		Ignoring, saying nothing in response, changing the subject, or leaving
	Symmetry	Unequal air time: monologues and silences
	Summary statement of "our" problem	No summary. Problem is seen as yours or mine, not "ours"
Exploring Underlying Concerns	Saying, listening and symmetry as above	Same as above
		No shift from positions to concerns
	Exploring	Bullying, insisting on one point of view as more valid than the others
	"We" attitude	Competitive instead of cooperative Trying to show how the other is wrong rather than to build a common understanding
	Summary of concerns on both sides	No summary. Points left hanging Only one side's concerns included in the summary
Choosing Solutions	Suggestions are win-win	Suggestions meet concerns of only one side
	Explicit choice of options to be implemented	No clear commitment or choices made
	Summary statement, "So let's do x"	Plan of action left vague and ambiguous
	"Are any pieces still unfinished?"	No final checking over for unfinished loose ends
	Final clear closure on full solution plan	No final sense of closure. Discussion ends with problem feeling unfinished

Lastly, this model of patient-therapist cooperation in the assessment process differs from the notion of the therapist who collects data and determines a diagnosis which s/he then feels almost uncomfortable about sharing openly with the patient. The patient-therapist interactions in the assessment process parallel the kind of cooperative interchanges that the overall treatment in a conflict resolution framework attempts to convey.

Table 18.1 is a checklist that summarizes the communication skills and maladaptive habits to listen for when assessing conflict patterns with any of the above techniques.

With a clear assessment that has identified which communication and negotiation patterns patients are utilizing, which need to be weeded out, and which need development, a therapist is ready to launch into corrective coaching.

CHAPTER 19

Coaching: Improving Cooperative Problem-solving Skills

WHEN THERAPY FOCUSES ON the *content* of patients' conflicts, the therapist's role is to guide; explicit teaching is seldom necessary. Uncovering underlying concerns and buried feelings can liberate patients, relieving them of long-troubling emotions. A therapist's guidance in finding new solutions that better gratify newly understood underlying concerns completes the unlocking of difficulties and opens new passageways to more satisfying living. By contrast, when conflict *processes* are the focus of a treatment session, explicit skill training is often necessary. In order to negotiate effectively and to reduce the number of issues that become conflictual in their lives, patients need to be able to communicate effectively within themselves and with others. The habits described in Chapter 2 and summarized in Table 18.1 need to become comfortable and automatic.

My experience supervising therapists has been that the training of psychotherapists of all types tends to overlook the coaching dimensions of treatment. The result can be considerable naivete about techniques for facilitating skill development. For instance, many therapists are susceptible to the illusion that understanding how and why something can be done in a better way equals ability to act in that new manner. Explaining may be essential in classroom teaching of a subject like history or calculus, but conflict resolution, like sports or playing a musical instrument, requires habit development as well as understanding. Therapists also sometimes wrongly assume that if a patient is able to demonstrate a constructive behavior once, that behavior has become an integrated part of the patient's response repertoire. As athletes know, one good forehand volley needs to be followed by many repetitions before the volley can be reproduced with regularity in practice sessions. Many more repetitions will be necessary before the volley can be relied on under the pressure of a real game. New skills require practice. Communciation and negotiation skills need practice, practice, practice. Good coaching therefore involves setting up exercises that convey and then establish each specific new habit.

This kind of active coaching may appear antithetical to the kind of therapist behavior that is encouraged in traditional psychoanalytic training. Therapist activity interferes with patients' transference reactions, and therefore tends to be looked upon with disfavor by therapists who rely heavily on transference as the primary technique for uncovering patients' underlying concerns. In order for transference phenomena to occur strongly, the analytic therapist must remain a relatively "blank screen." Transference still occurs even if a therapist colors the "blank screen" by utilizing active treatment interventions, but it occurs with less frequency and immediacy, particularly with healthier patients. A therapist who is going to coach effectively therefore needs facility in visualization, depth diving, identifying reciprocal interactions (vicious circles), working in a marital therapy format, and other techniques for uncovering core conflicts. If a therapist maintains a broad repertoire of exploratory techniques so that transference interpretation is just one of many options for facilitating resolution of patients' dilemmas in living, coaching does not threaten, and instead vastly augments, the therapist's effectiveness.

Psychodynamically trained therapists do tend to receive excellent training in exploring the origins of poor habits. This kind of rear view mirror work on conflict processes seems to be helpful, provided that it is coupled with explicit skill training in new communication and conflict patterns. Understanding what one has been doing wrong, without knowing what to do right, can become demoralizing rather than enlightening. Knowing where poor habits were learned does not necessarily indicate the way to improvement. Historical perspective needs to be combined with a forward-looking perspective on the skills patients need to acquire.

The coaching techniques suggested here come in part from psychological learning theory and and also from the educators — violin teachers and tennis coaches — I have found most helpful in my own learning experiences. Learning theory has contributed the theoretical notions of positive reinforcement, breaking large skills into small learning chunks and then shaping by successive approximations (operant conditioning), modeling, and visualizing prior to doing. My violin teacher and a number of tennis coaches have provided the models and given me the personal experiences that have brought these learning theory conceptualizations to life.

This chapter begins with a review of some of the ways in which therapists can impart new skills to patients. Within each of these broad categories there is ample room for therapist creativity. The latter part of the chapter suggests exercises for building the specific skills that I find patients most frequently are missing. These exercises, like most of the strategies described in this book, are meant to be suggestive rather than exhaustive. As a therapist becomes skilled in recognizing deficits and in thinking of treatment as a coaching endeavor, inventing new drills can contribute to the creative challenge of therapeutic work.

POSITIVE REINFORCEMENT

The most powerful positive reinforcement comes when patients find that their new skills work. When a therapist walks patients through an effective negotiation of one conflict, patients usually become motivated to reproduce this success in subsequent conflicts. As patients see their negotiation skills growing, they typically feel positive about themselves and about their treatment, as well as eager to continue to grow in this way.

The therapist can enhance this process in two ways. The therapist's belief that patients can learn to be more effective serves as positive reinforcement for continuing to build new conflict patterns. Each time the therapist points out evidence of progress, of ways in which patients are utilizing more effective communication and negotiation strategies, this increases the likelihood that patients will continue to develop these new skills. The therapist's genuine assurances to patients that they do have a quiet voice within saying what they want, that that voice deserves permission to speak, and that they have inborn empathic abilities if they listen closely to others are essential to the growth process.

Second, the therapist needs a positive format for giving feedback when patients are falling back on self-defeating conflict habits. Rather than communicating that habits are poor in a critical fashion, the goal is to give this feedback in a way that blocks the old and immediately brings forth new behavior. This new behavior can then be positively reinforced by the therapist with acknowledgment, "Look; you did it!"

A tennis coach, for instance, can show a player that he is mistakenly starting volley shots by pulling his racket back; this feedback needs to be followed immediately, however, with instruction on where the racket should be positioned at the outset of the shot. What is wrong needs to be followed by how to do it more effectively, which prepares the way for subsequent positive reinforcement, "Yes! That's good!"

SHAPING AND MODELING

The effectiveness of conveying new skills by shaping and modeling is well established. Nonetheless, these techniques are sometimes underutilized in therapy. To utilize these coaching techniques a therapist first must be clear about the specific skills to be improved. Shaping and modeling then can be used as primary interventions in process-focused sessions and can be interspersed with problem-solving guidance in content-focused sessions.

Shaping refers to the move-by-move feedback that hones a new behavior pattern. Every move of the subject is responded to with feedback encouraging more of this, less of that, until the subject has the new action just right. In behavioral learning theory terms, shaping is a method of teaching via reinforcement of successive approximations, with immediate reinforcement (positive or negative) of each behavior (Lieberman, 1976). Meyer and Chesser (1970) describe shaping, also known as operant conditioning, in early animal experiments:

> It has been possible to produce progressively more complex forms of behaviour in gradual stages from a preceding simpler form. Suppose one wishes to teach a pigeon to peck at a small disc on the wall. Reinforcement is first given when the bird moves toward the disc and remains there. The next reinforcement is given as the bird progresses further towards the target and pecks it. This type of operant conditioning or shaping has successfully produced quite complex behaviour patterns. (pp. 32-33)

The power of shaping has been reinforced for me in working with various tennis instructors. A coach with whom I learn most quickly gives me a steady stream of feedback and encouragement. Standing by the net, he feeds balls rapidly, following each of my strokes with brief instruction that will improve my stroke on the next ball and offering ample appreciation on good strokes. "Meet the ball out in front. . . . Bend your knees. . . . Stay low all the way through the shot . . . lean on your front foot. . . . Excellent . . . . You're late; start running sooner. . . . Small steps. . . . Very good. . . . Again. . . . Perfect!" The frequency and immediacy of feedback, advice, and encouragement maximize the learning of new skills. As the skills become consolidated, less detailed shaping and conscious programing are necessary to override poor habits and produce instead the new ones.

Ideally a tennis coach alternates intensive drills with more relaxed periods of talking about the skills that are being developed. Similarly, the therapist needs to watch the pacing of the session to be certain that the patient understands the skills being coached and does not become overwhelmed by too much feedback.

Connie, a woman in her late thirties, always questioned her own thoughts and feelings. When she felt angry, a voice within her said, "You shouldn't feel that way." When she wanted to rest instead of doing the dishes, a voice within her said, "You can't." When she felt that her neighbors were being unreasonable, she thought, "That's not a fair way to think."

To counteract this pattern I suggested that Connie practice consciously responding to each self-observation with a positive self-statement. If Connie thought, "I feel so depleted today," she was to add a legitimizing self-response, "and that's understandable because. . . ."

When Connie gave evidence of self-negation in the sessions, I similarly encouraged self-acceptance. For example, when Connie criticized herself for having angry feelings, I validated the angry feelings and encouraged Connie to verbalize how feeling angry was understandable in reaction to something that had happened. Similarly, when Connie said, "I would like so much to go to law school and become a lawyer, but that's ridiculous," my corrective response was "Sounds like an interesting possibility. What sounds attractive to you about law school?"

This intensive shaping was coupled with insight about where Connie had learned to doubt herself (from a continuously critical mother). The combination of the insight and the operant conditioning (shaping) had clear therapeutic impact.

Modeling, based on imitative learning, refers to a person's intentional and unintentional example-setting. As Lieberman (1976) writes, modeling

. . . enables the learner sometimes to short-circuit the tedious and lengthy process of trial-and-error (or reward) learning. . . . Much of the behaviors which reflect the enduring part of our culture are to a large extent transmitted by repeated observation of behavior displayed by social models, particularly familial models. If performed frequently enough and rewarded in turn with approval by others, the imitated behavior will become incorporated into the patient's behavioral repertoire. (pp. 122-123)

Modeling may need to be explicit to counteract the extensive learning that has occurred if patients have had prolonged exposure to unfortunate interactions. Therapists can probably assume that patients unconsciously identify with them and pick up their ways. The impact of modeling, however, can be enhanced. Taking seriously the coaching role, the therapist can suggest, "Now watch me closely. Notice how I begin here, and then do x, and finally I end up here with y." We would certainly expect this kind of explicit modeling from a tennis coach or a violin teacher. It is equally helpful fron a therapist teaching new communication and negotiation skills.

I modeled acceptance instead of criticism by responding consistently to what made sense, rather than what was wrong, with whatever Connie expressed. Sometimes I further enhanced this modeling by calling Connie's attention to these responses. "How did you feel when I treated your thoughts about law school as worth considering?"

When Connie expressed distrust of her neighbors, I augmented the impact of modeling by first calling attention to it. "What do you think I am going to say about your hunches about your neighbors?" Then, after validating Connie's reactions to her neighbors, I again asked, "How would you describe the way I responded to your thoughts about your neighbors?"

Negating instead of listening to her thoughts and feelings, Connie had been perpetually stuck in the first stage of conflict resolution, never able to gather even the basic data in troubling situations. For Connie, learning to listen to herself and to trust her readings of reality removed a major roadblock on the way to healthier emotional living.

The impressively successful Suzuki method of violin teaching has students listen repeatedly to recordings of new pieces before they even begin to try playing them themselves. Likewise, the tennis coaches from whom I seem to learn the most utilize both shaping and modeling, starting with the modeling. When a tennis pro demonstrates a good forehand volley, I develop a mental image of the kind of stroke I am trying to produce. If we start purely with shaping, I feel barraged with guidance messages but with the destination unclear.

A pure shaping procedure can feel like the game children play, "hot and cold." One child, blindfolded, sets out to find a hidden object. When he is getting closer the other children, serving as coaches, clap louder and with more frequency. But when he strays far from the object, only silence greets him. I remember from my childhood the distressing feeling of being blindfolded, not knowing where I needed to turn to find the treasure, and dependent upon chance moves to point me in the right direction.

Modeling that is not followed by frequent and detailed feedback is frustrating, as learning is likely to proceed slowly. Tennis instructors who show and explain a stroke, but then allow ten minutes of practice before they give more feedback, are not maximizing their coaching impact. If explicit modeling followed by steady feedback is a formula for efficient teaching of music and athletics, odds are good that communication skills can be coached similarly.

VISUALIZATION

When I was in high school my violin teacher used to have me sing difficult passages of a new sonata before trying to master the fingerings and bowings that made it difficult. "If you can sing it, you can play it," was her maxim. A related principle seems to hold true for patients trying to increase their communication and negotiation repertoire: "If you can visualize it, you can do it."

When the patient envisions the use of new skills prior to actually trying them out in real life or even within the therapy hour, the odds of success seem to be increased. Equally important, misfirings from beginners' mistakes with new skills will be minimized because they can be anticipated from the visualization. That is, the reverse of my violin teacher's maxim may be true: If you can't see it, you probably can't do it.

> Jason, a small, quiet and kindly man, was married to Gloria, who was larger and more energetic. For many years she had been the leader in virtually all of their interactions. Both spouses wanted to develop at least an egalitarian relationship, and preferably a traditional male-female relationship with Jason in the dominant role, but for various reasons Gloria was not willing to participate in treatment.
>
> Working within an individual treatment format with Jason I suggested situations in which Jason was to visualize himself and his wife interacting. The idea was for him to picture himself acting in more virile, interactive, and assertive ways prior to trying the new behaviors out at home. Jason's initial visualizations were extraordinarily passive. For instance, when I asked him to visualize himself taking a more active and assertive stance arriving home after work in the evenings, his image was to say to his wife, "You cook dinner while I sit in the family room with the paper and a beer." That is, he could visualize himself giving an order and then becoming passive, but not interacting.
>
> Jason's next attempt to visualize more assertive interactions with his wife was somewhat more active, but still in a demanding rather than cooperative mode. "You cook dinner while I take it easy to get my mind off business. Then after dinner you take some time for yourself while I take care of cleaning up. Then I'd like for us to spend some time together, to go for a walk or do something together." The you-statements at the outset were certainly likely to antagonize his wife, even if she appreciated his attempts to act more assertively and to initiate more interactions between them.
>
> By the third visualization Jason began to glimpse himself acting in a more cooperatively assertive way. "Hi Gloria. How did your day go? . . . I'd like to take a few minutes to get my mind off business, and then I'd be glad to help you out in the kitchen. How would that be for you? . . . I'd like if we could have some time together tonight too. What would you think about taking a walk together after dinner?"
>
> At the conclusion of several months of therapy Jason reported that his marital relationship had improved significantly. Meanwhile, at work, in the corporate environment where he had always been technically capable but had blended into the woodwork, Jason's competency ratings soared. He was offered a financial bonus and promoted for "leadership abilities."

DRILLS AND EXERCISES

Drills and exercises expedite and consolidate learning. They offer a format for learning by successive approximations, as well as repetitions to enable a new behavior to become "easy" and habitual. Drills also build awareness of when a counterproductive habit is occurring. Awareness of problematic behavior is a critical early step in behavior change. Yet behaviors that are obviously counterproductive in the eyes of the therapist may occur completely out of the patient's awareness.

Becoming aware of a provocative vocal tone, for instance, may require time and considerable practice. Patients who sound angry often have no idea when their voice is on the attack. It may take explicit exercises for them to learn to hear when they are undermining their effectiveness by speaking in a critical tone.

> Vicki and Eric routinely spoke to one another in critical and insinuating tones. Both had grown up in households where perpetual argument was the rule. The goal of the following exercise was to learn to recognize angry voice tones, and then to resume the discussion in a more cooperative voice. Both spouses were encouraged to see how often they could notice their own departures from cooperative voice tones. I kept score, giving two points each time either spouse could recognize his/her angry voice tone, and one point for recognizing anger in the spouse's voice. The couple lost four points if either spouse used an angry voice without either of them recognizing it before the next person spoke. The goal was to maximize the number of points the couple could cooperatively amass. The exercise was designed to make a playful exercise out of what might otherwise be a self-critical or embarrassing endeavor.
>
> The homework assignment that week built on this awareness skill. I instructed the couple to sit down at least one night after dinner with a three-minute timer. The objective was to talk together about a sensitive topic for three minutes without either one slipping into the old negative voice tones. To monitor their progress they were to record how long, in minutes and seconds, they lasted each try. Talking together for three minutes without anger would constitute "winning."
>
> The following week Vicki and Eric reported that they had not succeeded in doing their assignment. They had begun talking, but then they had become so engrossed in their productive, forward-moving discussion that they forgot to set the timer. This experience marked a turning point in their treatment, as it was the first time that they had managed to discuss difficult topics on their own without antagonism.

Drills provide the repetitions necessary for new behaviors to become automatic. It is stressful and frustrating to try to maintain skills that require conscious control and effort. As repetitive drills begin to bring these skills to the automatic pilot level, patients begin to feel that the new ways of interacting are really "them," not just role-playing. Patients are correct when they complain, "but that's not *me!*" New behaviors do not feel like *them* until they have become a part of their automatic behavioral repertoire.

Drills and exercises need to be tailored to each patient, simplified as necessary so that patients can experience success. By dividing new skills into manageable learning bits, repeating each bit until it has been mastered, and then putting these new bits together into sequences, learning is accelerated. My violin teacher taught me to tackle new music by playing a sequence of only two or three difficult notes, then the measure, then a neighboring measure, followed by joining these two measures. Proceeding in this manner until all the difficult passasges were learned and linked together yielded efficient mastery of new material.

Similarly, patients may learn to say what they feel or think without resorting to negative you-statements. They may need to learn to listen for what is right instead of what is wrong. Then they are ready to put these skills together into interactional sequences.

One of the signs of a consummate violin teacher, tennis instructor, or psychotherapist is an ability to identify precisely which specific skill is most crucial at a given time, that is, which skill, if improved, will cause most of the others to fall in line. My general strategy is to try to stay organized by beginning with the skills needed at the beginning of a negotiation, and working my way gradually to the end. By the time we are working on skills like generating solutions and obtaining closure, I usually find we are nearing the end of treatment. Nonetheless, I sense that, whereas skills can be listed and representative exercises can be suggested, decisions about which skill to emphasize when seem to be a matter of art.

EXPLORATION OF THE ORIGINS OF DYSFUNCTIONAL COMMUNICATION HABITS

Understanding where and why dysfunctional habits were learned in the family of origin can facilitate habit change. Family-of- origin explanations alleviate the onus of blame and shame from patients, giving them a plausible reason for why they have been engaging in clearly counterproductive behaviors and leaving them feeling more sympathetic toward their communication foibles. These habits may have been serviceable in the family culture in which they grew up.

The explanation that we acquire patterns of communication and negotiation just as we acquire language, by assimilation of what we see and hear in our families, frees up patients to see these patterns as learned rather than as inherent in their personality. If the patterns are learned rather than innate, they can be augmented or relearned, just as adults add to their vocabulary or learn a second language. Such learning is not necessarily easy or fast, but it can be accomplished.

A sympathetic understanding of why the family of origin developed these patterns is also important. Viewing parents compassionately, as having done their best given their own limitations and inadequate upbringings, seems to leave patients feeling calmer and better prepared to move on to learning new skills. The point is for patients to understand that their *current* family will work better with cooperative negotiation strategies, which they can learn.

Barbara and Tom illustrate how patients develop listening deficits. Both were high-functioning professionals, well-educated, creative, and personally charming, but their marriage was disintegrating. Each experienced major frustration because the other seemed unable or unwilling to listen to what he or she said. Interestingly, Barbara and Tom come to their listening deficits from opposite family of origin patterns.

Barbara grew up in a household with a mother who meant well, but because of her own neediness looked to her daughter to mother her. Consequently Barbara learned too well and too early the role of listener, and later felt exploited when put in that position. In addition, because she seldom had received appropriate mirroring from her mother, she was uncomfortable talking about her own feelings. Her mother's chronic neediness left Barbara feeling that her own needs were always of lesser importance than those of others.

Barbara's father had also been a taker more than a caretaker toward her. Turning away from his wife (which in turn fueled his wife's distress), he sought intimacy from his daughter. Their overly close relationship included sexualized contact. Barbara, thirsty for positive attention, received at least some gratification from this contact. On the other hand, the contact was essentially exploitative, clearly not responsive to her developmental needs, and consequently again made her feel used. With this background, Barbara's discomfort with giving empathic nurturing (verbally and in sexual encounters) was quite understandable.

Tom also had difficulties listening, which added reality to Barbara's fears that listening would be asymmetrical. If she listened to Tom, she felt used, as he did not reciprocate in a balanced give-and-take fashion.

Tom's difficulties with listening to his wife came from excessive experience being the listened-to. He had been a model child in a large family and one of his parents' favorite children. They dwelled on and marveled over his many successes in school, with friends and leadership, and in athletics. He grew up accustomed to being treated as special, and this attitude carried over into his marriage. He felt uncomfortable being asked to reciprocate with attention to the wife's successes and dilemmas. He was used to being the star on center stage and had not learned to be a co-star or member of the audience. This understanding of the family roots of his reluctance to listen enabled Tom to feel less defensive about his dearth of listening habits and to want to learn to share the spotlight with his wife.

COMPENSATORY DRILLS FOR SPECIFIC SKILL DEFICITS

In order to proceed through the three conflict resolution stages, people need at least the two basic skills—saying what they feel and want, and listening to what others feel and want. These skills are so rudimentary that they seem obvious, so essential that without them the process is hopeless, and yet they so often are missing, particularly in people whose distress leads them to seek therapy.

The I-statements drill

The habit of talking about one's own feelings rather than about the other person's deficits often needs direct coaching. The indications may be an individual who is incessantly self-critical, or a couple that engages in bickering and fighting. Long-established linguistic patterns of you-statements generally include patterns of focusing attention on the other rather than the self and on what is wrong rather than what is sought.

The following exercise is described for use with a couple. With an individual the same principles would apply, but the interactions generally would be between the voice of conscience and the voice of feelings and concerns.

In teaching skills it is generally helpful to start with a simple and nonthreatening version and from there to proceed to more complex and more sensitive examples. Following this principle I begin by having each spouse interact with me. I ask them to tell me how they feel when I address them in style A, then style B. I tell them I will pretend to be a friend of theirs.

Style A: "You ignore me. You never take time to do things with me."

Style B: "I would like more time with you. I would love to arrange a plan to get together, maybe for lunch or dinner, or to watch the football game."

When they chuckle and say, "Of course, Style B," we then tease out what the differences are between the two. I check that they hear the tone of voice differences. I want to be certain that they have heard the focus on I versus on you, which I describe as their "sphere of attention."

With respect to intrapsychic battles, the following example can be used (as if I am talking to myself):

Style A (in a disgusted voice): "'You're so selfish. You never do things for other people."

Style B (thoughtfully): "I know it's important to do things for others, and yet I notice that I seldom seem to put this principle into action."

One or two examples generally suffice to clarify the difference in emotional impact, and in likely outcome, of these two modes of expression. The next step is to have patients experience the shift in focus from the other person to their own feelings and thoughts. I say a Style A you-statement to them. They need to transmute this critical statement into an I-statement. For example, I suggest, "You are unreliable. You're never ready when I pick you up for us to go out together." The patient then needs to invent a revised version, which might be something like, "I feel anxious to get going and irritated at the delay when I come to pick you up and you're not ready."

Usually the therapist needs to offer several examples to be certain that patients not only understand but are beginning to integrate the habit of looking inward instead of outward when they feel uncomfortable about something. As patients understand how to make the attentional shift from the other person to their own inner experience, the examples can shift to their actual, real-life complaints/concerns. Gradually, the exercise can be continued with spouses interacting with one another instead of with the therapist. The key, however, is to restrain patients from getting caught up in discussion of content and to keep the focus instead on their patterns of expression, specifically, I-statements rather than you-statements.

This exercise generally helps patients to understand that they need to make not only a change of pronouns but a total shift in attention. If attention is thought of as a beam of light (Wachtel, 1987), this beam can be focused on self or on other. I use the phrase "sphere of attention" to help patients picture where this beam of light is being directed. Chronically angry, critical and blaming patients can learn to tell themselves, "OK, if I want things to change I'll have to switch my sphere of attention now." Similarly, patients can learn to monitor for symmetry by monitoring the sphere of attention. If they notice that it has been excessively focused on themselves, they then can say, "OK, now I'd better switch my sphere of attention to get the other half of the data."

Coaching effective listening: The "Yes, and . . ." drill

When patients do not really listen, they may hear but not take seriously others' perspectives. In the Martin family, for instance, Jim and his Dad seldom listened to other family members. They took a "my way or else" stance, setting up a wall that blocked them from hearing anyone else's opinions, concerns or wishes. The underlying belief that every discussion would have a winner and a loser made them reluctant to let themselves hear what anyone else said. If the other person was in any way right, that would mean that they were wrong and therefore undeserving of getting what they want. Even when Jim and Dad understood this pattern, the nonlistening habits persisted, indicating time for explicit listening drills. While understanding was helpful, it clearly needed to be augmented with practice.

One exercise for teaching listening skills involves setting a strict struc-

tured pattern of discussion. In what I think of the "yes, and . . ." drill, one
participant starts off with a brief statement about anything, preferably a
neutral topic such as the weather, clothes, the furniture in the therapy
room, etc. The other is instructed to respond by reiterating what the prior
speaker has just said and then adding a personal opinion. The additions are
all to begin with the conjuction "and" to counteract the tendency to undo
what the other has just said by starting off with "but."

"I had to rush to get here."

"You had to rush to get here, and I didn't rush, but was late."

"Yes, we both had trouble getting here on time, and I'm glad we made it
anyway."

"You're glad we made it, and I am too. . . ."

Individuals who routinely counter what others say by showing what is
wrong with it, or who routinely are thinking about their own point of view
when the other is talking, have a difficult time with this simple exercise.
Argumentative couples in particular find the drill amusing but challenging
and may need to repeat it in many sessions, as well as to practice it at home
as a homework assignment, before it will become automatic. The observation, "But in real conversations people don't do this," is true and false. In
successful real conversations, the reiteration is not necessary because it is
habitual. As the new pattern becomes established, couples cease to need the
more formalized and explicit structure.

Chronically disengaged as well as chronically antagonistic couples seem
to benefit from this exercise. The dialogue of chronically antagonistic
couples is oppositional. Whatever one says, the other counters with the
opposite, so there is no sense of forward momentum. Disengaged couples
sometimes show a non-interactive pattern in which their thoughts are put
forth but never linked. The discussion feels like two separate discussions,
parallel like the rails on a train track. By contrast, this "yes, and . . ." format
structures discussion so that the dialogue feels like two people traveling on
one track. The ensuing ideas include joint input, with each participant
adding dialectically to the prior participant's input instead of deleting or
ignoring it.

Teaching an understanding of the impact of "but"

A reliable clue that a patient is not engaging in effective and genuine
listening is the occurrence of the word "but." The "but" indicates that the
listener has taken in the words but is not taking the other person's point
seriously. A reiteration followed by "but" is like putting food in one's
mouth and then spitting it out instead of swallowing it.

An exercise between therapist and patient can be very useful in conveying the impact of "but" on discussions. The patient is told to say something, anything, to the therapist. The therapist then responds to each patient comment with a statement that begins with "but." After several interactions the therapist asks what the word "but" seemed to do and what feelings it evoked. For example,

PATIENT: You seem to have new shoes on.
THERAPIST: Yes, but they already are scuffed up and dusty.
PATIENT: They do compliment your outfit and look very professional.
THERAPIST: Yes, but they hurt my toes and were a big mistake. I shouldn't
    have bought them. I wish I could take them off, but I can't exactly go
    around as a barefoot therapist.

In the debriefing, patients usually describe their subjective experience as having felt erased or negated at each juncture in the dialogue. They generally express having felt mildly frustrated, saying (rightfully) that the buts conveyed that I hadn't taken in what they had said to me.

The particular metaphor that a patient uses to describe his or her subjective reaction to this exercise will generally indicate that patient's unique way of using or experiencing "but." Patients have said,

"It felt like you brushed away and ignored what I said."

"I felt like you were just looking for what was wrong in what I said."

"Your 'but' felt like a big eraser that came along and erased what I said so that you could write instead what *you* wanted to say."

"I put a thought out like I was adding a brick to a wall we were building together. Your 'but' took my brick down, and then you put your brick up. If I added a but to take down your brick, and so on, that would be just the kind of never-get-anywhere discussion that my husband and I continually experience."

A next step can add considerably to the potency of this exercise. The patient can be asked to take a turn responding to each statement the therapist says with a comment beginning with "but." Most patients respond to this exercise, and particularly to this last paradoxical step, with amusement.

Listening for what is wrong versus listening for what is right

Some patients habitually respond with negatives (either toward the self or toward a spouse). At some point it may be helpful to notice whether attention to negatives, to what is wrong, is not just a verbal style but a whole perceptual style.

When an individual attunes only to negative data, love, affection, and enjoyment are diminished or negated altogether. People experience feelings of love when they notice qualities or behaviors that they like in the other person. Similarly, self-love requires that people notice things that please them about themselves. For these feelings to emerge, attention must be focused on the positive attributes. The relationship is probably reciprocal; that is, when one feels love, one notices the positives; when one notices positives, one feels loving feelings. Likewise, a negative perceptual set will eventually undermine love and self-love feelings. Some negativity, of course, is the product of dominant-submissive interactions and resultant depression, and must be treated as such. In other cases, however, the negativity has become a characterological and perceptual style.

Conflicts may get resolved, new conflict negotitation patterns may become established, and the individual or couple may still not experience joyful and loving feelings. An additional focus on building habits of noting and verbalizing positives can inject vitality and enthusiasm into these patients' lives.

> Jeanne, in treatment with her husband Bart, realized that she, like her mother before her, was locked into a negative mental set. To alter this pattern she was given a series of homework assignments. The first week she was to focus on her daughter, keeping count of the number of positive comments she could make to her. This assignment went well, and Jeanne came into the next session relatively elated with her progress.
>
> The second assignment was to make and count positive comments to her husband. In the following session, Bart, who was unaware of Jeanne's homework assignment, came in expressing optimism about his marriage and enthusiam about his home life. But even though Jeanne could see the effects of her changed orientation, the habitual pull of her negative mental set shifted only after repeated assignments. The exercise, to focus on positive things to notice and comment upon to her husband, had to be reassigned from time to time over a several-month period.
>
> To further complete Jeanne's perceptual shift I assigned her the same exercise with respect to self-commentary. Again the outcome was positive, with Jeanne reporting an increased sense of self-acceptance and even glimmerings of joy. As should be clear from the other descriptions of Jeanne and Bart in this book, this one intervention alone probably cannot account for the changes in their attitudes toward themselves and each other. At the same time, this assignment clearly affected both of them.

A CHALLENGING CASE

Alas, pattern recognition is rewarding, but pattern change, to use Beitman's terms (1987), does not necessarily follow. Some patients need considerably

more drills to overcome the use of "but," to learn to change "yes, but . . ."
to "yes, and. . . ." What if even this coaching does not end the habit? It is
likely then that the words are not weeds that can easily be pulled out of the
vocabulary. Instead, they may have deep roots in an egocentric or oppositional stance. The following case illustrates skill-building attempts with a
particularly challenging case.

Ron and Shelly had been in therapy for ten months. Positive feelings had
been restored to their relationship, and they both said they wanted a more
cooperative mode of communicating. Nonetheless, they still both quickly
bristled whenever they tried to discuss any mutual decisions. The only way
they could cooperatively get through to decisions was to short-circuit the
exploration of concerns and leap as quickly as possible into brainstorming
on solutions.

As they would dip their toes into brief explorations of concerns, both
Shelly and Ron feared that they would become bogged down forever in
feelings and escalations of feelings. That pattern had in fact been one that
had recurred all too often. Tensions would build and crying seemed
inevitable.

I knew from prior sessions that the problematic skill in exploring
concerns was in the listening rather than saying. Each spouse felt that
his/her point of view was more important than the other's. They had
learned that validating the other's was vital, but they did so via pseudo-
validations such as "I understand your concern, but. . . ." Even when they
did not include the blatant giveaway, "but," the formulaic and perfunctory
way in which they performed their reiteration duty belied the sincerity of
their "yes, and . . ." responses.

We had laid a foundation for addressing this problem in the prior session
by discussing family-of-origin sources of egocentricity. Ron's mother and
Shelly's father each had expected all other family members to revolve
around them and always to agree with their positions. These insights were
helpful but not sufficient for changing Ron and Shelly's replications of their
parents' stances. They could each recognize the self-centered orientation of
their parents, but neither could feel or identify when they were acting the
same way themselves. Furthermore, neither had images of more empathic
responses.

I reminded myself that effective coaching combines chunking, stepwise
increases in the challenge level of the exercise, shaping via successive
approximations, modeling, positive reinforcement, and multiple repetitions. I decided to utilize all of these vehicles in a last determined attempt
to teach the skill of responding empathically when someone else has
expressed a concern.

I began by giving Shelly and Ron a hypothetical situation to discuss in order to establish a diagnostic baseline. Then, testing the limits of how well they could communicate, I offered them re-do opportunities. Like multiple drafts of a written document, these repeated efforts sometimes enable patients to radically improve their dialogue patterns.

The topic I selected was a problem Shelly and Ron had discussed (and, I thought, had fully resolved) in a prior session. My intent was to start with nonthreatening content. I suggested that they pretend that Ron's mother had just phoned to say that she and Ron's father would soon be coming for a week's visit.

Shelly started the discussion well. "Gee, your folks are coming for a week. How are we going to handle this?"

It immediately became clear that Ron especially, and Shelly to a lesser extent, simply could not come up with empathic responses. Shelly said, "I'm worried that we won't take enough time away from them to maintain our good feeling as a couple. In the past we have both just hovered around your mother, who becomes the prima donna whom everyone caters to."

Ron responded, "I agree that she creates that when she visits, but I'm worried that we'll go overboard and ignore them."

Shelly, exquisitely sensitive to the negation of her concern with the "but," unconsciously reacted by trying to show how foolish Ron's concern was. "We couldn't possibly ignore them," she returned.

In no time Shelly and Ron were arguing about whether or not they could ignore Ron's parents. Feeling that Ron had not heard her, Shelly was reiterating repetitively, "We have to take time to stay a couple." This kind of going-on-and-on about the same point triggered Ron's worst fears and irritated him intensely. His mother used to go on eternally saying the same thing over and over. Eventually, however, Ron caught himself reacting in his old ways and tried to right the discussion, saying, "We have to do both — take time for ourselves and be sure we don't ignore my parents." By this time, alas, Shelly was too locked in her resentment to hear this well-intentioned but too-little-too-late attempt.

After enough exchanges to get a full picture of their baseline starting patterns, I stopped the exercise. We debriefed, listening first to the tape-recorded replay of their interaction. (I often tape sessions on cassettes that patients can take home for review or leave with their files in my office. Then, when we want an instant replay, it is available.)

Ron observed, "It was clear that she felt her point was more important than mine." Reflecting on her experience, Shelly said, "It felt like he erased my point in his first response, and I didn't hear anything else he said after that. I just kept trying to get my point accepted. I guess that's why I kept saying the same thing over and over. It felt to me that he believed his point was more important than my concern."

I instructed Ron and Shelly to try a re-do of the same discussion, this time paying closer attention to what the other person was saying and making an effort to make both people's concerns equally important. "I want you to make a real effort to make sure that the other person can feel your equal weighting."

Shelly began, "My major concern is being able to be a couple while they are here with us."

Ron responded, "I hear that concern. *And* (dutifully emphasizing the 'and'), what I would like to do is to spend some time with them."

There was a long pause. Finally Shelly spoke hesitantly, "I agree that we need to spend time with them, . . ."

I cut in, zeroing in on these initial exchanges. The first draft had given us a clear diagnostic picture. Now we were working on improvements. At this point nothing would have been gained by letting the exercise go on, amassing too much data to process. It was preferable to call attention to breaks in the communication as they occurred.

Shelly had again felt that Ron was not taking her point seriously. And Shelly's extreme hesitation in her response indicated that she was working on genuinely hearing Ron, but still was more locked into seeing what was wrong with his statement than in seeing his legitimate concern. Again she realized that she had focused on what was wrong, instead of what was understandable, in what Ron had said. She realized that this negative focus emerged each time she sensed that their discussion had a greater emphasis on what Ron wanted than on what she wanted. We again recalled that in her family of origin her father's needs counted; her mother was just there to respond to his wishes. And in fact Shelly's super-attuned radar for being ignored had been accurate. Ron was still giving pseudo-validations. Reacting with the right, if formulaic, words does not accomplish validation if there is no appreciation of the other's concern.

We went for a third try. This time the instruction was even more explicit. "Look for everything that's right about what the other person says, and then elaborate that. Make it a caricature of super-validating." To make it even easier, I switched to totally nonthreatening content and to interactions with me instead of with each other. In order for exercises to be effective the therapist has to keep simplifying them until the patient(s) can be successful. Then the skills can be graduallly built up for handling more difficult situations.

I turned to Ron and, having glanced out my window for something to comment on, said, "I'm worried that the grass won't get green this spring."

To my surprise, Ron was still unable to respond with cooperative validation. "It is a concern," he said, attempting to do what he thought "validating" involved. But then he went on, spoiling his response, saying, "I think it's going to be very green this year."

Note that in ordinary conversation Ron's response, expressing an opposite opinion, would have been perfectly normal. We were working, however, on the explicit skill of empathic listening, and in this context the response was poor. I asked Shelly if Ron had accomplished the assignment. She immediately pointed out that he had not repeated what I had said. To the contrary, he had contradicted what I said.

We tried the same example a second time. I said to Ron, "I'm worried about the grass never turning green this year." Then, to be sure he would have the idea, I coached him further, adding, "Now listen closely to the concern I said, and elaborate on it."

Ron responded, "I'm *very* worried about the grass being green this year," which was clearly not a truthful response, and which indicated that he still did not understand what it is to listen to what is right in a person's statement of concern. This skill was clearly much harder to communicate than I had anticipated.

I was determined to convey the idea. I decided to switch to modeling, as I had clearly tested the limits of what, even with careful shaping and coaxing, Ron was able to come up with in the way of empathic listening. I suggested that he tell me the same worry about the grass, and listen to my response.

Ron responded, "Gosh, I'm really worried about the grass being green this year."

I elaborated, "I hadn't thought about it before, but now that you say that I can see that the grass may have a problem. It has been a dry winter, with not nearly as much snow as we usually get."

I asked Ron how he experienced my response. For the first time I began to feel that he was catching on.

"Well, you sort of talked about what I was talking about," he said with surprise.

"In what way? Was I in opposition to it?"

"No," he said musingly. "Actually, you were sort of adding supporting facts; you didn't just repeat."

"Right!" I answered. "Instead of automatically repeating, I was making a real attempt to slip into your understanding about the grass, and even to add to it." I was feeling jubilant, my hope that empathy could be taught returning.

I turned with enthusiasm to launch into the same process with Shelly. "Your turn. I'm going to give you a concern and I want you almost to caricature an empathic response by listening to what's right in what I say and then adding supporting facts.

"It may be April, but it's hard for me to get out my spring wardrobe when it keeps snowing," I said, again making up whatever came to my mind as a nonthreatening example.

Shelly responded, "I understand what you mean. It's really hard to figure out what the weather is going to be like, to know which way it's going to be, if it's spring, or winter."

To my surprise Shelly had had no difficulty with the assignment. Her empathic skills were excellent; she just didn't use them whenever she felt her own concerns were being ignored.

Having the idea does not guarantee that patients can put it into action, and certainly does not suggest that the new responses will become automatic. To engrain empathic responses, we took more practice runs, with Ron and Shelly alternately responding to my nonsense statements. I tried to keep the examples coming fast, like a tennis drill. "Ron, I've never noticed before that there are awnings on that building that I see out the window. It's a vanilla building; the awnings help it a little bit."

Ron answered (craning his neck to look out the window, a good indicator that he was trying to see it as I was seeing it), "Yes. The awnings do dress it up a bit."

"Bravo!" I said. "What made that such a good response?"

"I was building on what you said."

I continued, "OK, you guys are ready for your final exam. Shelly, I'm worried that we'll go totally overboard on being a couple when my parents come to visit and we'll just ignore my parents."

Shelly paused at length. "I'm trying to figure out how to build on that one. . . . I think we can figure out some activities that they would like. We could repeat what we've done before with them, and also find some different things to do to spend time in nice ways with them."

I faced Ron again, "Ron, your turn. I'm worried that we'll go overboard and just ignore my folks."

"I don't know how to build on a statement like that." He was stymied.

I encouraged him, "You did it before, when you first expressed this concern. It's the habit of building on what someone else has said that is new for you. . . . Focus on what was right about my statement."

"I just can't seem to come up with anything."

I needed to make the assignment easier, and to add more modeling. "You give the statement to me. We'll switch roles."

Stating his own feelings was easier. "I'm worried we'll go overboard with the folks."

"I guess that's possible," I responded. "Everytime I learn something new I have a tendency to go from one extreme to the other. I guess what might save us is just having talked about finding a balance, with both time for us as a couple and time for entertaining them."

At this point we were running out of time and needed to move toward closure. I wanted to bring the content of the issue to resolution, as well as to summarize the pattern skill we had practiced. I asked each spouse what his/her understanding of the skill was, and did one last example with each of them. They both did well, and then Ron astounded me. Apparently the exercises tapped a rich vein of insight. Ron reflected on how he had been responding to his children when they came to him with a problem.

"I think part of the problem is my attempt to take a comforting reassuring role. I'm thinking of what I do when one of my kids comes to me with a problem. They say, 'Dad, I blah blah blah . . .' and my response is always, 'Don't worry, everything is going to be all right. Just relax.' The same kind of attitude comes out when Shelly and I have discussions. I try to respond in a reassuring fashion, 'Oh, don't worry about it. It's not as bad as you think.' And the more I say that to Shelly, the more she goes on and on. I'm trying to prevent the matter from becoming a big deal, but my response instead fans the fire."

Therapist: "Amen."

CHAPTER 20

Resistance

RESISTANCE CAN BE UNDERSTOOD as a form of conflict that frequently emerges in the course of psychotherapy. Resistance can be the manifestation of patients' conflicts between wanting to improve their lives and their fears of new difficulties that could emerge with any changes they might make. The term is also used to describe tensions that develop between a therapist and patients.

Most people cling to the safety of the familiar, which is at least predictable if not effective. At the same time, patients come to treatment because they want to make changes. A tug of war may ensue between the urge to move ahead and the fears and difficulties of change. This tension can block the smooth flow of treatment.

Wachtel, drawing a similar conclusion, writes that therapists, and particularly behaviorally trained therapists,

> . . . are hampered, I believe, by their lack of attention to conflict. In important ways, in fact, the concepts of resistance and of conflict are almost identical. Resistance is not something that periodically comes up to disrupt the therapy. It is the track of the patient's conflict about changing, the way in which the sincere desire to change confronts the fears, misconceptions, and prior adaptive strategies that make change difficult. (Wachtel, 1982, p.xix)

Resistance of this type is likely to be experienced as an intrapsychic battle. It can be seen as the tendency to try to fit new data into old schemas and to rely on old ways of doing things rather than to continually modify the old schemas (Wachtel, 1981). The more rigid and inflexible a person's cognitive schemas, the more resistance may be seen in therapy.

Resistance may be manifest in attempts to squelch awareness of feelings,

315

indicated by what gestalt therapists describe as breaks in the flow. At these times the individual

> . . . interrupts his own functioning. These interruptions can be thought of as the resistances, or the evidence of resistances . . . a person blocks or interrupts his communications, either within his internal self-system or with the interpersonal system. (Kepner & Brien, 1970, p.43)

> Renalda had closed her eyes to visualize her dilemma about continuing to carry certain burdens in her life. She pictured herself carrying a heavy load of snow. She became aware of wanting to let down the load. At that point she abruptly opened her eyes. The wish to set down her load felt unacceptable. Eye-opening signaled resistance, discomfort with continuing the visualization task that was bringing uncomfortable thoughts into her awareness.

> Similarly, Karen longed to move out of her lonely world, to make friends, to socialize after work, to expand her interests, and to interact more with other people. At the same time, moving into the world of social contacts would mean crossing the frontier of the familiar. Moving from the painful yet familiar isolation of her apartment to venture out to the mainstream world felt terrifying. As she began to focus in treatment on her loneliness problem, Karen became reluctant to talk. Her eyes downcast, she looked withdrawn, almost despairing.

In other cases resistance may be manifested in the contrast between what patients say they want to do and what they actually do. For instance, they may say, "yes, yes," to a homework assignment, and then not do it. Sometimes they intend to handle new situations in a new way, and then react powerlessly against the power of habit. Wanting to improve a tennis forehand, and even knowing how to do it better, may still not override the forces of prior patterning.

Resistance may also be enacted between patient and therapist, particularly when the therapist is encouraging more or different changes than patients feel comfortable with. Delightful as it might be if patient and therapist always worked together like hand and glove, with perfect coordination and teamwork, the reality of therapy is that patient and therapist sometimes clash. Therapists trained in a psychodynamic tradition might call the breakdown in cooperation resistance (as well as transference). Behaviorally trained clinicians are more likely to label the phenomenon noncompliance. Whatever descriptive label is used, when patients and therapist seem to be pulling in opposite directions, resolving the conflict and restoring cooperation are critical to the success of treatment.

When Karen suddenly stopped the flow of her talk in therapy, inappropriate therapeutic intervention and Karen's transference issues were both involved. I had suggested that she participate in an evening therapy group. This idea felt overwhelming to Karen. In addition, the suggestion of group treatment triggered strong transference issues for her. Karen heard my suggestion as an indication that I wanted her to start exploring social activities in the evenings after work. Although expanding her social contacts was an objective that she had specified, Karen feared that she would disappoint me (and herself) if she tried and failed. Since in the past she had not been able to socialize, she saw little hope for the future. Soon she felt that she must already have disappointed me. She felt certain that I was angry at her (and she was angry at herself) for not being able to go out on her own.

The path out of the resistance involved exploring Karen's feelings on both sides of her conflict. Karen was surprised to hear that I was neither angry nor disappointed. She seemed to relax hearing me empathize with how frightening the prospect of tackling her long-standing pattern of social isolation must be. As she heard empathy instead of the critical response she had expected, the perceived conflict between her concerns and mine melted away, and she also relaxed her harsh self-criticism. Clarification of the family roots of her expectation that I would be angry and disappointed added to the relief.

Resolution of this conflict necessitated also my open acknowledgment that her fears were understandable in light of my too challenging suggestion. We carefully scaled down the first steps of our social interaction plan so that each step would feel less awesome, more manageable.

The term "resistance" has several advantages over the term "noncompliance." "Noncompliance" tends to focus excessively on the patient-therapist interaction, as noncompliance implies noncooperation with assignments from the therapist. By contrast, the term "resistance" can encompass both patient-therapist conflicts and intrapsychic struggles that interfere with treatment progress. At the same time, behavioral therapists' reluctance to use the word "resistance" reflects an important consideration. Behaviorists point out that the term "resistance" has sometimes been used to blame the patient for breakdowns in therapeutic teamwork when in fact the therapist's unrealistic demands or provocative manner have initiated the difficulties.

A focus on the phenomenon from a conflict resolution perspective has the advantage of overcoming both of these limitations. Both intrapsychic and patient-therapist friction are encompassed in the one framework. And in a conflict resolution framework "blame" resides neither in just the patient nor just the therapist, but in both the patient's "resistance" and the therapist's difficulty in correctly ascertaining the patient's readiness for certain tasks.

From the perspective of conflict resolution theory, the keys to overcoming resistance are the same as those for resolving any conflict, i.e., clarification of the conflict, exploration of the underlying concerns, and then discovery of mutually satisfying solutions. Whether resistance manifests an intrapsychic conflict, an interpersonal patient-therapist conflict, or both, exploration of the specific concerns underlying patients' resistance can lead to resolution of the problems that have been making change difficult. Resistance can be exacerbated, however, to the extent that conflict resolution attempts take the form of positional bargaining. If a resistance conflict gives rise to a win-lose, lose-lose, or no settlement outcome between the wishes and fears about change, or the wishes of patient and therapist, therapeutic progress can be slowed.

The following instances of resistance illustrate a conflict resolution perspective on resistance and suggest some therapeutic options for dealing with this process.

RESISTANCE AS FEAR OF CHANGE

Ralphine sought treatment to explore why she was pushing away her fiancé.

A relatively subtle moment of resistance occurred midway through treatment. I had suggested that tape-recording the session could be helpful, both so that Ralphine could review her session later in the week and so that I could use the tape for research purposes. Although Ralphine agreed to this suggestion, the tape recorder's placement in the room necessitated that she move from the couch upon which she had sat in prior sessions to a chair across the room. Ralphine balked. She hesitated, grimaced, and then, sighing "Oh well . . ," rose and moved.

"I don't like change," Ralphine explained. We explored Ralphine's concerns about change and preferences for continuity. Old patterns of behavior were familiar and hence felt safe even when they were unsatisfactory. Change connoted fright and difficulty. Ralphine noted many instances in her life where she had stayed in bad situations rather than risk trying to move on—at jobs, in her first marriage, and in a negative therapy experience with a prior therapist.

These insights led Ralphine to a sudden realization of her intent when she pushed away men who sought close relationships with her. Intimacy meant change. Marriage meant leaving her familiar, if lonely, lifestyle for the challenges of unknown territory.

Later, at her final therapy session, Ralphine recalled the sense of liberation she had experienced in that therapy session. Ralphine's self-report corroborated the traditional psychoanalytic hypothesis that analysis of resistance (in the terms of this book, exploration of the underlying concerns motivating resistant behavior) can be a powerful treatment intervention.

RESISTANCE AS SELF-PROTECTION

Jim was a college student, the only son in the Martin family of six. When the family wanted to discuss how to bring Jim's new fiancée into their large family group, Jim did not want the topic brought up.

Like most behavior, Jim's resistance was multidetermined. The Martin family had a long history of arguing about problems, of stirring up bad feelings with no positive outcomes. Jim's resistance to discussing his fiancée's entry into the extended family stemmed in part from a desire to avoid further contentious talk about his plan to get married.

Second, Jim and other family members saw conflicts in terms of right and wrong. Attempts to discuss problems tended to become like the game "Pin the tail on the donkey," i.e., attempts to determine who should be stuck with the blame. Jim's reluctance to discuss the problem served to protect him from being designated the one in the wrong. He sensed that the rest of the family was allied against him on this issue, so the likelihood of his escaping the donkey tail seemed low.

To deal with Jim's resistance I encouraged him to verbalize his concerns. Hearing his sensitivity on the topic of his marriage, family members reassured him that they were not interested in either criticizing or blaming. The ensuing discussion, which, aware of Jim's concerns, I tightly refereed to keep safe, turned out to be very helpful in maintaining the family's closeness. Family members noted that Jim had been withdrawing from them. They expressed concerns about how they could make both Jim and his fiancée feel more comfortable in the family circle. Jim felt relieved hearing that his parents and siblings had accepted his marriage decision. They mapped plans together for helping his fiancée overcome her wariness of them, so that she could look forward to joining their extended family system.

PATIENT-THERAPIST CONFLICTS ABOUT TREATMENT

Because of her generally frightened view of life and living, Karen gave me many opportunities to practice patient-therapist conflict resolution. She resisted virtually anything new in her life, including new treatment options. The following instance occurred within the context of a hospitalization for severe depression. The dialogue illustrates how a conflict resolution model of resistance can guide a therapist to resolution of what initially feels like an irresolvable treatment blockage. Clarification of Karen's underlying concerns, with maximum specificity, followed by careful explanation of my concerns, opened the way to a mutually acceptable solution.

Karen was resisting taking the medication that the psychiatrist and I had agreed was imperative. Her initial response was "No, I don't need it. And I don't want it." She and I then conversed as follows.

THERAPIST: You sound very certain about not wanting medications, almost angry that I even suggested it. Is that accurate?

KAREN: *Yes.* (spoken with finality)

THERAPIST: I see that you have strong feelings about not taking medications. Maybe you can help me to understand what it is about medications that makes them out of the question.

KAREN: (silence)

THERAPIST: What is your understanding of why medication is not necessary?

KAREN: I'm just lazy. Just not a strong enough person. That's why I can't make my life work. I don't need medication. I just need to shape up.

THERAPIST: In what ways lazy? Can you give me some specific examples?

KAREN: I just hibernate. I don't even try to meet people or to get a better job so that my life would be better. All I do is withdraw and hide from everything, and just go to my job that I hate. That's why I'm miserable. I make myself miserable by not doing anything to make things better. Medications won't help.

THERAPIST: That helps me to understand what you mean by lazy. You mean hibernating, putting out a minimum of energy in your life, just enough to keep your job. Is that right?

KAREN: Yes.

THERAPIST: We've talked before about how little energy you have when you are depressed. That you get like a battery that's run down. And then because you can't sleep and have to force yourself to eat, that battery never gets adequately recharged. You get caught in a vicious cycle. The more run down the battery gets, the less energy you have to try to find a different job. The more stuck you feel in the job you hate, the more depressed you feel.

KAREN: Right. If I were just a stronger person then I wouldn't be stuck. I would do something. But we talk and talk in therapy sessions, and I still never do anything about making things better. I'm just lazy. All I do is hide.

THERAPIST: I agree. As much as we've talked about your job, and about ways to go about finding a better job, you don't seem to be able to do anything about it. It's like the energy isn't there. As you say, you're not strong enough. In fact, I think your policy of hibernating, of hiding from social contacts and anything in life other than your job, has been a very smart one. You have had so little energy with that

major depression in your system that you do have to be extremely
judicious about spending energy on anything beyond survival. That
job enables you to survive.

KAREN: My biggest fear is that I could end up a bag lady. I hate that job, but
it does give me income enough that I can pay my rent and for food and
not end up on the street.

THERAPIST: (summary statement of concerns) So we agree. You are worried
that you are lazy, that you can't seem to summon up enough energy to
begin making changes in your life. You call that lack of energy lazy
and I call it depression, but what we both are referring to is your
strategy of hibernating from life in order to survive, in order to save
all of the little bits of energy that you have to put into earning a living.
And I think that has been a very smart strategy, because in fact you
have managed, even amidst severe depressions that would have
incapacitated most other people, somehow always to keep going to
work.

KAREN: I guess that's so. And I don't want to take medications because last
time I took medications they made me sleepy all day, and that just
made it even harder to wake up in the mornings and to keep myself
going.

THERAPIST: So if you're already pushing yourself to your limit, and it's clear
that you're barely managing to survive as it is, the idea of trying
anything different, especially something that might make you sleepy
and therefore make things worse, harder, must sound too risky.

KAREN: Yes.

THERAPIST: Are there other concerns too, or is that pretty clearly what you
are worried about that makes you not want medications?

KAREN: That's it.

THERAPIST: Can you handle trying to hear what my concern is? It's actually
similar to yours. (eliciting cooperation)

KAREN: OK.

THERAPIST: I feel the same as you do about our therapy. We talk about what
you need to do, and then you can't seem to take any of the first next
steps we discuss in our sessions. I also see you as barely staying alive
and needing to use all your energies just to hold onto your job and to
combat your suicidal thoughts. And I agree that tackling anything
beyond those goals when you're hanging on by your fingernails as it is
could jeopardize your ability to stay alive. So mostly we agree.
(emphasizing points of agreement)

KAREN: (a barely visible head nod in agreement)

THERAPIST: So we're stuck. The only way I can see to intervene in this cycle is to find some way to give you more energy. And that's why I want you to take pills. You still will have to make the life changes that will make you happy. You're absolutely right only you can make your life better. All the pills will do is give you a little more energy to make that happen.

KAREN: Yes . . . but last time they made me too sedated. I could hardly keep my eyes open at work. I can't risk that.

THERAPIST: I agree. That would be counterproductive. We have to be very careful that the medication we give you is one that does not generally have sedative side effects. And we also have to give it to you inititally in small dosages, increasing the dosage slowly enough that your body doesn't have to make big adjustments that might make you feel sedated.

KAREN: Are you saying I have to take the medication?

THERAPIST: I'm saying we have to be very careful not to disrupt your strategy of hibernation, of focusing all your energy on just keeping yourself going at work. And I'm saying that one way to help you with that strategy is to take a medication that will give you a little bit more energy, that will charge your batteries enough that work will be less of a constant struggle. And also, that we have to be very careful in our choice of medications so that you don't become burdened with an antidepresssant that makes you sleepy, and therefore less able to function, during the day.

KAREN: Well . . . I guess maybe that's OK.

TIT FOR TAT

Cooperative problem-solving is not always an option. If this route is blocked by psychotic thought, for instance, unilateral decision-making may be necessary. The therapist still listens closely for the patient's underlying concerns but then, for the patient's benefit, may need to implement a "my way or no way" solution. For various reasons Karen some months later eventually ceased taking her medications. To the dismay of the several of us who had been working with her, she gradually sank into a severely suicidal and psychotic depressive state of mind. I was determined to find some way to get her to agree to hospitalization and/or medications. She refused everything. If I could not convince her, I was prepared to hospitalize her under Colorado's laws for involuntary commitment.

Casting about for ways to influence Karen toward voluntary treatment, I mentioned that by state law I was mandated to contact her relatives if I felt she posed a serious suicidal risk. "Don't you *dare* do that!" Karen insisted, her eyes growing wide. "I would do *anything* before I would let you do that!" "All right," I responded, relieved to have found a point of leverage. "You have three choices: medications for a minimum of three months, voluntary hospitalization, or I call your mother." She chose immediate medications, and I cheered silently.

CHAPTER 21

Ethical Perspectives

THIS BOOK HAS A MORAL point of view. The treatment ideas it proposes are not "value free"—but then, no treatment is value free. Therapy cannot be conducted without underlying ethical assumptions any more than a language can be spoken without an accent. People who think they have no accent may lack the breadth of perspective to hear how their way of talking differs from others'. Belief in the ideal of conducting therapy free of a values, like a belief in an ideal of speaking without an accent, suggests that the speaker or therapist is egocentrically assuming that his/her way is the true way, with other ways viewed as deviations.

REALMS OF ETHICAL CONCERNS

Professionals involved in disciplines such as politics, law, medicine, and business confront similar questions of values, of the role of moral issues in the conduct of their work. One political theorist writes instructively that the study of ethics in government has had two branches (Lilla, 1981). One branch has been concerned with the morality of the practitioners. In political life, public servants are expected to adhere to a generally accepted moral code. These rules concern refraining from accepting bribes, honesty in the conduct of political campaigning, etc. If followed, these rules lead government officials to conduct themselves as at least ethical if not necessarily competent public servants. The second branch of moral concerns in government addresses the morality of decisions made by public servants, e.g., decisions to wage war, to distribute tax responsibilities, to pay out governmental benefits, to intervene in other nations' affairs, etc.

Discussions of ethical issues in psychotherapy have had a similar two branches. With respect to the first branch, ethical behavior for practitioners includes refraining from sexual interactions with patients, avoiding dual relationships, and maintaining confidentiality (Conte, Plutchik, Picard, & Karasu, 1989). Exposure to ethical principles is included in the education of therapy professionals. The psychology licensing exam, for instance, includes testing of applicants' knowledge and understanding of the American Psychological Association's ethical code, *Standards for Providers of Psychological Services* (APA, 1977).

The second branch of ethical questions in the practice of psychotherapy focuses on the therapist's moral responsibility and culpability vis-à-vis actions and decisions patients make while they are under the therapist's guidance. Behavior that is hurtful to oneself or to others, decisions to end or to continue a marital relationship, to pursue an extramarital affair, to terminate the use of alcohol, to pursue particular career paths, etc., all inherently involve ethical issues.

Therapists have shown ambivalence about involving themselves in this second branch of moral concerns, in the decisions that we are party to by dint of our therapeutic involvement. We want our patients to develop in positive moral directions, yet we feel uncomfortable about imposing our own moral viewpoint on them. In many ways we reparent our patients, yet we are not their actual parents and feel uncomfortable taking on the responsibility of real parents to impart moral standards. How can we resolve these dilemmas, these conflicts between our responsibilities for patients and our realization of the limitations of this responsibility? How do we distinguish when responsibility for clients veers into excessive influence, intrusion, or domination—or, at the other extreme, into neglect and inadequate guidance?

One way that we resolve this dilemma is by saying that our moral obligation is to be certain that patients become aware of and take into account ethical dimensions in their decision-making. However, the particular ethical code of any given patient is not ours to dictate. Thus we can, do, and should encourage patients to consider ethical aspects of decisions and behaviors. Making underlying value assumptions explicit is as important as bringing to the light of full awareness the impulses, wishes and feelings underlying our patients' behaviors. At the same time, it is not for us to judge, advise, or recommend that our patients should or should not do this or do that, unless there is a clear and present danger to someone as a result of our patients' actions.

The "unless" clause in this latter principle is critical. Most therapists agree that, except for pastoral counselors, for us to assert what is moral and what is not, or which moral rules to adhere to, is generally not appropriate.

On the other hand, a therapist, as a publicly licensed professional, is responsible to the community at large as well as to specific clients. By law as well as by our profession's conventions, professional intervention must include an active response when breaches of law have occurred or the safety of other members of society is at stake. For instance, in most states therapists are required by law immediately to report instances of child abuse to governmental authorities. In this case the therapist's duty to protect others rises above the immediate wishes of the client s/he is treating. Similarly, therapists have a duty to warn potential victims when a patient has homicidal thoughts. Patients carrying sexually transmitted illnesses pose a somewhat more subtle moral dilemma for therapists. In these instances no law requires the therapist to protect the community, and yet a therapist who is treating an infected person and witnessing sexual behavior that could endanger unknowing sexual partners has a moral obligation at least to raise the issue with the patient and perhaps even to notify relevant authorities or victims.

Instances in which the client may pose a danger to him/herself or others are, in fact, relatively uncommon, particularly in private psychotherapy practices. On the whole, therefore, the *content* of patients' concerns, values, and decisions is their responsibility and outside of the therapist's control.

Viewing therapy from a conflict resolution perspective reveals that there is a third arena, a third branch of ethical concerns, namely, the *process* by which we are encouraging our patients to address their problems. Conflict resolution treatment is explicitly value-laden in this third realm. This book posits that coercion is less morally desirable than cooperation, and that a mutually optimizing outcome is to be favored over a settlement that harms one side. Settlements that balance altruism and self-interest are ethically as well as functionally preferable. That is, the *content* of patients' conflicts requires guided exploration by a relatively neutral therapist-guide, but the *process* of resolution necessitates therapist coaching based not only on what works but also on explicit moral values. Acknowledgment of the feelings and needs on all sides is morally preferable to subduing or ignoring one party's concerns to the benefit of another.

A cooperative conflict resolution process hones in on the essential sine qua non of moral behavior. Individuals, as well as civilizations, can be judged by the extent to which they are able to hear accurately and respond constructively both to their own concerns *and* to the concerns of others. Some moral and religious thinkers emphasize the ability to be attuned to one's own flow of feelings and thoughts. Others stress responsivity to the needs of others. The conflict resolution perspective posits that it is the ability to do both — to hear and respond to both self and other, and in the intraspsychic sphere to integrate both wishes and values—that constitutes the fundamental basis of moral action and ethical living.

By teaching cooperative dispute resolution process to our patients, we are committing an act of moral education. We are offering a process that works efficaciously, bringing more satisfaction and less emotional distress to our patients' daily lives. At the same time we are addressing the moral core of our patients' lives.

THE THERAPIST'S MORAL BURDEN

One therapist colleague, reading an early draft of this book, confessed that he was bothered by the implication that yelling at one's spouse is an inferior mode of problem-solving, and maybe even morally reprehensible. "Are you telling me I should feel guilty every time I get mad at my wife?" he asked me.

This question made me quite uncomfortable. I sensed that my friend wanted me to say, "Of course not. I am writing only descriptively, not prescriptively. You can draw your own conclusions. I'm just a psychologist talking about what communication patterns work best in what circumstances. I don't operate in the realm of shoulds." I wanted to be able to reassure him further, saying, "You don't have to examine your personal life or make changes. I'm just talking about patients."

And that answer would have had some truth. Certainly, for everything there is a time, and there are indeed times when yelling is an appropriate behavior. Yelling gets the other's attention and can shake up the status quo and open spaces for new solutions. The other extreme, doing nothing, is sometimes desirable also. Some problems do work themselves out over time, and more successfully than if they had been addressed directly. Alas, that answer is not enough to quell my discomfort. A full and flexible response repertoire may be necessary for dealing with the many kinds of people and problems a mature adult is likely to confront in life. Still, for ongoing interactions with family, friends, and colleagues, cooperative and open discussion of problems is clearly preferable to flight, fight, immobilization or avoidance. And a process of settlement that acknowledges and looks to satisfy the concerns of all participants is preferable, ethically as well as practically, over one that yields winners and losers.

Furthermore, our patients, like our children, learn as much or more from what we do as from what we say. When we set an appointment, do we look to find the time that is best for both ourselves and for the patients? In establishing payment schedules do we rigidly insist on what is best for us, do we bend too flexibly to our own detriment, or are we dually responsive to both our patients' needs and our own?

An intellectual understanding of how people can resolve their conflicts, internal and interpersonal, is not enough for a therapist. This way of interacting must become a part of our basic grammar of living. Only then will we reflexively respond to the many conflicts, small and large, that emerge between ourselves and our patients, in a way that is attuned and responsive to both our own and our patients' concerns.

THE HURTFUL PATIENT

This line of thinking leads to another uncomfortable dilemma. What do we do with patients who do not accept our moral system? What about patients who are unremittingly selfish? How do we respond to those whose sadistic impulses are ego-syntonic, who believe that hurtful behavior toward their spouse or children is somehow acceptable? To those who justify their behavior by insisting that the victim deserves or has provoked their anger?

As therapists we can "lead the horse to water but we cannot make him drink." There are limits to our abilities to guide and coach patients, limits because of our always imperfect guiding and coaching skills, and limits because of our patients' desires, values, and capacities for making changes.

A dramatic illustration of predispositions toward selfish or altruistic behavior is suggested in a study of onlookers' responses to the persecution of Jews in World War II. Oliner and Oliner (1988) interviewed subjects from a number of European nations, matching those who rescued their fellow countrymen and those who withdrew or stood by indifferently while the Nazi forces arrested Jews and sent them to death camps. Factors such as social status, intelligence, education, talent and creativity did not distinguish those who stood by silently from those who took risks, often great personal risks, to reach out and help endangered friends and even strangers. Rather, the Oliners conclude, the key factors yielding selfishness or altruism seem to have been "the values learned from their parents which prompted and sustained their involvement."

In an article reviewing the Oliner research, Adelson (1988) sums up the study's findings regarding individuals who did nothing to help their neighbors at risk:

> The by-standers are constricted, cold, distrustful. They do not expect much goodness from others, having experienced so little of it at home. It is every man for himself. They are in the Kleinian sense paranoid personalities, sour, suspicious, vigilant, self-absorbed. (p. 42)

By contrast, individuals who were sensitive to the dangerous situation of Jews and who took action to provide safety for them showed quite another picture. For these individuals:

> The essential value involved caring for others. That of course is a value most of us learn and teach, but much of the time we give it only lip-service. For the individuals the Oliners studied, it was a force too strong to shrug off or cast aside. Faced with the choice of whether or not to help those in peril, the rescuers found that for them there was no choice. "While some tried to resist the burdens . . . their sense of personal obligation did not allow them to do so." In some cases it was "a matter of heightened empathy for people in pain." Others had internalized the helping norms of the groups — often religious — to which they were attached. For a small minority, strong principles of justice or caring were prepotent. In all these cases the need to help others was preemptive, imperative. Their values had the force of drives.
>
> What we learn from the Oliners is that such values will be internalized under certain conditions. The parents themselves live by them, practicing what they preach, hence offering a model of altruistic behavior. The children are raised gently but firmly. Moral standards are high, yet the parents avoid harsh discipline. The family atmosphere is affectionate. Children are encouraged to understand the feelings of others; that empathic outlook seems to structure the moral code. (Adelson, 1988, pp. 41-42)

As therapists we do well to bear in mind the Oliners' study. First, the study helps us to understand those individuals who, despite our best intentions, our most attentive nurturing, and our repeated expressions of understanding, are not able to grasp the idea of cooperative or empathic interactions and leave therapy before this transformation has been accomplished. We cannot succeed in helping everyone.

Second, the Oliner study reminds us of the climate of warmth, firmness, and clear guidance that enables the emotional and moral development of children in families. Such a climate suggests a standard for therapists looking to see their patients flourish. In the conduct of therapy, the psychotherapist's role is analogous to the role of parents. We are offering a reparenting opportunity, and like parents we are inherently, in the nature of our work, offering guidance as well as a climate of appreciation and caring.

THERAPISTS, NOT MORALISTS

The therapist must be master of many arts — a master communicator, parent, negotiator, teacher, guide and coach. I am not suggesting that we add moral judge to our list of credentials or to our therapeutic mission. In day-to-day work with patients we have enough challenges dealing in the

realm of what is without venturing into preaching about what *should be*.
Moreover, a moralistic stance would undermine our effectiveness as
clinicians. Yet, I have asserted that psychotherapy is inherently a morally
based endeavor. Patients ask us to help them live more satisfactorily. To
pretend otherwise can cause us to neglect the moral ramifications of our
work, to our own and our patients' detriment.

Heeding the moral foundations of psychotherapeutic work highlights the
responsibility carried by those who practice in the psychotherapy professions. We are not mechanics fixing cars. Like it or not, we address the core
issues of how people live their lives and of how we are raising upcoming
generations. With this awareness we can choose most carefully what we are
modeling for our patients and what we are teaching them. Rather than
abstain from coaching for fear we are encroaching on patients' moral
territory, we must be thoughtful about when and how to advise. Though
decisions must be up to patients, our responsibilities are to guide patients
from conflict to resolution so that they will be able to make sound choices,
and to teach them to negotiate the path toward resolution more cooperatively and thereby more effectively.

> If I am not for myself, then who will be for me? If I am for myself
> alone, what am I? And if not now, when?
>
> — from *Sayings of the Fathers*

References

Ables, B. S., in collaboration with J. M. Brandsma. (1977). *Therapy for couples*. San Francisco: Jossey-Bass.

Abraham, K. (1948). Notes on the psycho-analytical investigation and treatment of manic-depressive insanity and allied conditions. In *Selected papers of Karl Abraham*. New York: Basic Books. pp. 137-156. Reprinted in W. Gaylin, Ed., *The meaning of despair*. (1968). New York: Jason Aronson.

Abramson, L., Seligman, M. E., & Teasdale, J. (1986). Learned helplessness in humans: critique and reformulation. In J. C. Coyne, (Ed.), *Essential papers on depression*. New York: New York University Press.

Ackerman, N. W. (1958). *The psychodynamics of family life: Diagnosis and treatment of family relationships*. New York: Basic Books, 1958.

Adelson, J. (1988). The psychology of altruism. *Commentary*, 86(5).

American Psychological Association. (1977). *Standards for providers of psychological services*. *Washington, DC: Author*.

American Psychiatric Association. (1987). *Diagnostic and statistical manual*. (3rd ed., rev.). Washington, DC: Author.

Angyal, A. (1951). A theoretical model for personality studies. *Journal of Personality, 20*, 131-135.

Angyal, A. (1965). *Neurosis and treatment: A holistic theory*. New York: John Wiley & Sons.

Arieti, S. (1962). The psychotherapeutic approach to depression. *American Journal of Psychotherapy, 16*, 144-145, 397-406.

Arieti, S. (1978). Psychodynamics of severe depression. In S. Arieti & J. Bemporad (Eds.), *Severe and mild depression*. New York: Basic Books.

Arkowitz, H. & Messer, S. B. (1984). *Psychoanalytic therapy and behavior therapy*. New York: Plenum.

Auerswald, E. H. (1987). Epistemological confusion in family therapy and research. *Family Process, 26*(3), 317-330.

Axelrod, R. (1984). *The evolution of cooperation*. New York: Basic Books.

Barlow, D. H. (1988). *Anxiety and its disorders*. New York: Guilford.

Bateson, G. (1972). *Steps to an ecology of mind*. New York:
Ballantine Books.

Bateson, G., Jackson, D. D., Haley, J., & Weakland, J. (1956). Toward a theory of schizophrenia. *Behavioral Science, 1*, 251-264.

331

Beavers, W. R., (1985). *Successful marriage: A family systems approach to couples therapy.* New York: Norton.

Beck, A., & Emery, G. R. (1985). *Anxiety disorders and phobias.* New York: Basic Books.

Beck, A. T. (1976). *Cognitive therapy and the emotional disorders.* New York: International Universities Press.

Beck, A. T. (1967). *Depression: Clinical, experimental, and theoretical aspects.* New York: Harper & Row.

Beck, A. T. (1985). Cognitive therapy, behavior therapy, psychoanalysis, and pharmacotherapy: A cognitive continuum. In M. J. Mahoney & A. Freeman (Eds.), *Cognition and psychotherapy.* New York: Plenum.

Beck, A. (1986). Maladaptive cognitive structurs in depression. In J. C. Coyne (Ed.), *Essential Papers on Depression.* New York: New York University Press.

Beitman, B., Basha, I., Flaker, G., DeRossear, L., Mukerji, B., & Lamberti, J. (1987). Non-fearful panic disorder: Panic attacks without fear. *Behavior Research Therapy, 25,* 6, 487-492.

Beitman, B. (1987). *The structure of individual psychotherapy.* New York: Guilford Press.

Berman, E., Lief, H., & Williams, A. M. (1981). A model of marital interaction. In G. Pirooz Sholevar (Ed.), *Handbook of marriage and marital therapy.* New York: Spectrum Medical and Scientific Books.

Bibring, E. (1953). The Mechanism of Depression. In *Affective Disorders.* New York: International Universities Press. pp. 14-47.

Blum, R. (1972). *Deceivers and deceived.* Springfield, IL: Charles C. Thomas.

Bowlby, J. (1973). *Attachment and Loss,* Volume II: Separation, anxiety and anger. New York: Basic Books.

Bowlby, J. (1975). Attachment theory, separation anxiety, and mourning. In S. Arieti (Ed.), *American handbook of psychiatry,* VI, 302. New York: Basic Books.

Bruch, H. (1973). *Eating disorders.* New York: Basic Books.

Burton, J. W., & Sandole, D. J. D. (1986). Generic theory: The basis of conflict resolution. *Negotiation Journal, 2,* 333-344.

Carter, B., & McGoldrick, M. (1989). *The changing family life cycle: A framework for family therapy.* Boston: Allyn & Bacon.

Cohen, B., Baker, G., Cohen, R., Fromm-Reichmann, F., & Weigert, E. (1954). An intensive study of twelve cases of manic-depressive psychosis. *Psychiatry, 17,* 100-137. Reprinted in J. C. Coyne (Ed.), (1986). *Essential papers on depression.* New York: New York University Press.

Conte, J. R., Plutchik, R., Picard, M. A., & Karasu, T. B. (1989) Ethics in the practice of psychotherapy: a survey. *American Journal of Psychotherapy. 43*(1), 32-42.

Coyne, J. C. (Ed.) (1986). *Essential papers on depression.* New York: New York University Press.

Crary, E. (1984). *Kids can cooperate: A practical guide to teaching problem solving.* Washington: Parenting Press.

Dancy, B. L., & Handel, P. J. (1984). Perceived family climate, psychological adjustment, and peer relationship of Black adolescents: A function of parental marital status or perceived family conflict? *Journal of Community Psychology. 12,* 3, pp. 222-229.

Dare, C. (1986). Psychoanalytic marital therapy. In N. S. Jacobson & A. S. Gurman (Eds.), *Clinical handbook of marital therapy.* New York: Guilford.

Deutsch, M. (1973). *The resolution of conflict.* New Haven: Yale University Press.

Dollard, J., & Miller, N. (1950). *Personality and psychotherapy.* New York: McGraw-Hill.

Ellis, A., & Bernard, M., (1985). *Clinical applications in rational-emotive therapy.* New York: Springer.

Enos, D. M., & Handal, P. J. (1986). The relation of parental marital status and perceived family conflict to adjustment in white adolescents. *Journal of Consulting and Clinical Psychology*, *54*, 6. pp. 820-824.

Erikson, E. H. (1950). *Childhood and society*. New York: Norton.

Fagen, J. (1976). Critical incidents in the empty chair. In C. Hatcher & P. Himelstein (Eds.), *The handbook of gestalt therapy*. New York: Jason Aronson.

Feldman, L. (1976). Depression and marital interaction. *Family Process*, *15*(4), 389-396.

Festinger, L. (1957). *A theory of cognitive dissonance*. New York: Row, Peterson.

Fisher, R., & Ury, W. (1981). *Getting to yes*. Boston: Houghton Mifflin.

Foa, E. (1989). *Prescriptive matching in psychotherapy: Psychoanalysis for simple phobias?* Symposium at Society for Exploration of Psychotherapy Integration, Conference V, Berkeley, CA.

Fogarty, T. (1976). Marital crisis. In P. J. Geurin (Ed.), *Family therapy*. New York: Gardner Press.

Follett, M. T. (1940). Constructive conflict. In H. C. Metcalf & L. Urwick (Eds.), *Dynamic administration: The collected papers of Mary Parker Follett*. New York: Harper.

Ford, E. (1983). *Missed connections*. New York: Random House.

Fossum, M., & Mason, M. (1986). *Facing shame*. New York: Norton.

Frank, J. D. (1976). Restoration of morale and behavior change. In A. Burton (Ed.), *What makes behavior change possible?* New York: Brunner/Mazel.

Framo, J. L. (1985). Foreword. In W. R. Beavers, *Successful marriage: A family systems approach to couples therapy*. New York: Norton.

Freud, A. (1936). The ego and the mechanisms of defence. In *The writings of Anna Freud*, 2, New York: International Universities Press, 1966.

Freud, S. (1917 [1915]). Mourning and melancholia. In J. Strachey (Ed. and Trans.). *Standard edition of the complete psychological works of Sigmund Freud* (*14*, 239-258). New York: Norton.

Gilbert, R. (1988). The dynamics of inaction: Psychological factors inhibiting arms control activism. *American Psychologist*, *43*, 755-764.

Gill, M. (1981). Analysis of the transference. In H. J. Schlesinger (Ed.), *Psychological Issues Monograph Series* (No. 53). New York: International Universities Press.

Ginott, H. (1965). *Between parent and child*. New York: Macmillan.

Goldfried, M. R. (1980). Toward the delineation of therapeutic change principles. *American Psychologist*, *35*, 991-999.

Goodstein, R. K., & Swift, K. (1977). Psychotherapy with phobic patients: The marriage relationship as a source of symptoms and focus of treatment. *American Journal of Psychotherapy*, *31*, 285-292.

Gottman, J. M. (1979). *Marital interaction: Experimental investigations*. New York: Academic Press.

Greenberg, L. (1984). A task analysis of interpersonal conflict resolution. In L. Rice & L. Greenberg (Eds.), *Patterns of change*. New York: Guilford.

Guidano, V., & Liotti, G. (1983). *Cognitive processes and emotional disorders*. New York: Guilford.

Hafner, R. J. (1977). The husbands of agoraphobic women and their influence on treatment outcome. *British Journal of Psychiatry*, *131*, 287-294.

Hafner, R. J. (1980). Marital homeostasis and spouse-aided therapy in persisting psychological disorders. *Australian Journal of Family Therapy*, *2*, 2-8.

Haley, J. (1963). *Strategies of psychotherapy*. New York: Grune & Stratton.

Haley, J. (1973). *Uncommon therapy: The psychiatric techniques of Milton H. Erickson, M.D.* New York: Norton.

Haley, J. (1976). Marriage therapy. In G. D. Erickson & T. P. Hogan (Eds.), *Family therapy: An introduction to theory and technique*. New York: Jason Aronson. Reprinted from *Archives of General Psychiatry*, 1963, *8*, 213-234.

Hanasi, Yehudah, *The sayings of the fathers*. P. Blackman (Ed.) (1980) New York: Judaica Press.

Hand, I. and Lamontagne, Y., (1976). The exacerbation of interpersonal problems after rapid phobia removal. *Psychotherapy: Theory, Research and Practice, 13*, pp. 405-411.

Harlow, H. F. (1961) The development of affectional patterns in infant monkeys. In B. M. Foss (Ed.), *Determinants of infant behaviour*, Vol.1. London: Methuen; New York: Wiley.

Heitler, S. (1975). *Post-partum depression: A multi-dimensional study*. Doctoral dissertation, New York University, New York.

Heitler, S. M. (1985). *David decides about thumbsucking*. Denver: Reading Matters.

Heitler, S. M. (1987). Conflict resolution: A framework for integration. *Journal of Integrative and Eclectic Psychotherapy. 6*, 3.

Hiroto, D. S. (1974). Locus of control and learned helplessness. *Journal of experimental psychology, 102*, 187-193.

Jacobson, N. S., & Holtzworth-Munroe, A. (1986). Marital therapy: A social learning-cognitive perspective. In N. S. Jacobson & A. S. Gurman (Eds.), *Clinical handbook of marital therapy*. New York: Guilford.

Johnson, S. M., & Greenberg, L. S. (1987). Emotionally focused marital therapy: An overview. *Psychotherapy, 24*, 552-560.

Jordan, C. S. (1979). Mental imagery and psychotherapy: European approaches. In A. A. Sheikh & J. T. Shaffer (Eds.), *The potential of fantasy and imagination*. New York: Brandon House.

Kagan, J., Reznick, J. S., & Snidman, N. (1988). Biological bases of childhood shyness. *Science. 240* (4849), 167-171.

Kelman, H. (1971). *Helping people: Karen Horney's psychoanalytic approach*. New York: Science House, Inc.

Kepner, E., & Brien, L. (1970). Gestalt therapy: A behavioristic phenomenology. In J. Fagen & I. L. Shepherd (Eds.), *Gestalt therapy now*. New York: Harper & Row.

Kiesler, (1971). *The psychology of commitment: Experiments linking behavior to belief*. New York: Academic Press.

Klein, D. F. (1981). Anxiety reconceptualized. In D. F. Klein & J. G. Rabkin (Eds.), *Anxiety: New research and changing concepts*. New York: Raven Press, pp. 235-263.

Klinger, E. (1980). Therapy and the flow of throught. In J. E. Shorr, G. E. Sobel, P. Robin, & J. A. Connella (Eds.), *Imagery: Its many dimensions and applications*. New York: Plenum.

Knobloch, F., & Knobloch, J., (1979). *Integrated psychotherapy*. New York: Jason Aronson.

Kovacs, M., & Beck, A. T. (1986). Maladaptive cognitive structures in depression. In J. D. Coyne (Ed.), *Essential papers on depression*. New York: New York University Press.

L'Abate, L., Ganahl, G., & Hansen, J. C. (1986). *Methods of family therapy*. Englewood Cliffs, NJ: Prentice-Hall.

Lazarus, A. (1977). Has behavior therapy outlived its usefulness? *American Psychologist, 32*, 550-554.

Lewin, K. (1951). *Field theory in social science*. New York: Harper and Row.

Lieberman, R. (1976). Behavioral approaches to family and couple therapy. In G. Erickson & T. Hogan (Eds.), *Family therapy: An introduction to theory and technique*. New York: Jason Aronson.

Lilla, M. T. (1981). Ethos, "ethics," and public service. *The Public Interest, 63*, 3-17.

Linehan, M. (1988). *Alternative model and treatments of patients with borderline personality disorder*. Plenary address to Society for Psychotherapy Integration. (Tape 88.23, 1 of 2). Fairfax: CADET.

Lishman, W. A. (1972). Selective factors in memory: Part 2, affective disorder. *Psychological Medicine, 2*: 248-253.

Lloyd, G. G., & Lishman, W. A. (1975). Effect of depression on the speed of recall of pleasant and unpleasant experiences. *Psychological Medicine, 5*: 173-180.

London, P. (1986). *The modes and morals of psychotherapy*, 2, Washington: Hemisphere Publishing.

Luborsky, L., Crits-Christoph, P., & Mellon, J. (1986). Advent of objective measures of the transference concept. *Journal of consulting and clinical psychology. 54*, 39-47.

Luborsky, L. (1977). Measuring a pervasive psychic structure in psychotherapy: the core conflictual relationship theme. In N. Freedman & S. Grand (Eds.), *Communicative structures and psychic structures*. New York: Plenum Press, pp. 367-395.

Luborsky, L. (1987). Research now can affect clinical practice: A happy turnaround. *The Clinical Psychologist*. Summer, 56-60.

Luce, R. D., & Raiffa, H. (1957). *Games and decisions*. New York: Wiley.

Madanes, C. (1984). *Behind the one-way mirror*. San Francisco: Jossey-Bass.

Madanes, C. (1981). *Strategic family therapy*. San Francisco: Jossey-Bass.

Mahoney, M. J. (1984). Psychoanalysis and behaviorism. In H. Arkowitz & S. B. Messer (Eds.), *Psychoanalytic therapy and behavior therapy: Is integration possible?* New York: Plenum.

Markman, H. J. & Floyd, F. (1980) Possibilities for the prevention of marital discord: A behavioral perspective. *American Journal of Family Therapy, 8*, 29-48.

Marmor, J. (1971). Dynamic psychotherapy and behavior therapy: Are they irreconcilable? *Archives of General Psychiatry, 24*,22-28.

Marshall, J. R., & Neill, J. (1977). The removal of a psychosomatic symptom: Effects on the marriage. *Family Process, 16*, 273-280.

Martin, F. (1977). Some implications from the theory and practice of family therapy for individual therapy (and vice versa). *British Journal of Medical Psychology, 50*, 53-64.

Mayo, J. A. (1979). Marital therapy with manic depressive patients treated with lithium. *Comprehensive Psychiatry, 20*, 419-426.

McKinney, M. E., & Whitte, H. (1985). Dietary habits and blood chemistry levels of the stress prone individual: The hot reactor. *Comprehensive Therapy. 11* (8), 21-28.

McLuhan, M. (1964). *Understanding media: The extensions of man*. New York: McGraw-Hill.

Messer, S. B. (1986). Behavioral and psychoanalytic perspectives at therapeutic choice points. *American Psychologist. 41*(11), 1261-1272.

Meyer, V., & Chesser, E. S. (1970). *Behaviour therapy in clinical psychiatry*. Middlesex, England: Penguin Books Ltd.

Milton, F., & Hafner, R. J. (1979). The outcome of behavior therapy for agraphobia in relation to marital adjustment. *Archives of General Psychiatry, 36*, 807-811.

Minuchin, S. (1965). Conflict-resolution family therapy. In G. D. Erickson & T. P. Hogan (Eds.), *Family therapy: An introduction to theory and technique*. New York: Aronson.

Minuchin, S. (1974). *Families and family therapy*. Cambridge: Harvard University Press.

Moore, C. W. (1986). *The mediation process: Practical strategies for resolving conflict*. San Francisco: Jossey-Bass.

Nelson R. E., & Craighead, W. E. (1977). Selective recall of positive and negative feedback, self-control behaviors, and depression. *Journal of Abnormal Psychology, 86*, 379-388.

Nierenberg, G. (1968). *The art of negotiating: Psychological strategies for gaining advantageous bargains*. New York: Hawthorn Books.

Norcross, J. (1986). Levels of change. In J. O. Prochaska (Ed.), Integrative dimensions for psychotherapy. *International Journal of Eclectic Psychotherapy, 5*(3), 256-274.

Omer, H., & Spivak, M. (1987). Contacting the acutely disorganized person. *Psychotherapy, 24*, 3, 368-374.

Oliner, S. P., & Oliner, P. M. (1988). *The altruistic personality: Rescuers of Jews in Nazi Europe*. New York: Free Press.

Papp, P. (1981). Paradoxes. In S. Minuchin, & H. C. Fishman. *Family therapy techniques.* Cambridge: Harvard University Press.

Pittman, F. (1987). *Turning points: Treating families in transition and crisis*. New York: Norton.

Prochaska, J. (1986). Integrating the integrative dimensions. *International Journal of Eclectic Psychotherapy 5*(3), 269-274.

Pruitt, D. G., & Rubin, J. Z. (1986). *Social conflict: Escalation, stalemate, and settlement.* New York: Random House.

Rae, J. B. (1972). The influence of wives on the treatment outcome of alcoholics. *British Journal of Psychiatry, 120*, 601-613.

Raiffa, H. (1982). *The art and science of negotiation*. Cambridge: Harvard University Press.

Rapaport, A., & Chammah, A. (1970). *Prisoner's dilemma*. Ann Arbor: University of Michigan Press, Ann Arbor Paperbacks.

Restak, R. (1982). *The self seekers*. New York: Doubleday.

Reyher, J . (1963). Free imagery, an uncovering procedure. *Journal of Clinical Psychology, 19*, 454-459.

Rice, L. N., & Greenberg, L. S. (1984). *Patterns of change*. New York: Guilford.

Ricks, D. F. (1974). Supershrink: Methods of a therapist judged successful on the basis of adult outcomes of adolescent patients. In D. F. Ricks, M. Roff, & A. Thomas (Eds.), *Life history research in psychopathology* (Vol. III). Minneapolis: University of Minnesota Press.

Rounsaville, B. J., Weissman, M. M., Prushoff, B. A., et al. (1979). Process of psychotherapy among depressed women with marital disputes. *American Journal of Orthopsychiatry, 49*, 505-510.

Saltzman, N. (Ed.) (1989). Clinical exchange: Gifts. *Journal of Integrative and Eclectic Psychotherapy. 8* (1), 68-84.

Satir, V. (1972). *Peoplemaking*. California: Science and Behavior Books.

Scarf, M. (1987). *Intimate partners: Patterns in love and marriage*. New York: Random House.

Schlesinger, H. (1982). Resistance as process. In P. L. Wachtel (Ed.), *Resistance: Psychodynamic and behavioral approaches*. New York: Plenum.

Schultz, J. W., & Pruitt, D. G. (1978). The effects of mutual concern on joint welfare. *Journal of experimental social psychology. 14*, 480-492.

Schwartz, G. E. (1989). *How people change: A systems perspective on integrating psychotherapies*. Invited address, Society for Exploration of Psychotherapy Integration, Berkeley, CA.

Seixas, J. S. & Youcha, G. (1985). *Children of alcoholism: A survivor's manual*. New York: Crown.

Seligman, M. (1975). *Helplessness: On depression, development and death*. San Francisco: W. H. Freeman.

Shaprio, D. (1965). *Neurotic styles*. New York: Basic Books.

Sheikh, A. (Ed.) (1984). *Imagination and healing*. New York: Baywood Publishing.

Sims, A. (1975). Factors predictive of outcome in neurosis. *British Journal of Psychiatry, 127*, 54-62.

Singer, J. L. (1974). *Imagery and daydream methods in psychotherapy and behavior modification*. New York: Academic Press.

Skinner, B. F. (1969). *Contingencies of reinforcement: A theoretical analysis.* New York: Appleton-Century-Crofts.

Slater, E. J., & Haber, J. D. (1984). Adolescent adjustment following divorce as a function of marital conflict. *Journal of Consulting and Clinical Psychology, 52,* 5, pp.920-921.

Stewart, D. (1988). How to talk with the Russians. *Harvard Magazine, 1,* 21-23.

Strupp, H. H. (1977). A reformulation of the dynamics of the therapists contributions. In A. S. Gurman & A. M. Razin (Eds.), *Effective psychotherapy: A handbook of research.* New York: Pergamon.

Stuart, R. B. (1980). *Helping couples change.* New York: Guilford.

Tryon, G. S. (1989). Study of variables related to client engagement using practicum trainees and experienced clinicians. *Psychotherapy, 26,* 54-61.

Wachtel, P. (1977). *Psychoanalysis and behavior therapy: Toward an integration.* New York: Basic Books.

Wachtel, P. L. (1981). Transference, schema and assimilation: The relevance of Piaget to the psychoanalytic theory of transference. *The annual of psychoanalysis. 8,* 59-76. New York: International Universities Press.

Wachtel, P. L. (Ed.) (1982). *Resistance: Psychodynamic and behavioral approaches.* New York: Plenum.

Wachtel, P. L. (1984). On theory, practice and the nature of integration. In H. Arkowitz & S. B. Messer (Eds.) *Psychoanalytic therapy and behavior therapy.* New York: Plenum.

Wachtel, E. F., & Wachtel, P. L. (1986). *Family dynamics in individual psychotherapy: A guide to clincial strategies.* New York: Guilford.

Wachtel, P. L. (1987). *Action and insight.* New York: Guilford.

Weissberg, M. (1983). *Dangerous secrets: Maladaptive responses to stress.* New York: Norton.

Weissman, M. H., & Klerman, G. L. (1977). The chronic depressive in the community: Unrecognized and poorly treated. *Comprehensive Psychiatry, 18,* 523-532.

Weston, D. (1985). *Self and society: Narcissism, collectivism, and the development of morals.* Cambridge: Cambridge University Press.

Weston, D. (1987). *Cognitive-behavioral interventions in the psychoanalytic psychotherapy of borderline personality disorders.* Paper, Society for the Exploration of Psychotherapy Integration, Chicago.

Wile, D. (1989). *Resistance in psychotherapy.* Panel, Society for Exploration of Psychotherapy Integration. Berkeley, CA.

Wilmot, J. H., & Wilmot, W. W. (1978). *Interpersonal conflict.* Dubuque, Iowa: Wm. C. Brown Company.

Wolfe, B. (1989). Phobias, panic, and psychotherapy integration. *Journal of Integrative and Eclectic Psychotherapy, 8,* 3.

Zartman, I. W., & Berman, M. R. (1982). *The practical negotiator.* New Haven: Yale University Press.

Index

INDEX OF CASES

GENERAL INDEX